HELPS FROM HEBREWS

Other Books In The

BIBLE STUDY TEXTBOOK SERIES:

- ACTS MADE ACTUAL
- SACRED HISTORY AND GEOGRAPHY
- ROMANS REALIZED
- THE CHURCH IN THE BIBLE
- LETTERS FROM PETER
- THE GLORIOUS CHURCH IN EPHESIANS
- THE GOSPEL OF JOHN VOL. I
- THE GREATEST WORK IN THE WORLD
- GUIDANCE FROM GALATIANS
- PAUL'S LETTERS TO TIMOTHY AND TITUS
- SURVEY COURSE IN CHRISTIAN DOCTRINE VOL. I
- SURVEY COURSE IN CHRISTIAN DOCTRINE VOL. II

BIBLE STUDY TEXTBOOK

HELPS FROM
HEBREWS

A NEW
Commentary
Workbook
Teaching Manual

DON EARL BOATMAN

President of
Ozark Bible College
Joplin, Missouri
Paraphrase by JAMES MACKNIGHT
Summary by T. R. Applebury

College Press, Joplin, Missouri

LIBRARY OF HANK KERR

Copyright 1960
Don Earl Boatman

Drawings by Daniel DeWelt
after Horace Knowles

DEDICATION

I dedicate this book to my wife with affection, and with appreciation for her labors of love in typing my three college theses as she assisted me in furthering my education.

I likewise dedicate this book to my children, Dona and Roger, who of necessity were denied my attention in the hours which were required to prepare the notes which now form this book.

HELPS FROM HEBREWS

CONTENTS AND ANALYTICAL OUTLINE OF THE EPISTLE TO THE HEBREWS

PART ONE

THE SUPERIORITY OF CHRIST AS THE FOUNDER OF CHRISTIANITY 1:1-4:13 14

I. He is superior to the prophets 1:1-3
   A. He is the complete and final Revelation of God 1:1, 2a.
   B. He is the Son of God 1:2b, 3

II. He is superior to the angels 1:4-2:18
   A. In name: "My Son" 1:4, 5
   B. In worship: "Worship Him." 1:6, 7
   C. In universal rule 1:8-2:4
      1. Because of character and creation 8-12
      2. Served by angels 13, 14
      3. Hence, the certainty of punishment to those who neglected God's Revelation through His Son is shown 2:1-4
   D. In recovering man's dominion of the earth 2:5-18
      1. Original dominion of the earth by God's people was lost through sin. This dominion is to be restored through Christ. (cf. Gen. 1:28) 5-9
      2. The necessity of Christ becoming a human being in order to accomplish this 2:10-18
         a. To demonstrate His power over Satan 10-15
         b. To sympathize with men through experience 16-18

III. He is superior to Moses 3:1-4:13
   A. The comparison of Jesus and Moses with respect to greatness and glory 3:1-6
   B. Warnings and exhortations with respect to pilgrimage 7-19
      1. Israel's. (cf. Num. 13 and 14) 7-11
      2. Ours 12-19
   C. Warning and exhortation in respect to rest: promises under Moses and Christ 4:1-13

1. Danger of losing the heavenly rest through unbelief and rebellion 4:1-3
   2. This heavenly rest in type 4-8
      a. The seventh day 4-5
      b. Canaan 6-8
   3. Conclusion from the above premises 9-10
   4. Exhortations and warnings 11-13

PART TWO

THE SUPERIORITY OF CHRIST AS HIGH PRIEST 4:14-10:39........138

I. Purpose of and His fitness for the priesthood 4:14-5:10
   A. The fact of Christ's priesthood stated, and an appeal to the reader 4:14-16
      1. Because of His greatness, "Let us hold fast our confession" 14
      2. Because of His human experience, "Let us draw near" 15-16
   B. The office of the priesthood 5:1-4
   C. Christ's qualifications for the priesthood 5-10

II. Necessity of growth in knowledge in order to realize the hope of the priesthood 5:11-6:20
   A. Difficulty of explaining the priesthood because of the low stage of the knowledge of his readers 5:11-14
   B. Exhortation to go on to perfection 6:1-3
   C. The awful consequences of falling away 4-8
   D. Encouragement 6:9-20
      1. The apostle's hope for them 6:9-12
      2. The example of Abraham 13-20

III. Seven proofs of the superiority of Christ's priesthood 7:1-10:39
   A. He is a Priest after a higher order than Aaron 7:1-19
      1. As seen in Melchizedek as a type 7:1-3
      2. As seen in Melchizedek's greatness in his relation to Abraham 7:4-10
      3. As seen in the imperfection of the Levitical priesthood 7:11-19
   B. He is a Priest made with an oath 20-22

C. He is an unchangeable Priest 23-25
D. He is a sinless Priest 26-28
E. He is a Priest of a better covenant 8:1-13
  1. Officiates in the true tabernacle, of which the earthly was a type 1-5
  2. Is a Mediator of a new covenant 8:6-13
F. He is a Priest in a better tabernacle 9:1-28
  1. The old tabernacle and its imperfect services 9:1-10
  2. The superiority of Christ's ministry in the heavenly tabernacle 11-14
  3. The effectiveness of the new covenant based upon the death of Christ 15-22
  4. Necessity and adequacy of the better sacrifice 23-28
G. He is a Priest of a better sacrifice 10:1-39
  1. The impossibility of the Mosaic sacrifice to take away sins 1-4
  2. The efficacious and final sacrifice of Christ 5-10
  3. Finality of Christ's priestly ministration 11-14
  4. Finality of Christ's sacrifice confirmed by prophecy 15-18
  5. Exhortation based on the priesthood of Christ 19-39

PART THREE

The nature, development and duties of faith 11:1-13:25 343

I. The nature of faith 11:1-3
  A. Definition 11:1
  B. Illustration 11:2, 3
II. Progressive development of faith during Patriarchal and Mosiac dispensations 11:4-40
  A. The antediluvian: faith in God 11:4-7
  B. The patriarchal: faith in God, plus faith in His promises 8-27
  C. Israelitish nation: faith in God's promises of the coming Messiah 28-40

III. The perfect and final faith of the Christian dispensation 12:1-29
   A. Jesus, the Author and Perfecter of our faith 1-3
   B. Perils threatening the life of faith 1-17
      1. Failure to respond to chastening 4-13
      2. Falling short of the grace of God 14-17
   C. The nature of the old covenant in contrast with that of the new 18-24
      1. The terror of the old 18-21
      2. The mercy of the new 22-24
   D. Warning 12:25-29
IV. Final exhortation regarding duties pertaining to the truth 13:1-25
   A. Social duties 1-7
   B. Doctrine and worship 8-16
   C. Obedience to elders 17
   D. Request for prayers 18-19
   E. Prayer for them 20-21
   F. Exhortation 22
   G. Information concerning Timothy 23
   H. Salutation 24
   I. Benediction 25

PREFACE

It is my sincere hope that *Preaching and Teaching Helps from Hebrews* will indeed be to many what the title suggests. The verse-by-verse commentary, given in outline form, should prove useful both in the classroom and in the pulpit. In addition to the exegetical analysis of the book of Hebrews, a great number of expository sermon outlines have been correlated into the comments.

Being very zealous for expository preaching, I have used this approach often in the classroom of Minnesota Bible College where I formerly taught, and more recently in Ozark Bible College.

With sincere gratitude the author wishes to express appreciation to many friends whose work helped to make this book possible.

The outline for the book of Hebrews was gleaned from Professor Victor Hoven's classroom lectures in Eugene Bible College.

It is an honor to have Professor Ralph Applebury contribute his chapter summaries.

Esther (Mrs. Daniel) Burris volunteered to type and mimeograph my notes making them available to my students while I was teaching several years ago in Minnesota Bible College.

Edeana White, a student in Ozark Bible College, prepared my class discussion questions, incorporating them into the manuscript.

Professor Don DeWelt recently urged me to make the notes available for this book, and with the assistance of Professor Woodrow Phillips planned for its production.

Marjorie (Mrs. Woodrow) Phillips did the proof reading, and has contributed much to the original manuscript with her ability to improve sentence structure.

I believe this book will prove to be very helpful to those who desire a practical application to life from the Word of God. Only one Book is inspired, and as I have prepared these notes I have sought diligently to teach and to write in full accord with the will of God as found in His Book.

Don Earl Boatman

INTRODUCTION

I do not believe there is a textbook in print, or an older one which may be reprinted, which deals with the book of Hebrews more adequately and accurately than this one.

In the first place, Don Earl Boatman, president of Ozark Bible College, believes that God — through His Holy Spirit — is the ultimate author of Hebrews, and of all the Bible. Therefore, *Helps from Hebrews* is a labor of love, permeated by reverence and faith.

Following a rich educational preparation and several years of successful preaching ministry, the author became a Bible college teacher. Assigned the class in Hebrews, he approached it with the most thoroughgoing preparation possible — as he did all of his classes. Then, each year was made the occasion and opportunity for further research and prayerful meditation.

The present volume is the outgrowth of mimeographed class notes, which, in turn, were the outgrowth of this teaching experience. For several years, when I have had occasion to restudy some section of Hebrews, these class notes have had high priority among my reference materials. I have found them most helpful.

I anticipate for *Helps from Hebrews* an enthusiastic reception and a widespread and long continued use. It is sufficiently scholarly and complete to be highly acceptable as a college textbook. As do all of the College Press — Bible Study Textbook Club publications, it incorporates several features which make it especially valuable for such use.

The simplicity of the book, together with its thoughtful questions and other textbook techniques will make it quite practical for study groups in the local church.

Every preacher, elder, deacon, Bible School teacher — in fact, every Bible student — will want to give it a place among his "easiest to reach" and "most frequently to be used" reference and study volumes. And the fact that it is prepared with textbook use particularly in mind makes its factual content the more easily accessible, and adds to its suggestive and stimulative value.

Chester A. Williamson

GENERAL INTRODUCTION TO THE EPISTLE TO THE HEBREWS

1. *The people addressed* — The letter to the Hebrews was evidently addressed to Jewish Christians who were in danger of apostatizing from Christ and returning to Judaism. They were subjected to persecution by their own race and treated as apostates and unclean because they had left Moses and accepted Christ.
2. *The purpose of the epistle.*
   a. To exhibit the unsurpassed glory of the new convenant in contrast with the old.
   b. To exhort the Hebrew Christians to steadfastness in Christ. cf. 3:12; 4:14; 6:4-8; 10:23; 13:22.
3. *Authorship.*
   a. Tradition of the church in the East, where the epistle was first received, is unanimous in ascribing authorship to the Apostle Paul, as did also the council of Carthage, 397 A.D., and Clement of Alexandria, 165 to 220 A.D.
4. *Internal evidence as to Paul's authorship.*
   a. Figures of speech are similar to those used in his other letters. cf. I Cor. 9:24-25; Gal. 2:2; 5:7; Phil. 3:13-14; II Tim. 4:7-8 with Heb. 12:1-2.
   b. Paul's view of the law as expressed in his other letters is the same view expressed in Hebrews. cf. Acts 13:39; Rom. 7:1-6; I Cor. 9:20-21; II Cor. 3:6-13; Gal. 3:16 to 4:31; Eph. 2:14-18; Col. 2:13-17 with Heb. 8:7 to 10:18.
   c. The word "mediator" is used by Paul only. cf. Gal. 3:19-20; I Tim. 2:5 with Heb. 8:6; 9:15; 12:24
   d. Conditions in the life of Paul are true to those of the writer of the Hebrew letter.
   1) The writer was a prisoner in Italy. Heb. 13:19-24.
   2) The writer was a friend of Timothy. Heb. 13:23.
   3) The writer asks for prayers of brethren that he might be set free. Heb. 13:18-19.
   e. The word "covenant" is found only seven times in the New Testament outside of Paul's writings. Paul uses it nine times in other writings. It is used seventeen times in Hebrews.
   f. No other writer invokes grace upon readers.
5. *Date.*
   Though much is said of the worship and sacrifice in the

temple, there is an entire absence of any intimation that the temple had been destroyed. cf. 8:4; 10:11. Since the temple was destroyed in A.D. 70, the letter must have been written before that date. From 13:24 it seems to have been written in Italy.
6. *Place* (supposition).
   According to the references in 13:24 to the prayers, it must have been written during his first imprisonment from 61-63 A.D. in Rome, Italy.

ANALYSIS:
1. The great proposition of this epistle is: *The superiority of Christianity to Judaism is seen in its Founder and Mediator, Jesus Christ.*
2. The Book Has Three Divisions.
   Part I. The superiority of Christ as Founder of Christianity — 1:1-4:13.
   Part II. The superiority of Christ as High Priest — 4:14-10:39.
   Part III. The nature, development and duties of faith — **11:1-13:25**
3. In this letter, *Christ is shown* to be superior to: Prophets 1:1-3; Angels 1:4-2:18; Moses 3:1-4:13.
4. Alexander Campbell's estimation of this letter and also of Romans:
   "The epistle to Romans and Hebrews contains the most comprehensive and complete exposition of all that enters into Christian faith and worship ever spoken or written."

QUESTIONS ON THE OUTLINE

I. *On the introduction.*
1. Is the epistle addressed to a specific area, or to a person?
2. What nationality seems to be in the mind of the author?
3. What can we judge their spiritual condition to be?
4. What seems to be the purpose of the epistle?
5. What bearing has tradition upon ascribing the authorship to Paul?
6. What authorities ascribe Paul's authorship?
7. Who else is suggested?
8. What is meant by "internal evidence of authorship"?

9. What is the evidence of internal authorship in regard to figures of speech?
10. If you feel that Paul wrote this letter, how do you explain Heb. 2:3? (See my notes.)
11. Do you feel that Paul's view of the law is a strong argument for authorship? Why?
12. Explain the value of the argument from the word "mediator".
13. Are the conditions in the life of the author true to Paul? Name three.
14. "A prisoner in Italy" is suggested as one condition. Could this be true of others?
15. Could others have been a friend of Timothy?
16. Do you feel that his prayer for deliverance to be with them carries much evidence?
17. Was Paul primarily a missionary to the Jews, therefore making this a strong argument?
18. Tell of the use of the word "covenant" in New Testament writings.
19. What can be said of the date of the authorship?
20. What is the evidence for the place where it was written?
21. Do we have any other evidence from other epistles that Paul may have been the author?
22. What does the salutation or benediction at the close indicate as to authorship?

II. *On the analysis.*
1. What seems to be the great proposition of the book?
2. Is the entire book given over to this?
3. If not, what is the nature of the balance of the book?
4. Name the three divisions of the book.
    a. Superiority of Christ as the Founder of Christianity — 1:1-4:13.
    b. Superiority of Christ as High Priest — 4:14-10:39.
    c. Nature, development and duties of faith — 11:1-13:25.
5. According *to this letter,* to whom is Christ superior?
    a. Prophets — 1:1-3.
    b. Angels — 1:4-2:18.
    c. Moses — 3:1-4:13.

PART ONE

THE SUPERIORITY OF CHRIST AS THE FOUNDER OF CHRISTIANITY
1:1-4:13.

I. *He is superior to the prophets.* 1:1-3.
   A. *He is the complete and final revelation of God.* 1:1, 2a.

Text
1:1-2a

1 God, having of old time spoken unto the fathers in the prophets by divers portions and in divers manners, 2a hath at the end of these days spoken unto us in His Son . . .

Paraphrase

1 The same God, who in sundry parts and in divers manners anciently revealed His will to the fathers of the Jewish nation by the prophets, Enoch, (Jude, ver. 14), Moses, Samuel, David, Isaiah, etc.

2a Hath in these last days of the Mosaic dispensation spoken the gospel to mankind, all at once and after one manner . . .

Comment

God

The book begins with an assumption of God's existence. Like Genesis, it makes no attempt to prove the existence of God. The Psalmist said that fools do not believe in God. cf. 14:1; 53:1. The author of Hebrews must have felt the same way.

This wonderful God of man is not appreciated, so a brief study of Him is in order. This study is far from exhaustive — but is practical:

a. The Being of God:
1) He is Spirit — John 4:24.
2) He is Eternal — Romans 16:26; II Peter 3:8.
3) He is Living — Matt. 22:32; 16:16.
4) He is One — Rom. 16.27; I Tim. 1:17; Jude 25.
5) He is Ultimate (alpha and omega) — Rev. 21:6.

b. The Character of God:
1) Omnipotent — all-powerful — almighty — Rev. 19:6; Rom. 13:1.
2) Omniscient — all-wise — knoweth all things — Rom. 16:27; Eph. 3:10 — manifold wisdom.
3) Holy — John 17:11; Rev. 4:8; 6:10.

4) Righteous — John 17:25; Matt. 6:33; Phil. 3:9.
5) Good — Rom. 2:4; Luke 18:19.
6) Kind — Titus 3:4.
7) Merciful — Rom. 12:1; II Cor. 1:3; Luke 6:36.
8) Just — Gal. 3:8; Rom. 3:26.
9) Loving — John 16:27; II Cor. 13:11; II Thes. 2:16.
c. In relationship to the world:
1) This is of primary importance, for God has not been far removed from man, but has sought to win man to Himself.
2) Below are listed some phases of His relationship:
a) Omnipresent:
Acts 17:24-25 — "dwelleth not in temples — "
Acts 17:28 — "in Him we live — "
b) Creator:
Acts 17:24 — "the God that made the world"
Mark 13:19.
c) Sovereign — Ruler, Lord, Monarch:
Acts 17:24 — "He being Lord of earth — "
d) Savior:
Luke 1:47 — "in God my Savior."
I Tim. 2:3 — "in the sight of God our Savior — "
Jude 25 — "God our Savior."
e) Revealer:
Phil. 3:15 — "God shall reveal this unto you — "
I Cor. 2:10 — "God revealed them unto us — "
Rom. 1:17 — "therein is revealed — "

having of olden time spoken

This refers to God's contact with man from the very beginning. God has always spoken to man:
a. In the patriarchal time God spoke face to face:
1) To Adam.
2) To Noah.
3) To Abraham, Isaac and Jacob.
b. He spoke to man through prophets in a great attempt to win man:
1) Moses the lawgiver was a mighty voice for God.
2) The major and minor prophets had a major message.
Some doubt that God spoke. Aside from the Word that says He did, it seems likely that He would.

a. If He could, but would not, He would not be a just and righteous God; therefore, He would not be worthy of worship.
b. If He would but could not, then He would be weaker than man, and therefore, unworthy of worship.

spoken unto the fathers

Who is referred to?
a. Possibly the patriarchal fathers are included.
b. No doubt the Jewish race as a whole under the Mosaic law should be considered as included.

A problem with the patriarchal consideration is that he says "unto the fathers in the prophets."
a. The prophets appeared during the Mosaic dispensation.
b. However, the word "prophet" is not limited to the idea of foretelling of events.
c. Prophecy means "to tell," and on occasions the patriarchs may have served as prophets to their generation.

in the prophets

The meaning of the word:
a. One who speaks for another — a "forth-teller."
b. Foretelling of the coming of Christ was by no means their only task.

The prophets are divided into two groups:
a. Major prophets — Isaiah, Jeremiah, Ezekiel, and Daniel.
b. Minor prophets — The names of the last twelve books of the Old Testament are the minor prophets.

There are others who are considered prophets:
a. Moses — Deut. 18:15.
b. Aaron — Exodus 7:1 — "Aaron shall be thy prophet."

The preaching of the prophets may be generally summarized under three phases:
a. Judgments upon kingdoms.
b. The coming kingdom.
c. The King of kings.

in divers portions

This suggests that God's revelations to man have been in different dispensations:
a. Covenants of faith with the patriarchs were made in the Patriarchal or Starlight Dispensation.

b. Covenants with Moses were made in the Moonlight Dispensation.
1) During this period, the prophets gave further light to the people of the day.
2) The prophets also enlightened men about the Sunlight Dispensation to follow.
3) John the Baptist removed the final clouds.
God spoke more fully following these two dispensations with two others:
a. The revelation of Jesus is the Sunlight Dispensation.
b. The message of the apostles is the Holy Spirit Dispensation. The "divers portion", then, may be called progressive revelation. The portions put together make one book.
a. The portions have a unity when read as one book:
1) Its history is a unit.
a) A history of the past.
b) Teaching for a satisfactory present.
c) A prophecy of the future.
2) Man's salvation is in it:
a) A scarlet thread runs throughout all the Word.
b) Blood atonement is the theme that ties the Word together from Genesis to Revelation.
3) A Person is there, although revealed in different portions:
a) Gen. 3:15 speaks of Him bruising the serpent's head.
b) Isaiah 53 speaks of Him being bruised.
c) Revelation pictures Him destroying all wickedness and rewarding righteousness.
4) A kingdom is there:
a) A prophetic kingdom — Dan. 2:44.
b) A present kingdom — Matt. 16:18.
c) A world-wide victorious kingdom — Matt. 24:44; Rev. 11:15 — "kingdom of the world is become the Kingdom of our Lord."
b. Since Christ gave credence to the portions, the critic must destroy Christ before he can destroy the Old Testament. cf. Luke 24:44; Matt. 12:39-41; 16:4.

in divers manners
This suggests that God has used various methods to make known His message:

a. He spoke with a voice:
   Exodus 24:4 — "all the words which Jehovah hath spoken will we do —"
   Isaiah 38:4 — "Then came the word of the Lord to Isaiah, saying —"
b. He wrote with His fingers:
   Dan. 5:5 — Belshazzar saw the handwriting on the wall.
   Ex. 31:18 — The law was written by the fingers of God.
c. He spoke in action, demonstrating his power:
1) Miracles were of several kinds:
a) Burning bush — Ex. 3:2.
b) Daniel in the lions' den — Dan. 6:22.
c) Walls of Jerico fell — Joshua 6:20.
d) Thundering and lightning when the law was given — Ex. 20:18.
2) Temple veil rent in twain — Matt. 27:51. This spoke of the ending of the earthly Holy of Holies.
3) Victory in war for his people showed that righteousness must prevail.
a) Gideon's victory — Heb. 11:32 and Judges 7:22
b) Egyptians defeated in the Red Sea.
d. He spoke in dreams and visions:
1) Daniel 2:1 — Nebuchadnezzar's dream and interpretation by Daniel in 2:17-49.
2) Joseph interprets dreams of fellow prisoners in Gen. 40.
3) Joseph's dream in Gen. 37.
4) See Hosea 12:10.
   Romans 1:4 is proof that "spoke" may refer to more than vocal words:
   cf. Ps. 19:2 — "day unto day uttereth speech."
   cf. Rom. 1:20 — "even His everlasting power and divinity."

hath at the end of these days

What days?
a. The days of the prophets just referred to.
b. The prophets' days seemed closed for about 400 years after Malachi, but John broke the silence.
c. These days may refer to the end of the Jewish age, which was a prophetic age.

spoken unto us in His Son

How did God speak through Him?

HELPS FROM HEBREWS 1:2

a. Not always vocally.
1) Christ's compassion and love spoke.
2) Christ's resurrection spoke. cf. Rom. 1:4 — "who was declared to be the Son of God with power — "
In Christ's voice God spoke:
John 8:28 — "but as the Father taught Me, I speak these things."
John 12:49 — "For I spake not from Myself but the Father that sent Me, He hath given Me a commandment what I should say and what I should speak."
John 14:10 — "the words I speak, I speak not of Myself — "

Study Questions

1. Does the book of Hebrews begin with the word "God"? Does the original Greek manuscript begin this way?
2. In what way is Hebrews like Genesis?
3. Name the three divisions in my outline about God.
4. Tell of the being of God.
5. Tell of the character of God.
6. What can be said about God's relationship to the world?
7. What is meant by "olden times"?
8. In patriarchal times, how did He speak?
9. What would you think about God if He could but wouldn't speak to man?
10. What would you say about God if He would but couldn't speak to man?
11. Who is meant by the term "fathers"?
12. When did prophets first come into Bible history?
13. Did prophets speak to the patriarchs? If not, can "fathers" refer to them?
14. What is the responsibility of a prophet?
15. Name a prophet who spoke to Abraham.
16. Into what two groups are the prophets divided?
17. Explain the term, "divers portions".
18. What is meant by "different dispensations"?
19. Explain the expression, "progressive revelation".
20. Do these portions comprise a unit.
21. Do you see a theme running through all the revelation of God?
22. Does Christ give credence to the Old Testament?
23. What were the ways God spoke?

24. Tell of some actions of God that revealed something about Him.
25. What message was spoken by the temple veil being rent?
26. What was spoken concerning God in His helping the people in war?
27. Name some dreams in which God spoke.
28. Name some visions in which God spoke.
29. Are all of God's messages vocal?
30. What is meant by "end of these days"?
31. What days are referred to?
32. How did God speak through Christ?
33. Did Christ claim to speak for God?

B. *He is the Son of God.* 1:2b, 3.

Text
1:2b-3

2b ... whom He appointed heir of all things, through whom also He made the worlds; 3 Who being the effulgence of His glory, and the very image of His substance, and upholding all things by the word of His power, when He had made purification of sins, sat down on the right hand of the Majesty on high;

Paraphrase

2b ... by His Son made flesh whom He constituted heir of all things; through whom also He made the worlds.

3 This great personage, even in His incarnate state, being an effulgence of His Father's glory, and an exact image of His substance, and upholding all things (namely, the worlds, ver. 2.) by His powerful command, when He had made atonement for our sins by the sacrifice of Himself, and not of beasts, sat down at the right hand of the manifestation of the divine presence in the highest heavens, by invitation from God, who thereby declared His ministrations as a priest both acceptable and effectual.

Comment

in His Son

This Sonship is in a unique sense:
a. He is the only one of His kind.
b. He is not a son — but *the Son.*

His Sonship was established by many proofs:
a. He is the Son in the parable of the husbandman. Luke 20:9-18; cf. Matt. 11:25.

b. Jesus claimed to be the Son.
   John 14:2 — "in My Father's house."
   John 4:26 — "I am He — "
c. Son — as seen in His miracles: John 20:30-31.
d. Son — as seen in His superior teaching.
   John 7:46 — "never man so spake."
e. Son — as seen in His superior life:
   Luke 23:4 — Pilate: "I find no fault — "
   Heb. 4:14 — "Having then a great high priest . . . the Son of God . . ."
   John 8:46 — "which of you convicteth Me of sin . . ."
f. Son — as seen in His resurrection:
   Rom. 1:4; Acts 17:30-31.
g. Son — as seen in the acclamation of God:
   Matt. 3:17 — at His baptism.
   Matt. 17:1-8 — at His transfiguration.

Whom He appointed heir of all things
   The word "heir" suggests something to inherit. What was it?
a. An excellent name. Heb. 1:4. cf. Phil. 2:5-11.
b. Lordship. Acts 2:36. Matt. 28:18.
c. Power and judgment. John 5:22 — "given judgment unto the Son."

through whom also He made the worlds
   Christ was present in creation:
   John 1:3 — "all things were made through Him . . ."
   Gen. 1:26 — "Let us make man in *Our* image, after *Our* likeness . . ."

the worlds
   The Greek word here translated, "worlds", is disputed by translators.
a. The footnote is "ages".
b. The singular form has three meanings:
1) Endless duration.
2) Any age or period.
3) Anything that lives or exists.
   We may assume that it refers to the processes in each age by which God is bringing to pass His great purposes.

who being the effulgence of His glory
   The word "effulgence" is also translated "brightness".

a. This word appears only once in the New Testament.
b. "Effulgence" means a reflected splendor.
   Jesus made it plain that those who saw Him could say that they had seen the Father.
   John 14:8-9; 14:11; 17:21.
   They saw the Father only as they saw His qualities in Christ.
a. John 1:18 — "No man hath seen God at any time."
b. All that God is, has been expressed in Jesus.

and the very image of His substance

This makes Him deity, which should be theological enough for us!
"Image" means "impress".
a. The word in the Greek is *charaktei*.
1) In the primary sense, it denotes the instrument used in engraving or carving.
2) The whole expression, "the very image of His substance", is used to set forth the dignity of Christ, in order to build up our faith.
b. Calvin says, "He is called the 'impress of His substance', because the majesty of the Father is hidden until it shows itself impressed as it were on his image. They who overlook this connection and carry their philosophy higher, weary themselves to no purpose, for they do not understand the design of the Apostle; for it was not his object to show what likeness the Father bears to the Son!" (p. 35.)
c. cf. II Cor. 4:4 — "Christ who is the image of God."
"Substance" is translated "person" in the King James version.
a. The word is *hupos* and means "what lies under".
b. This is not the same word used in Heb. 11:1 — "faith is the *substance* of things hoped for."
c. "Substance" or "essence" was the controversial topic of Arius and Athanasious.
1) The Council called by Constantine tried to settle the problem, but failed.
2) Trying to fully understand divine reality with human terms is too much for man.
d. God is Spirit. Man doesn't think of Spirit as having substance, although He does have form.
   Deut. 4:15-16, Exodus 24:9-10; 33:20 — "Thou canst not see My face for man shall not see My face — "

upholdeth all things

The word here translated "upholdeth", is *phero* in the original manuscripts, and has the idea "to bear", or "to carry". What is included in the word, "upholdeth"?
a. Man is upheld:
Acts 17:28 — "In Him we live — "
Job 12:10 — "In whose hand is the soul of every living thing — "
b. The world is supported by God:
Job 26:7 — "He hangeth the earth upon nothing — "
Col. 1:17 — "In Him all things consist — "
The above verses, Col. 1:17 excepted, speak of God's action, while Heb. 1:3 refers to Jesus' action.
The harmony of the problem lies in the fact that Jesus is spoken of as "the Word".

by the word of His power

In Genesis are recorded the creative words, but here are the sustaining words.
a. Material substance has no resident power in it.
b. The "laws of nature", so-called, are only a manifestation of the uniformity of God's activity.
While Jesus was on earth, He demonstrated the power of His words:
a. He cast out spirits with a word. Mark 9:25.
b. He said, "Be thou made clean", and a leper was made whole. Matt. 8:3.
c. The centurion asked Jesus, saying, "Only *say the word* and my servant shall be healed." His faith was rewarded with a healing word from Jesus. Matt. 8:8; 8:13.

when He had made purification of sins

The cross is the method of taking care of sins.
a. All Old Testament sacrifices were a type of the blood sacrifice of Jesus.
1) John used the type of animal sacrifices as a figure of speech, saying: "Behold the Lamb of God who taketh away the sin of the world." John 1:29.
b. Jesus came into the world to endure the cross.
Luke 9:51 — "He steadfastly set His face to go to Jerusalem — "

Heb. 12:2 — "endured the cross — "
c. It is the blood that purifies:
Rev. 1:5 — "unto Him — that loosed us from our sins, by His blood."
Heb. 9:28 — "So Christ was once offered to bear the sins of many."
To have this cleansing, we must have our own crucifixion service:
Acts 22:16 — "be baptized and wash away thy sins — "
Titus 3:5 — "by the washing of regeneration."
Rom. 6:3 — "baptized into His death."

sat down on the right hand

This truth is spoken by others:
a. Stephen saw Him there. Acts 7:56.
b. Peter preached that He was there. Acts 2:33.
c. John pictured Him at the throne of God. Rev. 5:6, 7:17.
The author of Hebrews makes much of this point:
a. In 1:4, we see His person — King.
b. In 8:12, we see His ministry — Priest.
c. Hebrews 10:12 and 12:2, He is seated at the right hand of the throne of God after one complete and final sacrifice.
d. In 12:1-2 we see Him as the joyful leader of a great cloud of witnesses.
On earth, truth is often on the scaffold, and wrong on the throne, but not so in Heaven.

of the majesty

The Greek word for "great" is here translated, "majesty".
a. Jesus at the throne signifies power and authority serving as the special chosen one of God.
b. He is to be loved for His redemption of mankind, but ought to be honored on account of His royal magnificence.

Special Outline of 1:1-3

Threefold place of Jesus:
1. Prophet — "spoken unto us" — 1:2.
2. Priest — "made purification" — 1:3.
3. King — "at the right hand" — 1:3.

Study Questions

34. Discuss the divine sonship of Christ.

35. What is meant by "only begotten"?
36. Name various ways Christ's sonship is proven.
37. If Christ is appointed heir, what is He to inherit?
38. What scriptures enlarge upon the work of Christ in creation?
39. Define the word "worlds." Does he mean our earth?
40. What may we surmise then if the word has this translation?
41. What is meant by "effulgence"?
42. Is it a common word in the New Testament?
43. Describe how the glory of God is seen in Christ.
44. What is meant by "image"?
45. What is meant by the word, "substance"?
46. How does the King James version translate it?
47. What problem arose in church history over the word, "substance"?
48. What is meant by "upholdeth all things"?
49. Does the scripture speak of God or Christ being the sustainer?
50. How harmonize?
51. Did Jesus ever demonstrate that His words have power?
52. Name the instances.
53. When did Jesus make purification for sins?
54. What scriptures of the New Testament connect Jesus with cleansing from sin?
55. Is there a cross for us?
56. When Jesus finished the work of the cross and His earthly ministry, where did He go?
57. What other passages of scripture support Christ's right-hand glory?
58. What is meant by "the majesty on high"?

II. *He is superior to the angels* 1:4-2:18.
A. *In name:* "My Son" 1:4, 5.

Text
1:4-5

4 having become by so much better than the angels, as He hath inherited a more excellent Name than they. 5 For unto which of the angels said He at any time,

Thou art My Son,
This day have I begotten Thee? and again,
I will be to Him a Father.
And He shall be to Me a Son?

Paraphrase

4 The Son, by Whom God hath spoken the Gospel, is by so much greater than the angels, by how much He hath inherited by descent a more excellent Name than they.

5 For although in your scriptures angels have been called the Sons of God, to which of the angels did God ever say, by way of distinguishing Him from all other beings, My Son Thou art; to-day I have begotten Thee? See chap. v. 5. And again, I will declare Myself His Father, and Him My Son.

Comment

having become

   This suggests a time when He was not better than the angels. When could this time have been?
a. Perhaps just after the emptying spoken of by Paul. Phil. 2:5-10.
b. While Christ was in human flesh and before He was refilled with His original glory.
   During the time of His humility on earth, He was at least in some respect lower than the angels:
a. "made a little lower than the angels." cf. Heb. 2:9.
b. "a body didst Thou prepare for Me." cf. Heb. 10:5.

so much better than the angels

   What is meant by "so much better"? The word in the Greek is *Kreithan*.
a. It very likely means a measure of place or position, not quality of being.
b. Moral or spiritual excellence is not included.
c. Glory — honor — reverence, He had less while on earth, being obedient to the cross.
d. Ways in which He is better than angels:
   1. He is the Son — they are servants. 1:5-7
   2. He is worshipped by angels. 1:6
   3. He may be addressed by God. 1:8
   4. He is a king with a sceptre of righteousness. 1:8
   5. He was annointed with the oil of gladness above His fellows. 1:9
   6. He is addressed as "Lord". 1:10
   7. He is seated at the right hand of God. 1:13

8. Angels minister to those who inherit salvation made possible by Christ. 1:14
9. Not to angels did He subject the world to come. 2:5

e. The word "better" appears frequently in Hebrews:
1. Better than angels. 1:4
2. Better things. 6:9
3. Better person than Abraham. 7:7
4. Better hope. 7:19
5. Better covenant. 7:22
6. Better covenant and promises. 8:6
7. Better sacrifice. 9:23
8. Better possessions. 10:34
9. Better country. 11:16
10. Better resurrection. 11:35
11. Better things. 11:40
12. Better than that of Abel. 12:24

f. Paul elsewhere says that to depart and be with Christ is "better". Phil. 1:23

than the angels

Who are angels?

a. Generally, it can be said that they are beings less than God, and other than men.
b. Specifically, here are some facts about them:
1. They are intelligent beings, showing some characteristics of men:
I Peter 1:11-12 — "which things angels desire to look into."
2. They are messengers:
Rev. 4:8-11; Gen. 19:15 — Message to Lot.
3. They praise God and sing before Him.
Rev. 4:8-11; 5:9.
4. They are emotional. Luke 15:7, 10: Angels rejoicing over sinners who repent.
5. They are sexless creatures.
Matt. 22:30 — "neither marry or are given in marriage."
6. They are creatures of choice.
II Peter 2:4 — "when they sinned — "
Jude 6 — "kept not their own principality — "
7. They seem to be winged creatures, in some instances at least.
a) Six wings. Isaiah 6:2.
b) Four wings. Ezekiel 1:6.

c) Wings. Exodus 25:30; 37:9
c. There are two classes of angels:
1. God's angels who serve:
a) I Tim. 5:21 — "the elect angels."
b) Rev. 14:10 — "holy angels."
2. Evil angels:
a) Ephesians 6:12 — "spiritual hosts of wickedness."
b) Rev. 12:9 — "dragon was cast out and his angels."

A. *Superior to angels in name: "My Son"*
   as he hath inherited a more excellent Name

   This is a reward for His obedience, and thus His Name is above every name:
   a. What name is foremost in the world but the name of Jesus?
   b. We might argue over the second place name, Paul, Augustine, Lincoln, etc., but Jesus stands alone.
   c. What is the Name referred to here? "Jesus", "Christ", "Immanuel", etc.? The Name is "Son", as seen by verse 5. Observe the importance of the Name of Jesus:
   a. Acts 4:12 — In none other is there salvation.
   b. Eph. 1:21; Phil. 2:9 — Name above every name.
   c. Phil. 2:10 — Name to bow before.
   d. Phil. 2:11 — A Name to confess.
   e. Matt. 28:19 — Baptism in His name.
   f. Col. 3:17; Matt. 10:42 — All good to be in His Name.
   g. John 14:13; 15:16 — Prayer in His Name.
   h. Eph. 5:20 — Prayer in His Name.
   i: Matt. 18:20 — Assemble in His Name.
   j. Eph. 3:14 — His is the family Name.

v5 *for unto which of the angels said He at any time, Thou art My Son*

   This is a question with an implied answer. He has never at any time said this to any of the angels.
   a. Christ is unique; He is not one of the many hosts of angels, but the only Son of God.
   b. We should not consider Christ as man or angel, but as Son of God.

Thou art my Son

   This is a quotation from Ps. 2:7.
   "Son" is the "more excellent name" spoken of in verse 4.

Paul in Acts 13:33 says Jesus fulfilled the prophecy of Psalms 2:7.
Mary was told by the angel that her child would be called "Son of God".
Luke 1:35 — " .... shall be born of thee shall be called the Son of God."
God acclaimed Him as Son twice while He was on earth:
Matt. 3:17 — at His baptism.
Matt. 17:5 — at His transfiguration.
When did He become the Son of God?

a. This is a useless theological question based on the assumption that perhaps once He was not the Son.
b. The important thing is the fact that He was called the Son as against the fact that no angel was ever referred to as the Son of God.
c. These words were spoken of Christ as the son of David — as Man:
1) As God He was eternally in this relationship.
2) Isaiah 7:14 spoke of Him as "Emmanuel".

this day have I begotten Thee? ←

The meaning of "beget":
a. It means to procreate as a sire, generate.
b. It means to produce as an effect.
Paul seems to connect the begetting with the resurrection of Jesus.
Acts 13:33-34.
a. If the resurrection is the begetting, then it is God's declaration of Him as Son referred to in Rom. 1:4 — "declared to be the Son of God with power — "
b. Thus He was produced from the grave rather than produced as a child in a normal physical sense.

I will be to Him a Father and He shall be to Me a Son

This is a fulfillment of the royal covenant with David. cf. I Chron. 17:13; II Sam. 7:14.
Jesus spoke often of this relationship:
Matt. 11:25 — "I thank Thee, Father."
Luke 22:42 — "Father, remove this cup — "
Luke 23:46 — "Father, into Thy hands — "

Study Questions

59. Does "having become so" infer that one day He was not?
60. In what way was He below them?
61. How is Christ so much better than the angels?
62. Is it quality of which he is speaking, or one of place?
63. Find in this chapter ways in which He was superior.
64. How does the author prove that Christ has inherited a more excellent name?
65. When did God call Jesus his Son?
66. Does this Psalm 2:7 actually refer to Christ?
67. What is the day that Christ was begotten?
68. When did God beget Christ?
69. What does Romans 1:4 say of his Sonship?
70. Is the statement of Fatherhood a fulfillment of prophecy?
71. Did Jesus ever call God Father?
72. Name some instances when He did.

B. *Superior to angels in worship: "worship Him".* (cf. Acts 13:33); 1:6, 7.

Text
1:6, 7

6 And when He again bringeth in the firstborn into the world He saith, And let all the angels of God worship Him. 7 And of the angels He saith,
Who maketh His angels winds,
And His ministers a flame of fire:

Paraphrase

6 But, instead of calling any of the angels His begotten Son, when God foretells His bringing a second time the first-born into our world, by raising Him from the dead, to show that He hath subjected the angels to Him, He saith, Ps. xcvii. 7. Yea, worship Him, all ye angels of God.

7 Besides, of the angels indeed David saith, Ps. civ. 4. Who made His angels spiritual substances, and His ministers a flame of fire; — that is, the greatest thing said of angels is, that they are beings not clogged with flesh, who serve God with the utmost activity;

Comment

and when He again bringeth in the firstborn
The word "again" creates a problem.

a. It seems unlikely that this refers to Christ's birth, for His second coming would then be His third; the birth was not "again in the world."
b. A clarification of the problem of "again" may be in the alternate translation: "and again, when He bringeth in — "
1. This means He spoke again, rather than again bringing Him into the world.
2. The angels worshipped at His birth for they spoke — perhaps sang — from the heavens. Luke 2:14.
It can be said God "brought Him in", for the Scriptures teach it.
Luke 1:35 — To Mary: " . . . and the power of *the Most High* shall overshadow thee — "
John 3:16 — "that *He* gave — "

firstborn

This is a descriptive title and is used in at least two senses:
a. Firstborn of creation — Col. 1:15-18.
b. Firstborn from the dead — Rev. 1:5.
This is "firstborn." God desires Him to have many brethren: Rom. 8:29 — "that He might be the firstborn among many brethren."

into the world

The Greek word, here translated, "world", suggests "the *inhabited* world."
a. Christ came to man, for man needed a helper, an example, a Saviour.
b. Heb. 4:15 — "tempted as we are — "
c. Heb. 2:18 — "able to succor them."
God was able to do the most for man by bringing Christ into the inhabited earth.

He saith, and let all the angels worship Him

When did God say this?
a. Some commentators say the time is uncertain.
b. Some strain to suggest Ps. 97:7 or perhaps Deut. 32:43.
c. We do not need an Old Testament quotation; if the author were inspired as I believe he was, he spoke this by revelation, just as did John on Patmos.
The important thing is that the angels did worship Him while He was on earth, and now do so in heaven.

Luke 2:13-14 — "Glory to God — "
Rev. 5:11-12 — "and the number of them was 10,000 times 10,000 and thousands of thousands — saying — worthy — "

winds and His ministers a flame of fire

This is a quotation from Ps. 104:4
In Psalms it reads a little differently — "who maketh winds His messengers, flames of fire his ministers."
Differences occur among the translators here:
a. Calvin: "The passage quoted seems to have been turned to another meaning from what it appears to have; for as David is there describing the manner in which we see the world to be governed, nothing is more certain than the winds are mentioned, which he says are made messengers by the Lord. — this testimony is brought forward for this purpose, that it might by a similitude be applied to angels." (p. 44)
1. Calvin thinks that in this way David compares winds to angels because they perform offices in this world similar to what the angels do in heaven.
2. Hebrews seems to use winds to illustrate angels.
b. The correct thought of this phrase seems to be that angels move to serve Him — as spirits:
cf. Dan. 9:21 — "they swiftly — "
cf. Heb. 1:14 — "they are ministering spirits — "

His ministers a flame of fire

Angels are related to fire.
Rev. 14:18 — Angels have power over fire.
Rev. 16:8 — An angel gives power to the sun to scorch men with fire.

Study Questions

73. What is meant "when He again bringeth"?
74. Does it change the meaning to move the word "again"?
75. What is meant by "firstborn"?
76. Does this refer to Bethlehem birth?
77. Are there second-born ones?
78. In what way is Christ firstborn? See Col. 1:15-18; Rev. 1:5.
79. How, when others were resurrected before Him, could He be firstborn from the dead?
80. When did God say, "Let all the angels worship Him"?
81. Was He worshipped by angels? When?

82. Where is a heavenly worship described?
83. How many angels worshipped Him in this instance?
84. Give an explanation of "Who maketh His angels winds".
85. Where is the quotation found?
86. Do God's angels move as wind?
87. What is meant by "ministers a flame of fire"?
88. Where is a New Testament scripture that may clarify this?

C. *Superior to angels in universal rule* — 1:8-2:4.
1. Because of character and creation.

Text
1:8-12

8 but of the Son He saith,
 Thy throne, O God, is for ever and ever;
 And the sceptre of uprightness is the sceptre of Thy Kingdom.
9 Thou has loved righteousness, and hated iniquity;
 Therefore God, Thy God, hath anointed Thee
 With the oil of gladness above Thy fellows,
10 And,
 Thou, Lord, in the beginning didst lay the foundation of the earth,
 And the heavens are the works of Thy hands:
11 They shall perish; but Thou continuest:
 And they all shall wax old as doth a garment;
12 And as a mantel shalt Thou roll them up,
 As a garment, and they shall be changed:
 But Thou art the same,
 And Thy years shall not fail.

Paraphrase

8 But to show that the Son is Governor of the world, He saith to Him, Ps. xlv. 6. Thy throne, O God, is for ever and ever. And, Of this government Thou art worthy, because the sceptre of Thy kingdom is a sceptre of rectitude: Thy government is exercised for maintaining truth and righteousness in the world.

9 By coming to destroy the devil and his works, Thou hast showed the greatest love of righteousness and hatred of wickedness; therefore, O God, Thy God (John xx. 17.) hath bestowed on Thee as a king, and a priest, and a prophet, endowments whereby Thou excellest all Thy associates in these offices.

10 And, still farther to display the greatness of the Son above

all the angels, (see ver. 14.), it is said, Ps. cii. 25-27. Thou, Lord, in the beginning didst firmly build the earth, and the works of Thy power are the heavens.

11 They, though firmly founded, shall perish, but Thou, their maker, possessest an endless existence; and they all, as a garment becomes useless by long wearing, shall grow old, unfit for answering the purpose of their creation;

12 And then, as a worn-out upper garment, Thou wilt fold them up, and lay them aside as useless, and they shall be changed for the new heavens and the new earth to be substituted in their place: but Thou, their maker, art the same, without any change, and Thy duration shall never have an end.

Comment

Thy throne, O God, is for ever and ever

This passage has various readings.

a. The original is found in Ps. 45:6 — In the footnote of the A.S. version it reads, "Thy throne is the throne of God."
b. In Hebrews the footnote reads, "Thy throne is God forever." This is the problem: is Christ addressed here as "God"?
a. Calvin says: "The Jews, in order to avoid owning Christ, make an evasion by saying that the throne of God is spoken of; whoever will read the verse who is of sound mind and free of the spirit of contention, cannot doubt, but the Messiah is called God. (p. 45)
b. To back up Calvin's position, note verse 9. "Therefore God, Thy God, hath anointed Thee."
1. The commas could be removed so it would read, "God Thy God hath — "
2. The Psalm is addressed to Jesus, so the commas are correctly placed.

The main point should not be lost in the above discussion:

a. The point is the eternality of Jesus.
b. He is not just a minister of God as are the angels, but He has an eternal throne.

and the sceptre

This is a baton or staff borne by a sovereign as an emblem of authority.

of uprightness

    In a world of corruptness and graft, we need one who rules with uprightness. Ps. 37:18; Isaiah 26:7.
    Jesus' baptism was on the basis of righteousness.
    Matt. 3:15 — "to fulfill all righteousness."

is the sceptre of Thy kingdom

    "Thy kingdom" is also translated "His kingdom".
    Some make a distinction between kingdom of God and kingdom of heaven.
a. One view: The kingdom of God includes all saints from Adam to the present, and the church is a part of it.
b. Second view: The kingdom of heaven will be set up by Jesus when He comes, and the church is not a part of it.

SPECIAL OUTLINE
The New Testament Teaching on the Kingdom

I.   The first preaching of the kingdom.
A. John, in Matt. 3:2: "Repent ye for the kingdom of heaven is at hand."
B. Jesus in Matt. 4:17: "From that time Jesus began to preach, and to say, Repent ye; for the kingdom of heaven it at hand."
C. Matt. 10:7 to disciples: "As ye go, preach saying the kingdom of heaven is at hand."
D. Luke 10:9 — the seventy: " . . . and heal the sick that are therein, and say unto them, the kingdom of God is come nigh unto you."
E. Two questions to be asked:
1. Were the seventy preaching differently than the twelve? No, all eighty-four were preaching the same message.
2. How near was the kingdom to them?
a. This is about six months before the death of Christ.
b. Within their lifetime: Mk. 9:1 — "Verily I say unto you, That there be some of them that stand here, which shall not taste of death till they have seen the kingdom of God come with power."
3. The conclusion is that the kingdom and the church are the same.
II. The names of the kingdom
A. "His kingdom"
    Matt. 16:28: Verily I say unto you, there be some standing

here, which shall not taste of death till they see the Son of man coming in *"His kingdom."*

cf. John 18:36 where Jesus said to Pilate: *"My kingdom* is not of this world; if My kingdom were of this world then would my servants fight, that I should not be delivered to the Jews, but now is *My kingdom* not from hence."

"The kingdom of God" in the same instance:

Mark 9:1 "Verily I say unto you that there be some of them that stand here, which shall not taste of death till they have seen the *kingdom of God* come with power."

Luke 9:27: "But I tell you of a truth, there be some standing here, which shall not taste of death, till they see *the kingdom of God."*

We are not discussing two different kingdoms; they are the same:

B. "The kingdom of heaven"

Matt. 19:23 — right after the rich young ruler went away sorrowing: "Verily I say unto you, that a rich man shall hardly enter into the *kingdom of heaven."*

Mat. 16:19: "And I will give unto thee the keys of *the kingdom of heaven,* and whatsoever — "

C. "The kingdom of God"

Mark 10:25 — The rich young ruler provoked this:

"It is easier for a camel to go through the eye of a needle than for a rich man to enter into the *kingdom of God."*

John 3:5: "Except a man be born of the water and the spirit, he cannot enter into the *kingdom of God."*

D. "My church"

Matt. 16:18: "I say unto thee — upon this rock I will build *my church."*

E. "The church of the firstborn"

Heb. 12:22, 23: "But ye are come — to the general assembly and *church of the firstborn,* which are written in heaven, and to God the Judge of all, and to the spirits of just men made perfect."

F. "A kingdom"

Heb. 12:28: "Wherefore we *receiving a kingdom* which cannot be moved, — let us have grace whereby we may serve God acceptably with reverence and godly fear."

G. "The church of God."

I Cor. 1:2 "Unto the church of God which is at **Corinth** to

them that are sanctified in Christ Jesus, called to be saints, with all that in every place call upon the name of Jesus Christ our Lord, both theirs and ours."
H. "The churches of Christ."
Rom. 16:16 "The churches of Christ salute you."
Ecclesia is the Greek word here translated "church." It means "called out"! Who are its members?
I. "Church His body."
Eph. 5:23 "For the husband is the head of the wife, even as Christ is the head of the church and He is the Saviour of the body."
I Cor. 12:13: "For by one spirit are we all baptized into one body, whether we be Jews or Gentiles, whether we be bond or free; and have been all made to drink into one Spirit."
J. "The regeneration":
Matt. 19:28: "And Jesus said unto them, Verily I say unto you, that ye which have followed me, in *the regeneration* when the Son of man shall sit in the throne of His glory, ye shall also sit upon twelve thrones, judging the twelve tribes of Israel."
III. The purpose of the kingdom
Luke 22:29-30: "I appoint unto you *a kingdom,* as my Father hath appointed unto Me; that ye may eat and drink at My table in My kingdom and sit on thrones judging the twelve tribes of Israel."
A. They would rule while Christ was reigning.
B. They would be the authority — keys to the kingdom.
1. *Superior to angels in universal rule because of character and creation*

Comment

Thou hast loved righteousness
What is righteousness?
a. It is in the realm of good beyond that which is demanded, but that which comes with love.
b. A man is right when he supports his family, but he is in the realm of righteousness when he goes beyond.
What evidence do we have that He loved righteousness?
a. His teaching emphasized it.
1. Matt. 5:20.
2. Luke 10: parable of the good Samaritan.

   b. It was proved by His sinless life.
1. Luke 23:4: Pilate found no fault in Him.
2. Matt. 4: He insisted on righteousness when the devil tempted Him.
3. Heb. 4:15: "was without sin."
   c. His obedience to the Father's will proves His love for righteousness.

and hated iniquity

   How do we know He did?
a. By his teaching.
1. The woes to the sinner. Matt. 11:21; 23:13-29; Luke 6:24.
2. His condemnation of hypocrisy. Matt. 6:16; 15:7.
   b. He proved it by His actions.
Matt. 21:12. The cleansing of the temple.
Jesus hated evil, but not the evildoer.
a. He looked upon the rich young ruler and loved him. Mk. 10:21.
b. He ate with publicans and sinners. Matt. 9:10.
c. He forgave the vilest of sinners, those who crucified Him. Luke 23:34.
d. He came to die for sinners.
We are expected to be like Christ.
a. Ps. 97:10: "Oh ye that love Jehovah, hate evil."
b. Matt. 6:15; 18:35: Forgiveness.

therefore God, Thy God hath anointed Thee

   Is Christ addressed as God here?
a. Yes, if the comma is left after "God", if read as addressed to Jesus Christ.
b. No, if the comma should be removed and placed after "therefore", for it then reads, "God Thy God."
1. This means then that God is the God of Jesus.
2. It should be remembered that commas are arbitrarily placed in the scripture by men.
3. This is a quotation from Ps. 45:6 and appears the same in the Old Testament as in the New Testament.
   c. God is the God of Jesus.
Matt. 27:46: "My God, My God, why hast Thou forsaken me —"
Anointing was a familiar practice in the scriptures.

a. There were two kinds, perhaps three.
1. The ordinary anointing of head and body. cf. Deut. 28:40; Ruth 3:3; Micah 6:15; Ps. 23:5.
2. The official anointings:
a) Prophets were anointed at their inauguration to office. I Chr. 16:22; I Kings 19:16; Ps. 105:15.
b) Priests were anointed:
1) At the institution of the Levitical priesthood, they were anointed to office. Ex. 40:15; Numbers 3:3.
2) The anointing for the high priesthood. Ex. 29:29; Lev. 16:32.
a) Kings were anointed in a divinely appointed ceremony. I Sam. 9:16; 10:1; I Kings 1:34, 39.
3. The anointing of inanimate objects. Gen. 31:13 — Jacob anointed the pillar at Bethel. cf. Ex. 30:26-28.
   Jesus was anointed, as other scriptures indicate:
a. Acts 4:27: " — Jesus whom Thou didst anoint — "
   Acts 10:37-38: " — how God anointed Him with the Holy Spirit."
b. Jesus was and is Prophet, Priest and King, so He is deserving of anointment.
1) Prophet — Deut. 18:15-18.
2) Priest — Heb. 4:14.
3) King — Rev. 17:14.

with the oil of gladness

Jesus was glad — Heb. 12:2: " — who for the joy that was set — "
God was pleased with him; thus He was glad:
Matt. 3, at His baptism: " — in whom I am well pleased — "
Matt. 17, at His transfiguration: " — well pleased — "
There are two means or materials used for anointing, one material, and one figurative:
a. Material — oil. Luke 7:46: respect paid to a friend or guest. Ps. 23.5.
b. God's anointing for man.
   II Cor. 1:21: " — anointed us in God."
   I John 2:27: " — the anointing which ye received — "
   The "oil of gladness" is figurative, and we may believe the Holy Spirit is referred to.
   Acts 10:37-38: " — anointed Him with the Holy Spirit."

above Thy fellows

Who are the "fellows"?
a. Obviously the Godhead is not referred to.
b. He is above all others:
1. He is above man with whom He dwelt, as He took upon Himself the form of a servant, for these men must confess Him. Phil. 2:9-11.
2. He is above all rulers, for He is "King of kings and Lord of lords." Rev. 17:14; 19:16.
3. He is above all saints, for He is their priest. Heb. 4:14.

the foundation of the earth

This is a quotation from Ps. 102:25.
a. It seems not to refer to Christ at the first reading.
b. Christ's name is not mentioned in the Psalm.
c. Calvin says, " — but it is yet plain that He is so pointed out, that no one can doubt but that His kingdom is there avowedly recommended to us." (p. 47)

New Testament verses that suggest the same idea: Jn. 1:1; Col. 1:16. The eternality of Christ over the inhabited world is established.

and the heavens are the works of Thy hands

This refers to the creation above the earth.

"Heavens" is in the plural form. The completeness of His power is established. There is not one God who made heaven, and another God who made earth.

They shall perish

What is meant by "they"?
a. Specifically, "the foundations of earth and the heavens."
b. This world will perish. See other verses: Matt. 24:35; II Peter 3:7-13; Rev. 21:1: "The first heaven and first earth are passed away."
c. Other things will likewise perish:
1. Evil angels will perish. II Peter 2:4; Matt. 25:41.
2. Sinful men will perish. Jn. 3:16; Rev. 20:15; II Peter 3:7.

but Thou continuest

This is called "immutability" by the theologians. Christ is

not mutable — not changing. Christ is invariable — unchangeable. Note His eternality as seen by other verses. Heb. 1:8; 13:8; II Cor. 1:19.

they shall wax old as a garment

Scientists agree to the ageing of the world.
They say that the sun is losing its heat, but of course tomorrow they may change their mind. They say the soil is wearing out, so our vegetables need vitamins added.
Obviously man grows old.
James verifies this — 4:14: Man is "as a vapor."

and as a mantle shalt Thou roll them up

The mantle was a loose sleeveless garment worn over other garments. God is powerful enough to roll up the earth as easily as man cares for his coat.

and as a garment they shall be changed

Peter expresses this thought likewise in II Peter 3:10.
God is able to make changes quickly. I Cor. 15:52: "in a twinkling of an eye — "

but Thou art the same

In what ways is He the same?
a. He is the same in *dependability,* so His words will abide. Matt. 24:35.
b. He is the same in *character,* so His love will save us in the end.
c. He is the same *in any age.* Heb. 13:8 — "yesterday, today, yea and forever."

and Thy years shall not fail Thee

Old age is no factor with Jesus.
Time does not enter in for He is eternal. Death could not corrupt Him. Ps. 16:10: " — Holy One did not see corruption." Acts 2:31: " — nor did His flesh see corruption."

Study Questions

89. What is the duration of God's throne?
90. How does this prove His superiority over angels?
91. What is a sceptre?
92. What is its significance?

93. What is the nature of His reign? cf. Psalm 37:18; Isaiah 26:7.
94. Does Matt. 3:15 add to the idea of reign of righteousness?
95. Does Jesus have a kingdom?
96. What words are connected with the term, "kingdom"? What is the difference between the terms, "kingdom of heaven", and "kingdom of God"?
97. Is it possible to have a kingdom without a king?
98. When was Jesus king?
99. When is He your king?
100. How did Christ feel concerning righteousness?
101. What is righteousness?
102. What evidence do we have that Christ loved righteousness? By His preaching? By His life?
103. How strongly was Jesus against iniquity?
104. Did Jesus hate the sinners?
105. Name some times that Jesus preached against sin.
106. Did He ever display wrath against sin?
107. Is God the God of Christ?
108. Is Christ spoken of as being God?
109. Did Jesus ever call God His God? cf. Matt. 27:46.
110. Describe the various kinds of anointing in the Old Testament.
111. When was Christ anointed?
112. What about Jesus caused Him to deserve anointing? (Prophet — Priest — King.)
113. What is the significance of the expression, "oil of gladness"?
114. Did Jesus ever hear of an expression of gladness from God?
115. What other means has God used to anoint people?
116. In what way have we been anointed? cf. II Cor. 1:21; I John 2:27; Acts 10:37-38.
117. Who are the fellows of Christ?
118. Could "fellows" refer to the Godhead?
119. Is He above man? How do we know this is true?
120. Is He above rulers? Rev. 17:14; 19:16.
121. Is He above priests? Heb. 4:14.
122. "And Thou Lord" — To whom does this refer?
123. Read Psalm 102:25, which is quoted in Heb. 1:10.
124. Did He make the heavens? cf. John 1:1; Col. 1:16.
125. What is the main idea established here?
126. What is meant by, "they shall perish"?

127. Does the scripture back up this teaching that the worlds and heavens will perish?
128. Will anything else perish?
    1. Evil angels: II Peter 2:4; Matt. 25:41.
    2. Sinful men: John 3:16; Rev. 20:15; II Peter 3:7.
129. "But Thou continuest" carries what idea?
130. Do other verses establish His eternality?
131. What figure of speech is used to describe the ageing of the earth in v. 11?
132. Do scientists agree?
133. Does man grow old? cf. James 4:14.
134. What figure describes the end of the world in v. 12?
135. What is a mantle?
136. What other scriptures teach that God is able to change things? II Peter 3:10; I Cor. 15:52.
137. In what ways are God and Christ the same?
138. Are the Godhead members subject to failing years?
139. Can the Godhead be corrupted by failing years? cf. Psalm 16:10; Acts 2:31.

2. *Superior to angels in universal rule because He is served by angels* 4:13-14

Text
1:13-14

13 But of which of the angels hath He said at any time, Sit thou on my right hand, Till I make thine enemies the footstool on thy feet?

14 Are they not all ministering spirits, sent forth to do service for the sake of them that shall inherit salvation?

5. Some are sent to take care of the living saints.
   Matt. 18:10: "In heaven their angels do always behold the face of My father who is in heaven." Acts 5:19; Acts 12:7.
6. "They are all sent forth to minister in some way directly or indirectly, for the benefit of those who are the heirs of salvation." Milligan. (pp. 73-74)

Paraphrase

13 Moreover, none of the angels have any proper dominion over the world. For, to which of the angels did God at any time say, as He said to His Son in the human nature, Ps. cx. 1. Sit thou at my right hand; reign thou over the universe, till I utterly subject all thine enemies to thee?

14 Instead of exercising sovereign dominion, are not all the angels called, Ps. civ. 4., ministering spirits, subject to the Son, (v. 6.), and by Him, sitting at God's right hand, (v. 13.), sent forth to minister for them who shall inherit immortality as the sons of God?

Comment

any time

1. This is a question with an implied answer. The answer is "none." Jesus was spoken to in words that were never spoken to any angels.

sit thou on my right hand

This is a quotation from Ps. 110:1.
It is not unusual to have God spoken of as having bodily organs:
a. Face: cf. Gen. 32:30 — "God face to face." Ex. 33:11 — spoke to Moses "face to face."
b. Hand: cf. Ezra 7:9 — "according to the hand of God." Job 2:10 — "receive good at the hand of God."

till I make thine enemies the footstool

God and Christ have their enemies:
a. In Acts 4:24-28, Psalm 2 is shown to be fulfilled in Jerusalem by Pilate; the Jews and the Gentiles in the crucifixion of Christ.
Enemies seem to combine forces when they have a common enemy or objective. The Sadducees and Pharisees joined forces against Jesus.
b. James 4:4: Friendship of the world is enmity with God.
c. Rom. 8:7: A carnal mind is at enmity with God.

the footstool of Thy feet

This is a familiar expression:
a. Christ is waiting to do this. Heb. 10:13.
b. Christ will reign until this is a reality. I Cor. 15:24-25.
c. Christ's victory will come. Rev. 19:11-21.
Enemies of Christ will be punished. Heb. 10:27 — "a fierceness of fire which shall devour the adversaries."
"Footstool of thy feet" alludes to an ancient custom of princes and kings to tread on the necks of their vanquished enemies, in token of their complete victory over them.

are they not all ministering spirits
    This is an interrogative type of expression:
a. The question form is just as strong as a positive statement.
b. Angels are ministering spirits, for v. 13 verifies that "they" refers to angels.
    This establishes the superiority of Christ over angels.
a. Angels may minister, but Christ is Saviour.
b. Angels only serve those who have salvation made possible by Christ.
    We have examples of different classes of angels that serve man and God:
a. The Cherubim and Seraphim:
1. Cherubim
a) Cherubim guarded Eden. Gen. 3:24.
b) Figures of them were placed on the mercy seat. Ex. 25:18.
c) Figures of colossal size, with extended wings, were in Solomon's temple.
2. Seraphim
a) The name means, "burning, glowing".
b) Isaiah saw them in his vision. Is. 6:2.
c) They had three sets of wings; one set covered the face in humility; the second covered the feet, showing respect; the third was used to fly.
d) They resembled men. Is. 6:3.
e) They had a twofold purpose; Is. 6:3, to praise God; Is. 6:6, to communicate.
b. Michael and Gabriel
1. Michael:
a) His name means, "who is like God".
b) He is one of the chief princes or archangels. Dan. 10:13; Jude 9.
c) He was the "Prince of Israel". Dan. 10:21.
d) He is spoken of as "Great Prince". Dan. 12:1.
e) He is the leader of the hosts of God in war. Rev. 12:7.
2. Gabriel:
a) His name means "man of God".
b) He is an angel of high rank.
c) He made two great announcements: the birth of John, Lu. 1:11-22, to Zacharias; the birth of Jesus, Lu. 1:26-31, to Mary.

1:14 HELPS FROM HEBREWS

    d) He was sent to Daniel to explain his visions. 8:16; 9:21.
  c. Elect angels
  1. Paul speaks of them, I Tim. 5:21: "— and elect angels."
  2. These are in opposition to the evil angels spoken of in Eph. 6:12: "spiritual hosts of wickedness"
  d. Let us see their work in the past:
  1. Old Testament ministry:
  a) Appeared to warn Abraham and Lot. Gen. 18:1-2; 19:1.
  b) Protected the men in the fiery furnace. Dan. 3:19-28.
  c) Stopped the mouths of lions for Daniel. 6:22.
  d) Helped God's people in war. Psalms 34:7: "angel of Jehovah encampeth —" Exodus 23:20-21: "angel before thee —" Joshua 5:13-14 — before Jericho's battle: "— prince of host of Jehovah." Judges 2:1-5 — angel from Gilgal, telling them to destroy all paganism.
  2. New Testament ministry:
  a) Gabriel announced the birth of both John and Jesus in Luke 1.
  b) Angels ministered unto Jesus after His temptation, Matt. 4:11 and in Gethsemane, Luke 22:43.
  c) Angels carried Lazarus to Abraham's bosom, Luke 16:22.
  d) An angel directed Philip to the Ethiopian, Acts 8:26.
  e) An angel appeared to Cornelius, Acts 10:7.
  f) An angel comforted Paul, Acts 27:23.
  g) An angel released Peter and John from prison, Acts 5:19.
  h) An angel saved Peter from Herod, Acts 12:7-11.
  i) Churches in Revelation had angels, Rev. 2:1, 8, 12, 18.
  j) They will be present when Christ comes. Matt. 16:27; 24:31.
  e. Do they minister to us today?
  1. The *International Standard Bible Encyclopedia* says, "The modern conception of the possession by each man of special guardian angels is not found in the Old Testament." (p. 132)
  2. Milligan believes they serve us:
  a) He believes that they aid in the work of redeeming man; and in carrying out this work of its final consummation.
  3. Some may be sent to frustrate the wiles and devices of Satan and his fallen angels. Jude 6.
  4. Some are sent to punish wicked men. Acts 12:23.

Study Questions

140. Did God ever speak to Christ something not said to angels, according to this verse?

141. Is it common for God to be spoken of as possessing organs, such as hands? cf. Gen. 32:30; Ex. 33:11; Ezra 7:9; Job 2:10.
142. What enemies does God have?
143. What makes us enemies of God? cf. James 4:4; Rom. 8:7.
144. What is the significance of "footstool"?
145. Describe this time of waiting. cf. Heb. 10:13; I Cor. 15:24-25.
146. Will God see to it that Christ will be victorious? cf. Rev. 19:11-21.
147. If angels minister, how is Christ greater?
148. What are the different classes of angels?
149. Where do the Cherubim and Seraphim appear?
150. What does *Seraphim* mean?
151. What can be said of Michael and Gabriel?
152. What does the name Michael mean?
153. What is the nature of his work?
154. What is the meaning of the name Gabriel?
155. Tell of some of his work.
156. What are "elect angels"?
157. What would be their opposites?
158. Tell of some of the work of angels in the past in the Old Testament.
159. What classes of work did they participate in?
160. Tell of the work of angels in the life of Christ.
161. What was their work in Acts?
162. What is their work described in the book of Revelation?
163. What passages teach that angels may minister to us today?

Chapter One — True or False

_____ 1. When God spoke to the men in the Old Testament, He made his way known in just one way.

_____ 2. The revelation of Christ came at the end of certain days.

_____ 3. Christ was present at the time of creation.

_____ 4. The author of the Hebrew letter states in this chapter that now Christ is preaching to the souls in prison.

_____ 5. This epistle points out that since Christ came into this world as man, we have abundant evidence that Christ is mutable (changeable).

HELPS FROM HEBREWS

_____ 6. There is only one kind of angel, those that serve the devil.

_____ 7. Jesus loved righteousness and hated iniquity, according to the Hebrew letter, and therefore He asked His angels to sit at His right hand.

_____ 8. One way Christ is superior to the angels is in His name.

_____ 9. In spite of the fact that we have just one Old Testament, Hebrews speaks of God speaking in divers portions.

_____10. Jesus sat down at the right hand of God prior to the atonement, according to Hebrews.

_____11. Since Christ was begotten of the Father, we may assume that Christ came into existence after God had made the heavens and the earth.

_____12. Malachi was the last prophet through whom God has spoken.

_____13. This epistle speaks of the earth growing old.

_____14. A vision was one method God used to speak in the Old Testament, but He has never used the method since.

_____15. The prophets, priests and kings were anointed in the Old Testament, but we have no mention of anointing in this chapter.

_____16. Since Christ assisted God in creation, and in Him all things exist, He is the only person who ever lived who did not look forward to an inheritance.

_____17. Since the world and the heavens are to perish, Christ's throne will not be forever, for His throne will not have anything upon which to rest.

_____18. Christ's enemies are to be considered as candidates for Christ's footstools.

_____19. The name God is a name that belongs only to Jehovah.

_____20. The Son can be spoken of as being a reflection of God's glory.

_____21. Revelation of God has been progressive.

_____22. The heirs of salvation have angels serving them as ministering spirits.

_____23. The world is growing old, and as a garment it shall be changed.

_____24. The sceptre of Christ is spoken of as a "sceptre of righteousness".
_____25. This chapter speaks of God working with His hands.

SUMMARY OF CHAPTER ONE

God's final word to man was spoken through His Son, although He had revealed His word through the prophets in the ancient times. The superiority of this last message is related to the superiority of the One through whom it was revealed. Seven points of His superior excellence are given:

(1) Heir of all things.
(2) Creator of the world.
(3) The effulgence of God's glory.
(4) The image of His substance.
(5) The One who upholds all things.
(6) The One who made purification for sins.
(7) The One exalted to the right hand of the throne of God.

The Son is greater than angels, as indicated by the name which He inherited — the name "Son".

A series of Old Testament quotations proves His superiority. No angel was ever called "Son". They were commanded to worship the firstborn, for they are ministering servants.

The Son is King eternal, and righteousness characterizes His reign. The things which He created will be changed like a garment that grows old, but He will remain the same. He will conquer all His enemies, while angels will serve those who shall inherit salvation.

Preliminary Discussion of Chapter Two

The first chapter is an exaltation of God's revelation.

1. God tried to speak to man in several manners.
   A. God, being what He is, was obligated to reveal Himself.
   B. In His love, He sent prophets and angels to teach man.
2. After every effort He finally sent His Son.
   A. Chapter one is an exaltation of Christ and His message.
   B. He is not merely a prophet or an angel.
      1. He is heir of all. v. 2.
      2. He made the world. v. 2.
      3. He is the brightness of God's glory, and the image of His substance. v. 3.

4. He upholdeth all things. v. 3.
   5. He brought purification.
   6. He is seated.
   7. He is superior to angels.
   8. He has a greater name than they.
   9. He was begotten in the resurrection.
   10. All angels shall adore Him. v. 6.
   11. He has an eternal throne.
   12. He has the sceptre of righteousness. v. 8.
   13. He was anointed with the oil of gladness above all.
   14. All other things perish, but years shall not fail Him.
3. Some have allowed themselves to slip and fall after hearing other revelations. How awful for us to neglect this great revelation!
   A. A more earnest heed should be given to the things that we have heard.
   B. Simply because God makes such great efforts to love and win man, man should not place the responsibility on God for man's salvation.
4. Notice how personal this Chapter Two is.
   A. *We* ought to give more earnest heed.
   B. Things *we* have heard. v. 1.
   C. *We* drift away. v. 2.
   D. *We* escape. v. 3.
   E. *We* neglect. v. 3.
5. In an exegesis class we take verses apart to find the truth and depth of truth by studying words, phrases, verses. There is danger here; however. Note these admonitions:
   A. Don't lose sight of the greatness of God's Word.
   B. See the whole revelation — see it as a unit.
   C. Study the outline of the book so that you will see the purpose and plan of the book.
6. In Chapter Two, verses one and four, we have a great warning because we have a great salvation.
   A. The warning is of the danger of slipping and neglecting from which there is no escape.
   B. The danger is illustrated by the judgment of God in the Old Testament.
   C. If God punished for neglect in the Old Testament, how much more sore will be His judgment for neglect of His Son.

7. In verse one, we have an exhortation to give earnest heed.
   A. We must not be careless, indifferent.
   B. If this is God's final revelation and His supreme effort to win man, we must not take it lightly.
3. *Hence, we see the certainty of punishment to those who neglect God's revelation through His Son.*

Text
2:1-4

1 Therefore we ought to give more earnest heed to the things that were heard, lest haply we drift away from them. 2 For if the word spoken through angels proved steadfast, and every transgression and disobedience received a just recompense of reward; 3 how shall we escape, if we neglect so great a salvation? which having at the first been spoken through the Lord, was confirmed unto us by them that heard; 4 God also bearing witness with them, both by signs and wonders, and by manifold powers, and by gifts of the Holy Spirit, according to His own will.

Paraphrase

1 Because the Son, by whom God hath spoken to us in these last days, is greatly superior to all the angels, both in His nature and office, we ought to pay the more attention to the things which the ministers of the word heard Him speak, (ver. 3.), lest at any time we should let them slip out of our minds.

2 For, if the law which God spake to the Israelites, by the ministry of angels, was so confirmed by the miracles which accompanied it, that every presumptuous transgression and disobedience received a just punishment,

3 How shall we escape unpunished, if we disbelieve and despise the news of so great a salvation? which began to be preached by the Lord Himself, and hath been fully published and confirmed to us Jews, not by a vague report, but by the credible testimony of the apostles and others who heard Him;

4 God himself bearing joint witness to the salvation preached of the Lord and His apostles, both by signs and wonders, and miracles of divers kinds, which He enabled these preachers to perform, and by distributions of the gifts of the Holy Ghost, which they bestowed, not according to their will, but according to His own pleasure?

Comment

Therefore we

    This suggests a conclusion to be drawn from previous points:
a. Since God has loved us, giving us a ministry, a word, a Christ, ministering angels, some duties must rest on us.
b. Salvation is not to be solely God's responsibility. It is time man should awaken, for God will not endure a wayward society.

to give the more earnest heed

    This calls for application of man's energies, and not a careless. carefree attitude:
a. God challenges men to hear — to reason.
1) Rev. 3:13: " — hath ears, let him hear."
2) Isaiah 1:18: " — let us reason."
3) Deut. 18:19: " — not hearken."
4) Matt. 7:27: " — heareth and doeth not."
b. Man is a creature of choice. Therefore, he must use his intellect for his self-preservation.
    Jesus spoke plainly concerning disbelief, saying that disbelievers will be condemned. (Mark 16:16)

to the things that were heard

    What had been heard?
a. This refers to the message heard from Christ and his Apostles.
1. Some might want to say that it refers to all the Old Testament scriptures, but this is not true, except as preached by the Lord and the apostles.
2. The content suggests the preaching of Christ and His apostles, and not the divers portions and manners of the Old Testament times.
b. The message that made them Christians is referred to here.

lest happily we drift away from them.

    Drifting is always downstream.
a. Like a man that is above the waterfall, he has only to fold his hands and drift to his destruction.
b. The man who would reach heaven must strive, not drift.
    An alternate translation is, "Lest at any time we should let them slip."

a. The Word will not slip — it is final and eternal.
1. Matt. 24:35: " — my word shall not pass away."
b. Man needs to guard himself lest he slip.
1. Luke 13:24: "Strive to enter in at the strait gate."
2. II Peter 1:10: "Make your calling and election sure."

for if the word spoken through angels proved steadfast
1. Milligan says this refers directly to the Mosaic law.
a. Gal. 3:19 — law was ordained in the hands of a mediator by angels.
b. Deut. 33:2. " — from His right hand went a fiery law for them."
c. Acts 7:53: — "who have received the law by the disposition of angels, and have not kept it."
God's words to Israel were filled with warnings, and the history of Israel proves that God meant what He said:
a. Exodus 23:20-21: "An angel before thee — provoke him not."
b. **Deut.** 17:12: There was a death penalty for rejecting the word of a priest.
The word "if" suggests a conclusion to be drawn — look for it.

a just recompense of reward
The penalty in the Old Testament was severe and quick. A few examples of its severity are given:
a. Deut. 19:16-21 — The penalty for a false witness.
b. Joshua 7:25 — Israel stoned Achan for disobedience.
c. Deut. 22:21 — A harlot stoned to death.
The New Testament gives us a picture of the seriousness of sin.
a. Acts 5:1-11 — Ananias and Sapphira — carried out dead.

a just
Israel agreed to the justice of it:
a. Deut. 27:26: "all the people shall say amen."
Who is man that he could challenge the justice of a Father who is so forgiving and loving?

recompense of reward
"Recompense" means compensation, award or payment:
a. Good, as well as bad, has its retribution.

b. We live in a dependable universe, where whatever a man sows, that will he reap. Gal. 6:7-8.
c. Every road has its ending.
d. Every law has its penalty, else it is no law.
Recompense is God's privilege, for it is He who has made the laws of the universe.
a. Heb. 10:30-31: "Vengeance belongeth to Me, I will recompense."
b. Rev. 19:15: "winepress of the wrath of the Almighty."

How shall we escape

This is the conclusion suggested by the "if" in verse two. There is no escape.
Three characteristics of God make it impossible for man to escape:
a. He is omnipresent — man cannot go where God is not.
b. He is omniscient — all-wise, so He cannot be outwitted by man.
c. He is omnipotent — all-powerful, therefore man cannot overpower Him.
1. He is almighty.
a) Gen. 17:1; 35:11; Rev. 21:22.
2. He is the source of all power.
a) Rom. 13:1: There is no power but of God.
Some have tried to escape from God, but found it impossible:
a. Adam and Eve tried to hide. Gen. 3:8.
b. Cain tried to hide, Gen. 4:10, but God said, "The voice of thy brother's blood crieth unto Me from the ground."
c. Jonah tried it, but he had more than a tribal deity.

if we neglect so great a salvation
1. In what ways is our salvation great?
a. I Peter 1:12: Angels desire to look into it.
b. John 8:56: Abraham rejoiced as he saw it coming.
c. Heb. 5:9; 12:2: Christ is the author of it.
d. John 3:16: God loved us.
e. Romans 1:16: It has power.
f. Heb. 2:3-4: It is confirmed.

the Lord

Was there no salvation until Christ?
a. Yes, in a sense:

1. Enoch was translated. Heb. 11:5.
2. Elijah went up by a whirlwind in a chariot of fire and horses of fire. II Kings 2:11.
3. Lazarus carried into Abraham's bosom. Luke 16:22.
4. Psalms 23: "through the valley of the shadow of death."
b. Old Testament salvation is not as clearly set forth as that which Jesus gives, which is the great salvation.
1. II Tim. 1:10: "brought life and immortality to light."
Of what did He the Lord speak?
a) He spoke of His Deity:
1. John 1:18: "Son who is in the bosom of the Father."
2. John 10:30: "I and the Father are one."
b) He spoke of Himself as "the Way."
1. John 14:6.
c) He spoke of repentance.
1. Luke 24:47; 13:3.
2. Luke 15:7.
d) He spoke of His authority.
1. Matt. 28:18-20; Mark 16:16.

was confirmed unto us

Who did the confirming?
a. No doubt those that heard Him is here meant:
1. The apostles were eye and ear witnesses of His personal ministry:
a) Acts 1:8.
b) Acts 1:21.
c) I John 1:1-3.
d) I Peter 1:20: " — but was manifested at the end of time for your sake."
e) **Acts 26:26:** "This thing hath not been done in a corner."
Does the word "us" destroy the apostleship of Paul?
a. Not necessarily, for he could be simply associating himself with his readers.
b. This is done frequently in other parts of the epistle. (See 3:14; 4:1, 2, 3, 11, 14, 15, 16; 6:1, 3.)

God also bearing witness with them

The apostles did not have to stand on their word alone:
a. They had proof that accompanied their message.
b. Thus the person who rejected the preaching rejected not only the word of God, but also His works.

The Jews in their heckling of Jesus had asked for proof. Matt. 12:39.

both by signs and wonders

What is meant by "signs"?

a. Hear Jesus name some signs: Mark 16:17-18; 16:20.
1. Cast out demons, v. 17.
2. Speak with new tongues, v. 17.
3. Take up deadly serpents, v. 18.
4. Drink deadly poison, v. 18.
5. Lay hands on sick and they recover, v. 18.

b. These signs were miracles:
1. They were not witch doctor trickery, but proofs of the origin of the message delivered.
2. They are called "signs" because they arouse men's minds to think of something higher than what appears.

What is meant by "wonders"?

a. This is not necessarily something different, but a different way of looking at the same thing:
1. Milligan quotes Ebrard as teaching that miracles may be regarded in a fourfold aspect:

a) First with regard to their *design* as signs — miraculous testimonies in behalf of the truth.
b) Secondly, with respect to their *nature* as wonders, supernatural acts calculated to excite wonder and amazement in the minds of those who witnessed them.
c) Thirdly, with respect to their *origin* as manifestations of supernatural powers.
d) Finally, in their *specific Christian aspects*, as gifts and distributions of the Holy Spirit imparted to the original witnesses and proclaimers of the truth. (See I Cor. 12; Eph. 4:11; Milligan, pp. 79, 80.)

A good example is Acts 2:43: "And fear came upon every soul, and many wonders and signs were done through the apostles."

a. Signs would set their thoughts to work.
b. Wonders would cause them to feel.
c. Miracles would cause faith. John 20:30-31.
d. Works beyond the uniformity of nature would cause astonishment.

and by manifold powers

"Powers" rather suggests the energy put forth in wonders:
a. It was seen in Jesus. Luke 9:43.
b. Christ always gave glory to God for the power that worked in Him.

The word "manifold" is suggestive, for Christ proved His power over many things:
a. Power to forgive sins. Matt. 9:6.
b. Power over unclean spirits. Matt. 10:1.
c. Power to heal sickness. Mark 3:15.
d. Power over nature. Mark 4:39: "Peace be still."
e. Power over death. John 10:18: "Power to lay it down, power to pick it up."
f. Power to transform human life abounds in the scripture and in human history.

These three expressions appear together to show the devil's powers likewise:

II Thess. 2:9: "Working of Satan, with all power and signs and lying wonders."
a. The devil deceives, while Jesus deals with truth.
b. The devil's servants can practice magic as well as a magician can fool people; but remember that it is deceit, not truth.

and gifts of the Holy Spirit

These gifts pertain primarily to the church, whereas the other expressions were definitely true of God in times past:
a. Eph. 4:11: " — He gave some apostles, and some prophets, and some evangelists, and some pastors and teachers — "
b. I Cor. 12:4-17 — diversities of the Spirit.
c. I Cor. 12:28-30 is a very good list.

according to His own will

God in His wisdom is able to distribute gifts arbitrarily in order to make them most efficient in His service.

Calvin says, "The words remind us that the miracles mentioned could not be ascribed to any except to God alone and that they were not wrought undesignedly, but for the distinct purpose of sealing the truth of the gospel." (p. 56)

Study Questions

164. Did God ever speak through angels a punishment or a warning?
165. "Just recompense of reward" means what?
166. Name some instances of fair punishment.
167. Did the people ever agree that God was just? (See Deut. 27:26.)
168. Is this a world that gives recompense of reward? (See Gal. 6:7-8.)
169. What is there about God that makes it impossible for man to flee from God? Explain.
170. Name some who have tried to escape.
171. What is referred to as "gifts of the Holy Spirit"?
172. Why did God give some people gifts? (See Eph. 4:11; I Cor. 12:4-17; I Cor. 12:28-30.)
173. What new discussion does Paul begin in verse 5?
174. What is meant by the expression, "world to come"?
175. Does he mean that in the new earth man will reign?
176. Was this world ever subjected to man?
177. Was it ever lost?
178. When? (See Gen. 3:15-24.)
179. Was it lost to anyone? cf. Psalm 68:18; John 14:30; II Cor. 4:4; John 12:31; John 16:11; II Cor. 2:2; I John 5:19; Rev. 12:9.
180. Did the Jews desire signs?
181. What is the difference between signs and wonders?
182. What is the real difference? Are not both miracles?
183. What power do we see in the apostles?
184. "Manifold powers" suggests many powers. Will you name some indications of Christ's power over many things?
185. Could power refer to the energy put forth in doing wonders?
186. Does the devil have similar power? cf. II Thess. 2:9; Eph. 6:12.
187. Is neglect a sin?
188. What will neglect do in other realms, such as a flower garden, a farm, a building, a baby?
189. Is the sin in proportion to the greatness of the thing neglected?
190. In what ways is salvation through Christ a great salvation?
191. What in this salvation was spoken by the Lord?

192. Did He add to what has been previously spoken?
193. Did He just add more light?
194. Name some things spoken of by Jesus.
195. Did Jesus speak of the death, burial, resurrection?
196. What do you understand by the word "confirmed"?
197. Who did the confirming?
198. Is the author stating that he received his message from the apostles who traveled with Jesus?
199. Is it characteristic of the author to identify himself with the reader?
200. Who is referred to by the expression, "them that heard"?
201. Explain the statement, "God bearing witness with them."

D. *He is superior to angels in recovering man's dominion of the earth*: 2:5-18

1) *Original dominion of the earth by God's people, lost through sin, to be restored through Christ*: 2:5-9.

Text
2:5-9

5 For not unto angels did He subject the world to come, whereof we speak. 6 But one hath somewhere testified, saying,
   What is man, that Thou art mindful of him?
   Or the Son of man, that Thou visitest him?
7 Thou madest him a little lower than the angels;
   Thou crownedst him with glory and honor,
   And didst set him over the works of thy hands:
8 Thou didst put all things in subjection under his feet. For in that He subjected all things unto him, He left nothing that is not subjected to him. But now we see not yet all things subjected to him. 9 But we behold Him who hath been made a little lower than the angels, even Jesus, because of the suffering of death crowned with glory and honor, that by the grace of God He should taste of death for every man.

Paraphrase

5 For although the angel (Exod. xxiii. 20.) who conducted the Israelites had Canaan subjected to him, to the angels God hath not subjected the world which is to come, the possession of which is the salvation of which we speak.

6 Now, that the Son of God was to be made flesh, and, in the flesh, was to be appointed King universal, David in a certain

place, Psal. viii. 4, plainly testified, saying, What is the first man that Thou shouldst remember him; or the posterity of the first man, that Thou shouldst take such care of them?

7 For, to save them from perishing, thou wilt make Him, who is thy Son, for a little while less than angels, by clothing Him with flesh, and subjecting Him to death: After that, Thou wilt crown Him with glory and honor, by raising Him from the dead, and wilt set Him over the works of Thy hands, as Ruler and Lord of all.

8 Thou wilt put all things under His feet. See Eph. i. 22. Wherefore, by subjecting all things to Him, God will leave nothing unsubjected; consequently, there is nothing over which His power will not at length finally prevail. But at present we do not yet see all things subjected to Him; for evil angels and wicked men are still unsubdued by Him:

9 But we see Jesus, who for a little while was made less than angels, by appearing in the flesh, that, through the gracious appointment of God, He might die, not for the Jews only, but on account of everyone: Him we see, for the suffering, of death, crowned with glory and honour, by His resurrection and ascension. And these are sufficient proofs, that all His enemies shall finally be subdued by Him.

Comment

1. The Catholic Bible (revision of the Challoner Rheims version) states it this way:
   "for He has not subjected to angels the world to come — ".
   C.B. footnote: "To come" here means the Christian dispensation, not the future life.
2. Footnote to American Standard version: "The inhabited earth." However, observe that it is the inhabited earth to come.
3. Was this world subjected to man?
   Yes:
   See Gen. 1:28: "And God blessed them, and God said unto them, Be fruitful and multiply and replenish the earth and subdue it and *have dominion over* the fish of the sea and over the birds of the heavens and over every living thing that moveth upon the earth."
4. Was it ever lost by man?

a. "Yes," says Calvin: "As soon then as Adam alienated himself from God through sin, he was justly deprived of the good things which he had received — The wild beasts ferociously attack us, those who ought to be awed by our presence are dreaded by us, some never obey us, others can hardly be trained to submit, and they do us harm in various ways; the earth answers not our expectations in cultivating it; the sky, the air, the sea and other things are often adverse to us." (p. 57)
b. "Yes," says Milligan: "But in consequence of sin, man has in a great measure lost his dominion. See Gen. 3:15-24." (p. 82)
5. Was it lost *to* everyone? Did someone take over when man lost the dominion?
Milligan believes this is what occurred. "For a time Satan got possession of this world." (p. 82)
a. Psalm 68:18: "Thou hast ascended on high; Thou has led away captives."
b. John 12:31: "Now is the judgment of this world: now shall the prince of this world be cast out.
c. John 14:30: "I will no more speak much with you, for the prince of the world cometh and he hath nothing in Me."
d. John 16:11: "The prince of this world hath been judged."
e. II Cor. 4:4: "In whom the god of this world hath blinded the minds of the unbelieving, that the light of the gospel of the glory of Christ, who is the image of God, should not dawn upon them."
f. II Cor. 2:2.
g. I John 5:19.
h. Rev. 12:9.

the world to come

What is the "world to come"?
a. Observe the footnote — "the inhabited earth."
b. Observe the Catholic Bible comment, which says that it means the Christian Dispensation, not the future life.
c. Milligan: "The world to come is not that which we hope for after the resurrection, but that which began at the beginning of Christ's kingdom; but it will no doubt have its full accomplishment in our final redemption." (p. 58)
d. Newell: "The thought of the world to come pervades the

book of Hebrews, and cannot here refer to present things." (p. 43)
e. Thayer defines "world to come": "That consummate state of all things which will exist after Christ's return from heaven."
f. Connybeare: "The world to come here corresponds with the city to come of 13:14."

what is man that thou art mindful of him

This is an interesting question. What *is* man?
a. He is very little, physically.
1. For labor in China, India, Tibet, he receives a few cents a day.
2. For length of life, very little.
a) James 4:14: "life is a vapor".
b) Animals and trees outlive man. Some turtles are centuries old.
3. His strength is very little:
a) A human baby is the most helpless of creatures.
b) Animals are faster and stronger.
4. Yet, man gives great significance to the flesh as he lives for its gratification.
b. Mentally, he is worth more.
1. He is able to rule the animals of the earth.
2. He can alter nature itself.
a) Harness the waterfalls to make power.
b) Capture the rivers to turn dynamos.
c) Improve upon plants, making hybrids.
3. He can discover the secrets of the world.
a) With the telescope, he scans the heavens.
b) With the microscope, he examines the unseen.
c) He combats disease.
d) He combines elements to build machines for man's own good.
4. Although man's mental attainments are temporary, people live as though they were of prime importance.
c. Spiritually, his worth is immeasurable:
1. God is interested in each person individually.
a) Physically, yes:
1) Matt. 10:30: " — hairs of your head are numbered."
2) Luke 12:27: " — consider the lilies — "
3) Malachi 3:10: " — open you the windows of heaven — "
b) Mentally, yes:
1) Man is made in the intellectual likeness of God. Heb. 2:7-8.

2) Gen. 1:26: "In Our image."
c) Spiritually, more so:
(1) Matt. 10:32: " — shall confess Me before man — "
(2) John 3:16. "God so loved the world — that He gave — His Son."
(3) James 4:14: "What is your life? It is even a vapor."
2. The giving of Jesus is God's attempt to show man's greatness:
a) He did not send an angel or offer an animal.
b) His Son's pain, sorrow, and death is proof of God's love.
Historically, what is man?
a. Man as God made him:
1. Gen. 2:7: He made him as dust.
a) Scientifically, man is: 10 gallons of water, 24 pounds of carbon, 7 pounds of lime, 1¼ pounds of phosphorous, ½ teaspoonful of sugar, 4½ teaspoonfuls of salt, some oxygen, hydrogen, nitrogen, enough iron for 1 large nail.
b) If this is all of which man consists, a man could be purchased for .79c (before inflation).
c) A scientist, curator of Northwestern Department of Chemistry, once valued man's body at .98c. Now, in 1960, it is worth $31.04.
d) An estimate of your day: Your heart beats 103,689 times a day. Your blood travels 168,000,000 miles. You give off 85.6 degrees Fahrenheit in heat, which means you generate 450 foot tons of energy. You exercise 7,000,000 brain cells.
b. Heb. 2:7-8: "Crowned him with glory and honor."
c. Made him a trinity:
1. I Thess. 5:23: "May your spirit, soul, and body be preserved."
2. Jesus — Matt. 22:37: "Love the Lord thy God, with all thy heart . . . thy mind and . . . thy soul."
What is man as sin makes him?
a. Sin makes him brutal.
1. Cain slew Abel.
2. The wealthy live in luxury, while the poor starve.
3. The powerful plunge men into war.
4. A man can kidnap babies for gold.
5. A man can live on an animal level, which will bring him to destruction. II Peter 2:10-12.
b. Sin makes him dirty and diseased.
c. Sin makes him rebellious toward God.

1. I John 3:4: Sin is transgression of God's law.
d. Sin makes him purposeless. Dr. Shirley once told of a certain youth who was seven days in New York. He saw eighteen shows, but was oblivious to the libraries, scenic, and historic spots there to see. He spent the last day reading a "true story".
Man as Christ remakes him.
a. See how Christ can change people:
1. Woman of Samaria — John 4:6: five husbands, but she came to Christ and became a soul-winner.
2. Paul, a cruel persecutor of church, was transformed.
3. Begbies, in *Twice Born Men,* proves His power. Get this book and read it!
b. He gives people a purpose in life.
1. Soul winning.
2. Helping the needy.
3. Working for the eternal, in place of the temporal.
c. He makes them rise above the temporal.
1. Riches — treasures laid up in heaven.
2. Emphasis is placed upon the eternal.

Son of Man

Who is referred to here, man or Christ?
a. Arguments for Christ being referred to:
1. Similar expressions are made in reference to Christ:
a   Matt. 21:16 — quotes from Psalms 8:2: "Out of the mouths of babes and sucklings Thou has perfected praise."
b) Eph. 1:22: "And He put all things in subjection under his feet and gave Him to be head over all things to the church."
c) I Cor. 15:27: "For, He put all things in subjection under His feet, but when He saith all things are put in subjection, it is evident that He is excepted who did subject all things unto Him."
1) The translator has noted in the margin that this is a quotation from Psalm 8:6.
2) This passage in Corinthians, some say, refers to Christ.
2. Much is made of the alternate reading of verse 7! **"A little while lower."**
a) Even Calvin, who holds that Psalms 8 refers to man, feels that Paul turns here from David and "designates the abasement of Christ's humiliation." (p. 58.)

b) Some insist that since the Logas could not die, a body was prepared for Him so that He could die.
b. Arguments for man in general being referred to:
1. Because it is a visitation of God from generation to generation.
2. When did God visit Jesus? God was with Jesus all the time; on the cross would be an exception.
3. Because we know what Christ is, who He is. It would not be necessary to raise such a question about the Lord.
4. Because God was in Christ, reconciling the world unto Himself.
5. Because the writer later calls specific attention to Christ. cf. v. 9.
6. God didn't visit His Son, but visited man through His Son.
7. The 8th Psalm is a discussion of man.
8. Man is lower than the angels. II Peter 2:11: "Whereas angels though greater in might and power bring not a railing judgment against them before the Lord."
9. Authorities who say Psalm 8 does not refer to Christ:
a) Milligan says: "That this has reference to mankind in general and not to Jesus Christ personally considered, as some have alleged, is evident from the Psalm itself, as well as from the scope of the apostle's argument." (p. 85)
b) John Calvin: "It seems to be unfitly applied to Christ . . . The Psalm speaks not of any particular person, but of all mankind — This affords no reason why the words should not be applied to the person of Christ." (p. 56)

that thou visitest him

What is the difference between "mindful and "visitest"?
a. "Visit" is the effect of God's mindfulness.
b. Since God recognized man, He visits man with blessings out of His loving heart.
God's visiting is twofold:
a. He visits for good to bring blessings.
1. Joseph said to his brethren: "God will visit you and bring you out of the land."
2. Luke 1:68: "For He hath visited and wrought redemption for His people."
a) This is the most important visitation, although dozens of verses can be quoted to show God's physical blessings such as named by Joseph.

      b) How grateful lonely people are when guests visit them, but here is named the greatest Visitor.
— b. He visits man to punish Him:
1. He has in the past:
    a) Exodus 32:34: "I will visit their sin upon them — "
    b) Psalm 89:32: "Then will I visit their transgression with the rod and their iniquity with stripes."
    c) Jeremiah 10:15: "In the time of visitation they shall perish."
    d) Exodus 20:5: "Visiting the iniquity of the fathers upon the children for the third and fourth generations."
    e) Exodus 34:7, Numbers 14:18, and Deut. 5:9.
2. He will in the future:
   II Peter 3:8-13.

Thou madest him a little lower

   Observe that the footnote in the A.S. version says, "For a little while lower."
   Milligan says, "It is still a question with the critics whether the word "little" is expressive of *time* or *degree*."
   Who holds for the *time* element?
a. Those who say "Son of Man" refers to Christ.
1. They say it means "a little while", and designates the abasement of Christ's humiliation.
2. Since Christ the Logos would not die, a body was prepared for Him so that He could die.
   If we do not try to push this theory, we have man a little lower than the angels:
a. Christ was praised by angels at His birth: "Glory to God in the highest," not because He was made lower than the angels.
b. Man is ministered to by angels (1:14); so we may conclude that, in some sense at least, we are lower.
   Is man lower than the angels according to other scriptures?
   Yes: II Peter 2:11: "Whereas angels though greater in might and power bring not a railing judgment against them before the Lord."

Thou crownedst him with glory and honor

   This was true of Adam in his pre-sin state.
a. Gen. 1: He was given dominion over fish, birds, cattle, over all the earth and every creeping thing.

b. Psalm 8:1-8.
   Milligan states that "glory" and "honor" are nearly synonymous in both Hebrew and Greek, and they are used for the sake of emphasis. (p 86) If this verse applies to Christ, it would apply after His resurrection.

and didst set him over the works of Thy hands

Critics reject this passage, but it occurs frequently in manuscripts:
a. Milligan says, "It is found in the original Hebrew, in the Septuagint and in several manuscripts. I am therefore inclined to retain it —" (p. 86)
b. It is in harmony with other scriptures.
   Note man's responsibility over the creation:
a. Gen. 2:15: "— dress it and keep it —"
b. Gen. 1:28: "— have dominion —"

under his feet

The scriptures quoted above verify this:
a. After Adam's sin things become different for man.
b. The earth brought forth weeds and animals turned upon him, so that they are now called wild beasts and domesticated beasts.
   Man was the crowning glory of God, but sin caused him to lose much of his dominion.

subjected to him

This fits man perfectly:
a. Once everything in the sea, air, and earth was beneath man.
b. Now it is a different picture. Who would dare to go unarmed into a jungle?
c. Man's lost estate is described.
   Some make it apply to Christ.
a. When was everything subjected to Christ? When was it taken away?
b. I Cor. 15:25-27 is quoted by those who hold this theory.
1. They do show similarity, but that is not proof.
2. Heb. 2:8, does not fit Jesus, although a stretching of points can make it fit.
   The verse's purpose is to show that man is no longer king.

a little lower than the angels, even Jesus

    Christ was lower only as He took upon himself the role of man:
a. In this way He was lower — in suffering.
b. In his flesh, He was lower than the heavenly bodies of angels. The author picks out the one Person lower than angels Who will be able to restore man to a place of glory and honor.

crowned with glory and honor

    On earth, Jesus became a wise being, humiliated and crucified. This He came to do, and His obedience brought Him to God's right hand. Without suffering, He could not have died; without dying He could not have made atonement; without the atonement man would yet be in his sins:
1) Matt. 26:28: " — shed for the remission of sins — "
2) Heb. 9:22: " — without the shedding of blood there is no remission — "

    When was this glory and honor given?
a. Not on earth, for here He had to suffer.
b. Peter preached this after Christ's ascension.

that by the grace of God He should taste of death for every man.

    This shows the impelling motive — grace:
a. Man rebels, but God seeks man.
b. Man is ungracious, but God is gracious.
    This states the importance of Christ's death:
a. Matt. 20:28: "a ransom."
b. I Pet. 1:18-19: "redeemed with precious blood."
    Why is blood used for man's redemption?
a. Let the scriptures speak:
Gen. 2:17: Life was lost.
Gen. 9:4: Life is in the blood. Compare Lev. 17:14.
Life being lost, blood which has life is the price of redemption.

Study Questions

202. What is man, according to James 4:14?
203. Where does man rate physically? cf. Matt. 10:30; Luke 12:27.
204. Where does man rate mentally? cf. Heb. 2:7, 8; Gen. 1:26.
205. Where does man rate spiritually?
206. Where does man rate as a ruler?

HELPS FROM HEBREWS

207. What is man, according to Genesis?
208. What is he according to I Thess. 5:23; Matt. 22:37?
209. What is man as sin makes him?
210. Give illustrations of people made over by Christ.
211. Who is referred to as Son of Man, Christ or man?
212. Where does the scripture concerning the Son of man appear originally?
213. Is it prophetic?
214. Does Paul in Corinthians throw any light on this subject? cf. I Cor. 15:27.
215. Why do some think the 8th Psalm is referred to here?
216. Give arguments to show that the 8th Psalm refers only to man.
217. If we are uncertain at this point, is the total teaching lost? What is being taught?
218. For what purposes has God visited man?
219. Are such visits all over, or will they be repeated? cf. II Peter 3:8-13. I Thess. 4:13-18.
220. Give an exegesis of "Thou madest Him a little lower than the angels."
221. If Christ is referred to, how long was He a little lower than the angels?
222. Is man lower than angels? cf. Heb. 1:14; II Peter 2:11.
223. Does the term "little" refer to time or degree? Give reasons.
224. If Christ is crowned with glory and honor, when was He crowned?
225. Did man ever rule over the creation of God's hands? cf. Gen. 1:28; 2:15.
226. Does verse 8 describe a lost dominion of man?
227. What is meant by "under His feet"?
228. Does the term "domesticated animals" indicate that all is not subject to Him?
229. What proof is there that man does not rule everything now?
230. What rebels against man?
231. What seems to be the purpose of verse 8?
232. Who is beheld in verse 9?
233. How was Christ lower than the angels?
234. Is there any doubt over verse 9 as there is over verse 8?
235. When was He crowned with glory and honor?
236. What is the difference between glory and honor?

237. What is meant by the "grace of God"?
238. Define the meaning of, "taste of death."
239. Why were death and blood used as the means of redemption? cf. Gen. 2:17; 9:4; Lev. 17:14.
240. Who is the one Person able to restore man to his dominion and power?
241. Was the thought expressed in v. 9 preached on Pentecost?
242. What does verse 10 say was becoming to God?
243. What about His nature would constrain Him?
244. Does it carry the idea of expediency?
245. What is meant by "for Whom are all things"?
246. Does Christ have all things now?
247. What does I Cor. 15:24 have to say in this regard?
248. Does "through Whom are all things" refer to God, Christ, or both?
249. Discuss Acts 17:28; John 1:3, 10; Col. 1:16, 17.
  2. *The necessity of Christ's becoming a human being in order to accomplish this:* 2:10-18.
     a. *To demonstrate His power over Satan:* 2:10-15.

Text
2:10-15

10 For it became Him, for Whom are all things, and through Whom are all things, in bringing many sons unto glory, to make the Author of their salvation perfect through sufferings. 11 For both He that sanctifieth and they are sanctified are all of one: for which cause He is not ashamed to call them brethren, 12 saying,

I will declare Thy name unto My brethren,
In the midst of the congregation will I sing Thy praise.

13 And again, I will put my trust in Him. And again, Behold, I and the children whom God hath given Me. 14 Since then the children are sharers in flesh and blood, He also Himself in like manner partook of the same; that through death He might bring to nought him that had the power of death, that is, the devil; 15 and might deliver all them who through fear of death were all their lifetime subject to bondage.

Paraphrase

10 The salvation of mankind through the death of the Christ need not surprise you: For it belonged to God, Who is the last

end as well as the first cause of all things, when bringing His many sons into heaven, to make the Captain of their salvation an effectual Saviour, through sufferings ending in death.

11 Wherefore, that He might be a perfect Saviour, both He Who with His own blood sanctifieth, or fitteth men for appearing in the glorious presence of God, (ver. 10.), and they who are sanctified, are all of one father, namely, Abraham, (ver. 16.) that, being his brethren, he might have a strong affection for them: for which cause, though Jesus be the Son of God, He is not ashamed to love mankind, and to call them His brethren,

12 Saying to His Father, when I appear in the human nature on the earth, I will declare Thy perfections to My brethren of mankind: In the midst of the congregation of My brethren I will sing praise to Thee for Thy goodness to men.

13 And again Messiah is introduced, saying, I will put My trust in Him. And again, in the same prophecy, Behold I and the children, that is, the disciples, whom God hath given Me, are for signs and for wonders in Israel. This likewise shows, that He was to appear in the flesh among the Israelites.

14 Since, then, the children given to the Son to be saved, participate of flesh and blood, by being born of parents who are flesh and blood, even He, to be capable of dying for them, in like manner partook of flesh and blood, by being born of a woman, that through death (the very evil which the devil brought on mankind by sin) He might render ineffectual the malicious designs of him who had the power of bringing death into the world, that is, the devil

15 And deliver from eternal death, those penitent persons who, through the fear of future punishment, have passed the whole of their life in a grievous bondage.

Comment

for it became Him

Paul, or the author, explained Christ's greatness. Now he shows why it was done:

a. It was expedient.
b. Because of the nature of God, it was "becoming" of God to do it.
c. Because He loves, He would be constrained to do something about lost man.

for Whom are all things

A loving Father will commit all to the consecrated Son:
a. Romans 8:17: "Heirs of God and joint heirs with Jesus Christ."
b. Heb. 1:2: " — whom He appointed Heir — "

Christ has proven His worthiness but has not come unto the inheritance as yet:
a. I Cor. 15:24: "When He shall deliver up the kingdom to God."
b. For the present, God is the owner of all things.

and through whom are all things

This can be said of both Christ and God.
a. Of God — Acts 17:28: "In Him we live."
b. Of Christ — John 1:3: All things were made by Him.
c. John 1:10: The world was made by Him.
d. Col. 1:16-17: By Him all things consist.

Creation is ascribed to the Son, but then all things are preserved by the power of God.

in bringing many sons unto glory

God is to add to His family through Jesus Christ:
a. He desires all men to become part of His family.
1) II Pet. 3:9: " — not wishing that any should perish."
2) John 3:16: " — whosoever believeth — "
b. We have the privilege of choosing to be born into this family, unlike into our earthly home, where we had no choice.

What is our glory?
a. Phil. **3:21**: " — fashioned like His glorious body."
b. I Cor. 15:43: "It is sown in dishonor; it is raised in glory."

When will we have glory?
a. We have some glory now:
1. Rom. 8:21: " — glorious liberty."
2: I Pet. 4:14: " — spirit of glory."
3. Eph. 3:13: " — tribulation which is your glory."
b. We have glory that is yet to come:
1) Col. 3:4: "When Christ shall be manifested, then shall ye also with Him be manifested in glory."

How do we receive this glory?
a. II Thess. 2:14: " — He called you through our gospel to the obtaining of the glory of our Lord Jesus Christ."

b. 1 Peter 5:10: "— God of all grace who called you unto His eternal glory in Christ."

to make the Author of their salvation perfect

The Greek word for "author" is *Archegos,* a combination of two Greek words:
a. The words mean "to begin" and "to lead."
b. The word "Author" is also translated "Captain."
c. Christ is our "leader", and a perfect one.
d. The idea of leadership is expressed elsewhere:
1. Acts 5:31: A Prince, a Saviour.
2. Acts 3:15: Prince of Life.
It is time the world should heed this Leader, Who alone can save.

perfect through sufferings

Suffering made Him perfectly qualified for the execution of His office:
a. Christ was perfect in character, being without sin, but His experiences as man perfectly qualified Him to be a merciful High Priest.
b. His perfection makes a good Bible study:
1. Perfect in His life.
a) Luke 23:4: Pilate found no fault.
b) Heb. 4:15: Tempted, yet without sin.
c) I Pet. 1:19: Without spot.
2. Perfect in His sacrifice.
a) Isaiah 53:7: Openeth not His mouth.
b) Luke 23:34: Prayed for His enemies.
c) I Pet. 1:19: Without spot or blemish.
Suffering, tribulations, etc., serve to perfect us.
Rom. 5:3: " — tribulation worketh stedfastness."

for both He that sanctifieth

What is meant by "sanctifieth"?
a. The word is also translated "consecrates."
b. It means to set apart for a holy use, or to an office.
1. Matt. 23:19.
2. John 17:17.
c. It means to purify from pollution, either ceremonially or spiritually.
1. Ceremonially — Heb. 9:9-10.

2. Morally or spiritually — I Thess. 5:23.
d. It means to purify from the guilt of sin by a free remission. Heb. 10:10; 14; 18.
  How are we sanctified?
a. It is done in obedience to truth:
1. John 17:19: Sanctified through the truth.
2. II Tim. 2:21: Vessels sanctified for the Master's use.
3. I Cor. 1:2: Sanctified in Christ Jesus.
4. I Tim. 4:5: Sanctified by the Word.
  Who is meant by "He"?
a. The connotation suggests Christ, for this one calls us brethren, and God does not do that.
b. The other members of the Godhead do sanctify too.
1. Holy Spirit — Rom. 15:16.
2. God — John 10:36.

and they that are sanctified are all of one

  What is meant by "all of one"?
a. Some suggest one race, one blood, one offering.
b. Newell: "It speaks of one kind of quality of being, rather than mere unity." (p. 52)
c. One inheritance (Rom. 8:17) is suggested.
d. Milligan says: "Of one Father."
1. This fits best, for we have a common Father with Jesus, Who calls us brothers.
2. We do not have the devil as father, but Jesus' own Father as our father.

for which cause He is not ashamed to call them brethren

  Christ will be ashamed of all who are not sanctified:
a. Matt. 10:33.
b. Mark 8:38.
  If He calls us brothers, should we call Him brother?
a. No, for we are brothers by grace.
b. He is so much more than brother; He is Lord, God, Saviour, Master, King of kings, High Priest.

saying, I will declare Thy Name unto My brethren

  This is a quotation from Psalm 22:22:
a. This is Christ speaking through David.
b. The word "declare" is also translated "proclaim."
  The name of God is to be declared:

a. Jesus in His miracles prayed and gave glory to God.
b. John 1:18: Christ declared the God Whom men could not see.
   Who is meant by "brethren"?
a. Some say, "Christ also spoke to the Gentiles, and they were not His brothers."
1. Mark 7:26: A Greek — a Syrophoenician.
2. John 4:9: Samaritan.
c. This probably refers to the great victory when Christ and His brethren will be around the throne of God. Rev. 19.

In the midst of the congregation will I sing Thy praise

This phrase verifies the idea of Christ being with His church. The church should praise God.
a. Eph. 5:19: "Speaking . . . in psalms and hymns."
b. Some churches roll up the rug on Sunday evening for dancing rather than for praising God.

And again I will put My trust in Him.

The source of this quotation is uncertain, for several places sound similar.
a. Psalm 18:2 is suggested, for much of this Psalm is Messianic.
b. II Sam. 22:3, Isaiah 8:17 and 12:2 are suggested.
   An alternate translation says, "I will confide in Him."
   Who is trusting who?
a. Is the Christ trusting in God?
b. Does Christ have faith in God, when He knows God personally?
1. It is true that knowledge eliminates faith.
2. Christ did not have faith in God's character or existence, for these He knew.
3. Trust enters in when God's purposes are yet to be fulfilled.
c. Christ is our perfect example of trust.

And again, behold I and the children whom God hath given Me.

This is a quotation from Isaiah 8:18.
a. "This quotation concerns Isaiah and his childern and is applied to Christ and God's children, His disciples." (Milligan)
b. The idea probably is that the elder brother and the children will trust in God. A warning is therefore needed. Heb. 3:12: "evil heart of unbelief."
   What is meant by "children given unto Me"?

a. It does not mean that we become children of Christ, but children of God in the church of Christ.
b. See John 6:37: "All that the Father hath given Me, will come unto Me."
Notice the similarity in names of the type, Isaiah, and the antitype, Jesus.
a. "Isaiah" means "salvation of Jehovah."
b. "Jesus" means "Jehovah's salvation."

Since then the children are sharers in flesh and blood

The King James version says, "partakers of flesh".
In flesh, man is sensuous, subject to infirmity and decay.

He also in like manner partook of the same

He did not become like an angel to save angels, but became like man to save man:
a. Heb. 10:5: " — a body Thou hast prepared."
b. Phil. 2:5-11: " — took the form of a servant."
An immortal being cannot die, so Christ became mortal so that He could die for man.

that through death He might bring to nought

The Catholic Bible and the King James version translate "nought" as "destroy."
a. "The word does not mean to annihilate, but to render useless." (Milligan)
b. "The devil is now only weakened; his power is gone." (Calvin)
c. If these men are right, will the devil ever be destroyed? Yes. See Rev. 20:10.
"through death" is suggestive:
a. Some accomplish in death that which they could not accomplish in life.
1. Death of a mother, a wife, sometimes leads to the conversion of a father, a husband, a child.
2. Death of men, when untimely, helps to make them national heroes, martyrs to a cause, and prompts men to arise to the cause.
b. Through death Jesus could prove He had power over it, and authority over the grave. He demonstrated that He was the one who had the power over death.

1) II Cor. 5:1.
2) I Cor. 15:

him that had the power of death, that is the devil

The devil has an ambition, but his power is weakened:
a. The meaning of his name:
1) "Diablos" in Greek means "accuser" or "slanderer".
2) "Satan" in Hebrew means "he who hates, an enemy".
b. Pride was probably his downfall:
I Tim. 3:6: " — lest being puffed up, he fall into the condemnation of the devil."
c. He works to control man:
1. John 12:31; 16:11: He is "Prince of this world."
2. John 8:34; I Tim. 3:7: He seeks to enslave and ensnare.
d. His power to accuse man as he did Job of old is gone:
1. He cannot slander us before God, for we have been accepted.
2. Jesus breaks the power of sin, and thus death, the result of sin, is broken.

and might deliver all them

Some feel that this refers directly to the Gentiles who had no revelation, but we may say that "all" is world-wide.
Christ is a deliverer for all men, not simply a national hero. This suggests that Christ is the help of man to escape the works of the devil.
a. This is proven by I John 3:8: "That He might destroy the works of the devil."
b. This word "might" is also translated "may", which suggests futurity.
c. Why does not God destroy the devil now?
1. It would leave a vast number of orphans, for the devil's children are numerous.
2. A destruction of the devil would change this world from one of choice.

who through fear of death

Why do men fear death?
a. Because of pain, misery.
b. Because of the darkness and corruption of the grave.
c. Because of the uncertainty of their condition and destiny beyond it.
For the Christian it loses its terror and sting:

a. I Cor. 15:55: "O death where is thy sting?"
b. Psalm 23:1 · "Thou art with me."
c. I Thess. 4:18: "Wherefore comfort one another with these words."
d. II Cor. 5:8: "at home with the Lord."

were all their lifetime subject to bondage.

Bondage is twofold:
a. Bondage to fear is the one specifically meant.
1. Men dread death, work against it, spend fortunes to prolong life and to escape it.
2. Death haunts us, if not for self, for our loved ones.
b. Bondage to sin is likewise present. See Romans 6:16-18: "Servants . . . of sin unto death."
What is the end of those who are in bondage to fear?
a. The answer is plain.
1. Rev. 20:14-15.
2. Matt. 25:46.
3. Rev. 22:11.
b. Christ delivers from this end.
Rom. 8:15: " — received the spirit of adoption."

Study Questions

250. How does God obtain sons?
251. Does God want many sons? See II Peter 3:9; John 3:16.
252. Harmonize the expression, "many" with Jesus' statement of the strait and narrow way.
253. What will be our glory?
254. Do we have any glory now?
255. How do we obtain glory?
256. Define the word "author". What is its origin?
257. What verses speak of Christ as a leader?
258. How is the word, "leader", translated by others?
259. What made Christ perfect?
260. Does this refer to His character?
261. Could it refer to His quality as a leader?
262. Discuss the verses that speak of Christ's perfection.
263. Does it refer to His being qualified by suffering?
264. Of what value are sufferings for us? See Rom. 5:3.
265. Give an exegesis of verse 11.
266. What does "sanctification" mean?

267. Who sanctified who, according to chapter 2?
268. When are we sanctified? See Eph. 5:26.
269. What is meant by, "are all of one"?
270. Does the author refer to God, or to Christ?
271. Does God ever call us brethren?
272. What verse teaches that Christ will not be ashamed of us?
273. Should we call Christ our brother?
274. Do we have any record of Jesus singing?
275. Where is this quotation found?
276. What is the purpose of the singing?
277. Who is meant by "brethren"?
278. Whose name is declared?
279. When will this singing take place? Rev. 19.
280. Who has faith in whom?
281. What is meant when it is said that Jesus would put His trust in God? Is faith present where there is knowledge? In what did He trust?
282. Who are the children given to Christ?
283. Are we children of Christ? cf. John 6:37.
284. Why did Christ share in flesh and blood according to 2:14?
285. Why did Christ not take up the flesh of an angel?
286. Why did He not remain immortal, and in heaven?
287. Why is "through death" significant?
288. What is meant by the word "nought"? Does it mean to annihilate?
289. Does death prove a blessing in other realms?
290. Could Christ die if He were not in the flesh?
291. What could Christ prove by death? cf. II Cor. 5:1; I Cor. 15.
292. How can it be said that the devil had the power of death?
293. Is the past tense significant in the words, "*had* the power of death"?
294. What does the word "devil" mean?
295. What is the Devil able to do according to John 8:34; I Tim. 3:7?
296. Verse 15 suggests deliverance from the fear of death. Do you feel that Christians are delivered, that they fear death less than non-Christians?
297. Why are people fearful of death?
298. Give verses that tell of man's freedom from the terror of death.

299. What bondage is referred to?
300. Is the devil's power destroyed outright? If not — why not?
b. *It was necessary for Christ to become human in order to sympathize with men through experience.* 2:16-18

Text
2:16-18

16 For verily not to angels doth He give help, but He giveth help to the seed of Abraham. 17 Wherefore it behooved Him in all things to be made like unto His brethren, that He might become a merciful and faithful high priest in things pertaining to God, to make propitiation for the sins of the people.

18 For in that He himself hath suffered being tempted, He is able to succor them that are tempted.

Paraphrase

16 Moreover, by no means doth He take hold of the angels who sinned, to save them; but of those who are the seed of Abraham by faith He taketh hold, to deliver them from death, and to conduct them to heaven.

17 Hence it was necessary He should be made like His brethren (ver. 11.) in all things, and particularly in afflictions and temptations, that, having a feeling of their infirmity, and being capable of dying, He might become a merciful as well as a faithful high-priest in matters pertaining to God, in order, by His death, (ver. 14.), to expiate the sins of the people, and to intercede with God in their behalf.

18 Besides by what He suffered Himself when tempted, He knows what aids are necessary to our overcoming temptations, so that He is able and willing, in the exercise of His government as king mentioned (ver. 9.) to succour them who are tempted.

Comment

For verily not to angels doth He give help
  Jesus' coming was for man, not angels.
  It is also translated, "He took not on Him the nature of angels." (KS)
a. He did not, as the next verse verifies.
b. He came not as an angel, but as man.

That He preferred us to angels was not owing to our excellency, but to our misery.

but He giveth help to the seed of Abraham

There are two groups for consideration:
a. The physical seed.
1. He came to the house of Israel, but this consideration alone limits the verse.
2. The good tidings announced concerning the birth of the Saviour in Bethlehem was for all men.
b. The spiritual seed, which includes all men of faith.
1. Gal. 3:9: " — are of faith are blessed."
2. Gal. 4:28: "Now we, brethren . . . are children of promise."
3. Rom. 9:8: "The children of the promise are reckoned for a seed."

Wherefore it behooved Him in all things

He felt a moral necessity, an obligation to do something for man:
a. The nature of God, loving, just, merciful, would require God to seek man.
b. Jesus was of the nature of God, so He would feel obligated to save man.

Two things should be considered in the expression, "all things":
a. Man has a twofold being.
1. Flesh.
2. Affection, feeling or emotion.
b. Jesus came as flesh, and He had sympathy, feeling, and emotion.

to be made like unto His brethren

Who were His brethren?
a. Some suggest His flesh and blood relatives.
b. Some suggest His Jewish brethren.
c. Some suggest His brethren in the church.
d. His brethren in the flesh — mankind in general — may be considered, for the emphasis is on becoming like man, and not upon the word, "brethren".

that He might become a merciful and faithful High Priest.

"Might become" suggests that living in the flesh was needed

in order to qualify Him:
a. We do not like to limit Jesus, but from our standpoint we cannot now excuse ourselves and say that Deity does not know our feeling since Jesus suffered as man.
b. We become the most sympathetic when we have experienced the same thing as the one who needs our sympathy.

"Merciful" is suggestive:
a. In Old Testament times, sin's punishment had no mercy. cf. Heb. 10:28: "Die without mercy."
b. Jesus was merciful:
1. His coming was an act of mercy.
2. He showed compassion on earth.
a) John 8:11: "— go and sin no more."
b) Luke 7:13. "— He had compassion on her."
c) Matt. 9:36: "— Jesus was moved with compassion."
c. Since Christ experienced all of life, we readily believe that He will be merciful to us.

faithful

Christ proved His faithfulness:
a. Luke 9:51: "— He stedfastly set his face to go to Jerusalem."
b. Matt. 26:39: "— not My will but Thine be done."
c. Matt. 26:52: "— Put up again thy sword into its place."
d. Heb. 3:2: "Jesus . . . was faithful."
Jesus was faithful to His purpose in this life. Therefore we feel He will be faithful as our High Priest.

High Priest in all things

On earth He was our sacrifice, in heaven He is our High Priest:
a. The High Priest on earth made sacrifices, then went into the Holy Place to make restitution for the sins of the people.
b. Jesus serves in the Holy Place as our Priest.
1. Heb. 3:1: "— High Priest of our confession."
2. Heb. 10:21: "— having a great High Priest."

in things pertaining to God

Jesus had many opportunities to leave God's way:
a. Men sought to make Him bow to their traditions.
b. The devil sought to receive His devotion. Matt. 4
He was pleasing to God rather than to men:

a. Baptism, Matt. 3:17: " — well pleased."
b. Transfiguration, Matt. 17:5: " — well pleased."
c. Acts 2:33: " — being at right hand of God."

to make propitiation for for the sins of the people

The word, "propitiation" means "a covering", "an appeasement", and is also translated "reconciliation".
a. His atonement is referred to.
b. This is the priestly function of Christ.
The Catholic Bible uses the word "expiate".

For in that He Himself had suffered being tempted.

Alternate translations should be seen here:
a. A.S. footnote: "for having been himself tempted in that wherein He hath suffered."
1. This suggests that there is suffering in temptation.
2. Temptation here "means no other thing than experience or probation," says Calvin. (p. 76)
a) Jesus is a good example of the distress of the soul:
Luke 22:44: " — great drops of blood."
Matt. 26:38: "My soul is exceeding sorrowful unto death."
b) Men who are not dishonest, but have great temptations before them, undergo great distress of soul.
b. Catholic Bible: "Himself has suffered and has been tempted":
1. This makes the experiences separate.
2. Of course He did experience suffering apart from being tempted.

He is able to succor them that are tempted

There are three things needed by the one tempted:
a. Strength to withstand.
1. Phil. 4:13: " — through Christ."
2. I Cor. 10:13: "God . . . will not suffer you to be tempted above that ye are able to bear."
3. Eph. 6:13: " . . . may be able to withstand."
b. Consolation for the spirit.
1. Matt. 5:11 "Blessed are ye."
2. I Pet. 1:6-7: "Rejoice."
3. Rom. 8:28: " — to them that love God, all things work together for good."
4. James 1:2 and 1:12.

c. Deliverance.
1. II Pet. 2:9: "— The Lord knoweth how to deliver the godly."
2. I Cor. 10:13: "— a way of escape."
The Great Shepherd will walk down the valleys and will prepare a table for us in the presence of our enemies.

Study Questions

301. Does Christ help angels, according to this chapter (v. 16)? Why not?
302. Why would He help us instead of angels?
303. Does this verse limit His help to the Jews?
304. What is meant by "seed of Abraham"?
305. Are we the seed of Abraham, too? cf. Gal. 1:1; 4:28; 3:7, 29; Rom. 9:6-8.
306. Verse 17 gives us another reason for Christ coming in human flesh. What is it?
307. What is meant by "behooved"?
308. What is meant by "all things"?
309. What is characteristic of man besides flesh?
310. Would "all things" refer to emotion — love, sympathy, etc.?
311. How could Christ's life on earth make Him a merciful high priest?
312. Was the Old Testament priesthood merciful? cf. Heb. 10:28.
313. Tell of Jesus' compassion on earth.
314. Are we the most sympathetic when we have suffered similar experiences?
315. Tell of Christ's faithfulness.
316. What might be included in "all things"?
317. Is the expression, "pertaining to God", significant?
318. Did God ever express pleasure in Christ on earth?
319. What is meant by "propitiation"?
320. What does verse 18 suggest about temptation? Does it describe its effect on the one tempted?
321. Does all temptation come through suffering, or are two different things named here?
322. What are the things needed by the person tempted?
323. Do we have the promise of Christ's strength?
324. Do we have consolation?
325. Is there deliverance in Christ?

326. What temptations did Jesus face?

Chapter Two — Multiple Choice

1. The word spoken by angels proved to be:
   1. Steadfast.
   2. Erroneous.
   3. Corrupted.
2. A just recompense of reward means:
   1. A joyful reward.
   2. Compensation.
   3. An expected one.
3. Christ came into the world in the form of:
   1. An angel.
   2. A spirit.
   3. A servant.
4. In Hebrews we are exhorted to give an earnest heed to the things:
   1. Which we have observed.
   2. Which we have seen.
   3. Which we have heard.
5. Christ was made lower than:
   1. The men who killed Him.
   2. Lower than animals, for they never have to pray to God.
   3. Angels.
6. The word was confirmed by:
   1. Angels, ministering spirits.
   2. Signs, wonders and miracles.
   3. The end of certain days.
7. Christ as a High Priest is:
   1. Ever busy.
   2. Merciful.
   3. Ready to enter the Holy of Holies.
8. Christ is not ashamed to call us:
   1. Saints.
   2. Down for sin.
   3. Brethren.
9. The Great Salvation was spoken first:
   1. By the Lord.
   2. At Pentecost.
   3. At Rome.

10. Christ tasted for every man:
    1. Of God's love.
    2. Death.
    3. The Lord's Supper.
11. The Captain of our salvation was made perfect through:
    1. Living in eternity.
    2. His deity.
    3. Suffering.
12. The quotation, "What is man that thou art mindful of him," is:
    1. Taken from the Psalms.
    2. Taken from the Prophets.
    3. A statement by Moses who marveled when he saw the waywardness of Israel.
13. Through death Christ brought to nought:
    1. The power of wicked men.
    2. The devil.
    3. Sin that caused death.
14. For not unto angels hath:
    1. He extended the right hand of fellowship.
    2. Shown sinners repenting.
    3. Subjected the world to come.
15. The word spoken by angels:
    1. Refers to the angels praising God at Christ's birth.
    2. The word of Cherubim and Seraphim.
    3. The Mosaic law.
16. We are to give earnest heed:
    1. Lest the scriptures die out.
    2. Lest God punish us.
    3. Lest we let slip the things that were heard.
17. The salvation is spoken of:
    1. As a great salvation.
    2. As a favor of the Trinity.
    3. As something yet to be revealed.
18. The salvation:
    1. Can be escaped.
    2. Can be neglected.
    3. Is for the Hebrews first.
19. Signs, wonders, and miracles are spoken of in relationship to the:

      1. Various gifts of the Holy Spirit.
      2. The falseness of the devil.
      3. Coming of Christ.
20. Jesus did not take upon Himself the nature of an angel:
      1. But the nature of the seed of Abraham.
      2. But great glory on earth.
      3. But the nature of men to come.

SUMMARY OF CHAPTER TWO

This chapter is the logical conclusion of the thought of God's final message which is presented in Chapter One. Since God has spoken in His Son, we ought to heed the message. Two reasons are given to show why we should pay attention to it.

First, disobedience to the Word spoken through angels was punished. That being so, how could one who disregarded the Word spoken through the Lord hope to escape punishment? Second, the Christian age is under the dominion of the Son, not angels. A quotation from the eighth Psalm, which tells of the dominion over creation which God gave to Adam, is applied to Jesus in support of this claim.

Jesus became identified with man through His suffering, that He might "taste death for all" and be able to call them brethren whom He saved. In His death, He destroyed the power of the devil and brought freedom to those in bondage to sin. He was made like His brethren and became for them a faithful High Priest, providing a covering for the sins of the people.

III. *He is superior to Moses.* 3:1-4:13
A. *The comparison of Jesus and Moses with respect to greatness and glory.* 3:1-6

Text
3:1-6

1 Wherefore, holy brethren, partakers of a heavenly calling, consider the Apostle and High Priest of our confession, even Jesus; 2 who was faithful to Him that appointed Him, as also was Moses in all his house. 3 For He hath been counted worthy of more glory than Moses, by so much as he that built the house hath more honor than the house.

4 For every house is builded by some one; but He that built all things is God. 5 And Moses indeed was faithful in all his

house as a servant, for a testimony of those things which were afterward to be spoken; 6 but Christ as a Son, over His house; Whose house are we, if we hold fast our boldness and the glorying of our hope firm unto the end.

Paraphrase

1 Since the author of the gospel is the Son of God, I exhort you, holy brethren, who by the preaching of the gospel (chap. ii. 3.) are partakers of the calling to enter into the heavenly country, (Eph. i. 18.) to consider attentively the dignity and authority of the Lawgiver and High-priest of our religion, Christ Jesus;

2 Who, in forming the gospel church, was faithful to God Who appointed Him His Apostle or Lawgiver, even as Moses also was faithful in forming all the parts of the Jewish church, God's house at that time.

3 But although the faithfulness of Jesus was not greater than that of Moses, He was counted by God worthy of more power than Moses, in as much as he who hath formed the services of the church, not for his own benefit, but for the benefit of others, is a more honourable person than any member of the church; such as Moses was, who needed the services of the Jewish church equally with the people.

4 Besides, every religious society is formed by some one: But He who hath formed all righteous communities and religious societies, is God; Who having delegated His authority to His Son, hath made Him Lord of all.

5 Now Moses indeed was faithful in forming all the parts of the Jewish church, as a servant who acted according to the directions which he received from God, without deviating from them in the least; because the Jewish church was designed for a testimony of the things which were afterwards to be spoken by Christ and His apostles.

6 But Christ, in erecting the gospel church, was faithful as a Son set over His Father's house as its Lawgiver: of Whose house we who believe, whether we be Jews or Gentiles, are members, if indeed we hold fast the bold glorying in the hope of resurrection to eternal life through Christ firm to the end, which we professed at our baptism.

Comment

Wherefore holy brethren

They are brethren, not by race or nationality, but by belief.
a. It is impossible to have brotherhood when the fundamentals of faith are denied.
b. International brotherhood will not be attained until men are brothers in Christ.
The verse speaks of "holy" brethren.
a. In what way are we holy?
1. We are made holy by sanctification at our baptism when we bury the old man of sin and rise to walk in newness of life.
2. We are holy if we walk in holiness.
b. None will see God unless holiness is present. cf. Eph. 5:5; Heb. 12:14.
c. Church people need to live up to the name, "holy brethren".

partakers of a heavenly calling

God's heavenly, or holy, calling comes through the Word:
a. Heavenly agencies sometimes are used to bring preacher and convert together, but the call comes through preaching.
1. Peter and the household of Cornelius were brought together, but the Word called Cornelius and his household to salvation.
2. Paul was brought to the preacher by a heavenly instrumentality, but he was *told* what to do to be saved. Acts 9:6.
b. This call is to a unique life:
1. I Cor. 1:2: " — called to be saints."
2. II Thess. 2:14: " — called .... to the obtaining of the glory of our Lord Jesus Christ."
3. Gal. 5:13: " — called for freedom."
4. Rom. 1:6: " — called to be Jesus Christ's."

consider the Apostle

Singular attention is now to be given to Jesus Christ for several reasons:
a. He was faithful. 3:2.
b. He was appointed. 3:2.
c. He was counted of more glory than Moses. 3:3.
d. He was a Son over His house. 3:6.
Consider the apostleship of Jesus:

3:1 HELPS FROM HEBREWS

a. The word, "apostle" means, "one sent". Jesus claimed to have been sent:
1. Luke 4:43: "I must preach . . . . for therefore was I sent."
2. Luke 20:9-16: He was the Son in the parable of the husbandman.
b. To whom was He sent?
1. Strictly speaking, to the Jews:
a) Matt. 15:24: " — unto the lost sheep of the house of Israel."
b) John 1:11: "He came unto His own."
2. Purposefully speaking, to all men:
a) I John 4:14:" — to be the Saviour of the world."
b) John 3:16: " — the world."

and High Priest

The priestly system is more easily understood by some than by others:
a. The Jews had a priestly system. See Lev. 16.
b. Most heathen groups have a priestly system, although it is a very corrupt one.
The Christian's High Priest is Christ, Who is perfect, without sin and at the right hand of God.

of our confession

The word "confession" is translated "profession" in the King James version:
a. It is the Greek word, *homologia,* used in several other places:
1. I Tim. 6:12: "Profession" in K.J.; "confession" in A.S.
2. II Cor. 9:13: "Profession" in K.J.; "confession" in A.S.
3. **Heb.** 4:14: "Profession" in K.J.; "confession" in A.S.
4. Heb. 10:23: "Profession" in K.J.; "confession" in A.S.
b. We do confess our faith in a person:
1. Matt. 10:32.
2. Rom. 10:9-10.
c. The confession of our faith *is* a profession; we confess faith, which obligates us to a way of life:
The idea of profession is challenged by Newell. (p. 80)
a. He seeks to emphasize that it is a confession in a person, and not a way of life.
b. In reality, he is correct. We do confess faith, but the idea of profession is too often left out, so people are baptized and come out "wet sinners."

even Jesus

    What are we to confess about Jesus?
a. Matt. 16:13-18: "The Christ, the Son of the Living God."
b. I John 4:15: "Jesus is the Son of God."
Some confess Him to be only a good, moral martyr.
What about those who will not confess the truth?
a. II John 7: They are deceivers, and the anti-Christ.
b. I John 2:22: They are liars.

who was faithful

    The faithfulness of Jesus stands out:
a. He was faithful to God in temptation.
b. He was faithful to God in the miracles, giving God the glory.
c. He was faithful in God's work, His Father's business. Luke 2:49; Heb. 3:2.
d. He was faithful even in death. Matt. 26:42; John 17:4; 19:30. We may believe that He is now faithful in being our High Priest.

to Him that appointed Him

    This word, "appointed", is also translated "advanced" or "made":
a. Milligan suggests that the word refers not to origin, nor to begetting, but to task.
1. His example is I Samuel 12:6: "The Lord advanced Moses and Aaron."
2. Christ was appointed to a task. John 9:4; Heb. 12:2; 3:2.
3. It was a timely appointment.
4. Jesus came willingly to His appointment.
There are some appointments that should concern men:
a. A day to repent, Acts 17:30-31.
b. A day to die, Heb. 9:27.

as also was Moses in his house

    Moses was a faithful person:
a. Heb. 11:25: He chose ill treatment with the people of God.
b. Exodus is a picture of wayward, whimpering Israel and faithful Moses:
1. They murmured, but Moses prayed.
2. They worshipped the golden calf, but Moses worshipped God.

c. Numbers 12:7 is a commendation of the faithful one.
Israel was the house of God, not the house of Moses:
a. Exodus 25:8: "Let them make me a sanctuary."
b. Exodus 29:45: "I will dwell among the children of Israel."

more glory than Moses in all his house

Moses was a glorious person:
a. He represents one division of the Old Testament. Luke 24:44.
b. He was selected to be transfigured with Jesus. Matt. 17.
c. Moses' glory vanished. Matt. 17:5-6.
What is meant by "glory"?
a. It means fame, honor, brightness, splendor, praise.
b. Jesus is the most famous person in the world. Washington and Lincoln, are national heroes, but Jesus is international.
What can be said about Jesus' glory, pertaining to time?
a. He had some glory on earth:
1. John 17:4: "I have glorified Thee."
2. John 7:37-39: "Jesus was not yet glorified."
b. He received glory after His earthly mission:
1. Acts 2:36: " God hath made Him both Lord and Christ."
2. I Peter 1:21: " God raised Him from the dead and gave Him glory."
c. The church is now glorifying Him: Eph. 3:21.
d. His glory is yet to come:
1. Matt. 16:27: He came in the glory of His Father.
2. I Thess. 4:13-18.

more honor than the house:

Does this infer that Jesus built the house of Israel?
a. "Yes," says Milligan. (p. 115)
b. Christ may be regarded as the Builder and Furnisher of the whole house of Israel, of which Moses himself was a member. Christ is eternal; He was the rock from which Israel drank, so this figure is reasonable.

He that buildeth all things is God

The purpose of this verse is to establish the deity of Jesus. Everything that is done should be ascribed to God.
I Cor. 3:6: "Apollos watered, but God giveth the increase."

Moses indeed was faithful in all his house as a servant

    Several verses establish Moses' faithfulness:
a. It is established in Heb. 11:24-30.
b. He was faithful in building the Tabernacle according to the pattern. Ex. 25:40.
c. Numbers 12:7: " — faithful in all my house."
God's house is referred to: cf. Numbers 12:7. "He is faithful in all my house."
Moses was a servant: Numbers 12:8.

afterward to be spoken

    In this sense, Moses was speaking as a prophet and giving an example of faithfulness:
a. He was a herald of a doctrine to be published later.
b. He was a forerunner of a coming prophet. Deut. 18:15.
c. His example is for all: I Cor. 10:11: "These things happened .... by way of example."

but Christ as a Son over his house

    Moses was a servant, but Christ was a Son in God's house:
a. This is only one of the many figures applied to Jesus:
1. Matt. 16:13-18: He is the Builder.
2. I Pet. 2:4-6: He is Cornerstone.
3. Heb. 3:6: Son in the house.
4. Heb. 10:21: High priest over the house of God.
b. The word "own" appears in the King James version: "... over His own house."
1. Milligan challenges this translation. "In this figure it is not His own house, but the house of God."
The expression "house of Christ" never appears, but always the "house of God."
a. Eph. 2:19: "Household of God."
b. I Tim. 3:15: " — in the house of God."
c. Heb. 10:21: " — over the house of God."
d. I Pet. 4:17: " — judgment begins at the house of God."
e. Eph. 2:22: " — in whom ye are builders together."
f. I Pet. 2:7: " — head of the corner."

Whose house are we

    The former house was presided over by the High Priest and by Moses:

- a. It was transitory and typical, a shadow of something better to come.
- b. Now we are the glorious eternal house of God.
  It is a joy to be a part of a house that cannot be destroyed:
- a. Matt. 16:13-18: The gates of Hades cannot prevail against it.
- b. Matt. 7:24-27: Storms of life will not destroy it.

if we hold fast our boldness

Faithfulness is an absolute essential to salvation, for the book of Hebrews eliminates the doctrine of "once in grace, always in grace."

- a. We are of the household *if* we "hold fast".
- b. The implication is that when we turn loose, we are no longer in the house of God.
- c. Many scriptures speak similiarly:
1. Matt. 10:22: " — endureth."
2. Luke 9:62: " — putteth his hand to the plow."
3. Rev. 2:10: " — faithful unto death."
4. Heb. 3:14: " — if we hold fast."
5. Heb. 6:5-6: " — fall away."

The word "boldness" is also translated "confidence":
- a. It has the idea of freeness and boldness of speech.
- b. "It means an inward state of full and undisturbed confidence." (Milligan.)

and the glorying of our hope

It is also translated, "the rejoicing of hope":
- a. This is a contrast to crying, complaining Israel.
- b. Hope refers to the object of our faith.
1. It is in the realm of the unseen.
   Rom. 8:24: "Hope that is seen is not hope."
2. We hope for the glorious body, the new heaven and the new earth.

firm unto the end

Our task is to complete a course that we have started:
- a. God will save us because of our effort, not in spite of it.
- b. A person cannot become a willful weakling and expect God to save him.

Study Questions

327. What is the great theme of Chapter Three?
328. What is it that makes men brethren?
329. Can we be called brothers to those who deny the fundamentals of brotherhood?
330. In what way are we made holy?
331. What is the descriptive word used concerning brethren? Is it important? cf. Eph. 5:5; Heb. 12:14.
332. Do we live up to the term?
333. Of what are we partakers?
334. How is it a "heavenly" calling?
335. What heavenly agencies are used?
336. What agencies were used in the life of Peter? Paul?
337. Name some things related to our call concerning our character, relationship, etc.
338. Who is the apostle to be considered?
339. How can He be called an apostle? cf. Luke 4:43.
340. Name the various things said about Jesus in this verse.
341. To whom was Jesus sent primarily?
342. Did He claim to be sent to all men? cf. I John 4:14.
343. Does the Christian have a priest?
344. Is the idea developed in this verse? In the book of Hebrews?
345. How is Jesus our High Priest?
346. How often does He sacrifice?
347. What can be said about His sympathy?
348. What can be said about His character?
349. What is meant by the expression, "of our confession"?
350. What is the alternate word used for "confession" in the King James version?
351. Is our confession of faith in Christ also a pledge of profession?
352. What do we confess?
353. What do we confess about Him?
354. What does the scripture declare concerning those who will not confess that He is the Christ? cf. II John 7; I John 2:22.
355. Discuss the faithfulness of Christ throughout His life on earth. cf. Luke 2:49; Heb. 12:2.
356. If Christ was faithful on earth, what may we suppose about Him now?

357. To whom was He faithful?
358. What does the word "appointed" mean?
359. Is the word "advanced" a good translation?
360. Does the word "made" carry the idea?
361. What appointment is referred to in verse 2?
362. Who appointed who? To what was He appointed?
363. Did Jesus approach the appointment gladly?
364. What appointments has God made for the sinner?
365. Does the Christian have any appointments?
366. Discuss Jesus' faithfulness on the cross. Matt. 26:42.
367. Discuss Moses' faithfulness in the building of the Tabernacle.
368. Compare the waywardness of Israel with the faithfulness of Moses.
369. Discuss the house referred to here.
370. Is it God's house or Moses' house?
371. Was the Tabernacle, or sanctuary, ever spoken of as belonging to Moses?
372. Does the name of God appear in the original manuscript, as the new version would lead you to believe?
373. Tell of the glory of Moses in the Old Testament and in the New Testament.
374. What does "glory" mean?
375. What glory had Jesus on earth?
376. What glory is ascribed to Christ in Acts; in the Epistles; in Revelation?
377. Should the church glorify Christ? cf. Eph. 3:21.
378. Does verse 5 infer that Moses did not build the house?
379. Does verse 6 infer that Jesus built the house of Israel?
380. What scriptures teach Christ's presence during the wilderness journey?
381. Should everything be ascribed to God?
382. Does everything that is made necessitate a builder?
383. Is there room for evolution in this verse?
384. Check different versions. Do they translate it (v.6) "His house", or "God's house"?
385. Consult verses that speak of Moses' faithfulness. cf. Ex. 25:40; Numbers 12:7, 8.
386. Whose house is spoken of in Numbers 12:8?
387. What relationship did Moses have to the house?
388. What is meant by "afterward to be spoken"?

389. Was Moses speaking a prophecy through his life or by an oral message?
390. Were these Old Testament experiences an example to us? cf. I Cor. 10:11.
391. If Moses was a servant, what was Christ in God's house?
392. Was Christ *in* the house or *over* it?
393. Is the idea of the faithfulness of Christ inferred here?
394. Is the word "own" that appears in the King James version a problem of exegesis? Whose house would it be if the word "own" is allowed?
395. Do we have the expression, "house of Christ", in the New Testament?
396. Compare the verses that speak of the house of God. Eph. 2:19; I Tim. 3:15; Heb. 10:21; I Peter 4:17.
397. Who is in the house of God? Do Christians comprise it?
398. What qualification is made in this verse?
399. If we turn loose of our boldness, can we be of the house of God?
400. Is this true, "once in grace, always in grace"?
401. What are we to hold to?
402. What will keep us in God's house?
403. Name some other scriptures which speak of man's need for faithfulness.
404. What is "boldness"? What other word could be used.
405. How do we hold fast to our boldness?
406. What does the word "glorying" mean?
407. How do we glory in hope?
408. Is there room for complaint when our hope is alive?
409. What is a firm hope? How does hope differ from faith?
410. How long is our hope to be firm?
411. What "end" is meant?

B. *Warnings and exhortations with respect to pilgrimage.* 3:7-19
1. *Israel's pilgrimage:* 3:7-11

Text
3:7-11

7 Wherefore, even as the Holy Spirit saith,
Today if ye shall hear His voice,
8 Harden not your hearts, as in the provocation,
Like as in the day of the trial in the wilderness,

9 Where your fathers tried Me by proving Me,
And saw My works forty years.
10 Wherefore I was displeased with this generation,
And said, They do always err in their heart:
But they did not know My ways;
11 As I sware in My wrath,
They shall not enter into My rest.

Paraphrase

7 Since the Son is the Father's faithful Apostle or Lawgiver in His church, I, by commission from Him, say to you, as said the Holy Ghost to the Jews by David, To-day when ye shall hear God's voice by His Son, commanding you to enter into the rest of heaven,

8 Be not faithless and obstinate as your fathers were in the bitter provocation at Kadesh, where they refused to go into Canaan, in the day of temptation in the wilderness.

9 Where your fathers, from the time of their departure out of Egypt until they arrived at Canaan, tempted Me by their disobedience, and proved Me by insolently demanding proofs of My faithfulness and power, notwithstanding they saw my miracles forty years. See Deut. ix. 7.

10 Wherefore I was exceedingly displeased with that generation which I had brought out of Egypt, and said, They always err, not from ignorance, but from perverseness of disposition; and they have utterly disliked My method of dealing with them.

11 So, to punish them for their unbelief, I sware in My wrath, they shall not enter into My rest in Canaan.

Comment

Wherefore even as the Holy Spirit saith
   This is a quotation from Psalm 95:7.
a. He attributes these words to the Holy Spirit, thus establishing the inspiration of the scriptures.
b. Men who question the inspiration of the Bible have hundreds of such verses of which to dispose.

Harden not your hearts
   This suggests immediate action in favor of God, not against Him.
a. This subject is emphasized all through the New Testament:

1. John 9:4: " — while it is day."
2. Acts 22:16: "Now why tarriest thou?"
3. Rom. 13:11: " — awake out of sleep."
4. Acts 16:33: " — same hour."
   Man is able to receive the word, but has the choice of hardening his heart.

as in the day of provocation

There were two reasons why the Jews needed to be reminded:
a. They were foolishly inflated on account of the glory of their race:
1. They needed to be reminded of their own sinfulness.
2. Their feeling of superiority blinded them to the reality of their condition.
b. They needed to know that falling away was dangerous.
   To what does the provocation refer?
a. Two possibilities:
1. Numbers, chapters thirteen and fourteen: Spies bring back a report: "We are as grasshoppers." (13:33)
   "And all the children of Israel murmured against Moses and against Aaron and the whole congregation said unto them, Would that we had died in the land of Egypt or would that we had died in the wilderness." (14:2)
2. Exodus 17 may be referred to:
a) Here the Israelites cried against Moses and complained. (See 17:1-7)
b) Moses gave the places names. (17:7)
1. *Massah* — proving — tempting.
2. *Meribah* — chiding — strife.
b. We do not know to which of the two places David referred.

Like as in the day of the trial in the wilderness

The term "wilderness" refers to any waste land, and this was the type of country in which the Jews traveled. They were led through the wilderness because:
a. It was less likely to lead to war.
b. It gave God a chance to prove His power and love.

where your fathers tried Me by proving Me

God brought them gifts — water, manna and quails for food, the cloud and the pillar of fire for guidance and pro-

tection — yet they asked, "Where is His power?"
It increased their guilt, when in spite of so many evidences of His power they made so little progress.
Trying by proving illustrated:
a. Newell — A boy says, "Father has forbidden me to do this and says I will be punished. I do not believe it. I will do what he said not to do and see if he will."
b. The action of Israel was a trying thing upon the patience of God; yet it also proved that He meant every word spoken.

and saw My works forty years

Not once or for a short time — but for forty years.
History of their waywardness:
a. First, in the wilderness of sin — when they murmured for bread and God gave them manna. Exodus 16:4.
b. Second — they murmured because of lack of water. Ex. 17:2-9. This place is called Massah and Meribah.
c. Third — During the third year after their departure from Egypt, they provoked God at Sinai by making the golden calf. Ex. 32:10.
d. Fourth — At Taberah (Numbers 11:3) they murmured for want of flesh, and were smitten with a plague, v. 33. Many were buried here. v. 34.
e. Kadesh — Caleb and Joshua as spies are rejected.
1. Num. 14:30: God says all shall die but Caleb and Joshua.
2. Deut. 1:34-35: God ordered them to turn into the wilderness, where they wandered 38 years. Deut. 2:14.
f. Wilderness near Mt. Hor. Num. 21:4-5. No bread or water. God sent serpents, and finally a brazen serpent was erected to save them.
3. Newell says it refers to the eleven-day journey from Horeb by way of Mt. Sinai unto Kadesh Barnea that because of unfaithfulness took forty years.

Wherefore I was displeased with this generation

"Generation" means race, or men of one age.
Here was God, their Father, grieved at their refusal to follow His leading.

and said, They do always err in their heart

"Err" means to wander, go astray.

but they did know My ways

Their consistent errors must have brought the longsuffering Father to the breaking point.

but they did know My ways

They were as ignorant of God as they were of the paths of the desert.
They seemed senseless, unable to understand the ways of God.
a. This was not an excuse, but an accusation.
b. This condition did not save them, but destroyed them.

as I sware in my wrath

"Sware" refers to what God spoke.
Numbers 14:30-35: God here stated they shall not enter, because they listened to the report of the ten spies.
"Wrath" refers to His condemnation:
a. God has a right to be wrathful.
1. A lack of anger is a weakness.
2. Tolerance is to be desired above intolerance, but it can also become a vice rather than a virtue.
b. God has wrath when His longsuffering comes to an end.
c. It is not good for man to reap and not sow.
1. It is not good for man to sow wickedness, and not reap the same.
2. God has made a consistent world for us.
d. God used them as an example unto us.
1. I Cor. 10:11-12: " — happened by way of example."

They shall not enter into My rest

Num. 14:20 is the place where God reached this decision.
The generation that showed a lack of faith was not given the privilege to enter Canaan.

Study Questions

412. Where is the quotation from the Holy Spirit found?
413. Does this establish the inspiration of the scriptures?
414. Who can harden or soften hearts in this verse?
415. Can you name other scriptures that place the responsibility upon man? cf. Rom. 13:11.
416. What day of provocation is referred to, Pharaoh's or Israel's?
417. Is it a certain time, or the whole exodus?

418. Name some instances of provocation. cf. Numbers 13:32; Exodus 17:1-7.
419. Could it be at Massah and Meribah alone?
420. What is meant by "trial in the wilderness"?
421. What is a "wilderness" in the scriptures?
422. Why did the Israelites go into the wilderness?
423. Who are the "fathers" referred to here?
424. How did they try God?
425. What is meant by "try"?
426. What did the trial prove concerning God?
427. How long did they try God?
428. What is meant by "works"?
429. Tell of the Israelites' provocation of God that brought about works of God.
430. What is meant by "generation"?
431. What did God declare concerning that generation?
432. What is meant by "err"?
433. Where was the seat of their trouble?
434. Why didn't they know God's ways?
435. Is ignorance a sufficient excuse for disobedience?
436. What is meant by "swear"?
437. What is the wrath of God — anger, or condemnation?
438. Is wrath a good quality or a bad one?
439. Would it be good for man if God were a weakling?
440. Would it be good for man not to reap what he sows?
441. Where and when did this swearing take place? cf. Numbers 14:23.

2. *Our pilgrimage* — 3:12-19.

Text
3:12-19

12 Take heed, brethren, lest haply there shall be in any one of you an evil heart of unbelief, in falling away from the living God: 13 but exhort one another day by day, so long as it is called To-day; lest any one of you be hardened by the deceitfulness of sin: 14 for we are become partakers of Christ, if we hold fast the beginning of our confidence firm unto the end: 15 while it is said,

To-day if ye shall hear His voice,
Harden not your hearts, as in the provocation.

16 For who, when they heard, did provoke? nay, did not all they that came out of Egypt by Moses?

17 And with whom was He displeased forty years? was it not with them that sinned, whose bodies fell in the wilderness?

18 And to whom sware He that they should not enter into His rest, but to them that were disobedient?

19 And we see that they were not able to enter in because of unbelief.

Paraphrase

12 Brethren, this example of sin and punishment should make you take heed, lest there be in any of you an evil heart of unbelief, by departing from the living God: which ye will do, if ye reject the gospel, or renounce it after having embraced it.

13 Instead of exhorting one another, after the example of your fathers, to depart from the living God, exhort one another every day to obey Christ, while He calls you today to enter into the rest of heaven, lest any of you should be hardened against his call, through the deceitful suggestions of an unbelieving, timorous, sinful disposition, which magnifies the hardship of suffering for the gospel.

14 For we are partakers of the blessings of Christ's house, the gospel church, only if we hold fast the faith we have begun to exercise on Him as our Saviour (chap. v. 9.) firm unto the end of our lives.

15 Perserverance in faith and obedience is requisite to your enjoying the privileges of Christ's house; as ye may know by the saying of the Holy Ghost to the Israelites in David's days, Today, when ye shall hear His voice commanding you to enter into His rest, harden not your hearts as your fathers did in the bitter provocation.

16 For many, when they heard the command to enter into Canaan, bitterly provoked God by their disobedience, and were excluded from His rest in Canaan. However, not all who went out of Egypt with Moses provoked God by their rebellion, and were so punished.

17 But, to show you the infectious nature of disobedience, I ask you with whom was God displeased forty years? was it not with them who rebelled, (Josh. v. 6.), even all the men of war who were numbered, whose carcasses fell in the wilderness?

18 Farther, to make you sensible of the evil of disobedience,

to whom did God swear that they should not enter into His rest, but to them who, notwithstanding they had seen God's miracles, did not believe He was able to bring them into Canaan, and absolutely refused to enter?

19 Thus we see that the Israelites could not fight their way into Canaan, because they did not believe the promises of God.

Comment

Take heed, brethren

"Profit by their mistake," the author is saying.
Society makes a fool of itself every generation:
a. One generation seemingly has to try everything for itself rather than to be warned.
b. Foolish is the man who will not learn from others.

lest haply

"Perhaps", or "lest there be", is the meaning of this expression.
There is a likelihood of falling away unless a person is careful.

there shall be in any one of you

This is personal — "*any* one of you".
We need warning, and we have it.
a. I Cor. 10:12: "Wherefore let him that thinketh he standeth take heed lest he fall."
b. I Cor. 9:27: " — I buffet my body."
c. I Cor. 10:5, 10.
d. II Peter 2:4.
e. II Peter 2:7.
f. Jude 5: "Now 1 desire to put you in remembrance, though ye know all things once for all, that the Lord, having saved a people out of the land of Egypt, afterward destroyed them that believed not."

an evil heart of unbelief

Sin will cause people to disbelieve.
The so-called "good moral man" does not exist:
a. Unbelief is evil — sufficient to keep one out of God's rest.
b. Mark 16:16: "He that disbelieveth shall be condemned."
The devil seems to sow doubt.

a. To Eve, Gen. 3:4-5: "Ye shall not surely die — ye shall be as God."
b. To Jesus. "If." Matt. 4.
1. Matt. 4:3: "*If* thou art the Son of God command that these stones become bread."
2. 4:5, 6: On pinnacle of temple: "If thou are the Son of God, cast Thyself down."

in falling away from the Living God

You can not fall away unless you were there.
Some say: "You never had it if you lost it."
The Jews fell away after believing and being saved.
This falling away is falling from fellowship, and results in falling into the hands of God.
Heb. 10:31: "It is a fearful thing to fall into the hands of the living God."

but exhort

To "exhort" is to give a pep talk:
a. We should not let another's spiritual enthusiasm freeze up.
b. This young Timothy was told to do.
I Tim. 6:2: "These things teach and *exhort*."
c. Be careful lest you get into a rut of browbeating. People need feeding as well as rebuking. "Exhort" means to encourage.

one another day by day

We have a responsibility to one another daily:
a. We should have a constant interest in our brethren.
b. A day missed in encouragement may result in an eternity lost.

so long as it is called To-day

It includes every time that God addresses us.
Every time that God's sacred mouth speaks, remember, "To-day if ye shall hear His voice."
Jesus warned about the passing of the day:
a. John 12:35: "Yet a little while is the light with you. Walk while ye have the light, lest darkness come upon you."
b. John 9:4: "The night cometh when no man can work."
A seasonable time will not always last.

lest any one of you

This makes it broad enough to include all:
a. I Cor. 10:12: "Let him that thinketh he standeth take heed lest he fall."
b. Overconfidence in any endeavor is dangerous.

be hardened

He is talking to Christian people, yet some say, "once saved, always saved."
Sin makes one tough, calloused:
a. Saul, a wonderful specimen of mankind, became hardened against David.
b. Judas was trained among the other disciples, yet his heart was hardened against Jesus.

by the deceitfulness of sin

Sin is seductive:
a. Col. 2:8: " — maketh spoil of you through . . . vain deceit."
b. Matt. 13:22: " — deceitfulness of riches."
The sin here of primary concern is apostasy.
Ways to be deceived:
a. Deceive self. I Cor. 3:18; Gal. 6:3; I John 1:8; James **1**:22.
b. Fair speeches deceive the simple. Rom. 16:18.
c. Deceitfulness of riches. Matt. 13:22.
d. False teachers. Matt. 24:24: " — lead astray . . . the elect."
e. Deceived by the devil. Rev. 12:9: "Satan, the deceiver of the whole world."

for we are become partakers

It is also translated, "made partakers".
a. We become partakers in faithfulness to our call.
b. We cannot expect a faithful Christ to save an unfaithful person.

partakers of Christ

Christ partook of man's flesh that man might partake of Him. Being a partaker entitles one to the benefits:
a. It has the idea of sharing in, participating with.
b. The true calling of all true believers is meant here.

firm unto the end

"As long as life shall last" must be the determination of the child of God:

a. There is no time for relaxation, compromise, or half-heartedness.
b. "Hold fast" is the exhortation in Rev. 3:11.
We do not know when the "end" will be, so we must be firm always.

Today if ye shall hear His voice

The warning from Psalms 95:7 is quoted:
a. It suggests the urgency of action, the very day one hears.
b. We have only one chance. Heb. 9:27.
No purgatory, or second chance, is taught in this book.

For who when they heard did provoke?

This passage is translated differently:
a. The King James version says: "For some, when they had heard . . ."
b. It also is translated: "Who were those hearers who did bitterly provoke."
How does the difference arise?
a. The early manuscripts did not have punctuation or accent marks.
b. In 240 B.C., Aristophanes introduced an imperfect system for the benefit of scholars and teachers.
c. In the fifth century, Christian writers began to use accents.
d. Not until the tenth century did accents have a universal usage.
e. The problem arises in the word "who". Either:
1. "Who" is an interrogative and requires a question mark at the end of the sentence. Or,
2. "Who" is an inadequate pronoun equivalent to "some" and requires a period at the end of the sentence.
The word "some" suggests that some did not provoke, but this group was very small:
a. Joshua and Caleb were two of the hundreds of thousands, so even the word "all" in this verse is justified.
b. The lesson to be gained is to avoid being like the Israelites.

nay did not all they that came out of Egypt by Moses

The King James version translation may give room for some exceptions:
"Howbeit not all that came out . . .":

a. Joshua and Caleb are exceptions.
b. Clarke suggests: "... all the priests and whole tribe of Levi, for they were not of the ones to fight."
1. Num. 26:63-65 seems to eliminate this.
2. Some may have lived, however, for Eleazar, the son of Aaron, was one who did take possession:
a) See Num. 26:60: "— Eleazar son of Aaron."
b) See Num. 34:17 and Joshua 24:33.

And with whom was He displeased forty years

The King James version states, "But with many of them God was not well pleased."
Disbelief or doubt displeases God, as it breaks fellowship, or is a barrier to fellowship:
a. Disbelief drove Adam and Eve out of the garden.
b. Disbelief drove Israel into the wilderness.
c. Disbelief keeps men away from God. Heb. 11:6.

was it not with them that sinned whose bodies fell in the wilderness?

Individuals are not discussed, but a disbelieving nation is.
a. Joshua and Caleb were the exceptions.
b. Moses and Aaron did not enter Canaan.
c. I Cor. 10:5-13 suggests that not all perished, so we must conclude that those innocent ones who were too young to disbelieve did not perish.
d. Numbers 14:29 says that all who were twenty years old or under should enter.
Funerals must have been often and sad, as a generation perished in the wilderness because of unbelief.

and to whom sware He that they should not

This refers to God's condemnation and punishment. This is pronounced in Num. 14:20-38. Num. 14:22 says that they tempted God ten times.

not enter into His rest

It was a land of rest as God planned it:
a. No more bondage and oppression.
b. Cisterns, cities, farms, etc., were to be taken over. Deut. 6:10-11.

Those who did enter were disobedient like their parents, hence Canaan really never did become a place of rest.

but to them that were disobedient?

King James version: "But to them that believed not."
a. Mark 16:16 expresses the awfulness of disbelief:
1. You do not have to be a great worker of evil, only a disbeliever.
2. Disbelief in the love, providence and gift of Jesus Christ is sufficient to condemn a man.
Disbelief is equivalent to disobedience.

And we see

God's word is for us to study so as to find out how God deals with man:
a. I Cor. 10:11: "Now these things happened unto them by way of example; and they were written for our admonition, upon whom the ends of the ages are come."
b. Wise men profit by others' mistakes; fools never learn.

they were not able to enter in

This then is a warning to all Christians.
If every word spoken by angels was stedfast, Heb. 2:2, then this word must be heeded.
Reward goes only to the faithful:
a. Rev. 2:10.
b. I Cor. 9:24-27.
c. Matt. 10:22.

because of unbelief

They were believers who became unbelievers:
a. This is a lesson against backsliding, trifling.
b. Is this unbelief the same as infidelity?
1. No — it is not believing God.
2. There is a difference in believing God and believing *in* God.
3. Paul believed God. Acts 27:25: "For I believe God, that it shall be even so as it hath been spoken unto me."
This was backsliding for Israel:
a. Hosea describes Israel as a "backsliding heifer". See Hosea 4:16.
b. Revised Version: "Israel slideth back as a backsliding heifer. Israel hath behaved himself stubbornly like a stubborn heifer."

If you have worked on a farm you can understand this. Some say it is impossible for men to fall away and be lost. If you point out a backslider, they say he was not saved in the first place. It amounts to, "If you get it, you can't lose it; if you lose it, you never had it." It is a dangerous doctrine, "If you can't be lost — ." People can take all kinds of advantages of God, yet be saved.

c. Let us study the Scriptures on the subject:
1. Notice the many names given to backsliders.
a) Prov. 14:14: " — shall be filled with his own ways — "
Hosea 11:7: "People who are bent to backsliding —"
b) "Shrinking back": Heb. 10:38: " — righteous shall live by faith."
Some people shrink back. They lack courage. Some are like a horse with a collar sore; they never get in and pull.
c) Falling away: Heb. 3:12: " — evil heart of unbelief in falling — "
Luke 8:13: " — and in time of temptation fall away."
Heb. 10:26-31: " — sin wilfully."
Heb. 6:4-6: "For as touching those who — fell away."
d) Falling from grace: Gal. 5:4: " — ye are fallen away from grace."
How can man promote the doctrine that man can't fall away from grace?
e) Being hindered: Gal. 5:7: "Ye were running well, Who hindered you . . . "?
f) Removed from the faith: Gal. 1:6: " — ye are quickly removing from him that — "
g) Again entangled therein: II Pet. 2:20: " — they are again entangled . . . the last state is become worse with them than the first." cf. v. 21, 22.
2. Some examples of backsliding:
a) Israel: Hosea 4:16: "Israel slideth back." Exodus 32 records Moses on the Mount and Israel making a golden calf.
b) Solomon: I Kings 11:4: "When Solomon when he was old, his wives turned away his heart after other gods." cf. v. 9.
c) Simon Peter: Matt. 26:69-75: cursing, "I know not the man."
d) The Galatians: Gal. 1:6: "I marvel that ye are so quickly removed."
e) Simon the Sorcerer: Acts 8:13: "He believed and was baptized."

Acts 8:23: "Thou art in the gall of bitterness — "
f) Judas: Matt. 26:48.
g) Ananias and Saphira: Acts 5:1-11.
3. Some practical thoughts in relationship to backsliding:
a) Our duty to one who errs.
Matt. 18:15-17: "If thy brother sin against thee, go to him."
I Cor. 5:1-5: "Deliver such a one to Satan."
Gal. 6:1: "Restore such a one."
b) Some things that will keep one from backsliding:
1) Lord's Supper rightly observed:
I Cor. 11:30: " — for this cause many among you are weak and sickly, and not a few sleep."
2) Christian fellowship that exhorts:
Heb. 10:25: "Not forsaking the assembling of yourselves together — "
3) Guarding one's life with doctrine:
I Tim. 6:20: "Guard that which was committed unto thee."
I Cor. 11:2: "Hold fast the traditions even as I delivered them unto you."
4) Prayer and meditation: Matt. 26:41.
c) A realization that we need not fail, but that we can escape backsliding: I Cor. 10:13.
d) The backslider is not fit for the kingdom: Luke 9:62.
e) The way back to God for the backslider: Acts 8:22: "Repent and pray."
4. A warning on backsliding. For the willful sinner there is no way back. Heb. 4-6:
a. Simon Peter's fall was a spur-of-the-moment sin not planned at all; he was sorry, and so he repented.
b. Ananias and Sapphira, and Judas each planned their sin; it was willful, and there was no repentance.

Study Questions

442. Does God feel that one generation should learn from another?
443. Define "lest haply".
444. Does He make the application personal?
445. Give some warnings to man in the New Testament. cf. I Cor. 10:12; I Cor. 9:26; I Cor. 10:5, 10; Jude 5, 7.
446. What is the significance of "take heed"?
447. Is unbelief a serious matter according to verse 12?

448. Can a moral man who is an unbeliever be rightly spoken of as a good moral man"?
449. How serious is unbelief in the category mentioned in Revelation?
450. What did unbelief do to Adam and Eve?
451. What did it do to Israel after the Egyptian bondage?
452. Did the devil try to work on Christ in this realm?
453. What is implied in the expression, "falling away from God"?
454. Were they once with God?
455. Can you fall from a building without first being in it or on it?
456. Does this verse give encouragement to the doctrine of man that "if you had it, you can't lose it; if you lose it, you never had it?"
457. What is our estate if we fall? cf. Heb. 10:31.
458. Define the word "exhort".
459. How are we to exhort? cf. I Tim. 6:2.
460. How frequently should we exhort?
461. What is meant by, "so long as it is called today"? cf. John 9:4.
462. Does "any one of you" include you?
463. Is v. 12 a warning against overconfidence? cf. I Cor. 10:12.
464. What will harden man?
465. How does sin harden?
466. Give example of hardened hearts in the word of God.
467. What does sin do to people, according to v. 13? Discuss deceit.
468. What is the kind of sin that is involved here?
469. Can you name some verses that speak of various kinds of deceit?
470. Who is deceived in I Cor. 3:18; Gal. 6:9; I John 1:8?
471. What method is used in Rom. 16:18; II Peter 2:18?
472. What deceives, according to Matt. 13:22?
473. Who deceives in Matt. 25:24?
474. Who deceives in Rev. 12:9?
475. Define "partakers".
476. Why should we be partakers of Christ? Does it entitle us to anything?
477. What qualifies us to be a partaker of Christ?
478. How many evil situations could be avoided "if"? v. 14.

479. Explain "hold fast".
480. What is meant by, "beginning of our confidence"?
481. "Firm unto the end" — end of what?
482. What is the value of the uncertainty of the time of the end?
483. What is the significance of "today if ye shall hear His voice"?
484. Whose voice is referred to?
485. What Psalm is quoted?
486. If God has spoken, has man a right to expect more?
487. What did the Jews want from Jesus?
488. What was a "sign"? What did Jesus answer?
489. "Harden not your hearts" puts the responsibility upon whom?
490. How did God harden Pharaoh's heart? Was God to blame?
491. "As in the provocation": would this refer to the day when the Jews provoked Jesus?
492. What "day" is referred to?
493. Does "day" always mean 24 hours?
494. "For who, when they heard" refers to whom?
495. Is the word "who" always translated "who"?
496. What is implied by the word "provoke"?
497. Is it an accurate literal translation to say that all who came out of Egypt did provoke God?
498. Who were some exceptions?
499. Who does Clarke think may have been exceptions?
500. Cf. Numbers 26:63-65 to see if Clarke's view can be substantiated.
501. Did any live besides Joshua and Caleb? Cf. Numbers 26:65.
502. How long was God displeased?
503. Show other instances in the life of people when God was displeased.
504. What happened to those with whom God was displeased?
505. If their bodies did not fall, was it an inference that God was not displeased with them?
506. What was the age of those who did get to enter? Cf. Numbers 14:29.
507. How many funerals a day did it require?
508. To whom did God swear?
509. What did He pronounce at this time? Cf. Numbers 14:20-28.

510. What number of times did they provoke God? See Numbers 14:22.
511. In what way was Canaan to be a place of rest? Cf. Deut. 6:10-11.
512. The author has talked about disbelief all the way through, but now he uses the word "disobedient". Why?
513. Are "disbelief" and "disobedience" the same?
514. "And we see" has what significance?
515. "They were not able" carries what warning to us?
516. "Because of unbelief" — were they ever believers?
517. If so, what warning do we have?
518. Were they rank infidels?
519. Is there a difference in believing God and believing *in* God? Cf. Acts 27:25.
520. Was disbelief equivalent to backsliding?
521. What terms or synonyms are used for this condition of disbelief?
522. What are some examples of backsliding?
523. What should we do to the backslider?
524. What would you suggest doing to keep people from backsliding?
525. What is the way back to God for the backslider?
526. Is there a way for all backsliders to repent?
527. Why could Simon repent, but Ananias and Sapphira couldn't?

Chapter Three — Multiple Choice

1. Jesus Christ may be considered:
    1. An apostle.
    2. A martyr since he was crucified.
    3. A man of high estate.
2. Jesus is compared with:
    1. Isaiah.
    2. Enoch.
    3. Noah.
    4. Moses.
3. The third chapter of Hebrews mentions the children of Israel:
    1. Tempting God.
    2. Loving the Lord with all their heart, mind and soul.

3. Wandering forty-five years in the wilderness.
 4. The person spoken of as being faithful in all his house was:
   1. Elijah.
   2. Jeremiah.
   3. Moses.
 5. The frequency of exhortations on our part is to be:
   1. Semi-annually.
   2. Month by month.
   3. Week by week.
   4. Day by day.
 6. The certainty of our being made partakers with Christ is based upon:
   1. Our holding fast the beginning of our confidence firm to the end.
   2. Our knowledge of the will of God.
   3. The ability to give a testimony of our salvation by faith only.
 7. What expression summarizes the reason why the Jews could not enter into God's reward for them:
   1. Self-conciousness.
   2. Hatred.
   3. Unbelief.
   4. Poor leadership.
 8. The Christ in relationship to our confession is:
   1. Pope.
   2. High Priest.
   3. Rabbi.
   4. Author.
 9. Every house is built by some man, but He that built all things, according to this chapter, is:
   1. Paul, who built the Gentile house being sent to them.
   2. Christ, who said He would build His church.
   3. God, Who is the builder of the household.
 10. Our hearts are hardened by sin by:
   1. The pleasure of it.
   2. The deceitfulness of it.
   3. The beauty of it.
 11. This chapter is addressed to:
   1. Holy brethren.
   2. Backsliders.
   3. Gentiles.

12. Christ is counted worthy of more glory than:
    1. God.
    2. Adam.
    3. Moses.
13. God was displeased with the Israelites for:
    1. Ten days.
    2. Six months.
    3. Forty years.
14. Chapter three warns about:
    1. Evil heart of unbelief.
    2. False teachers.
    3. Following Moses.
15. Moses was a servant in God's house, but Christ:
    1. Was a builder.
    2. Was a Son.
    3. Had no part in a house.
16. We are exhorted to hold fast the beginning of our confidence:
    1. Firm unto the end.
    2. Because God will not let us go.
    3. Because we are weak.
17. The group that provoked God was:
    1. The males of Israel.
    2. They that came out of Egypt.
    3. Few.
18. The words of David in the ninety-fifty Psalm are attributed:
    1. To false teachers.
    2. To a lack of evidence.
    3. To the Holy Spirit.
19. The bodies of them that sinned in the wilderness:
    1. Fell in the wilderness.
    2. Were buried in one grave.
    3. Were over thirty years of age.
20. The disbelief in this chapter is called:
    1. The day of provocation.
    2. A minor offense to God.
    3. A rebellion against Moses.

SUMMARY OF CHAPTER THREE

Chapter three begins the development of the principal theme of Hebrews by calling attention to the faithfulness of Jesus, the Apostle and High Priest of our confession. In the first two chapters, He is contrasted with angels, for it is His message that is superior to that spoken through angels. In this chapter, He is contrasted with Moses for, although Moses was faithful, the quality of Jesus' faithfulness is superior.

This superior faithfulness is the basis of the appeal for Christians to be true to Christ instead of failing as the Israelites did in the wilderness journey because of their unbelief. Those who accept Christ as Leader are urged to hold steadfastly to their convictions to the end of the journey of life, remembering the fate of those who came out of Egypt under the leadership of Moses. They were refused entrance into the promised rest because of disobedience and unbelief.

C. *Warning and exhortation in respect to rest: promises under Moses and Christ.* 4:1-13.
1. *Danger of losing the heavenly rest through unbelief and rebellion.* 4:1-3.

Text
4:1-3

1 Let us fear therefore, lest haply, a promise being left of entering into His rest, any one of you should seem to have come short of it. 2 For indeed we have had good tidings preached unto us, even as also they: but the word of hearing did not profit them, because it was not united by faith with them that heard. 3 For we who have believed do enter into that rest; even as he hath said,

As I sware in My wrath,
They shall not enter into My rest:

although the works were finished from the foundation of the world.

Paraphrase

1 Wherefore, since the Israelites were excluded from Canaan for their unbelief and disobedience, let us be afraid, lest a promise of entrance into God's rest being left to all Abraham's seed in the convenant, any of you should actually fall short of obtaining it.

2 For we also who believe, being Abraham's seed, have in that promise received the good tidings of a rest in the heavenly

country, even as the Israelites in the wilderness received the good tidings of a rest in Canaan. But the good tidings which they heard had no influence on their conduct, because they did not believe what they heard.

3 Wherefore, according to God's promise, we, the seed of Abraham who believe, shall enter into the rest of God. But it is a rest different from the seventh day rest, seeing He said, con-concerning the unbelieving Israelites in the wilderness, So I sware in My wrath, they shall not enter into My rest, notwithstanding the works of creation were finished, and the seventh day rest was instituted, from the formation of the world: consequently the Israelites had entered into that rest before the oath was sworn.

Let us fear

He must be talking to Christian people:
a. I Peter 1:17: " — pass the time with fear."
b. Christians must take heed to the dangers that confront all Christians.

fear therefore lest haply

A trail of bleaching bones and graves in the wilderness, and their wandering in the wilderness forty long years ought to startle us:
a. Rom. 11:20: " — by their unbelief they were broken off, and thou standest by thy faith. Be not high minded but fear."
b. It is not a fear that shakes the confidence, but one that fills with concern and alerts one.

a promise being left

Milligan: "The participle 'being left' is in the present tense":
a. This implies the promise is here now, but is made sure to only those who, like Joshua and Caleb, continue faithful to the end.
b. We will be disappointed by failure unless we by fear work at our salvation.

should seem to have come short of it

Sin is "to miss the mark":
a. "Come short" alludes to the Grecian games, and is applied to the loser, no matter how close he came to being the winner.
b. At the end of the day, if you are not finished, you fall short.

c. In the day of judgment, if you have failed to arrive and have never crossed Jordan, you will not be saved.

For indeed we have had good tidings preached unto us even as also they

They had an earthly rest preached; we have a heavenly rest.
a. Milligan says: "Literally it should read 'we are evangelized as well as they'."
b. This ties in with Heb. 1:2: " — spoken to us in His Son."
c. See Eph. 1:9: " — making known unto us the mystery of His will according to His good pleasure which He purposed in Him."
The church is to preach these good tidings:
I Peter 4:10: " — steward of the manifold grace of God."
Eph. 3:10: " — that might be made known through the church."

but the word of hearing did not profit them

They would not go up.
a. Deut.1:20-21:" — and I said unto you, ye are come unto the hill country — go up — take possession — fear not; be not dismayed." 1:26: " — yet ye would not go up, but rebelled against the commandment of Jehovah, your God."
b. Good tidings were rejected for the ten spies' evil reports.
2. Jesus spoke of a similar people. Matt. 23:37: "Ye would not."
a. The test of a sermon is, "what profit?"
b. Some preaching is beautiful, but to no profit.

because it was not united by faith

Hearing is useless unless tied to or laid hold of:
a. The word "united" is also translated "mixed."
b. The place of faith is described in Heb. 11.
"Mixed" is described by Milligan: "This is metaphorically used and seems to have reference to the mixing of food with digestive fluids in order to be appropriated to the wants of the body."
Faith is to affect one's actions, character and destiny:
a. Jesus likened the hearer who does not obey to the foolish man building upon the sand. Matt. 7:26-27.
b. Of the spies, only Joshua and Caleb, "mixed faith".

with them that heard

Faith is the person's responsibility:
a. God gives us grace, not faith.
b. We do the uniting, the mixing.

We have been given ears to hear along with God's grace; now, as hearers we are to unite the message with faith.

a. Grace saves, Eph. 2:8, but only by faith on man's part.
b. Heaven is not a place for faithless people. If heaven were obtained by the grace of God only, everyone would be there.

For we who have believed

Is faith all that is necessary?
a. Let James answer. James **2:17**: "Even so faith, if it hath not works is dead, being alone." **2:24**: "We see then how that by works, a man is justified and not by faith only."
b. Faith discussed here is the active kind like Joshua's.

He talks of faith, for it is the beginning of our experience.

do enter into that rest

What is our "rest"?
a. Scriptures that show kinds of rest:
1. II Tim. 1:7: From fear — "not given us a spirit of fear." Rom. 8:15: "For we have not received the spirit of bondage again unto fear."
2. Rom. 8:2: Bondage to sin — "For the law of the spirit of life made me free from the law of sin and death."
3. Gal. 5:1: Bondage from law — "Be not entangled again in a yoke of bondage."
4. Rom. 8:1: From condemnation — "There is therefore now no condemnation."
b. McKnight says that the rest here spoken of is all future rest. It is an inward rest on earth for us, although the final rest will be future.
a) Peace of conscience.
b) Joy in the Holy Spirit.
c) Saved from the guilt and power of sin.

Rest is obtained by accepting the words of God:
a. *Illustration of it:* II Chronicles 32:8 — Hezekiah spoke to his people when the Assyrians came against them. "With him is an arm of flesh: but with us is Jehovah **our God to help us**, and to fight our battles. And the people rested them-

HELPS FROM HEBREWS 4:3

selves upon the words of Hezekiah king of Judah."
b. Sinners are restless, for sin does not satisfy.
Use of the word "rest" in the New Testament:
a. Jesus and rest:
Matt. 11:28-29: "I will give you rest."
b. Rest and persecution:
1. Acts 9:31: "Then had the churches rest."
2. II Thess. 1:7: "And to you that are afflicted rest with us, at the revelation of the Lord Jesus from heaven with the angels of His power in flaming fire."
c. Rest as a blessing on man by God.
I Peter 4:14: "Spirit of God resteth upon you."
II Cor. 12:9: "Power of Christ may dwell upon you."
The word "rest" should be understood in the same way as "salvation".
a. We are saved, but salvation includes now, as well as our experience of heaven.
b. We have rest now, but rest in heaven will be the greatest joy of us all.

even as he hath said, As I sware in My wrath

Psalm 95:11 is quoted here in rather a strange setting, it seems, on the first reading of it.
The author, like Jesus, quoted often from the Old Testament, which proves its accepted inspiration.

they shall not enter into My rest

King James version: "If they shall enter":
a. Milligan: The word should not be rendered "if" but "not".
b. This expression "if" seems not widely accepted.
Why this negative statement is to verify a positive one preceding it:
a. He argues that, since men are by the oath of God excluded from God's rest on account of unbelief, this implies that all who believe shall enter into His rest.
b. It is an argument from what is contrary.

although the works were finished from the foundation of the world

Some suggested explanations of this expression:
a. It probably means the completion of the creation in six days, followed by a rest.

1. The rest of God was after the creation. God looked upon it and saw that it was good.
2. Sin broke the rest of God.
b. McKnight says that this rest is mentioned to show it was not the seventh day, but a future rest which they could have had by believing.
c. Calvin says: "To define what our rest is, he reminds us of what Moses relates, that God, having finished the creation of the world, immediately rested from His works; and he finally concludes that the true rest of the faithful will be when they shall rest as God did."
d. Milligan feels that it is used to point out the sabbatical rest sanctified by God for His glory and all mankind.

Although there was a rest from the beginning, we can miss it by unbelief:
a. Reading it with the warning, we can see the danger of our not entering God's eternal rest, just as Israel missed their rest.
b. Man and God will have rest when sin and unbelief are ended.

Study Questions

528. The expression "let us" would include whom?
529. Who does he say should fear?
530. What kind of a fear is it?
531. What does I Peter 1:17 say about fear?
532. What have we seen from Chapter Three to cause fear?
533. What are we to fear?
534. Define "lest haply".
535. Does the expression, "being left", indicate a present promise?
536. If we should fear, then does it sound as though all will be saved — eternal security?
537. If a generation could be lost, is it not a serious warning to us?
538. What has he stated here that should cause us to fear?
539. What is the promise referred to here?
540. What is meant, "come short of the promise"?
541. How can you come short of a promise?
542. Why had good tidings been preached to them? Why did it fail?
543. How do our good tidings compare with theirs?
544. What would have been the profit to them?
545. Compare Deut. 1:20, 26 with our backsliding.

546. Is it inferred that faith alone is sufficient?
547. Give an exegesis of the expression, "not united by faith".
548. Compare Matt. 7:26-27 with the idea of mixing faith and obedience.
549. Does faith affect one's character and conduct?
550. Is faith our part, or God's part, in salvation?
551. How does the word of hearing profit us?
552. Does God give grace, or faith? cf. Eph. 2:8.
553. How does the hearer unite his faith?
554. If God gives faith, who might we expect to see in heaven? How many?
555. What good does food do if it is not mixed with the bloodstream?
556. Compare Jerusalem on the subject of hearing Christ.
557. Compare James 2:17-24.
558. "We who have believed" would refer to whom?
559. Is it persons who have believed the Old Testament example?
560. The word "rest" seems to have a prominent part here. What is involved? Of what are we free?
561. Is rest all future?
562. Read these verses to see what our rest might be. II Tim. 1:7; Rom. 8:2, 15; Gal. 5:1.
563. What kind of experiences are eliminated by the peace and rest of the Christian?
564. What use is made of the term "rest" in other places in the Bible? cf. Matt. 11:28-29; Acts 9:31; II Thess. 1:7; I Peter 4:14.
565. Read II Chronicles 32:8 for an example of a faith that "rests".
566. Does the word "rest" carry a similar idea as the word "saved"?
567. Discuss the King James translation, *"if* they shall enter."
568. What works are referred to in v. 3?
569. What opinions do commentators have on the "works" here referred to?
570. Does this make God's plan of salvation of long standing, if it refers to God's early plan of giving man rest from sin?
571. If God has always had provision for man's rest, and it was lost by unbelief, what should we conclude?
572. Does the scripture back up this logic?

573. What does the "seventh day" refer to? cf. Gen. 2:2-3 and Exodus 31:17.
2. *This heavenly rest in type.* 4:4-8.
a. *The seventh day.* 4:4-5.

Text
4:4-5

4 For He hath said somewhere of the seventh day on this wise, And God rested on the seventh day from all his works; 5 and in this place again,
They shall not enter into My rest.

Paraphrase

4 That the seventh day rest is God's rest, and that it was instituted at the creation, is evident, for Moses hath spoken somewhere concerning the seventh day rest thus: And God completely rested on the seventh day from all His works.

5 Moreover, in this ninety-fifth Psalm, the Holy Ghost said again to the unbelieving Israelites in David's time who were living in Canaan, They shall not enter into My rest. This shows, that another rest besides that in Canaan was promised to Abraham's seed, which would be forfeited by unbelief, but be obtained by believing.

Comment

For He hath said somewhere of the seventh day on this wise.

    Moses spoke of the first day of rest.
a. Gen. 2:2-3.
b. Ex. 31:17: "For in six days Jehovah made heaven and earth, and on the seventh day He rested and was refreshed."
Why does the author mention it here?
a. Milligan says: "To amplify and illustrate further what he has spoken in the preceding verse."
b. Milligan feels that this rest cannot be identical with that from which a whole generation of the Israelites were forever excluded.

and God rested on the seventh day from all His works

    This day of rest was instituted by God from the foundation of the world. Twenty-five hundred years later God spoke of a future rest which the Israelites were to be denied.

What is God doing now? The scriptures indirectly answer for us.

Heb. 1:3: Christ is spoken of as "upholding all things by the word of his power". John 5:17: "My Father worketh until now and I work — ." John 6:29: "This is the work of God, that ye believe on Him whom He hath sent." Acts 17:28: "In Him we live and move."

and in this place again

Ps. 95:11: Most authorities agree that "place" is to be in italics — not in the original manuscript.

They shall not enter into My rest

Clarke says that this was a second rest promised to the obedient seed of Abraham — spoken in the days of David, when the Jews actually possessed the land.

McKnight feels that it refers to the rest in Canaan, and was God's rest for two reasons:

a. God rested from introducing them after their settlement.
b. They were free to worship, free from the fear of their enemies.

Study Questions

574. When did God first speak of a rest for His people?
575. God's rest after six days of creation was what kind of a rest?
576. Why does Paul mention it here? What is the lesson?
577. Why the indefinite "somewhere"?
578. How many years after the first seventh day did God give man a seventh day?
579. Does God work today?
580. Are two different rests referred to here as seen by the word "again"?
581. In what ways could the Israelites' experience in Canaan be considered a rest?

b. *Canaan.* 4:6-8.

Text
4:6-8

6 Seeing therefore it remaineth that some should enter thereinto, and they to whom the good tidings were before preached failed to enter in because of disobedience, 7 He again defineth a certain day, To-day, saying in David so long a time afterward (even as hath been said before),

To-day if ye shall hear His voice,
Harden not your hearts.

8 For if Joshua had given them rest, he would not have spoken afterward of another day.

Paraphrase

6 Seeing, then, after the Israelites were living in Canaan, it still remained for them to enter into God's rest through believing, and seeing they who first received in the wilderness the good tidings of the rest in Canaan did not enter in on account of their unbelief, it follows, that they who receive, or have received the good tidings of the rest in the heavenly country, shall not enter into it if they do not believe.

7 Moreover, seeing the Holy Ghost specifieth a particular time for entering in, saying to the people by David, To-day, so long a time after the nation had taken possession of Canaan; as it is written, To-day, when ye shall hear God's voice commanding you to enter into His rest, harden not your hearts against entering.

8 For if Joshua, by introducing the Israelites into Canaan, had caused them to rest according to the full meaning of God's promise, the Holy Ghost would not after that, in Divid's time, have spoken of another day for entering into God's rest.

Comment

Seeing therefore it remaineth that some should enter thereinto

The King James version says "some must enter":
a. This carries the idea of necessity.
b. God did not forsake all men, but some did receive the promise, the faithful ones, Joshua and Caleb.
God's promise to Abraham must not fail, so God used the next generation to conquer the land.

and they to whom the good tidings were before preached failed to enter in

    Good news of freedom from bondage, news of prosperity, were all rejected for a discouraging report of ten spies:
a. Read the good news in **Ex. 3:8, 17; 13:5, and 33:3.**
b. How they could turn away from God's providential care seems a mystery to us.
    Before we condemn that generation, look at the warnings for our generation:
a. Acts 20:29-30: " — speaking perverse things to draw away the disciples."
b. II Tim. 3:1-5: " — form of godliness."
c. II Tim. 1:15.

because of disobedience

    Faithlessness is an equivalent to disobedience.
    Believers need to watch out today:
a. They can fall away and be lost, or Israel's example means nothing.
b. If a believer, a Christian, cannot be lost, then Paul wasted much time in this book.

he again

    (Ps. 95:7-8 very likely).
    The frequency of Old Testament quotations indicates why the gospel was to the Jew first:
a. The Old Testament was the Word of God, much of it a type of the New Testament, and much of it a lesson.
b. The Jew had a background which gave him an advantage.

defineth

    It is also translated "limited":
a. A certain time in which God's grace will work, for He limits man.
b. See Gen. 6:3: "My spirit will not always strive with man." God is no weakling. He practices longsuffering, but there is a line man cannot cross.

a certain day To-day

    When God decides on the day, it will not be tomorrow, but today:

a. Parents in their weakness say "tomorrow," and then forget to discipline tomorrow.
b. Parents do much threatening which means little but not so with God.
Some feel that this section was David's way of referring back to Moses' day for a lesson in David's day.

saying in David so long a time afterward

David by the Spirit is warning the people of his own day — living later by about 500 or 600 years, of the danger of unbelief:
a. Such a warning is never out of date.
b. Every generation needs to be warned, for men always err and disobey.

(even as hath been said before), To-day if ye shall hear His voice harden not your hearts

One generation can harden its heart as easily as another. The Christian dispensation is no different than any other, so we must heed this warning.

For if Joshua had given them rest

"Joshua" in the Greek is "Jesus". In Acts 7:45, it is translated "Jesus". Both names mean "saviour".
The people did enjoy comparative rest. Joshua 1:15: " . . . until the Lord have given your brethren rest." Joshua 22:4: "And now the Lord your God hath given rest." This was not the true rest. God has something better in store for His people.
They to whom David addressed the Psalm were in possession of that land, but they were reminded of the duty of seeking a **better rest**.

he would not have spoken afterward of another day

Who is "he"?
a. If it is Joshua, when did he speak it?
1. Newell feels it refers to Joshua's farewell address in Joshua 23:1-4, where he tells them to complete the conquest.
2. It shows the incomplete work of Joshua; more rest was needed.
b. "He" must refer to God, who spoke afterward through David, says Milligan.

1. This is not the best rendering.
2. The context has shown that Joshua failed, so he had to speak again in his farewell address of rest.
3. To clinch his argument, David was quoted in v. 7.

Study Questions

582. Is a second rest promised in the days of David correct according to Clarke?
583. What is implied by the expression, "some should enter"?
584. Would God's plan of salvation have failed if all had failed to enter?
585. What were the good tidings of God? of the ten spies? of Joshua?
586. What has been the main factor in man's failure in the past to enter into the rest of God?
587. What verses in the New Testament warn us against similar experiences?
588. If man, who had received the promise, lost out that day, should we not assume there is danger today?
589. What actually caused this disobedience?
590. If man can't be lost, what is the purpose of the teaching of this verse?
591. What other word may be used in place of the word "defineth" of verse 7?
592. Compare Gen. 6:3 for God's limitation.
593. What is the significance of this limitation?
594. Compare Gal. 4:4 with God's limitation of time.
595. If Moses and David found hardened hearts, is it likely that human nature has changed?
596. What hardens a heart?
597. Did Joshua ever promise another rest? Cf. Joshua 1:15 and 22:1-4.
598. Why is it likely not Jesus who is referred to here?
599. Why is "Joshua" also translated "Jesus" in the footnote?
600. Why is it likely Joshua is referred to and not David?
601. Who is referred to by "he would not have spoken afterward of another day"?
602. Was Joshua's rest complete? Is this why God declared it again through David in verse 7?

603. If the rest refers to Joshua's farewell words, then why is David quoted in verse 7?

3. *Conclusions from the above premises.* 4:9-10.

Text
4:9-10

9 There remaineth therefore a sabbath rest for the people of God. 10 For he that is entered into His rest hath himself also rested from his works, as God did from His.

Paraphrase

9 Therefore, seeing the Israelites did not, in Canaan, enter fully into God's rest, the enjoyment of another rest remaineth to the people of God, in which they shall rest completely from all the troubles of this life.

10 For the believer who is entered into God's rest, hath himself also rested from his own works of trial and suffering, Rev. xiv. 13. like as God rested from His works of creation.

There remaineth therefore a sabbath rest for the people of God

"There remaineth therefore" suggests that there is something better yet to follow:
a. Sabbath is a symbol of the rest yet to come.
b. This is the consummation of the new creature in Christ.
c. Jesus, Matt. 11:28-29: "Come unto me all ye that labor and are heavy laden —."
d. Rest fulfilled in Rev. 14:13: "And I heard a voice from heaven saying unto me, Write, Blessed are the dead which die in the Lord from henceforth. Yea, saith the Spirit that they may rest from their labors, and their works do follow them." cf. 21:1-5.

"Rest" here is sabbath rest, a state of rest:
a. It is not a state of inactivity, but release from the body of sin.
b. It is rest from this body of pain, sorrow and affliction.

for the people of God

There is the very opposite of comfort and rest for those who are not God's people. Luke 16:24: "For I am tormented in this flame." Rev. 14:11: "And the smoke of their torment goes up forever and ever; and they have no rest day and night, they that worship the beast and his image and receiveth a mark . . ."

For he that is entered into His rest

    Who is referred to here?
a. One view favors Christ:
1. For this view, we have only the idea that Christ is resting from his earthly mission.
2. Against it we have several factors:
a) First: Christ is not resting, since He is preparing mansions, making intercession for us, etc.
b) Second: Jesus is not mentioned here at all.
c) Third: We are exhorted by verse 11 to enter into the rest, as though it is the Christian's rest as referred to in verse 10.
b. A second view is that it is just a general statement of man entering into rest:
1. McKnight expresses it: "For the believer who is entered into God's rest, hath himself also rested from his works of trial and suffering."
2. Milligan says this view is most in harmony with the context.

hath himself also rested from his works, as God did from His.

    The Christian enters into a rest, just as did God when He rested:
a. Now every saint who, like Joshua and Caleb, is faithful enters into God's rest.
b. As certainly as God rested, so shall we rest.
    "His works" may refer to several things:
1. His own works that have no part in his salvation:
a. The Jew must give up the works of the old law.
b. The moral man must give up thinking that a moral life is able to save.
2. "That work which the child of God does in being faithful":
a. The work of God was good, and no doubt the good work of Christian people is referred to here in the parallel.
b. The life of self-denial comes to an end, and one enters into a rest with God.

Study Questions

604. Is David reminding them of seeking a greater rest?
605. What is the significance of the words "a sabbath rest for the people of God"?

606. When is this period of rest?
607. Is it a cessation of activity, or is another idea implied in our rest?
608. If the people of God have rest, what will the others have? Cf. Luke 16:24; Rev. 14:10.
609. Who is the "he" in verse 10?
610. Why is it not Jesus?
611. Is Jesus resting?
612. What are the works referred to?

4. *Exhortation and warnings.* 4:11-13.

Text
4:11-13

11 Let us therefore give diligence to enter into that rest, that no man fall after the same example of disobedience. 12 For the Word of God is living, and active, and sharper than any two-edged sword, and piercing even to the dividing of soul and spirit, of both joints and marrow, and quick to discern the thoughts and intents of the heart. 13 And there is no creature that is not manifest in His sight: but all things are naked and laid open before the eyes of Him with Whom we have to do.

Paraphrase

11 Since there remaineth such a happy rest to the people of God, let us carefully strive to enter into that rest, by obeying Jesus, lest any of us should fall, after the example of the Israelites, through unbelief.

12 For the Word of God, the preached Gospel whereby we are now called to enter into God's rest, and are to be judged hereafter, is a living and powerful principle, and more cutting than any two-edged sword, piercing not into the body but into the mind, even to the separating between both soul and spirit; showing which of the passions are animal and which spiritual: and to the separating of the joints also and marrows, laying open the most concealed parts of the animal constitution; and discerner of the devices and purposes of the heart.

13 But, not to insist farther on the rule of judgment, consider the omniscience of the Judge himself: there is no creature unapparent in His sight, for all things, the most secret recesses

of the heart, and stripped of every covering, both outwardly and inwardly, before the eyes of Him to whom we must give an account.

Comment

Let us therefore give diligence to enter into that rest

Here is an exhortation to labor:
a. Exertion of mind and body is a requirement of salvation.
b. This is a lawful work, in a world where men try other methods.
1. II Tim. 2:5: " — strive lawfully."
2. John 10:1: Some will be like thieves and robbers.

There is no room for predestination here, but there is an appeal to work.

that no man fall after the same example of disobedience

This does not sound like the position of some who say men are saved, not in spite of apostasy but from apostasy:
a. A person may make shipwreck of his faith, for God leaves man free to choose.
b. We are no different from the Israelites.
c. There are some who put people on probation for church membership, but refuse God the privilege of allowing man to prove his worthiness for eternal life.

The example of disobedience is recorded in Numbers 26:65.

for the Word of God is living

"Living" is also translated "quick":
Some dispute whether the "word" is referring to Christ or the scripture:
a. It is not the Old Testament law. See II Cor. 3:7. It was a ministration of death. Rom. 4:15: " — worketh wrath."
b. "The word" is probably not the personal word, but the word of the Person — the Gospel.

The Word of God does not beat the air with emptiness:
a. It leads some to triumph: II Cor. 2:14: "But thanks be to God Who always leadeth us in triumph in Christ."
b. It has the power of binding and loosing. Matt. 18:18:
1. Some, it draws to salvation; others, are driven to ruin.
2. It promises salvation to some, but pronounces vengeance on others.
c. It has the power of God in it. Rom. 1:16.

It is a living Word because it is backed by a living God and a living Christ.

and active

    It is also translated "powerful":
a. Rom. 1:16 — the power of God is the Gospel:
1. A person uses dynamite to move obstacles. The Word is God's means of action.
2. It is God's way to move man today.
b. No power or action is equal to it.
    God deals with men not by mere influences, but through His Word, whether written or preached.

and sharper than any two-edged sword

    The "sword" is a metaphorical word, military expression used to illustrate the character of the Word:
a. It is a part of the Christian's armor. Eph. 6:17.
b. It goes out of the mouth of the Rider, with which He smites the nations. Rev. 19:15.
    Two-edged sword:
a. It does double duty with one preaching or writing the Word.
b. This is simply to say that it is tremendously sharp.

and piercing

    The meaning is that it examines a man thoroughly:
a. It searches his thoughts and scrutinizes his will, with all of its desires.
b. Calvin insists that its character is to be confined to the faithful only, as they alone are thus searched to the quick.
    It is piercing for all, Christian and non-Christian:
    Titus 1:9: " — to convict the gainsayers."
    Jude 15: " — to convict all that are ungodly."
    John 16:8: "He will convict the world."

even to the dividing of soul and spirit

    Some claim only the Christian has a spirit, hence the word only deals with them.
    The Word is for all, and is active toward all:
a. John 16:8: " — when the Spirit is come He shall reprove the world of sin."
b. Rom. 1:16: "Jew and Gentile."
    What is the difference between the soul and spirit? Views differ.

a. "Soul" means all the affection; spirit, the intellectual faculty, according to Calvin. He quotes two passages to prove it:
1. I Thess. 5:23: "May your soul, body and spirit be preserved."
2. Isaiah 26:9: "My soul desired Thee in the night; I sought Thee with my spirit."
b. Soul is life, and spirit is personality, say others:
1. "We do not know whether Paul was speaking of man as he really was or using a current phraseology," says Milligan.
2. The inner man is emphasized to show how discerning the word is.
c. Greek words involved:
    Body — physical.
    Soul — animal soul or life.
    Spirit — immortal.

of both joints and marrow

Indicating that there is nothing so hard or strong in man that it can be hidden.

With a sword, man is content to pierce the heart, but God's word can delve into the inner man.

a. A sword can glance off the bone of an enemy, but nothing can resist the power of God's word.
b. Milligan thinks this is a proverbial saying indicative of the inmost parts of a person.

and quick to discern the thoughts

In the thick darkness of unbelief and hypocrisy is a horrible blindness, but God scatters this away.

Vices hidden under the false appearances of virtue are known by God:

a. Men may have good reputations, yet harbor evil thoughts, and God knows it.
b. God is all-wise, so we have no secrets.

and intents of the heart

Some people are evil, but lack the courage to act:

a. Many "embryo" Hitlers exist in the world, but they lack his initiative.

Some people have evil intents, but appear to work from good motives:

1. Rom. 16:18: " — by fair speech deceive."
2. Gal. 6:12: " — make fair show in the flesh."

3. II Peter 2:13: " — sporting while they feast."

And there is no creature that is not manifest in His sight

No creature can escape God:
a. Some have tried:
1. Adam and Eve hid.
2. Cain said he wasn't his brother's keeper.
3. Jonah ran away, but he wasn't away from God.
b. Some will try again, says Rev. 6:16, when they want rocks and mountains to hide them from God's wrath.

God knows us as we really are.
"Manifest in His sight" means to be made known:
a. Evil is manifested. Gal. 5:19: "Works of the flesh are manifest."
b. Good is manifested. I Tim. 5:25: The good words of some are manifest. I John 3:10: "Children of God are manifest."

but all things are naked

There is no covering, camouflaging, or deceit before God. "This may refer to a sacrificial term," says Clarke:
a. An animal prepared for sacrifice was slain, then cut open so that its intestines were exposed to view.
b. It was carefully examined for imperfections.
c. It was divided exactly in two, so that the spinal marrow was cloven down the center.

Adam and Eve were told by the serpent that when they ate of the tree they would be as God. Gen. 3:5:
a. Note that when they ate they saw their nakedness.
b. God has tried to cover man's sin since that time.

laid open before the eyes

It may mean as a criminal has his neck bent back so as to expose the face to full view so that every feature might be seen.

of Him with Whom we have to do

All men must give an account of themselves:
a. The wicked cannot die and go without judgment. Heb. 9:27; Rom. 2:6: "Render to every man according to his deeds."
b. Death does not end all; the skeptic cannot get by. We have to face God:

1. Vengeance is His. Rom. 12:19; Nah. 1:2.
2. Judgment is His. Heb. 10:27-31.
3. We must someday confess His Son. Phil. 2:10, 11.

Study Questions

613. What is meant by "give diligence"?
614. If man is saved regardless of what he does, would this exhortation to diligence be in order?
615. Compare the idea of diligence with II Tim. 2:15.
616. Does this eliminate the doctrine of predestination?
617. Is man saved in spite of his apostasy according to this verse?
618. Why should Baptists put people on probation if they believe "once saved, always saved"? Is it consistent?
619. If they can put people on probation, why not extend God the same right?
620. What example of disobedience is referred to in v. 11? Cf. Numbers 26:65.
621. Verse 12 speaks of the Word of God as "living". Is this a reference to Christ living?
622. Is the word referred to here an Old Testament word, or the Word of Christ?
623. What scripture would teach that it is not the Old Testament word? Cf. II Cor. 3:7; Rom. 4:15.
624. If it is not Christ, then how can it be spoken of as "living"?
625. Quote a verse that shows that the word makes "alive".
626. How can the Word be spoken of as being "active"? What other word could be used? Cf. Rom. 1:16.
627. On what does it act?
628. Explain the significance of the expression, "sharper than any two-edged sword".
629. Who wields this sword? Is it active without people to wield it?
630. Is it a part of a Christian's armor? Cf. Eph. 6:17.
631. Compare Rev. 19:15 for its use as judgment.
632. What other words could describe the idea of "piercing"?
633. How can the word of God be considered "piercing"? Cf. Titus 1:9; Jude 15; John 16:8.
634. Is the piercing of the spirit limited to the believers only, according to Jude 15; John 16:8?
635. Explain the expression, "dividing of soul and spirit".

4:14-16   HELPS FROM HEBREWS

636. Are "soul" and "spirit" different, or is this just a current phraseology of Paul's day?
637. Could the word "dividing" refer to a practice of the altar in dissecting the animals?
638. How can the word enter joints and marrow?
639. Is a real sword of man likely to pierce joints and marrow?
640. If not, what is meant?
641. How can the Bible discern man's thoughts and intents?
642. Does man always know his own intents?
643. Do we know the intent of others?
644. Do we ever misjudge intents?
645. Are there "embryo" Hitlers who lack the initiative to be tyrants?
646. Do false teachers have evil intents? Cf. Rom. 16:18; Gal. 6:2:4; II Pet. 2:1.
647. What is meant by "no creature that is not manifest in His sight"? What is meant by "manifest"?
648. Have some tried to escape His sight? Who?
649. Will they try it again, according to Rev. 6:16?
650. Does this word, "creature", include animals?
651. What is meant by, "all things are naked"?
652. Could this refer to the sacrifice being examined for flaws?
653. Who felt naked in God's presence because of sin?
654. "Laid open" would refer to what?
655. Who is the person with Whom we have to do — God — Christ? Cf. Heb. 9:24; Rom. 2:6; Rom. 12:19; Heb. 10:27-31.

PART TWO

The Superiority of Christ as High Priest. 4:14-10:39.
I. *Purpose of and His fitness for the priesthood.* 4:14-5:10.
A. *The fact of Christ's priesthood stated, an appeal to the reader.* 4:14-16.
1. *Because of His greatness, "Let us hold fast our confession."* 4:14.

Text
4:14-16

14 Having then a great High Priest, Who hath passed through the heavens, Jesus the Son of God, let us hold fast our confession. 15 For we have not a High Priest that cannot be touched with

138

the feeling of our infirmities; but One that hath been in all points tempted like as we are, yet without sin. 16 Let us therefore draw near with boldness unto the throne of grace, that we may receive mercy, and may find grace to help us in time of need.

Paraphrase

14 Now the unbelieving Jews, on pretence that the Gospel hath neither an high-priest nor any sacrifice for sin, urge you to return to Judaism: but as we have a great High Priest, who hath passed through the visible heavens into the true habitation of God, Chap. ix. 11, 12. there to officiate for us, even Jesus the Son of God, let us hold fast our religion.

15 To this constancy we Christians are encouraged by the character of our High Priest: For, though He be the Son of God, we have not in Him an High Priest Who cannot sympathize with us in our weaknesses, but One most compassionate, Who, being made flesh, was tempted in all points as far as the likeness of His nature to ours would admit, yet never committed any sin.

16 Let us, therefore, through His mediation as our High Priest, approach with boldness to the throne of grace on which God is seated to hear our addresses, that we may receive pardon; and, when tempted or persecuted, obtain the gracious assistance of His Spirit to help us seasonably in such times of distress.

Comment

Having then a great High Priest

Christ has two relationships, enabling man to come to God through Him:
a. An Apostle sent to teach. cf. Heb. 3:1.
b. A Priest:
1. This Priest has proven His character by His teaching.
2. This Priest has proven His love by His death.
3. This Priest has proven His superiority by passing through the heavens.

Christ's high priesthood met the argument of the critical Jew:
a. They could not say, "You have no tabernacle, no sacrifice, no city, no high priest." We have indeed!
b. The title "high priest" occurs first in Lev. 21:10:
1. There it is used to designate Aaron and his successors.
2. We have a High Priest in heaven itself, not in an earthly tabernacle.

4:14, 15   HELPS FROM HEBREWS

Who hath passed through the heavens

Only Christ has done this:
a. He lived in heaven, and passed through the heavens to earth.
1. Phil. 2:5-11.
2. I Cor. 10:4: " — they (the Israelites) drank of a spiritual rock that followed them: and the Rock was Christ."
b. He lived on earth, and then passed through the heavens to heaven:
1. Ascension: Acts 1:9.
2. Stephen: Acts 7:56.
3. **Peter Acts 2:34-36:** "seated."
c. He now works in heaven, and will pass again from heaven:
1. I Thess. 4:13-18.
2. Acts 1:11: " — Jesus — shall so come in like manner as ye beheld him going into heaven".
The Jewish high priest could pass only into the holy of holies on the great day of Atonement:
a. We have one who passed through the veil of skies.
b. Heb. 8:1-2 is very good: " — sanctuary which the Lord pitched."

Jesus the Son of God

This identifies our High Priest. He is not of the lineage of Aaron, but of the house of God.

let us hold fast our confession

Matt. 10:32: Our confession is in a Person: That confession gives us a profession.
a. It is a work of evangelism:
1. We are saved to serve.
2. We are won to win.
3. We were told to tell.
b. It is a way of life:
To renounce Christ is to seal our condemnation:
Heb. 6:4-6; Acts 4:12: "In none other is there salvation."
2. *Because of His human experience, let us draw near.* 4:15, 16.

For we have not a high priest that cannot be touched with the feeling of our infirmities.

He is a sympathetic, compassionate High Priest, who can be touched with our feelings. Heb. 2:17: "Wherefore it behooved

Him in all things to me made unto His brethren."
He is successful as a High Priest:
a. Jesus stands by us in temptation. Rev. 3:10.
b. His sacrifice is complete. Heb. 9:26: "But now once at the end of the ages hath He been manifested to put away sin by the sacrifice of Himself."

our infirmities

"Infirmities" is a word that may be taken in various senses:
a. II Cor. 12:10 suggests what might be included.
b. Probably the feeling of the soul should be included, such as fear, sorrow, dread of death.
Since He was made in the likeness of our sinful flesh, we know that he knows our feelings.

but one that hath been in all points tempted as we are

Christ's threefold temptation gives us the major threats of the devil:
a. Food — satisfy the physical.
b. Pinnacle of temple — to extend the mercy of God to selfishness.
c. Kingdom — lust for power — rulership.

yet without sin

Describe your mother and her virtues, but you can't use this expression.
Other verses tell us that He was perfect:
a. II Cor. 5:21: "Him who knew no sin, He made to be sin on our behalf that we might become the righteousness of God in Him."
b. I John 3:5: "And ye know that He was manifested to take away sins; and in Him is no sin."
Jesus was tempted without falling into sin, but this is not true of any other.

Let us therefore draw near with boldness

Because of the kind of High Priest we have, we should have courage to approach Him:
a. He is not a medicine man to Whom we have to bow and feel like a helpless creature.
b. Because of His love, we should come without hesitation.

4:16 HELPS FROM HEBREWS

  c. His experience with this life gives us encouragement. Boldness here is not brazen, but confident.

unto the throne of grace

The history of the throne of grace is interesting:
a. The ark was a symbol of God's grace. Jeremiah 3:16.
1. The lid was sprinkled with blood once a year. Lev. 16:14-15.
2. Here was the mercy seat. Lev. 16:2; Num. 7:89; Ex. 25:22.
3. Now we approach God through Jesus Christ Who sits at His right hand.
The throne of mercy is God's, but Christ is our access to God. Eph. 2:18.

that we may receive mercy

We have to make the approach, for God has done His share:
a. We must not be cast down with a sense of misery.
b. Since all have sinned and fallen short of God's grace, we need grace and mercy. Only God gives mercy:
a. The devil gives death, not life, and beyond this, he makes people unmerciful.
1. Hitler listened to no pleas of men.
2. Men possessed of the devil are unkind, unforgiving.
God has mercy only for those who merit it:
a. Look at these verses:
1) Heb. 10:27: " — fearful expectation of judgment."
Heb. 10:31: " — a fearful thing to fall into the hands of the living God."
b. If we fail to come to God for mercy, we should not expect it in the judgment.

and may find grace to help us

Observe why Christ can give us help which is superior to that of the priest of the old covenant:
a. The priest under the old system had to make atonement for his own sins. Heb. 5:2-3; Heb. 7:26-28; Heb. 9:7.
b. They were after the order of Aaron. Heb. 7:11; 7:11-17; 8:4-5.
c. The old was made without an oath. Heb. 7:20-22.
d. Theirs was temporary. Heb. 7:23-24.
e. They offered oftentimes the same kind of sacrifices. Heb. 9:25-26.
Heb. 9:28; Heb. 10:11-12. Heb. 10:14.

f. They entered into the holy of holies every year. Heb. 9:7-12.
g. Christ lives to make intercession. Heb. 7:25.

in time of need

Three great needs of man in the spiritual realm:
a. We are in need when saddened. John 14:1-4.
b. We are in need when tempted. I Cor. 10:13; Heb. 2:18.
c. We are in need at death. Ps. 23.
Jesus in his Sermon on the Mount said God would also care for our physical needs.

Summary — Exhortation

1. There is a throne of grace where God and man may meet.
2. The mercy place has the atoning blood of the Lamb of God.
3. We must come by faith. Faith and action must be mixed.
4. We may approach in boldness, confidence.
5. God still dwells with His people.

Summary - Warning

1. Faithfulness forfeited is a forfeit of eternal rest.
2. We cannot trifle with God's words. We must act *today*.
3. The great aim of life is to labor for the rest.

Study Questions

656. Christ is earlier described as an apostle. Where is He here?
657. What is the difference between the two works?
658. What has Christ done to prove that He is a great high priest?
659. When was the title of "high priest" first used? See Lev. 21:10.
660. What has Christ done that no other priest could do as far as the heavens are concerned?
661. What time of passing through is referred to here?
662. When will He pass through again?
663. What would the heavens be in type in relationship to the old system?
664. With what term does Paul identify our High Priest?
665. Since this is all true, what exhortation does he have for us?
666. What is our confession?
667. What do we confess concerning this Person.

668. Does this confession amount to a profession?
669. What can be said of our High Priest as far as sympathy is concerned?
670. How does this verse compare with 2:17?
671. What does the word "infirmity" mean?
672. Discuss Paul's bearing of infirmities, II Cor. 12:10.
673. What is meant by "touched with the feeling of our infirmities"?
674. Do pain, sorrow, suffering help one to be understanding of others?
675. Is God able to be more sympathetic since Christ lived in the flesh?
676. What three catagories of temptation did Jesus face?
677. How were the three so all-inclusive?
678. Was He tempted at other times?
679. Can you describe the most beautiful character whom you know with the expression "without sin"?
680. Is this a teaching limited to this verse? Cf. II Cor. 5:21; I John 3:5.
681. Have you noticed that with the great exaltation of Christ there is an exhortation to man? What is it in verse 16?
682. Do heathen people come boldly to their priests?
683. Does boldness allow brazenness and presumption?
684. What is meant by "boldness"?
685. What was the place of mercy in times past? Cf. Jer. 3:16; Lev. 16:2, 14, 15.
686. What is our throne of grace? Cf. Eph. 2:18.
687. What do we receive when we approach the mercy seat?
688. For whom does God have mercy?
689. Is God always merciful? Cf. Heb. 10:27, 31.
690. If we do not come to His mercy seat now, should we expect it at the judgment?
691. What is the purpose of grace which we may find there?
692. Could the Old Testament priest help?
693. When is man in need? What are his problems?
694. Is Christ able to help?

Questions on Chapter Four
True or False

_____ 1. Fear of God is an Old Testament doctrine and has no place in New Testament times.

_____ 2. Jesus is surely qualified to understand our needs, for He has suffered and has been tempted.
_____ 3. The sharpness of the Word of God is compared to a fine-grained, single-edged sword.
_____ 4. "Give diligence to enter into the rest" indicates that man has a responsibility.
_____ 5. The great High Priest of the Christian has yet to pass through the heavens.
_____ 6. The Word of God teaches humility; therefore, we ought not to approach the throne of grace with boldness.
_____ 7. The temptation of Jesus was in no respect like ours.
_____ 8. Unbelief has kept people who had received the promise of rest from receiving it.
_____ 9. The Word of God does not deal with the intents of the heart, but the thoughts of the heart.
_____ 10. This chapter warns lest we *go past* the rest of God.
_____ 11. The author speaks of a hearing that did not profit.
_____ 12. This chapter exhorts man as a creature who has no need.
_____ 13. This chapter seems to use soul and spirit interchangeably.
_____ 14. "The same example of disobedience" is an expression of this chapter.
_____ 15. Hearing needs to be united, or mixed, with faith.
_____ 16. The failure of Joshua's rest is a teaching in Chapter Four.
_____ 17. God completed His work on the seventh day, giving a few finishing touches, then rested.
_____ 18. A sabbath rest for the people of God remains.
_____ 19. "Good tidings were preached to Israel even as unto us" is an idea expressed in Chapter Four.
_____ 20. The Word is able to lay naked all things.
_____ 21. A description of Jesus includes, "yet without sin".
_____ 22. God is spoken of as one who has sworn.
_____ 23. The names "Joshua" and "Jesus" sometimes are used interchangeably.
_____ 24. We have been taught that God is a God of love, and yet this chapter pictures a different side — a God of wrath.
_____ 25. The Word of God is able to pierce both joints and marrow.

SUMMARY OF CHAPTER FOUR

Chapter Four consists of a series of exhortations based on the discussion in Chapter Three about the faithfulness of Christ and the failure of Israel because of lack of faith in the journey from Egypt to Canaan.

The first exhortation is in verse 1; "Let us fear." The second is in verse 11, "Let us enter the rest." The third is in verse 14, "Let us hold our confession." The last one is in verse 16, "Let us draw near with boldness to the throne of grace."

The first exhortation urges the Christian to remember that there is a rest for God's people in heaven. Evidence is presented to show why that rest could not have been either the sabbath that the Jews kept or the Promised Land into which Joshua led the Israelites. So there must be a heavenly rest for those who are faithful to Christ.

The second exhortation urges the Christian to be diligent and to strive eagerly to enter that rest, rather than follow the example of disobedience that proved fatal to Israel.

The third word of encouragement has to do with the necessity of holding fast the acknowledgment that Jesus, the Son of God, is High Priest, with sympathetic concern for the weaknesses of His people.

The closing word urges us to come boldly to the throne of grace for help in time of need.

B. *The office of the priesthood.* 5:1-4.

Text
5:1-4

1 For every high priest, being taken from among men, is appointed for men in things pertaining to God, that he may offer both gifts and sacrifices for sins: 2 who can bear gently with the ignorant and erring, for that he himself also is compassed with infirmity; 3 and by reason thereof is bound, as for the people, so also for himself, to offer for sins. 4 And no man taketh the honor unto himself, but when he is called of God, even as was Aaron.

Paraphrase

1 Now, to show that Christ is a real High Priest, I will describe the designation, the duties, and the qualifications of an high priest.

Every high priest taken from among men is appointed, by persons having a right to confer the office, to perform for men the things pertaining to the public worship of God, and especially that he may offer both free-will offerings and sacrifices for sins.

2 He must be able to have a right measure of compassion on the ignorant, and those who err through ignorance, because he himself also is clothed with infirmity; so that he will officiate for them with the greater kindness and assiduity.

3 And because he himself is a sinner, he must, as for the people, so also for himself, offer sacrifices for sins. (Lev. xvi. 6.)

4 Now, to apply these things to the Christ, I observe, first, that as in the gospel church no one can take this honourable office to himself but he who is thereto called of God, as Aaron was in the Jewish church;

Comment

For every high priest, being taken from among men

God's high priests were men:
a. The first indication that Aaron and his sons were to care for the tabernacle is found in Ex. 28:1.
b. Their first distinct separation to the office of the priesthood is recorded in Ex. 28.
c. After this, the legal head of the house of Aaron became high priest. Usually the eldest son succeeded in office.
The task was theoretically for life.

is appointed for men

God does not do things because of Himself, but because of men:
a. Mark 2:27: "Sabbath was made for man, and not man for the sabbath."
b. John 3:16: "God so loved the world."
The world is God's object of love, not Himself.

in things pertaining to God

Aaron and his sons were not appointed to secular things, but unto God:
a. They were to minister to holy things.
b. Their responsibility was not cultivation of the soil, commerce, etc., but to minister in holy things.

that he may offer both gifts and sacrifices for sins

What is the difference between gifts and sacrifices?
a. Gifts usually appear first. See 8:3 and 9:9.
1. Milligan says gifts and sacrifices are used interchangeably as in Gen. 4:3-5.
2. Milligan says "gifts" refer to bloodless sacrifices, and "offerings" to those that require the life of the sacrifice.
3. Mathew Henry says "gifts" refers to free-will offering.
4. Newell says gifts appear first because the chief and normal business of a priest was to receive the gifts and direct the worship.
b. "Sacrifices for sins" generally is understood to be the blood offerings:
1. All the sins and iniquities of Israel were confessed by the priest on the great day of Atonement, and during the year all sacrifices were under his direction.
2. The priest goes to God on man's behalf; the prophet comes from God representing God to men.

who can bear gently

The prophet can cry out against the sins of a people, "Repent or be destroyed."
a. The priest is to be sympathetic, and to aid in the forgiving of sins.
b. The word "bear gently" means "have compassion."
1. The priest had to decide whether a sacrifice for sin could be given legally. Lev. 10:8-11; Deut. 12:8-13; Deut. 24:8; Deut. 33:10; Mal. 2:7.
2. A bitter judge could be just.

with the ignorant and erring

The ignorant — see Lev. 5:17-19.
a. If a man sinned through ignorance or in error, or in an occasion where temptation might obscure for a time the guilt, a sacrifice could be given, sin be forgiven. Num. 15:22-29.
b. If it was the sin of the high hand, in the spirit of haughty insolence, there could be no sacrifice. He could be put to death at the testimony of two or three witnesses. Num. 15:30-31; Deut. 17:6.

The erring — those deceived by passions. See Lev. 6:1-7.

a. This was hard to judge, and the high priest hearing gently could sometimes bring a person to repentance.
b. Calvin feels that the word, "erring", does not refer to the sinners.

for that he himself is compassed with infirmity

The high priest was in a condition of temptation:
a. Paul could understand the Jew having infirmity, for he was one of the best Jews.
Rom. 9:2-3: "I have great sorrow and unceasing pain in my heart."
b. "Infirmity" was a physical condition, meaning "frailty, feebleness, distress of the soul." II Cor. 12:5-10.

And by reason thereof is bound, as for the people, so also for himself to offer for sins

Consider the Old Testament priest:
a. To offer for himself as well as for the sins of others. Lev. 4:3-12: v. 3, "If the priest that is anointed do sin according to the sin of the people, then let him bring for his sin, which he hath sinned, a young bullock without blemish unto the Lord for a sin offering."
b. Occasion of sacrifice for self:
1. He offered sacrifices for special sins. Lev. 4:3-12. On special occasions.
2. He, in the regular daily, weekly, monthly, yearly sacrifice, recognized his own sin.
3. On the day of Atonement he was required to go into the most holy place and there make an offering for his own sins first and then for the people. cf. Heb. 9:7, 12, 25.
Compare the priest with Jesus. He need not offer sacrifices for His sins:
Isaiah 53:9: "For He had done no violence, neither was there and deceit in His mouth."
Pilate, in Matt. 27:24, could find no sin in Christ's life. cf. Heb. 4:14.

and no man taketh the honor to himself

No priest can be self-appointed. It is a task appointed by God:
a. Where do priests get their appointments today? Not from God.

1. Some have been tried in the past and have suffered: Num. 16:10-11: When Korah sought the position of priest, the earth swallowed all of them up who were faithful to Korah.
2. Jude 11 speaks of the "gainsaying of Korah".
3. Uzziah meddled with an office and became a leper. II Chron. 26:18.
4. Saul. I Sam. 13:8-10.

b. A thousand priests can do no good, if not appointed, and it is a sin of which we must have no part.
Read the warning for those who follow false priests. Rev. 18:4.

but when he is called of God even as was Aaron

See Exodus 24:1 and Ex. 28 for his appointment.
See Num. 16:8 for the sons of Levi being made priests.

Study Questions

695. Describe the high priest "taken from among men".
696. When was the priestly system started?
697. What family was selected to serve?
698. When did the family first serve?
699. What is significant in the statement, "appointed for men"?
700. Does God do things for Himself or for men?
701. Was the high priest's job secular or religious according to this verse?
702. What is meant by "offer both gifts and sacrifices"?
703. Is there a difference?
704. Is this expression a common one? Cf. 8:3; 9:9.
705. Would "sacrifices" refer to the blood portion of worship?
706. What is the actual difference between the work of the prophet and priest?
707. What is significant in the expression, "bear gently"?
708. With what or whom was he to bear gently — the sacrifice or the sacrificer?
709. Did the prophet bear gently?
710. In what way did he have opportunity either to judge harshly or bear gently? Cf. Lev. 10:8-11; Deut. 12:8-13; Deut. 24:8; Deut. 33:10; Mal. 2:7.
711. Who would be "ignorant worshippers? Cf. Lev. 5:17-19.
712. Were they necessarily interested in being forgiven?
713. How could one sin ignorantly? Cf. Num. 15:22-29.

714. Were the "ignorant" and "erring" two different groups? Cf. Lev. 6:1-7.
715. How did the high-handed sinner fare?
716. Was there a sacrifice for him?
717. What could be done with him? Cf. Num. 15:30-31; Deut. 17:6.
718. In what way was the priest like the worshippers?
719. Can you name instances when priests fell in their infirmities?
720. What was the priest bound to do for the people? For himself? Cf. Lev. 4:3-12.
721. Did the high priest have sacrifices for special sins? Cf. Lev. 4:3-12.
722. Which sacrifice came first, the one for himself or for the people? Heb. 9:7, 12, 25.
723. Did Jesus need to make sacrifice for Himself?
724. How did a priest secure his position?
725. Could he usurp the privilege?
726. Did any men ever try? Num. 16:10-11; Jude 11.
727. How did Uzziah meddle with the office of priest. II Chr. 26:18.
728. Did Saul dare to act as a priest? I Sam. 13:8-10.
729. What is the danger of following a false priest? Cf. Rev. 18:4.
730. Whom did God call to be priest besides Aaron? Cf. Num. 16:8.
731. Would "calling" and "appointing" carry the same idea?

C. *Christ's qualifications for the priesthood.* 5:5-10.

Text
5:5-10

5 So Christ also glorified not Himself to be made a high priest, but He that spake unto Him,
> Thou art My Son,
> This day have I begotten Thee:
6 as He saith also in another place,
> Thou art a Priest for ever
> After the order of Melchizedek.

7 Who in the days of His flesh, having offered up prayers and supplications with strong crying and tears unto Him that

was able to save Him from death, and having been heard for His godly fear, 8 though He was a Son, yet learned obedience by the things which He suffered; 9 and having been made perfect, He became unto all them that obey Him the Author of eternal salvation; 10 named of God a High Priest after the order of Melchizedek.

Paraphrase

5 So also the Christ did not glorify Himself by making Himself an High-priest, but He glorified Him with that office, Who, after His ascension into heaven, said to Him, My son Thou art; to-day I have demonstrated Thee to be My Son by raising Thee from the dead.

6 As also He glorified the Christ to be an High Priest, Who in another psalm saith to Him, Thou art a Priest for ever, according to the order of Melchizedek: Thou art a human Priest, not like Aaron, but Melchizedek.

7 Secondly, as an High Priest, He can commiserate the ignorant and erring. For though He be the Son of God, He was subject to the infirmity of the human nature, and particularly to the fear of death, as is plain from this, that He in the days of His flesh, having offered up both deprecations and supplications, with strong crying (Psal. xxii. 1.) and tears, to Him Who was able to save Him from death, by raising Him from the dead; and being delivered from fear.

8 Although He was the Son of God, He learned how difficult obedience is to men, by the things which He suffered in the flesh while He obeyed God; and also what need men have of help to enable them to bear their trials and sufferings.

9 And being thus qualified to have a right measure of compassion on the ignorant and erring, He was made perfect as an High Priest; and He became, to all who obey Him, the Author of eternal salvation, by offering Himself a sacrifice for their sins:

10 As is evident from His being saluted by God, on His return from the earth, an High Priest, according to the order of Melchizedek.

Comment

So Christ also glorified not Himself to be made a High Priest
The devil offered Him glory, but He rejected it:

a. He asked God to glorify Him. John 17:5: "And now, Father, glorify Thou me with Thine own self, with the glory which I had with Thee before the world was."
b. He sought to glorify God:
1. John 17:4: "I have glorified Thee on earth: I have accomplished the work that Thou hast given me to do."
2. John 8:50: "I sought not My own glory."
c. He exhibited the glory of God:
1. John 1:14. "The Word became flesh and dwelt among us, and we beheld his glory, glory as of the only begotten from the Father, full of grace and truth."
2. II Cor. 4:6: "Seeing it is God, that said, Light shall shine out of darkness, who shined in our hearts, to give the light of the knowledge of the glory of God in the face of Jesus Christ."
3. Heb. 1:3: "Who, being the effulgence of His glory."
Christ was one who was willing to humble Himself, not to exalt Himself.

but he that spake unto Him

God planned for Christ to be High Priest. He said this in Psalms 2:7.

Thou art my Son. This day have I begotten Thee:

God prophetically called Jesus His "Son". The word, "begotten", does not refer to His origin but to His resurrection.

as he saith also in another place

This is found in Psalm 110:
a. This is one of the clearest of prophecies in the Psalms concerning Christ.
b. The Jew applies this to David:
1. This Psalm is applied to Christ by the apostles in Acts 2:34.
2. This cannot apply to David. It was not lawful for kings to exercise the priesthood.
3. Uzziah was meddling with an office that did not belong to him, so provoked God and was smitten with leprosy. II Chron. 26:18.

Thou art a priest forever, after the order of Melchizedek

This is rare: He was both king and priest. The comparison here is the important thing:
a. Aaron was temporary — Christ was eternal.

b. Aaron's office was successive — passed on to his children. Melchizedek's and Christ's office was personal, non heriditary.
c. Melchizedek's priesthood, then, is above Aaron's priesthood. "Without father and mother" is discussed in Heb. 7.
a. Matthew Henry says that this scripture is "not to be taken literally". His geneology is not given in order that he might be a type of Christ.
b. Archeologists have found this expression inscribed on tablets of that era.
"Forever" means "while time endures". When I Cor. 15:24 is fulfilled, His office will no doubt end.

Who in the days of His flesh

"While Christ was on the earth" is meant:
a. This word, "who", does not refer to Melchizedek, but to Christ.
b. It is obvious by verse 8 that Jesus is meant.

Having offered up prayers

"A request, petition" is meant by the word, "prayers":
a. John 17: great prayers of oneness.
b. He prayed before performing miracles.
c. He prayed before going to the cross. Luke 22:40-44.
If Christ prayed, then surely we need to pray, yet few have callouses on their knees.

and supplications

"Supplications" are prayers prompted by a deep sense of need, and our own helplessness.
a. When used separately, the words, "prayer" and "supplications" are used interchangeably.
b. When used together, it means a prayer prompted by a deep sense of helplessness.

with strong crying and tears

This is to show the intensity of His grief. These are the outward symptoms of grief. Examples of it:
a. Matt. 26:42: " — let this cup pass from Me."
b. Matt. 27:46: "My God, My God, why hast Thou forsaken Me?"

unto Him that was able to save Him from death

    He was not immediately delivered from death:
a. He obtained what He prayed for when He came forth a conqueror.
1. If the death referred to is physical death, God could have saved him. Angels could have saved Him. Matt. 26:53-54.
2. God could not save Him and still carry out His purpose. See Matt. 26:53-54.
b. God was able to do things not asked of Him by Christ.
    Death should be studied in the light of some prepositions:
a. The preposition:
1. "from."
2. "out of."
b. Newell says He did not ask God to save Him from dying, but to save Him out of death.

and having been heard

    Did not God forsake Him?
a. Yes, in order that the flesh could die.
b. If we live in God, He must forsake us in order for us to die.
    God heard his prayers, however, for Christ did not see corruption in the grave as do all others.
    Newell says His prayer was for the fulfillment of the prophecies concerning Himself.

for his godly fear

    Some interpret:
        "Having been heard for his piety."
        "He was heard by reason of His reverent submission."
        "Fear of responsibilities."
    What was the object of His fear?
a. Milligan: "He had a heart to fear and tremble, like other men in view of great undertakings:
1. The fact that Jesus told them to watch and pray lest they enter into temptation was proof of this.
2. It was not fear of death, but fear of being unequal to the occasion.
b. Matthew Henry says He was ready to sink under the heavy load of the world of sin and coming suffering. God heard His prayer and supported him in the agonies.

5:8, 9   HELPS FROM HEBREWS

Though he was a son

If God's Son had to be obedient, may we expect special favors, namely the right to disobedience?
a. May we impose upon God?
b. May we alter His teaching — climb up some other way?
Obedience is the natural thing for true family relationship.

yet He learned obedience

He was not driven to this by force:
a. He was not trained to it like an oxen, but He willingly submitted.
b. He learned it fully, for in a very special way He was called to deny himself.
Obedience made Him a consecrated one:
a. Jesus was consecrated, sanctified to the office of priest by obedience.
b. It was not a legal obedience, but an objective obedience.

by the things which he suffered

Obedience to the call of the cross was "becoming obedient." Phil. 2:6-8: "Suffered" must refer to all the experiences of Christ while in the flesh.

and having been made perfect

The Greek word means "sanctified" as well as "made perfect":
a. His obedience further consecrated Him to His task.
b. Nothing could make Christ move from His purpose.
What is meant by the word, "perfection"?
a. Newell: ". . . not moral perfection."
b. The perfection refers to His humiliation and suffering, culminating at the cross. Luke 13:32: "And He said unto them, Go and say to that fox, (Herod) behold I cast out demons and perform cures today and tomorrow, and the third day I am perfected."
c. Tested by every temptation.

He became unto all that obey Him

There is no room here for the false doctrine of "only believe":
a. We must obey, which is an imitation of Christ in obedience.
b. The obedience of Christ to the cross made Him the Author of our salvation.

As Christ became Saviour by obedience, so we must be saved by obedience.

the Author of eternal salvation

"Author" is from the Greek word, "cause":
a. "Cause" is used to denote that which constitutes an occasion of action. A rock may crush a house, but there was something that moved the rock.
b. Without Christ's cross there would be no blood for the remission of our sins. So Christ is our "cause" of salvation. "In none other is there salvation." Acts 4:12.
Eternal salvation is the joy of all who will obey.

Named of God a high priest after the order of Melchizedek

"Named of God" — the one Father appointed Him to the task. "Named" also means "called of God, saluted, acknowledged".
When did His priesthood begin?
1. Perhaps when He made purification for sins, which was the offering. Heb. 7:28.
2. After the offering, He went into the heavens to intercede at the throne of grace. 7:25.
The order of Aaron was only for the duration of the Mosaic system, but the order of Melchizedek is forever.
a. Melchizedek was singular in his office.
b. He had no predecessors or successors to his office.

Study Questions

732. According to verse five, did Christ seek the job of priest?
733. Did the devil tempt Him to glorify himself?
734. What does Heb. 1:3 say concerning Christ's glory?
735. When did God speak concerning Christ? v. 5b.
736. Does Psalm 2:7 refer to the day that Christ was begotten physically of God?
737. How do we know from other sources that this declaration refers to Christ, and not David? Cf. Acts 2:34.
738. Were kings allowed to serve as priests under the Mosaic law?
739. After what order was Christ?
740. In what way?
741. Was Melchizedek just a priest?

742. In what ways could Christ's and Melchizedek's priesthood be forever?
743. Was Aaron's priesthood a successive one?
744. What is meant, "who in the days of His flesh"?
745. Who is referred to, Christ or Melchizedek?
746. Is the doctrine that Christ lived in the flesh of great importance?
747. Did Christ offer up prayers?
748. On what occasion?
749. On whose behalf?
750. Could they be considered priestly prayers?
751. What are supplications?
752. Are the words "prayers" and "supplications" synonymous?
753. What is meant by, "strong crying"?
754. On what occasion did Christ pray with tears?
755. Was His grief prophesied?
756. To Whom did Christ pray?
757. Then are God and Christ two different persons?
758. Could God save Christ from death?
759. Why didn't He? Why did not Christ come down from the cross?
760. Did God answer Christ's prayer?
761. Did Christ's prayer concern death?
762. Did Christ pray to be saved *from* death, or *out of* death?
763. If it was death for which He prayed, why did He not ask for angels as He said He could do? Matt. 26:53-54.
764. Why did flesh have to die?
765. If God heard Him, as the text says, did not God answer His prayer?
766. Did God forsake Him on the cross? Harmonize.
767. What in the character of Christ caused God to hear Christ's prayer?
768. Was Christ fearful? Discuss.
769. What could have been an object of fear?
770. Did He have a heart to fear and tremble as others have?
771. If God's son had to be obedient, can we expect special favors?
772. Can we expect to impose our will on God and make Him obedient to us?
773. If God will save a man on man's terms, who is being obedient to whom?

774. What is meant by, "He learned obedience"?
775. Was He driven to it by force, or was it a sanctification to His office?
776. Was it a legal obedience, or an objective that caused obedience?
777. To what great act of obedience did Christ submit? See Phil: 2:5-11.
778. What taught Him obedience?
779. Would "things He suffered" refer to hardships only or all of the experiences in the flesh?
780. What did He suffer?
781. Define the meaning of the word translated "perfect."
782. Does "having been made perfect" refer to immediate or continuous action?
783. Does "made perfect" refer to moral excellence?
784. Would Luke 13:32 help to throw light on the question?
785. Could it be "proven perfect" that the author has in mind?
786. Did the testing of every temptation prove Him to be perfect?
787. Could we say that He was proven to be sanctified?
788. To whom does He prove to be the Author of salvation?
789. If it is for men that obey Him, can the moral man expect salvation?
790. Can the person who desires substitutes above obedience expect salvation?
791. Is there room for "only believe" here?
792. If we follow Christ, should we not follow the great virtue, the spirit of obedience?
793. If Christ became our Saviour by obedience, must we not be obedient, for salvation to be ours?
794. What is meant, "the author"?
795. In what way is He "the cause"? Isn't God the great primary cause?
796. How long is our salvation to last?
797. What is meant by, "named of God"?
798. What other word could be used than "named"?
799. When did Christ's priestly work begin? Cf. Heb. 7:28; 7:25.
800. Is it fair to name a beginning of the priesthood when it is after the order of one without *beginning* and *end*?
801. Of what duration was the Mosaic priesthood?

802. Why was Christ not named after the Aaronic priesthood?
803. Was He of the proper tribe for the Aaronic one?
II. *Necessity of growth in knowledge in order to realize the hope of the priesthood.* 5:11-6:20.
A. *Difficulty of explaining the priesthood because of the low stage of the knowledge of his readers.* 5:11-14.

Text
5:11-14

11 Of whom we have many things to say, and hard of interpretation, seeing ye are become dull of hearing. 12 For when by reason of the time ye ought to be teachers, ye have need again that some one teach you the rudiments of the first principles of the oracles of God; and are become such as have need of milk, and not of solid food. 13 For every one that partaketh of milk is without experience of the word of righteousness; for he is a babe. 14 But solid food is for fullgrown men, even those who by reason of use have their senses exercised to discern good and evil.

Paraphrase

11 Concerning Melchizedek I have much to say for the illustration of Christ's priesthood, which is difficult to be explained when spoken, not on account of the darkness of the subject, but because ye are of slow apprehension in spiritual matters.

12 For though ye ought to have been able to teach others, considering the time ye have professed the gospel, ye have need of one to teach you, a second time, some of the fundamental principles of the ancient oracles of God concerning the Christ; and have become such as have need of being taught the easiest doctrines, and are not capable of receiving the higher parts of knowledge.

13 Now every one who uses milk only, who knows nothing but the letter of the ancient revelations, is unskilled in the doctrines of the gospel: For he is a babe in Christianity.

14 But the matters concealed under the figures and prophecies of the law, which may be called strong meat, because they strengthen the mind, are fit for them who have made progress in knowledge, and who by practice have the faculties of their mind accustomed to discern both truth and falsehood.

Comment

Of whom

Of whom — who is meant?
a. It is applied to three different persons:
1. To Melchizedek.
2. To Christ.
3. To the endless priesthood.
b. So little is known of Melchizedek, we are quick to believe that he might be referred to here.

We have many things to say

Now he is discussing Christ's priesthood, so we may assume "of whom" refers to Christ. He is not speaking of Melchizedek except as an illustration; Christ is the main subject:
a. He has much to say about Christ and little about Melchizedek.
b. The many things are wonderful things.

and hard of interpretation

It is also translated, "hard to be uttered":
a. Difficulty of interpretation may lie in one of three directions: (Newell)
1. The teacher's inability.
2. The subject, deep and difficult.
3. The hearers.
b. It wasn't the teacher, it wasn't the subject, so the listener was at fault.

seeing ye are become dull of hearing

The brightness of His glory could not be seen because of their dullness, their darkness.
a. Their souls did not keep pace with the doctrines delivered.
b. They had a love for their brethren, but they were dull of hearing.
Jesus found the Jews this way and quoted Isaiah against them. cf. Matt. 13:14-15.

For when by reason of the time ye ought to be teachers

Time should have been used to advantage:
a. Newell: "Over 30 years from Pentecost to the writing of Hebrews."
b. Christians are to grow; they are not to be stunted.
Teaching should be the objective of all Christians:

a. People who attend Bible School, worship, prayer meeting, evangelistic services, ought to get to the place where they can teach others.
b. Most churches find it difficult to find a few teachers for their Bible School.

Ye have need again that some one teach you the rudiments

Literally, teach you a second time. Kindergarten lessons sometimes must be learned in adulthood.

of the first principles of the oracles of God

The average church member can't turn to God's word and point out the pattern for the church or its doctrine.
a. Church people complain at hearing old messages over and over again, but they often couldn't turn to a scripture on the subject.
b. Those who are teachers love to hear the Word taught.
"Of the oracles of God": what is meant?
a. It may refer to the notices which the prophets gave of the priesthood of Christ. Psalms 110; Isaiah 53.
b. "Oracle" simply means a divine utterance, and appears four times in the New Testament. (Milligan)
1. Acts 7:38.
2. Rom. 3:2.
3. Heb. 5:12.
4. I Peter 4:11.

and are become such as have need of milk

They once were in better condition than now:
a. When they first became Christians they were not so dull of hearing.
b. It is a sad day when men cannot digest God's deep treasures.
"As have need of milk".
a. "Milk", a metaphor, is used to indicate first principles. cf. I Cor. 3:1, 2.
b. These early principles are enumerated in 6:2-3.

and not of solid food

Deeper teaching — weightier problems — heavier responsibilities — they could not digest:
a. Babes are on a very weak diet.
b. They had not grown out of the high chair age.

c. The scaffolding of Christianity was the thing upon which they depended.

For every one that partaketh of milk is without experience

Babes can do only what they are taught, and that is very little:

a. The Hebrews had not experienced the things that mature Christians were to experience.
b. The walk of holiness, launching out on faith was needed. Babes have milk carried to them; adults take milk to babes.

of the word of righteousness

These have not been able to launch out into the sea of experience for Christ:

a. Matt. 6:33.
b. They were still in the crib.
"Word of righteousness" is suggestive:
a. Matt. 5:20: "Righteousness" is that which goes on beyond the right, the plain duty.
b. It means purity of heart, attitude of mind.

he is a babe

What are the characteristics of a "babe"?

a. They are tossed to and fro and carried about with every wind of doctrine. Eph. 4:14. So is a baby.
b. They belong to some special sect and cry, "My church".
c. They glory in men. I Cor. 1:12: "I am of Paul." "Apollos."
d. A babe sleeps instead of serving.
Our spiritual capacity suggests our spiritual age.

But solid food is for fullgrown men

Fullgrown men spiritually are needed. I Cor. 2:6; 14:20; Eph. 4:13.
The value of solid food is seen in Eph. 4:14.

who by reason of use have their senses exercised

Miserable is the person who fails to use his spiritual senses.

a. By believing, praying, thanking and by being obedient, we can make full use of our spiritual faculties.
b. The only way to exercise is by action, by using the abilities given to us.

c. People will be spiritually impotent until they use their senses. The word for "senses" is an interesting word:
a. Clark says it signifies the different sense organs as eyes, ears, tongue, palate, and nervous system in general.
b. The soul has its sensations: love, joy, compassion, etc.
c. The five senses of man have spiritual significance.
1. Taste: I Pet. 2:3; Ps. 34:8; Heb. 6:4; Matt. 5:6.
2. Hearing: Isaiah 55:3; Rev. 3:22.
3. Sight: Psalm 119:18; Eph. 1:18.
4. Smell: Phil. 4:18.
5. Feeling: Eph. 4:32.

Exercise is a requirement for one's spiritual development:
a. This word "exercise" is a metaphor taken from the athletes or contenders in the Grecian games.
b. These men applied all their powers that they might be ready for competition.

to discern good and evil

Those who do not exercise will see little or no harm in the pleasures of the world.
a. So many good people get into trouble, because, "I didn't see any harm in it."
b. The iceberg is dangerous because three-fifths of it is beneath the water, unseen, with jagged edges which may tear great holes in the ship.

Sin brings a tolerance for evil, so that men do not bother to discern good and evil.

Study Questions

804. Who is meant in the expression "of whom"? v. 11.
805. Are there many things to say of Melchizedek?
806. In what three matters may difficulty of interpretation be possible? v. 11.
807. Is it hard to interpret "of whom" "Christ" or "Melchizedek"?
808. Is it the teacher's fault here?
809. Is the subject hard to understand?
810. In the light of this verse, where is the difficulty? v. 11.
811. Do you understand what is hard of interpretation?
812. Is "dull of hearing" an offensive accusation?
813. What made Paul think that they were dull?

814. Did Jesus feel that His generation was dull? Cf. Matt. 13:14-15.
815. "Reason of time" would refer to what?
816. How much time had expired between Jesus' death and the writing of the Hebrew letter?
817. Is Paul inferring that all of them ought to be teachers?
818. How many of our converts aspire to be teachers?
819. How many become teachers?
820. How many are even interested in learning, according to Bible School, church, prayer meeting attendance?
821. Are elders expected to be teachers?
822. Should a man be an elder if he has all of the other qualifications? If he can't express himself, is he fit?
823. "Need again" would mean what?
824. What are "rudiments"?
825. "First principles" would mean what?
826. Do people complain at hearing simple things repeated over and over again?
827. Are the "dull of hearing" ones the complainers or the teachers?
828. What do "oracles of God" refer to?
829. Is "oracles" a common word in the New Testament? Cf. Acts 7:38; Rom. 3:2; Heb. 5:12; I Peter 4:11.
830. What would the "milk" refer to? Cf. I Cor. 3:1-2.
831. What does Peter say about milk? I Peter 2:2.
832. What does "solid food" refer to?
833. Why could they not digest it?
834. Did they not understand Aaron's priesthood?
835. Could it refer back to the priesthood of which he wanted to say many things?
836. Name some things that would be classed as "solid food".
837. Is there much hope of evangelizing the world with "high chair" Christians?
838. What is the future of the church when folk cannot wield the sword of the spirit?
839. What is meant by "experience"?
840. What experience does the baby in Christ lack?
841. Can a baby do more than it is taught? Is the same true of spiritual babes?
842. Would Romans 14:1-6 have a bearing on this subject?

843. Do we have any clues in Hebrews as to the particular shortcomings of the people which caused this to be written? For instance, in Corinthians and Galatians special problems are named.
844. What is meant by "word of righteousness"?
845. Can you define "righteousness"?
846. What could they have lacked that kept them from being righteous?
847. Did Jesus have anything to say concerning righteousness?
848. What does a baby do that weak Christians do?
849. Could our spiritual capacity be an indication of our spiritual age?
850. What do you consider "solid food" to be?
851. Observe that wisdom is connected with fullgrown men. I Cor. 2:6.
852. What comparison can be make with stature and Christ? See Eph. 4:13-14.
853. It is said of Jesus that he increased in wisdom and stature, in favor with God and man. Luke 2:52. What evidence do we have that He did?
854. Could these or the lack of them prove that we have or have not attained spiritual adulthood?
855. Do you know of anyone whom you consider to be fullgrown?
856. Should a man be an elder in the church if he is a babe?
857. What would the "senses" refer to?
858. What sensation does the spiritual person have?
859. What can you do to exercise your senses?
860. Are the five senses referred to in the Word? See I Pet. 2:3; Heb. 6:4; Psalm 119:18; Eph. 1:8.
861. Look at Eph. 4:32 for "feeling".
862. What does Phil. 4:18 say concerning smell?
863. Why should a person exercise himself?
864. What is meant by discernment?
865. Why is it an effort to detect evil? Isn't it obvious?

Questions On Chapter Five
Answer YES or NO

1. A high priest under the Jewish reign did not have to offer sacrifices for his own sins?

2. No man was able to take up the job of being a high priest but must have been called of God as was Aaron?
3. Strong meat of the gospel is for babies in order to hasten their spiritual growth?
4. Christ was a high priest before the days of Melchizedek?
5. Christ learned obedience by the things that He suffered?
6. If men were exceptional among the Jews, they could become high priests?
7. Jesus appointed Himself to be our High Priest?
8. Christ was descended of Aaron and hence from the tribe of Levi; therefore he could qualify as a priest?
9. Christ came willingly into the world, so He glorified Himself to be made a high priest?
10. God begot Jesus Christ?
11. The priesthood of Jesus was after the order of Melchizedek?
12. Jesus was God and therefore did not need to pray?
13. Man can exercise his body, but not his senses?
14. The author had some things to say that he said were hard of interpretation?
15. God's teachings have first principles in the oracles?
16. Christ was the only Person Who ever lived Who did not have a godly fear?
17. We may assume that Jesus did not weep over Jerusalem, for this chapter pictures Him as one Who never wept?
18. The priesthood of Christ is for a brief duration?
19. The priest's job is a limited one in that he offers only sacrifices?
20. This book seems to have been written to a people who were dull of hearing?
21. Christ is the Author of salvation for those who obey Him?
22. A fault with these people is that they had time to have been teachers but were not?
23. The word of God is likened unto milk?
24. The high priests of old were taken from among angels?
25. The high priest was in no sense bound to his responsibility?

SUMMARY OF CHAPTER FIVE

Frequent reference should be made to the condensed summary of the book. Thus far, two main points of Hebrews have been discussed: (1) the finality of God's revelation through His Son, and (2) the faithfulness of Jesus, our High Priest.

The first three verses of Chapter Five conclude the statement about the second point. The rest of the chapter introduces the important theme of the appointment of Christ as High Priest after the order of Melchizedek. He met all requirements necessary to become High Priest. Two things distinguished Him from Aaron: (1) His sinlessness; (2) His appointment after the order of Melchizedek. Christ's earthly ministry was marked by His devotion and obedience to God. He is the Cause of salvation since He completed the requirements for becoming the perfect Saviour; and because of this, God designated Him High Priest.

The mention of the change of order from Aaron to Melchizedek brought to mind the spiritually undeveloped state of Hebrew Christians and became the occasion for rebuking them because of their inability to appreciate this phase of Christ's ministry in their behalf. Chapters Six and Seven continue to enlarge upon this issue.

B. *Exhortation to go on to perfection.* 6:1-3.

Text
6:1-3

1 Wherefore leaving the doctrine of the first principles of Christ, let us press on unto perfection; not laying again a foundation of repentance from dead works, and of faith toward God, 2 of the teaching of baptisms, and of laying on of hands, and of resurrection of the dead, and of eternal judgment. 3 And this will we do, if God permit.

Paraphrase

1 Wherefore, since ye ought by this time to have been capable of strong food, dismissing the discourse concerning the principles of the Christian doctrine, as contained in the ancient revelations, let us proceed to the deep meaning of these revelations, and of the figures and prophecies in the law, which is the perfection of Christian knowledge, not explaining a second time the fundamental principles of repentance from works which merit death; and of faith in God;

2 Of the doctrine of baptisms, as emblematical of that purity of mind which the worshippers of God ought to possess; and of the laying on of hands on the sacrifices, as an acknowledgment

that the offerer deserved death for his sins; and of the resurrection of the dead; and of the eternal judgment, so called because its sentences will never be reversed.

3 And this more perfect instruction I will give you, if God permit, by preserving you from apostatizing till ye have an opportunity to read and consider this letter.

Wherefore leaving doctrine of the first principles

    The initial steps are the simple things:
a. Isaiah 35:8: Observe what Isaiah said: "Wayfaring man, though a fool, shall not err."
b. These first principles are named in verses one and two.
    They are not "left," but serve as the foundation.
a. Not left in the sense that they are forsaken.
b. Paul, in I Cor. 12 and 13, discusses the gifts of the Spirit and says, faith, hope and love are greater.

let us press on

    Paul set the example, saying, "I press toward the mark." Phil. 3:14.
    The Christian that isn't growing is going back toward the world.

to perfection

    Perfection is of God:
        Psa. 18:32: "The God that girdeth me with strength and maketh my way perfect."
        Psa. 138:8: "Jehovah will perfect that which concerneth me.
    Thy lovingkindness, O Jehovah, endureth forever."
    God is the standard:
        Matt. 5:48: "Ye therefore shall be perfect as your heavenly Father is perfect."
    The part of God's Word in perfection — our guide is perfect.
a. James 1:25: "But he that looketh into the perfect law, the law of liberty, and so continueth, being not a hearer that forgetteth but a doer that worketh, this man shall be blessed in his doing."
b. II Tim. 3:16-17: "Every scripture inspired of God, is also profitable for teaching — ."
    Our Saviour was perfect. See 4:15 and 5:9.

6:1

not laying again a foundation

In building a house we do not leave the foundation, yet to be always at work building it would be ridiculous.
a. The structure ought to rise above the foundation.
b. One foundation for a building is sufficient.
God speaks of us as His building.
I Cor. 3:9: "Ye are God's building."
Eph. 2:22: "In whom ye also are builded together — ."
Col. 2:7: . . . "rooted and builded up in Him."

of repentence

Some people are always in some scrape. They are always in need of forgiveness and repentance.
a. Repentance means that we do not continue in evil, occasionally regretting it.
b. John's listeners needed to bring forth fruits worthy of repentance.
We are not to live in constant need of repentance, but to avoid evil.

from dead works

The past of an individual is to be buried at baptism and ought never to need repenting of again.
What is "dead works"?
a. The vain effort to relieve a troubled conscience by legal obedience.
b. It is not service, but religious performances.
c. Newell has a unique idea here:
1. He says that Gentiles were commanded to repent of sins. Acts 8:22. They were never commanded to repent of dead works.
2. Milligan, however, feels that this is using the word in too limited a sense.
d. Works of the law were dead works, but surely "dead works" refers to all services of Satan.

and of faith towards God

The initial faith that caused one to act for God must not be considered sufficient.
a. Genuine faith produces righteousness.

b. Few men disbelieve in a higher Power, but this is not sufficient. The Jew had a faith in God. What he needed was a faith that included Jesus Christ.

of the teaching of baptisms

Why "baptisms" in the plural?

a. Chrysostom: Because they who returned to first principles abrogated their first baptism.
b. Calvin: "Baptisms" didn't have reference to many baptisms but solemn rites or the stated days of baptizing.
c. John Owen, translator of Calvin's commentary: "Some of these folk had been baptized by John, some were afterwards baptized only in the name of Christ (Acts 19:5); others were baptized in the name of the trinity."
d. This may allude to the Levitical law, says Clarke, for they had immersions, sprinklings, washings.
e. Some say the two baptisms that John preached, baptism in the Holy Spirit and in fire. Matt. 3:11.
f. Newell says, "Plural because unto the Jews God had prescribed."
1. John the Baptist's baptism.
2. Christian baptism.
g. Milligan says, (1) a baptism in water in which all penitent believers who confess Christ are introduced into his body; (2) a baptism in the Holy Spirit administered by Christ himself to all who are really begotten by the Spirit and born of the water; and (3) a baptism in fire by means of which the wicked will all be finally overwhelmed in sufferings.

The point to gain is that it is an initiatory step, and one is not to sit on the edge of the baptistry.

and of laying on of hands

The "laying on of hands" on the baptized was an apostolic practice by which miraculous gift of tongues, etc., was bestowed.

a. The evidence from scripture:
1. See Acts 8:14b, 15: "Peter and John, who, when they were came down, prayed for them, that they might receive the Holy Spirit." v. 17: "Then laid they their hands on them and they received the Holy Spirit."

2. Acts 19:6: Paul laid on his hands, and they spoke with tongues.
b. Two groups were able to impart gifts:
1. The apostles, Acts 19:6: "And when Paul had laid his hands upon them and they spoke with tongues and prophesied." II Tim. 1:6: " — gift in thee through the laying on of my hands."
2. The presbytery, I Tim. 4:14: "Neglect not the gift that is in thee, which was given thee by prophecy, with the laying on of the hands of the presbytery."
The laying on of hands was also connected with bodily healings. Acts 5:12: "By the hands of the apostles were many signs and wonders wrought among the people." Cf. Acts 9:41 and 28:8.
It was also done to set aside men for special tasks:
a. The seven in Jerusalem set aside for the care of Grecian widows. Acts 6:6.
b. Paul and Barnabas. Acts 13:3.
A warning as in order; laying on of hands was not to be done hastily. I Tim. 5:22.

and of resurrection of the dead

Does he mean "raised to walk in newness" from the dead, a spiritual condition, or does he mean a physical death?
a. Resurrection is a tenet of faith, a phase of the gospel.
1. Peter used the resurrection story to persuade the Jews of sin against God.
2. After this doctrine is believed, we are to press on to matters of life.
An Easter and Christmas religion is too apparent in our day, and no doubt was in theirs.
a. Many people go to church on Easter and sometimes on Christmas and never again during the year.
b. The resurrection is one of the primary things, for it is a part of the gospel. I Cor. 15:1-5.
It was the judgment to come, included in Paul's sermon, that terrified Felix. See Acts 24:25.
a. A fear or a confidence is not sufficient.
b. We are to build a wonderful Christian life on the foundation of our belief.

c. The fact that we are to be raised should be an inducement to repent and to live righteously.
Resurrection and judgment are connected with our Lord's resurrection. Acts 17:31 and Acts 24:25.

and of eternal judgment

An impelling motive is fear, a first principle.
a. A person who progresses in the Christian life has less fear in proportion to how much love is increased.
b. The reason some never repent is that they have never heard this doctrine of judgment.
The apostles were not afraid to preach this doctrine.
a. Paul used fear of judgment with Felix. Acts 24:25.
b. Peter used fear to move the people on Pentecost.
c. Jesus taught it.
Observe that six things have been named in the life that begin in relationship to Christ.
a. Repentance from dead works.
b. Faith toward God.
c. Baptisms.
d. Laying on of hands.
e. Resurrection from the dead.
f. Eternal judgment.

Building

Temperance

Meekness

Faith

Goodness

Gentleness

Longsuffering

Peace

Joy

Love

| Faith | Baptism | Resurrection |
| Repentance | Laying on Hands | Judgment |

Foundation

and this will we do

"And this will we do" refers to 6:1.
a. What will we do?

1. Leave the first principles. 6:1.
2. Press on to perfection. 6:1.
   Paul uses the word "we", perhaps to speak generally and personally.

if God permit

   This is a warning to the backslider.
a. Work now without delay, for there will not always be the opportunity for making progress.
b. Perhaps the Apostate has rejected God as in Noah's evil day when God will not always strive. Gen. 6:3.
c. Remember Jacob could not change his promise although Esau begged. Heb. 12:17.
   There are other views on this expression.
a. Milligan: "This we will do with the help of God."
b. Newell: "We beg you, guard your heart against that awful thought, that there are those truly seeking to get back to God whom He will not receive."
   Let us remember that there is an unpardonable sin.
a. The verses, Matt. 12:31-33: All sin be forgiven but against the Holy Spirit. Heb. 6:4: It is impossible to renew them who have turned back into sin.
b. Jesus did not say all would be forgiven if men desired it, but that one sin could not be forgiven.

Study Questions

866. What does verse one say to leave?
867. Does it mean to forsake them?
868. Do we actually leave them or build upon them?
869. What are "first principles"? Do they refer to "rudiments" in 5:12, or the "foundation" referred to in 6:1?
870. Define "pressing on".
871. Is a half-hearted attempt pressing on?
872. What did Paul say about pressing on in Phil. 3:14?
873. What is our standard of perfection?
874. Can we use God and Christ both as a standard?
875. How do we know Christ to be a perfect standard? Cf. 4:15; 5:9.
876. What part does the scripture have in perfection? See II Tim. 3:16-17.

HELPS FROM HEBREWS

877. Do we need any other guidebook according to this?
878. How many foundations are made when one is building a house?
879. How many should we have to build upon in our lives?
880. If a person spent a lifetime building a foundation on his house, would we consider him wise?
881. What verses speak of us as a building?
882. Does this verse condemn repentance?
883. What kind of person is in constant need of repentance?
884. What could be listed as "dead works"? Does "dead works" pertain to the law, since they were mentioned in Hebrews?
885. Should we have to continually repent of sins that have been buried in baptism?
886. Do we need to try to repent of some dead and buried sin?
887. If we truly repent of a sin, do we ever need to repent of it again?
888. Are we to repent of faith toward God, or does "faith" refer back to "Let us press on to perfection"?
889. How can we ever get to the place where we are not laying a foundation of faith?
890. What can you build upon if you are to press beyond the foundation of faith?
891. Does I Cor. 13:13 have a bearing on the subject?
892. Is a life prompted by love greater than one prompted by faith? Explain.
893. Why does he say "faith toward God"?
894. Is baptism in verse 2 singular or plural?
895. Why is baptism in the plural here? Did the Hebrews have two?
896. What baptism could be referred to? What have men suggested?
897. Is the Christian baptized more than once?
898. Were the early Christians who were first followers of John baptized the second time?
899. If baptism is an initial act of obedience, what should be expected to follow?
900. What does the laying on of hands refer to?
901. Who did the laying on of the hands?
902. Could all Christians impart special powers? Cf. Acts 8:15-17.

903. Could "the presbytery" refer to apostles who were considered elders?
904. What accompanied the laying on of hands?
905. Was it always to impart miraculous gifts? Cf. Acts 6:6; 13:3.
906. Was this to be done with great care? Cf. I Tim. 5:22.
907. What "resurrection of the dead" is referred to, ours or Christ's?
908. Is the doctrine of the Christ's resurrection something to build upon?
909. Is our resurrection from the watery grave to be built upon?
910. Does the observance of Easter and the indifference until a year later indicate a spiritual illness like the Hebrews had?
911. How often did the apostles refer to the resurrection? With what subjects is it connected? Cf. Acts 24:15; 17:31.
912. What special way did Peter use the doctrine of Christ's resurrection on the day of Pentecost?
913. Do you suppose that some assume we will inherit eternal life regardless of failure to grow just because it is so freely promised?
914. How can eternal judgment be a foundation?
915. Is fear a very strong impelling motive?
916. Does fear decrease as love increases?
917. Should we preach the doctrine of eternal judgment?
918. What will we do according to verse one?
919. Why does he use the "we"? Has Paul failed to see the need of learning first principles?
920. Is he saying we will do this, or is there some doubt about the ability to accomplish it?
921. Is it the same expression as in James 4:15?
922. Is it a warning lest they fall into a state of apostasy so severe as to keep them from finding God's help?
923. Name a day when God's Spirit would not strive.

C. *The awful consequences of falling away.* 6:4-8.

Text
6:4-8

4 For as touching those who were once enlightened and tasted of the heavenly gift, and were made partakers of the Holy Spirit,

HELPS FROM HEBREWS   6:4-8

5 and tasted the good Word of God, and the powers of the age to come, 6 and then fell away, it is impossible to renew them again unto repentance; seeing they crucify to themselves the Son of God afresh, and put Him to an open shame. 7 For the land which hath drunk the rain that cometh oft upon it, and bringeth forth herbs meet for them for whose sake it is also tilled, receiveth blessings from God: 8 but if it beareth thorns and thistles, it is rejected and nigh unto a curse; whose end is to be burned.

Paraphrase

4 For it is impossible for us to restore a second time, by repentance, those who have been once enlightened by believing the Gospel; and have tasted of the heavenly gift of freedom from the yoke of the law of Moses, and from the grievous superstitions of heathenism, which is bestowed on Jews and Gentiles under the Gospel; and have been made partakers of the gifts of the Holy Ghost at their baptism;

5 And have perceived the excellence of the Word of God, the doctrines and promises of the Gospel; and have seen the efficacy of the powers of the Gospel dispensation in reforming sinners;

6 And yet have renounced the Gospel, in the imagination that Jesus was justly punished with death as an imposter, crucifying a second time in their own mind, and making a public example of the Son of God, by inwardly approving of, and consenting to His punishment.

7 In giving up such wilful sinners as incorrigible, we act as men do in cultivating their fields. For the land which drinketh in the rain which often falleth upon it, and produceth fruits fit for the use of them by whom it is cultivated, continueth to be cultivated, and receiveth a blessing from God:

8 But that which, being duly cultivated and watered, produceth only thorns and briars, is reprobated by the husbandman as not worthy of culture, and soon will fall under the curse, and in the end will be burnt up with drought.

Comment

For as touching those who were once enlightened

Obviously, full Christians are up for discussion.
a. Clarke's commentary: "I do not consider them as having any

reference to any person professing Christianity. They are not applicable to backsliders of any kind."
b. Enlightenment refers to those who have known.
c. This expression is the mark of a true Christian.
1. 10:32: Paul points out that the Hebrew brethren were once enlightened and endured affliction.
2. Eph. 5:8 "Now are ye light in the Lord."
3. Col. 1:12: Saints in the light.
4. I Thess. 5:5: Sons of light.
5. I Peter 2:9: Into His marvelous light.
6. I John 2:10: "He that loveth his brother abideth in light."

If "once enlightened" does not refer to Christian people, how many repetitions of enlightenment does it take to make one a Christian?

Notice the word "impossible" appears in this expression in the King James version.
a. In the American Standard it appears in verse 6.
b. In the Greek it is in vs. 4: "For impossible (it is) those once for all enlightened —"

and tasted of the heavenly gift

God's word should always be sweet to us, but to some it is not.
a. Milligan: "The word 'tasted' means to experience, partake."
b. Newell: "— makes a difference in tasting and drinking." (p. 187)
1. A person can "taste" and be lost, he says.
2. The drinkers are truly saved.
a) The drinker commits himself to what he drinks and is therefore saved.
b) He says thousands taste of the heavenly gift, eternal life, who never drink that water.
c) The context shows that he is desperate for a point of view.

What is meant, "the heavenly gift"?
a. See the scriptures that offer suggestions.
1. John 6:51: Christ, the Living Bread that came down from heaven.
2. I Peter 2:3: "... if ye have tasted that the Lord is gracious."
3. Psalm 104:34: Meditation of Him shall be sweet.
b. Others say it refers to the Holy Spirit. Acts 2:38.
c. Others say it refers to the new life.

1. John 6:33: "The bread of God is He who cometh down from heaven and giveth life unto the world."
2. John 4:1-14: To the woman at the well.
3. John 3:36.
4. I John 5:12: " — He who hath the Son hath life."
   Salvation in Christ is most likely meant, for in this section he names the word of God, Holy Spirit; so salvation remains.
a. Christ is a gift; grace is a gift.
b. The gift of salvation and Christ were experienced by these Hebrews.

and were made partakers of the Holy Spirit

We are made partakers when we confess Jesus as Lord.
I Cor. 12:3: "No man can say Jesus is Lord, but in the Holy Spirit." John 14:17: "Even the Spirit of Truth whom the world can not receive; for it beholdeth Him not." John 7:39: "But this spake He of the Spirit, which they that believed on Him were to receive, for the Spirit was not yet given, because Jesus was not yet glorified."
We are made partakers when we are baptized. Acts 2:38: Gift of the Holy Spirit: Gal. 4:6: "Because ye are sons, God sent forth the Spirit of his Son into your hearts, crying, Abba, Father."
Newell says this is not the same as "sealed unto the day of redemption". Eph. 4:30.
Eph. 4:30: "Grieve not the Holy Spirit in whom ye are sealed."
Eph. 1:13-14: "Ye were sealed."
He says we can be a partner but never sealed, and uses Judas as an illustration.
Who but a Christian has been a partaker of the Holy Spirit?

and tasted the good word of God

Taste is a wonderful ability and is appreciated the most spiritually, for the Word of God is sweet. Ps. 19:10: "Thy word is sweeter than honey." 119:103: " — words sweeter than honey to my soul."
John speaks of the Word, Rev. 10:10: "It was in my mouth sweet as honey."

and the powers of the age to come

By faith we see in spirit the blessed immortality that is hid from our physical senses.
a. Milligan says this is the highest stage of Christian experience.
1. Enlightened.
2. Tasted of the heavenly gift.
3. Made to partake of the influences of the Holy Spirit.
4. Experience of the excellence of God's Word.
5. Participation in the full powers of the new dispensation.
b. The pull of eternity, longing for heaven, is an experience that the redeemed feel.
c. Clarke suggests two opinions:
1. It perhaps refers to all the miracles that Jesus did.
2. The communications and foretastes of eternal blessedness and joys of the world to come.
d. It must refer to the experience of divine things to the end that you feel a powerful longing for heaven. Phil. 1:23: "But I am in a strait betwixt the two, having the desire to depart and be with Christ, for it is very far better, 24 yet to abide in the flesh is far more needful for your sake."

and then fell away

Here we have a warning that much experience may be lost.
a. Let no man blame God after experiencing all this.
b. When we go astray, we are rushing headlong into ruin of our own accord.
c. Overconfidence may cause one to fall. I Cor. 10:12.
What is the meaning of "fall away"?
a. This is not a participation in some sin in which a person has been tempted.
1. It is a renouncing of the grace of God.
2. It is a forsaking of the Word of God, extinguishing the light.
3. It is a relinquishing of a participation of the Holy Spirit.
4. It is an abandonment of desire for the advocate.
b. When a person comes to the place where he can be shown a passage of scripture and says, "I don't care," then he has fallen.
Jesus taught that men could fall away. John 15:6: "If a man abide not in Me, he is cast forth as a branch, and is withered;

and they gather them, and cast them into the fire and they are burned."

"having fallen away" is a translation of this, as seen by the Word.

a. The Greek word is *parapesontas*.
1. It is an aorist participle of *parapipto*.
2. The word is *parapipto* — "fall away".
a) The word is compounded from *para* meaning "alongside", and *piptein*, "to fall".
3. Thayer: "Hence to deviate from the right path, to turn aside, to wander. In scripture to fall away from the true faith, from Christianity."
4. This is the only place in the New Testament that this word appears.
b. A second Greek word for "falling away" is *aphistemi*.
1. It means to separate from, either by one's will (voluntarily) or by the will of another.
2. Observe the use of the word. Newell, p. 192.
a) Four times in Luke: Luke 2:37: "Anna departed not from the temple." 4:13: "And when the devil had ended all the temptation, he departed from Him for a season." 8:13: Those on the rocky ground " — in time of temptation fall away." 13:27: "Depart from me, ye workers of iniquity." Observe here the will of another.
c. Other uses: Acts 19:9: Paul — "departed from them (the Jews) and separated the disciples." I Tim. 4:1: "And in later times some shall fall away from the faith." I Tim. 6:5: "From such withdraw thyself." II Tim. 2:19: "Let every one that nameth the Name of the Lord depart from unrighteousness."
d. A very specific use is in Heb. 3:12.
1. The Greek is *apostenai*.
a) From this word we get the word "apostasy".
b) Apostasy, Webster: "Abandonment of what one has voluntarily professed; total desertion of principles or faith."
2. The noun is *apostasia*. It appears twice: Acts 21:21: Here Paul is accused of abandoning Moses. II Thess. 2:3: Here is a general apostasy from God to the antichrist.

What is the extent of "falling away"?

a. What it is not.
1. It is not a falling into sin.

2. The sinner can return and be forgiven, if he has only sinned.
a) I John 2:1: "If any man sin, we have an advocate."
b. It is a falling away from God, from Christ, from salvation; a renouncing of the truth.
1. The "once" of v. 4 shows these acts to have been done in the past.
2. These referred to here have turned back to the sin they once loved.
3. These have turned away from the light and have come to hate it.
4. See Heb. 10:26-31.
   Life of repentance
   Life of unwilling sin
   1. Enlightened.
   2. Tasted of the heavenly gift.
   3. Made partakers of the Holy Spirit.
   4. Tasted the good Word of God.
   5. Tasted the powers of the age to come.
   I John 2:1 — Advocate — GOD
   for one who willingly sins, it is impossible to renew him again unto repentance. There is no more sacrifice for high-handed sin.

it is impossible to renew them again unto repentance

Observe that the word "impossible" appears in verse 4 in the Greek and in the King James version.
What is meant by "renew"?
a. It may be rendered, "restore".
b. Josephus used the word, and applies it to the restoration or renovation of the temple.
Does God cut them off, or is it that the sinner is too hardened to be restored?
a. There are arguments for both answers.
1. Old Testament scripture:
a) Those that say God gives man up: Gen. 6:3: "My spirit will not strive with man forever." Num. 15:30-31: " — soul that doeth aught with a high hand — shall be cut off." Pro. 1:26: " — I also will laugh in the day of your calamity." Pro. 1:28: "They will call upon me, but I will not answer." Josh. 24:19: "He will not forgive your . . . . sins."

b) Those that say God will forgive: Num. 30:5: "Lord will forgive." Hosea 4:16: Israel had behaved like a backsliding heifer, but God promises He will feed them as sheep."
2) New Testament passages:
a) That God will give man up: Rom. 1:24: "Wherefore God gave them up." Rom. 1:28: "Even as they refused . . . God . . . God gave them up." II Thess. 2:11-12: "God sendeth them a working of error."
b) Those that say God will forgive: John 3:16: "whosoever." John 6:37: "I will in no wise cast out." II Tim. 2:25: "If peradventure God may give them repentance."
b. Obviously the negative verses qualify the positive. God's grace can be extended only so far.
1. The reason why it is impossible is found in the word "rejected" of verse 8.
They have crucified Christ, put Him to an open shame, and God is unwilling for them to repent.
2. Of course, there is the possibility that such people will not want to repent.

seeing they crucify to themselves the Son of God afresh

When a person turns back to sin, it appears that he professes that Christ deserved to be crucified as an imposter.
a. They put a living Christ out of their life, and He is dead to them.
b. Notice that they who make sin their choice are the ones here discussed.
What actually takes place?
a. Their manner of life cuts off prayer and repentance.
b. They cut off His table for the table of demons.
c. Christian fellowship is replaced by that of the world.
d. Growth in grace is substituted by a sinking into sin.
The atheist or infidel cannot do this; only the Christian can "crucify the Son of God afresh".

and put Him to an open shame.

The person who goes back to the world brings shame upon Christ.
a. Christianity becomes a joke to the world when it is given up by a Christian.
b. It makes Christianity appear powerless.

c. Christianity appears as hypocrisy to the unbelieving when the believer denounces it.
If Christianity does not save one from sinning, the critic says, "I told you so".

For the land which hath drunk the rain that cometh oft upon it

Soil is used here to illustrate the Christian, of which much is expected.

a. The Christian drinks, tastes the good Word of God. But it does not always last.
b. The Christian should be like the good soil in Jesus' parable. Luke 8:4-8.
The Christian receives so much from God that it is inexcusable for him to do less than to produce fruit.

and bringeth forth herbs meet for them for whose sake it is also tilled, receiveth blessing from God

God's seed should strike root at once in our lives. "Herbs" is symbolic of the fruit desired in the life of the Christian.

a. Good seed and good soil, with refreshment from God, should produce a good harvest.
b. Let us consider how great an advantage the Christian has over the world.
Only good fruit may have the blessing of God.

But if it beareth thorns and thistles

Christian growth is the point of this parable, and thorns and thistles are the opponents of growth.

a. Herbs are the things that accompany salvation in vs. 9.
b. Thorns and thistles result when God is not allowed to be the husbandman.
The seed of the Gospel is sometimes destroyed by indifference and corrupt affections.

it is rejected

God cannot accept thorns and thistles, so rejection is needful.

a. The greater the expectation, the greater the disappointment in failure.
b. Thorns and thistles give no encouragement of harvest, so they must be rejected.
We must examine our lives to see if God will reject us.

and nigh unto a curse; whose end is to be burned

The rejected may look forward only to destruction.
a. Unless repentance takes place, the lake of fire will be their end.
b. Burning or blessing is our choice to make.
The only alternative for a good husbandman is destruction of the evil.

Study Questions

924. What is meant by, "for as touching"?
925. What kind of persons is referred to in Paul's discussion here?
926. Who is referred to by persons "once enlightened"?
927. Could it be persons who heard and saw the light, but did not embrace it?
928. What other part of the verse seems to indicate that Christian people are referred to?
929. Does not Heb. 10:32 make it specific that Christians are up for discussion?
930. Compare Eph. 5:8; Col. 1:12; I Thess. 5:5; I Pet. 2:9; I John 2:10 to see whether enlightenment is a mark of a Christian.
931. If "enlightened" is not referring to a Christian, how many times must one be illumined before he can become one?
932. In the King James Bible where does the word "impossible" appear? In the American Standard? In the original language?
933. What does "impossible" mean? Is it a final state?
934. What does the word "tasted" mean?
935. Is there a difference between "tasters" and "drinkers"?
936. Is it possible to "taste", but not be a "drinker" of eternal life?
937. Why do some try to make such close distinction here?
938. Observe that some commentators think that "tasters" can be lost but not "drinkers".
939. What possible explanations have been given for the expression, "heavenly gift"?
940. Why could it refer to water or bread of life as in John 6:51 and John 4:1-14?
941. What is the evidence in this verse that would rule the Holy Spirit and Word of God out as being the "tasted" gift?

942. Define the word "partakers". Is it the same as "tasting"? When are we made "partakers"?
943. Compare I Cor. 12:3 and Acts 2:38 and Gal. 4:6 to find when we experience the Holy Spirit.
944. Is "partaking" the same as being "sealed"? Eph. 4:30; Eph. 1:13-14.
945. Who but a Christian could be a "partaker" of the Holy Spirit"?
946. Why do some try to teach that "partaking" and "sealing" are not the same?
947. Is it fair to speak of Judas as being a "partaker", but not being a "sealed" one to illustrate the Christian state referred to here?
948. Is the word, "taste", here the same word of verse 4?
949. Do people consider God's words good tasting without accepting them?
950. Compare some attitudes found in Ps. 19:10; 119:103; Rev. 10:10.
951. Do the words "good Word of God" infer that some of it is not good?
952. Does the expression "powers of the age to come" refer to the very highest experience yet named in verses 4 and 5? Observe that four things are experienced ahead of this.
953. What could "powers of the age to come" refer to?
954. Could it be the experience of heavenly blessings of joy while we are yet on earth?
955. Why do you think it might be an experience similar to that faced by Paul in Phil. 1:23-24?
956. Is there any significance in the fact that he does not specifically say "fallen from the faith"?
957. Can a person lose all the former things named, at least for a time, according to verse 6?
958. What is this "falling away"? Is it a falling into some specific sin?
959. What is falling away? What is Thayer's definition?
960. Does the context suggest that it is serious?
961. Is this a common word in the New Testament?
962. What is a second Greek word for "falling away"?
963. Does *aphistemi* refer to a separate state that is voluntary, or one forced?

964. Compare Luke 13:27 for falling away by the will of another.
965. Compare the Word with Jesus' statement in regard to soil in Luke 8:13.
966. Is the word *aphistemi* always used to indicate "fall away"? Cf. Acts 19:9; I Tim. 6:5; II Tim. 2:19.
967. Compare the word as Paul used it in reference to falling from the faith in I Tim. 4:1.
968. Which Greek word is used in Heb. 3:12?
969. Which one of the Greek words is the root word for our word "apostasy"?
970. Notice that in II Thess. 2:3 an apostasy from God to the antichrist is pointed out.
971. Notice that in Acts 21:21 Paul is accused of "falling" from Moses.
972. Describe "fallen away" in relationship to each of the five experiences previously named.
973. A most important question here: is this falling away a permanent condition?
974. If it is not permanent, then what does the word "impossible" mean in vs. 4 of the King James version or vs. 6 in the American Standard?
975. If "fall away" means to deviate from the right path, to turn away, etc., can we justly infer that once they were in the Way?
976. Can you infer that "falling away" is to fall out of the "Way"?
977. If the word appears only this one time, can we be sure of its meaning when we can't judge its meaning by other texts?
978. Is there another word for "falling away"?
979. Is this the same condition as in Heb. 10:26-31? Why do you think so?
980. Could you say that the fallen one is no longer enlightened, but is in the dark?
981. Of what is such a one tasting in the fallen state?
982. Of what is he partaker?
983. Is he still tasting the Word of God?
984. Is he able to feel power?
985. Is he powerless, like a motor without electricity?
986. Does not God say we have an Advocate in I John 2:1 if we sin?

987. What kind of sin is the kind that makes a permanent barrier between God and Man?
988. Are there two kinds of sin involved in the ability to repent, and the inability to be restored?
989. Define the word "renew" in this expression, "renew again unto repentance".
990. Have the translators in the American Standard version made an error by placing the word "impossible" here, obviously teaching that some cannot be restored?
991. Do you feel that you have the right to conclude that some have fallen away, and therefore refuse any effort to restore them?
992. Where is the impossibility to be placed, in the heart of man, or in the attitude of God?
993. Cite some New Testament verses where God gives men up. Rom. 1:24-26; II Thess. 2:11-12.
994. Does God give men up? Note "rejected" in v. 8.
995. Cite instances in the Old Testament where He gave men up. Gen. 6:3; Prov. 1:28; Joshua 24:19.
996. Does He always give them up?
997. Observe that Num. 15:30-31 may be the clue as to why God cuts some off and does not others.
998. In this sixth verse, is the fault with man, that he is in such a state that he cannot be appealed to for repentance?
999. Is it in the mind of God? What does Paul think of God's mind in the matter? Cf. v. 10.
1000. What have such persons done to Christ in v. 6?
1001. Can the infidel or atheist crucify Christ afresh?
1002. Isn't the Christian the only one who can crucify Him afresh?
1003. Does this mean that they put a living Christ out of their life and make Him as one dead?
1004. Does it indicate that such ones consider Christ to be deserving of crucifixion as an imposter?
1005. What actually takes place in the life of such people who crucify Christ afresh and put Him to an open shame?
1006. Do they cut off Bible study, prayer, communion, fellowship, etc.?
1007. Could we say that growth in grace is substituted by sinking into sin?

1008. What is meant by the expression, "put Him to open shame"?
1009. If Christianity does not save the Christian from sinning, does it make Christ seem powerless and impotent?
1010. What illustration does the author use in verses 7 and 8?
1011. Could the land here be likened to Christ's parable in Luke 8?
1012. Should seed take permanent lodging and bring forth fruit?
1013. What does the "rain" compare to in our lives?
1014. Should showers of blessing not help us to be steadfast?
1015. What does Rom. 2:4 say concerning God's goodness? Cf. Exodus 34:6; Ps. 33:5.
1016. In this verse, what replaces "herbs"?
1017. Who does the rejecting?
1018. If we are "thistles", can we expect God to accept us?
1019. We are burned or blessed — is this Paul's teaching?
1020. Does the "burning" indicate finality in this impossible renewal state?
1021. Is "burning" a familiar expression in the New Testament? Cf. Matt. 3:11-12; II Peter 3:8-13.

D. *Encouragement.* 6:9-20.
1. *The apostle's hope for them.* 6:9-12.

Text
6:9-12

9 But, beloved we are persuaded better things of you, and things that accompany salvation, though we thus speak: 10 for God is not unrighteous to forget your work and the love which ye showed toward His name, in that ye ministered unto the saints, and still do minister. 11 And we desire that each one of you may show the same diligence unto the fulness of hope even to the end: 12 that ye be not sluggish, but imitators of them who through faith and patience inherit the promises.

Paraphrase

9 But, beloved, we are persuaded better fruits than those of apostasy will be produced by you, even such a firm adherence to the Gospel as is connected with salvation, though we thus speak to put you on your guard.

6:9, 10   HELPS FROM HEBREWS

10 For God, who hath promised to assist His sincere servants in time of temptation, is not unrighteous to forget, either His Own promise of the laborious and dangerous work by which ye showed your loce to Him, when ye assisted and comforted the persecuted disciples of Christ in Judea, and do still assist them.

11 Yet I earnestly desire every one of you to show the same diligence as formerly in assisting and comforting your brethren, in order that my hope concerning your perseverance in the faith of the Gospel may continue to the end of your lives.

12 This I desire, that ye may not be sluggards, but imitators of the believing Gentiles in their good works, who through faith in Christ, and patience under persecution, are, as Abraham's spiritual seed, now inheriting the promises in the gospel church.

Comment

But beloved we are persuaded better things of you

This is a word of encouragement to a people for whom Paul had affection. The better things would be the "herbs", rather than the "thorns and thistles".

The word "persuaded" indicates hopefulness on the part of the author.

a. Vincent: It is a past hesitation overcome.
b. Westcott: The form implies that the writer had felt misgivings and had overcome them.

The word "beloved" is one frequently applied to saints. See Rom. 1:7; 11:28; I John 3:2; 4:1; III John 1, 2, 5, 11.

and things that accompany savlation, though we thus speak

What are the things that accompanied the saved as seen in the Word of God?

a. Pentecostal brethren: fairer things. Acts 2:42.
b. Stephen: forgiveness. Acts 7:58-60. No retaliation.
c. Ethiopian eunuch: Rejoicing. Acts 8:39.
d. Paul: Straightway proclaimed Jesus. Acts 9:36-39.
e. Dorcas: Benevolent spirit. Acts 9:36-37.
f. Bereans: Examining hearts. Acts 17:11.

Though he has warned against backsliding and apostasy, he is hopeful that Christian fruit will be produced by them.

for God is not unrighteous to forget your work

God's character is at stake in relationship to memory.

a. A person who forgets leaves himself open for accusations.
b. He may be accused of intentional forgetting or carelessness if he forgets.
An honest person is obligated to remember to keep his promise.
a. These people had worked, and God is under obligation to honor faithful work.
b. We see the brethren, (5:12) had been neglectful of Bible study but they were to be commended for their work.

and the love which ye showed toward His name in that ye ministered unto the saints and still do minister

We serve God by serving our fellow man.
a. Ministering to saints is showing love to God.
b. Jesus emphasized this. Matt. 25:40.
c. John approaches the subject. I John 4:20.
These people seem to have been strong on the "social gospel".
a. It seems strange that neglected Bible reading would accompany this virture.
b. A national love, nurtured by persecution, may account for it in some measure.
c. The Jew has always looked out for the Jew.

And we desire that each one may show the same diligence

Desire for each individual to be faithful is expressed.
a. God is interested in each individual. Matt. 10:30: "Hairs of your head are numbered." Heb. 4:13: "There is no creature that is not manifest in His sight."
b. As individuals, we must stand before God, and not rest on the virtue of a group.
The Hebrews were benevolent in spirit, but each one was to be praised for this.

unto the fulness of hope

It may also be translated, "to the full assurance of hope". "Fulness of hope" refers to future glory intensified. Hope is an emotion, longing, fervent expectation.

even to the end:

Stedfastness is an exhortation oft repeated. Rev. 2:10: "Be thou faithful unto death." Matt. 10:22 and Col. 1:22-23. "The end" refers to their pilgrimage on earth.

that ye be not sluggish,

Some Christians lack fervor, and show sluggishness when fervency is needed.
a. James 5:16: "Fervent prayer of a righteous man availeth much."
b. Rom. 12:11: "Fervent in spirit, serving the Lord."
A sluggard condition is awful in the sight of God.
a. It is conceited. Pro. 26:16: "The sluggard is wiser in his own conceit."
b. It is sleepy. Pro. 6:9: "How long wilt thou sleep, O sluggard?"
c. It stands condemned. Rev. 3:16: "— so because thou art lukewarm."

but imitators (from Greek *mimic,* translated "followed")

This is a characteristic of people, for most people imitate. Observe passages on "imitator". I Cor. 11:1: "Be ye imitators of me even as I also am of Christ." I Cor. 4:16: "I beseech you therefore, be ye imitators of me." I Thess. 1:6: "And ye become imitators of us, and of the Lord." 2:14: "For ye brethren become imitators of the churches." We are also to imitate God, as mentioned in Eph. 5:1: "Be ye therefore imitators of God as beloved children."

who through faith and patience inherit the promises

Stedfastness is a characteristic of a strong faith. The backslider will not inherit the blessing, and should not be imitated. This passage does not sound as though salvation is a gift without works.

Study Questions

1022. Is the apostle hopeful for the Hebrews? (v. 9)
1023. Does the text suggest any affection?
1024. What would the expression "better things" refer to, "thorns" or "herbs"?
1025. What things accompany salvation?
1026. Name the conversions in Acts and point out things that could be considered "fruit" or "better things".
1027. Are the "better things" a return to repentance, or general good works? Is the conjunction "and" significant in v. 9?

1028. How is God's character involved in verse 10?
1029. What charges may be brought against a forgetter?
1030. Is God duty-bound to honor good works? Always? Cf. Matt.
1031. What is the work of the Hebrews which is deserving of honor?
1032. How is service to our fellow man an evidence of love for God?
1033. Is this always true?
1034. Is service to our fellow man service to God?
1035. What did Jesus say? Matt. 25:40.
1036. What did Jesus say? I John 4:20.
1037. What does Heb. 5:12 give as a clue to their trouble?
1038. How may we account for the fact that they were strong on the "social gospel"?
1039. What is Paul's desire for individuals in verse 11?
1040. Is he saying that, as a group, they could be commended for works, but, individually, they could not?
1041. What is meant by "fulness of hope"?
1042. How long is it to be maintained?
1043. Does this verse teach that there is no hope for people who lack diligence?
1044. Describe a sluggish spiritual condition.
1045. Compare James 5:16 and Romans 12:11 with regard to sluggishness.
1046. Could sluggishness and the lukewarmness of Rev. 3:16 be the same?
1047. What is meant by the exhortation to "be imitators"?
1048. Whose examples are we to follow?
1049. Could this be an allusion to the persons of Chapter Eleven?
1050. Why is he not urging us to imitate God as in Eph. 5.1?
1051. How do we know that he is not doing this?
1052. What two companionate virtues are linked with the receiving of promise?
1053. Is it possible to see the "faith alone" doctrine in this verse?

2. *The example of Abraham.* 6:13-20.

Text
6:13-20

13 For when God made promise to Abraham, since He could swear by none greater, He sware by Himself, 14 saying, Surely blessing I will bless thee, and multiplying I will multiply thee. 15 And thus, having patiently endured, he obtained the promise. 16 For men swear by the greater: and in every dispute of theirs the oath is final for confirmation. 17 Wherein God, being minded to show more abundantly unto the heirs of the promise the immutability of His counsel, interposed with an oath; 18 that by two immutable things, in which it is impossible for God to lie, we may have a strong encouragement, who have fled for refuge to lay hold of the hope set before us: 19 which we have as an anchor of the soul, a hope both sure and stedfast and entering into that which is within the veil; 20 whither as a Forerunner Jesus entered for us, having become a High Priest for ever after the order of Melchizedek.

Paraphrase

13 I say the believing Gentiles, who without doubt are heirs of the promises equally with the Jews: For when God made the promises to Abraham, after he had offered up Isaac, since He could swear by no one greater, He sware by Himself,

14 Saying, Surely I will greatly bless thee, by counting thy faith for righteousness; and I will greatly multiply thee, by giving thee a numerous spiritual seed, whose faith I will in like manner count to them for righteousness.

15 And so, having for many years, patiently waited, Abraham, in the supernatural birth of Isaac, obtained the beginning of the accomplishment of the promise concerning his numerous seed.

16 For men verily swear by greater persons than themselves, whose vengeance they imprecate if they swear falsely: and so an oath for the confirmation of any doubtful matter, is held by them a proper method of ending all contradiction.

17 Therefore, in accommodation to the sentiments of men, God willing more fully to show to all, in every age and nation, who are the heirs of promise, the immutability of His purpose to count their faith for righteousness, and to bestow on them the inheritance of the heavenly country, confirmed the declaration of His purpose with an oath:

18 That by two immutable things, the promise and the oath of God, in which it was impossible for God to lie, we might have strong consolation under the convictions of sin and the terrors of punishment, who have fled away from the curse of the law, like the manslayer from the avenger, to lay hold on the hope of pardon set before us in the promise confirmed by God's oath;

19 Which hope we have as an anchor to which our soul is fastened in this stormy sea of life, both strong and stedfast, because fixed into the place within the veil; that is, into heaven, whither we shall be drawn, by this anchor, as ships are drawn to the place where their anchors are fixed;

20 Into which place a Forerunner hath entered on our account, to fix our hope of pardon and eternal life as an anchor, even Jesus, Who, being made an High-priest for ever like Melchizedek, can procure pardon for us as a Priest, and save us eternally through His power as a king.

Comment

For when God made promise to Abraham

    The occasions of the promise, Gen. 12:1; his call, Gen. 15, Gen. 22:15-18. The content, 12:1-3.
    He was to be blessed in seven ways:
a. Abraham would be personally blessed.
b. He would have numerous descendants.
c. Through him the Messiah would come.
d. His spiritual followers would be great. Rom. 4:11, 16.
e. His name would be great.
f. God would curse them that cursed him.
g. He would be a blessing to the whole world.
    Observe that "promise" is singular, but has several features, Gen. 12:1-3. Abraham is a good example of faith and perserverence.

since He could swear by none greater He sware by Himself

    The occasion — Gen. 22:16-17: "By myself I have sworn, saith Jehovah, because thou hast done this thing, and hast not withheld thy son, thine only son — " The swearing is to make binding the promise.

6:14-17   HELPS FROM HEBREWS

saying, surely blessing I will bless thee, and multiplying I will multiply thee

    This is a Hebraism (Hebrew idiom) of intensity. This is expressed in Gen. 22:17.

having patiently endured

    What trials did we have?
a. Called to a strange land, living in tents, digging wells.
b. Lot was a source of worry.
c. Called to give his son. Gen. 22:15-18.
d. Sorrow for Sodom and Gomorrah.

    It covered about 100 years, from the departure from Haran to being gathered with his people. See Gen. 11:31; 12:4. Terah was 205, Abraham 75 when he departed out of Haran. We must patiently endure. Heb. 12:1: "Let us run the race with patience." 10:36: "For ye have need of patience, that having done the will of God, ye may receive the promise." Preachers must exercise it. I Tim. 6:11: "O man of God, flee these things and follow."

he obtained the promise

    Milligan: "The promise confirmed by the oath." Gen. 22:15-18.
    He lived long enough to see most of the promises fulfilled.
a. The promise had several features, and Abraham saw them fulfilled in Christ.
    Milligan, page 258, says that Abraham was received by God into His rest.

For men swear by the greater, and in every dispute of theirs the oath is final for confirmation

    In a promise, the assertation of an intention is made. In an oath, the person's character is publicly and solemnly put behind the assertion. In a promise, we look at words; in an oath, we look at who and what the promiser is.

Wherein God being minded to show more abundantly unto the heirs of the promise.

    God desired to show in a greater way his plan for his people.
a. Since man everywhere acknowledges the value of an oath, God condescended to give an oath.

b. This was to show to the family of Abraham God's plan to carry out His promise.

Primarily this was assurance intended to console and to encourage.

the immutability of His counsel

"Immutable" means to be unchangeable, invariable. Both Jew and Gentile are included in God's plan, Acts 2:39. God's good tidings are expressed as counsel.

a. Men need advice, counsel and guidance, and God is able to give it.
b. Man's changeable opinions are not to be compared with God's unchanging counsel.

interposed with an oath

"Interposed" is also translated "mediated." This is to make His promise double sure.

God calls attention to His divine being and pledges to fulfill His promises.

that by two immutable things

What are the "two things"?

a. Calvin says the two things are, (1) what He says; and (2) what He swears is immutable.
b. Some suggest the two things are:
1. The promise.
2. The oath.
c. Others say two oaths are referred to.
1. The promise — the oath made to Abraham respecting a Son, the Messiah.
2. The second refers to Christ's priesthood, recorded in Ps. 110:4: "Jehovah hath sworn and will not repent. Thou art a priest forever after the order of Melchizedek.
d. It seems the two immutable things appear in verse 17:
1. The promise.
2. The oath.
God's words are dependable words. Num. 23:19; Ps. 12:1-7.

in which it is impossible for God to lie

The character of God would be altered if He lied.
a. God would cease to be God if He were untruthful.

b. If He could not carry out His promise, He would not be all-wise.

God is absolute, hence there is the impossibility of Him being anything less than true.

we may have a strong encouragement

This may also be translated, "strong consolation." This is the influence of the two immutable things. With so much encouragement, why should we fail to find refuge?

who have fled for refuge

An allusion to the cities of refuge is made here. See Ex. 21:13; Num. 35; Deut. 19; Josh. 20. Three cities on each side of the Jordan afforded an opportunity of safety, or refuge, to evil men. The Christian has refuge in Jesus Christ.

to lay hold of the hope set before us

This we must do if we expect to attain. I Tim. 6:12: "Lay hold on eternal life, whereunto thou art also called and hast professed a good profession before many witnesses." I Tim. 6:19: "laying up in store for themselves a good foundation against the time to come, that they may lay hold on the life which is life indeed." This shows man's responsibility.

which we have as an anchor of the soul

An anchor gives stability.

a. A sea captain said once to young man, "Wherever you go, go to church. I find that it costs a little to anchor my ship, but that keeps it from drifting out onto the waves where it will be lost."
b. Observe that "fled" is past tense in v. 18b. This is present tense.

Our hope seems to be the "anchor".
a. Hope is an emotion of the heart. It is very important, for men will work, suffer, as long as there is hope.
b. Without hope, man grasps at straws and flounders in futility.

a hope

What is included?
a. Resurrection.
b. Mansions in the sky.

c. Second coming of Christ, I Thess. 4:13-18; II Peter 3:12-18.
Our hope rests in the Person of Christ.

both sure and stedfast

Until a soul enters into God, it finds nothing stable.
a. A ship is worth little if its anchor is not adequate.
b. Because of the nature of God and the accomplishments of Christ, we may rest in confidence.
As long as the anchor holds, the Christian rides the waves in spite of troubled waters.

and entering into that which is within the veil

Are we to enter? Who is referred to in this verse?
a. If this is so of us, he is teaching that the Christian by faith now should enter into the spiritual reward hidden behind the veil.
b. Forgiveness is within the veil, so in a sense the Christians enter within the veil as they enter into forgiveness.
Is he not saying Jesus entered, this verse going with the next?
a. No one claims inspiration for the insertion of verse numerals.
1. In 1551 Sir Robert Stephens was the first to divide any part of the Bible into verses.
2. This was done in a Greek New Testament about 300 years after the division into chapters by Cardinal Hugo.
b. The expression can well go with verse 19.
Milligan raises the question, "Is it the hope, or is it the anchor that enters within the veil?"
a. Let the expression go with verse 19 and his problem is solved.
b. The author surely is not mixing the figures of "anchor" and "veil".

whither as a forerunner

A forerunner is a common experience of men.
a. Pioneer travelers had their scouts.
b. Armies had their forerunners.
c. Children of Israel had theirs.
d. Jesus had John the Baptist.
e. We have Jesus.
The word is also translated "precursor."
a. "Precursor" means "runner, harbinger, omen".

b. It is used in the Septuagint to designate the first ripe grapes and figs. Num. 13:20; Isaiah 28:4.
   Vincent has the idea that Christ goes nowhere but where his people can go also.

Jesus entered for us

He entered ahead of us and for us.
Murray: "There was a veil that separated man from God. Jesus came from within to live without the veil and rend it and open a way for us. We may enter in and dwell therein the power of the Holy Ghost."

having become a high priest forever after the order of Melchizedek

The priesthood of Aaron was temporary, but Christ's priesthood is after an eternal one. A priest of Christ's ability eliminates any need for one on earth.
Who was Melchizedek?
a. He was a man. Heb. 7:4
b. He was a person of whom little is known.
1. He is named eight times in Hebrews.
2. He is named twice in the Old Testament. Gen. 14; Ps. 110.

Study Questions

1054. In verses 13-20, what great example has Paul given?
1055. What seven features appear in the promise in Gen. 12:1-3?
1056. The word "promise" is singular, but can you name various times that God promised?
1057. What clue is given in this verse as to what event in Abraham's life may be involved here?
1058. What is the swearing? When did God swear to Abraham?
1059. Does this verse refer to Gen. 12 or Gen. 22:16?
1060. Why did God swear by Himself?
1061. What singular act did Abraham do to cause God to swear? Cf. 22:16-17.
1062. What is the significance of the double expressions in vs. 14?
1063. What did Abraham patiently endure? Name some instances.
1064. How many years did he endure?
1065. Compare Paul's exhortation to us in Heb. 12:1 with 10:36.

1066. What did Abraham obtain — all of the seven promises in Gen. 12?
1067. If not, if Abraham did not see all of them fulfilled, how can it be said that he obtained?
1068. What is the significance of verse 16?
1069. What is the difference between a promise and an oath?
1070. For confirmation, which do we consider the most important?
1071. What is the difference between man's oath and God's oath?
1072. Define "God being minded".
1073. What was He minded to do?
1074. Is this what is meant by "more abundantly"?
1075. Who was this evidence for, Abraham or his descendants?
1076. Define the word "immutable".
1077. In what way could the promises and oath be considered counsel?
1078. Define "interposed with an oath".
1079. Explain what the oath does for a promise.
1080. What are the two immutable things of verse 18?
1081. Could it refer to two oaths, or to a promise and an oath?
1082. If God lied, what would it do to His character?
1083. If God could not carry out a promise, what would it do to His being?
1084. How can a swearing to Abraham be an encouragement to us of the 20th century?
1085. Describe the allusion to Old Testament cities of refuge.
1086. What is our refuge? Where is it stated?
1087. What are we to do with our hope?
1088. Whose responsibility is it?
1089. What figure of speech is referred to in v. 19?
1090. What is the purpose of an anchor?
1091. What is our "anchor"?
1092. How does our "anchor" serve to link us with the future?
1093. What happens when men give up hope?
1094. Can you tell the difference between faith and hope?
1095. In Whom is our hope?
1096. What things make up our hope?
1097. Is our hope a "what", or a "whom" here?
1098. What words describe our hope?
1099. Is this a description of Christ?

1100. Is it our hope that is described as sure and steadfast, or is Christ described as sure and steadfast?
1101. Who is referred to as entering into the veil?
1102. If Christ is referred to, why is it not expressed in past tense, — as being done at His ascension?
1103. Now look again at "lay hold" — are we to lay hold on hope, or on Christ?
1104. Is it "hope" or "anchor" that enters the veil?
1105. If the Christian is entering, what does he enter into?
1106. Is it the veil that he enters, or is it something contained within?
1107. Is verse 20 an enlargement on verse 19, that Christ entered the veil, or that we should be encouraged to enter since Christ entered ahead of us?
1108. What is the purpose of a forerunner?
1109. What is meant, "He entered for us"?
1110. If He did it for us, do we have to enter?
1111. What is the purpose of the entering?
1112. Why did He have to do it this way?

Multiple Choice Over Chapter Six

1. All of us should show diligence to the full assurance of hope:
   1. Until we are saved by faith.
   2. Unto the end.
   3. For we know we can't be lost.
2. The person whose seed was to be multiplied in generations to come, according to a promise was:
   1. Omri of Israel.
   2. Jonah of Ninevah.
   3. Abraham of Ur.
3. Therefore, leaving the principles of the doctrine of Christ, let us go on unto:
   1. A Christlike spirit.
   2. A likeness of Paul.
   3. Perfection.
4. The writer was persuaded of better things and the things:
   1. That characterize a converted Jew.
   2. That would prove that they listened to the preacher.
   3. That accompany salvation.

5. God's oath was made firm when He swore:
   1. By His only begotten Son.
   2. By Abraham.
   3. By Himself.
6. Those who were once enlightened and tasted the heavenly gifts Paul says were made partakers:
   1. Of the Holy Spirit.
   2. Of Paul's suffering.
   3. Of the vengeance of pagan rulers.
7. The Christian has a forerunner:
   1. He is John the Baptist because everyone knows that he prepared the way for Christ.
   2. Melchizedek, because he entered into Canaan, a type of Heaven.
   3. Christ, because the scripture says so.
8. This chapter speaks of some men:
   1. That put Christ to an open shame.
   2. Will help Him as a High Priest.
   3. That are to be excused for ignorance.
9. In this chapter a group is mentioned:
   1. That very likely would repent.
   2. That needed to be taught repentance.
   3. That it is impossible to renew them unto repentance.
10. The heirs of the promise of God have been shown:
    1. The immutability of His counsel.
    2. That He will readily change His mind.
    3. That it is easy to be a Christian.
11. The Christian has:
    1. An anchor of the soul.
    2. A chart of the dark valley.
    3. A blueprint for his life.
12. The author says God cannot lie, as seen by:
    1. The fact that it is wrong.
    2. Two immutable things.
    3. The fact that Jesus is the truth.
13. A commendable thing is stated about the people to whom this book was written.
    1. They defended the church.
    2. They refused all Judaistic practices.
    3. They ministered unto the saints.

14. The person who falls away is likened:
    1. To the soil that grows thistles.
    2. To a tumbling weed that is not anchored.
    3. To a mountain climber who slips on a treacherous trail.
15. We are told to press on to perfection, which is beyond:
    1. A foundation of repentance from dead works.
    2. The Mosaic law.
    3. The Sermon on the Mount.
16. Abraham obtained the promise:
    1. Having helped God to answer prayer.
    2. Having patiently endured.
    3. Since it was easily answered.
17. The "teachings of baptisms" is also translated:
    1. Baptism of the Holy Spirit.
    2. Immersion three times.
    3. Washings.
18. This chapter speaks of those who were once enlightened:
    1. Falling away.
    2. Being blinded by too much light.
    3. Always remaining in the light.
19. Speaking of encouragement, he says we may have:
    1. Everyone's encouragement.
    2. Self-encouragement.
    3. Strong encouragement.
20. One allusion to the Old Testament worship in the temple is:
    1. The veil.
    2. The court of Gentiles.
    3. The ark of the covenant.

SUMMARY OF CHAPTER SIX

Chapter Six is a continuation of the rebuke introduced in Chapter Five for failure to reach maturity in the Christian life. It begins with a strong exhortation to make progress, and points out the tragic consequences of apostasy. No new motive for repentance can be found for those who turn away from Christ to put themselves again in that group which crucified the Lord.

In spite of their sluggishness, the author hoped that those to whom he was writing would respond to his message about the completeness of Christianity as expressed in a life of faithful devotion to Christ. The example of Abraham is cited for their encouragement. They also are reminded that the sure, steadfast hope rests on Jesus, who is High Priest after the order of Melchizedek.

III. *Seven proofs of the superiority of Christ's priesthood. 7:1-10:39.*
A. *He is a Priest after a higher order than Aaron. 7:1-19.*
1. *As seen in Melchizedek as a type. 7:1-3.*

Text
7:1-3

1 For this Melchizedek, king of Salem, priest of God Most High, who met Abraham returning from the slaughter of the kings and blessed him, 2 to whom also Abraham divided a tenth part of all (being first, by interpretation, King of righteousness, and then also King of Salem, which is, King of peace; 3 without father, without mother, without genealogy, having neither beginning of days nor end of life, but made like unto the Son of God), abideth a priest continually.

Paraphrase

1 Now, that ye may know the nature of Melchizedek's priesthood, to which God likened the priesthood of his Son, I observe, that this Melchizedek, king of Salem, and priest of the Most High God, who met Abraham as he returned from the slaughter of the kings, and blessed him;

2 To whom Abraham imparted even a tenth of all the spoils, (v. 4.), being first, according to the interpretation of his name, King of righteousness, a most righteous king, and next also, King of Salem, which by interpretation, is King of peace, king of a peaceable and virtuous people;

3 Was without father without mother as a priest, so that he was not a priest by descent; and without genealogy in the scripture, consequently there is no evidence of his being related to Abraham in any respect. Moreover, having neither beginning of days nor end of life as a priest, but being made a type of the Son of God, he remained a priest all his life.

For this Melchizedek

No doubt it was a rare thing to find one like Melchizedek living in the midst of idolatry, superstitions, yet being true.

See Milligan for suggestions as to his identity. p. 195.
There are many theories concerning who he was:
a. Christ.
b. Holy Spirit.
c. An angel.
d. Enoch.
e. Shem.
f. An emanation from the Deity.
g. Melchizedek himself.

Scarcity of knowledge about him.
a. Gen. 14: Three short verses.
b. Psalm 110:4: Appears about 1,000 years later.
c. Heb. 7:1: Another 1,000 years later.
It is doubtful that he was Shem, for Shem's geneology is given.
Let him be Melchizedek — be himself.

King of Salem

What is Salem?
a. We know it as Jerusalem.
1. "Salem" meant "peace".
2. "Habitation of peace", or "city of peace", is its name, but it has seldom known peace.
b. This city David later chose as his capital when Hebron was too far south for his united kingdom.

Who were the people over whom he ruled?
a. Gen. 14:18 is the first mention of the City. Melchizedek was king and he was the priest of the Most High God.
b. He seems to have been an actual king, in that others such as the king of Sodom were mentioned in the same words.

priest of God Most High

It seems a little strange that in a country abounding in corruption, a man would be found preserving the pure worship of God.
a. Sodom and Gomorrah was on one side and the Canaanites on the other, yet here was a king who acted also as priest.
b. The world had seemed to turn from God, but here was Melchizedek remaining true.
Christ came into a world of sin, yet he remained true and faithful and became our sinless High Priest.

and met Abraham returning from the slaughter of the kings

    Lot had been taken prisoner, Gen. 14, by several kings.

a. Amrapheal, King of Shinar.
b. Ariock — King of Ellasar.
c. Chedorlaomer — King of Elam.
d. Tidal — King of Nations.

    Abraham completely routed these men and released Lot. Being a priest of the God that Abraham worshipped, we can see why these two would be on friendly terms.

and blessed him

    The blessing:

a. Gen. 14:19: "Blessed be Abraham of the Most High God, possessor of heaven and earth."
The word "who" establishes the fact that Melchizedek did the blessing. Newell, p. 211: "It is idle to contend that Melchizedek was not connected with sacrifice but with blessing only." See Heb. 7:15, 17, 24.

to whom also Abraham divided a tenth part of all

    In Gen. 14:20 it is difficult to find who paid tithes to whom, but this verse leaves no doubt. This act of devotion on the part of Abraham indicated a custom that was practiced in early times.

a. We see Jacob, Gen. 28:22, vowing to tithe.
b. There must have been a custom of divine origin going back to Adam, of which we know little.
Abraham paid voluntarily, but no doubt it was in harmony with what he knew to be an ordinance.

being first by interpretation

    The word or name is translated for us to give its meaning. Words were significant in those days, such as:

a. Eve: "mother of all living".
b. Joshua: "saviour".
Actually, he was king in a double sense.
a. Hebrews defines his name to mean King of **righteousness**, then points out the fact that he was King of Salem.
b. This double relationship likewise fits Christ.

King of Righteousness

    Jesus is also righteousness.
a. Zech. 2:10: "Rejoice, O daughter of Zion, behold thy righteous king cometh unto thee."
It is actually in Christ's priestly function that He becomes our righteousness. See Heb. 9:25-28.

and then also King of Salem, which is King of peace

    Abraham had moved into the territory of Melchizedek, but we see him making a peaceful gesture toward Abraham, the victorious warrior.
a. Gen. 14:18: He brought bread and wine.
b. In Psalm 104:15 we read: "Wine maketh glad the heart of man and bread strengtheneth the heart of man."
This gesture refreshed Abraham's servants, and thus proved Melchizedek's right for receiving the tithe, as well as being king of a city whose name is "peace".

without father without mother

    Since the archeologists find this expression, we know that it was a current expression.
Milligan says, "It is folly to ransack the archives of antiquity with the view of discovering more about him than Genesis 14 tells us." He comes out suddenly from the dark invisible background of the drama of human redemption, then retires forever without leaving any trace of predecessors or successors.
Greeks, Romans, and Jews spoke of a person as being without our parents:
a. When their names were not known — obscure parentage.
b. An orphan.
c. Their gods.

without geneology

    Without traced ancestry. This may mean in his position, for none are recorded before him or after him.

having neither beginning of days nor end of life

    His birth and death are not recorded, as though eternity were ascribed to him. Calvin says this omission of birth and life was done to give us an idea of one above the common order of men. Wescott agrees (p. 173).

The interference is that the silence is intentioned and significant.

but made like unto the Son of God

"Made like" is also translated, "being like". Some say he was like God's Son "in that no lineage is given", but Christ had lineage. Newell: "There is no note of the beginning of his priesthood nor of its ending. He comes on the scene as a continual priest without earthly or human connection."
Milligan says: "Like Jesus, he completely fills up the entire era of his royal priesthood in his own proper person."

abideth a priest continually

The words "continually", "perpetually", "forever" are related terms, and are simply indicative of the period to which they are applied, whether it be long or short. Newell, p. 219: "It does not say that the man Melchizedek is a continual priest today."

Study Questions

1113. Name some ideas that men have concerning who Melchizedek was.
1114. How can we rule Shem out?
1115. How may we account for him in a land of idolatry?
1116. Can we account for him the same as we do Abraham, who was living in a center of moon worship?
1117. What is "Salem", over which he was king?
1118. How do we know that he was not an idolatrous king?
1119. Who would be the "Most High God"?
1120. What is the slaughter of the kings referred to here?
1121. Who had been taken captive?
1122. Name the kings of Genesis 14.
1123. How may we account for the fact that Abraham was able to accomplish a great victory.
1124. May we assume that Abraham was a mighty chieftain leading a vast army?
1125. May we presume that Melchizedek's army helped since he met Abraham on his return?
1126. Who was blessed here? Who blesses, the lesser or the greater?
1127. What all is involved in blessing?

1128. Where did Abraham get an idea of a tithe?
1129. Could this custom be a part of God's original command when Cain disobeyed God?
1130. What is interpreted here?
1131. Was he doubly a king?
1132. Was Jesus King of Righteousness? Cf. Zech. 9:9.
1133. In what way was Melchizedek king of peace?
1134. If he were not, would he be inclined to make war on Abraham, an invader from Ur?
1135. What had he done to prove that he was peaceful? Cf. Gen. 14:18.

2. *As seen in Melchizedek's greatness in his relationship to Abraham. 7:4-10.*

Text
7:4-10

4 Now consider how great this man was, unto whom Abraham, the patriarch, gave a tenth out of the chief spoils. 5 And they indeed of the sons of Levi that receive the priest's office have commandment to take tithes of the people according to the law, that is, of their brethren, though these have come out of the loins of Abraham: 6 but he whose genealogy is not counted from them hath taken tithes of Abraham, and hath blessed him that hath the promises. 7 But without any dispute the less is blessed of the better. 8 And here men that die receive tithes; but there one, of whom it is witnessed that he liveth. 9 And, so to say, through Abraham even Levi, who receiveth tithes, hath paid tithes; 10 for he was yet in the loins of his father, when Melchizedek met him.

Paraphrase

4 Now, consider how great this priest was, to whom, without being either his kinsman or subject, or being commanded by God to do so, even Abraham the father of our nation gave a tenth part of the spoils of the conquered kings:

5 For they verily of the sons of Levi who receive the priesthood by descent from Aaron, have a commandment to tithe the people of Israel only according to the law, that is by tithing the tithes taken from the people by their brethren the Levites, although they have come forth of the loins of Abraham, and in that respect are equal in dignity to the priests;

6 But Melchizedek, who did not derive his pedigree from the progenitors of the sons of Aaron, (See v. 3. note 2.), and who, being a king as well as a priest, did not take tithes for his maintenance tithed Abraham a stranger, and blessed him, although he was the possessor of the promises.

7 Now, without all doubt, the inferior is blessed of his superior. Wherefore, by this transaction also, Melchizedek was shown to be greater than Abraham, both as a king and as a priest.

8 Besides, under the law verily men who at a certain age, ceased to be priests, as if they were dead, take tithes: but under the patriarchal dispensation one took tithes, of whom it is testified by God, that he lived a priest all his life.

9 And as one may say, even Levi, whose children receive tithes from Abraham's children, was tithed by Melchizedek in the person of Abraham:

10 For Levi was yet in the loins of his father Abraham, when Melchizedek met Abraham: So that the consequences of Levi's father's paying tithes and receiving the blessing, extended to Levi and to his children.

Comment

Now consider how great this man was

The apostle's aim here is to exalt the character of Melchizedek, with the view of still further exalting the character and priesthood of Christ.

"Great" — Few men are called great in the Bible.
a. Gen. 12:2: Abraham.
b. II Sam. 7:9: David, "I will make thee a great name."
c. II Kings 4:8: Shunem — a great woman.
d. Luke 1:15: John the Baptist.

upon whom Abraham, the patriarch

"Patriarch" defined:
a. A father or ruler of a family.
b. The progenitor of a race.

Abraham was a great person. Now if he paid tithes to Melchizedek then we can see how great Melchizedek was.

gave a tenth out of the chief spoils

The best tithe is suggested. Milligan says: "The top of the heap." Gen. 14:20 is the account.

The first cities conquered by the Israelites were to be devoted to God. The first fruits, the chief spoils were to be given to God.

and they indeed of the sons of Levi

There is not much difference in rank here, for the priests and people were brethren. There is not as much as in the case of Abraham and Melchizedek. Abraham was a great-grandfather of Levi, Aaron's ancestor.

that receive the priest's office

This refers only to the house of Aaron.
a. Exodus 28:1.
b. Numbers 17:1-11.
See also Numbers 18:22-32.
a. The people were required to pay tithes to the Levites.
b. The Levites were in turn to pay a tithe to the priests.
c. The Levites were the servants of the priests. Num. 18:2-6.

have commandment to take tithes of the people according to the law

This commandment is found in Numbers 18. Support of God's servants is a commandment of God and should be preached.

that is, of their brethren

Brethren received tithes of brethren, though actually we give unto God. The Levites, in receiving and using the tenth, were blessed as the servants of God.

though these have come out of the loins of Abraham

The argument is: Abraham, who excelled all others, was yet inferior to Melchizedek; then Melchizedek had the highest place of honor and is superior to all the sons of Levi. These Levites, although they received offerings, were of the same parents.

but he whose geneology is not counted from them hath taken tithes of Abraham

Melchizedek has no lineage, yet he received tithes from Abraham. This is stated to show the great and high place of Melchizedek.

and hath blessed him that hath the promises

    Abraham had the promise. This indicates the greatness of Melchizedek; the lesser individual had the promise but was blessed.

    There are three kinds of blessings in the scriptures:
a. Matt. 5:44: Prayer for a blessing.
b. Gen. 12: Prophetic blessings as in the case of the patriarchs.
c. Sacerdotal blessing: See Numbers 6:23-27. "Sacerdotal" means, "pertaining to a priest".

but without any dispute the less is blessed of the better

    Melchizedek blessed Abraham; hence, the "less" is Abraham. What does it mean: "bless"?
a. It is a symbol of greater authority.
1. Isaac blessed his son, Jacob.
2. Jacob blessed his grandsons, Ephraim and Manasseh. Gen. 48:20.
3. Priest blessed the people. Num. 6:23.
4. Luke 24:50: Christ blessed the apostles.
b. It indicates great power.

And here men that die receive tithes.

    The tithes were paid to men who died; thus it was an ever-changing priesthood. The word "here" refers to the Levitical system, and "there" to the administration of Melchizedek.

but there one

    Where is "there"? It refers back to Melchizedek. If it referred to paying tithes to Christ now, it would say "here" and not "there."

of whom is it witnessed that he liveth

    The silence of his death is an evidence of his life. He is showing that Melchizedek was perpetual; that of the Levites was temporary. He lives in type. Christ is the antitype. "Witness" is two kinds:
a. That of the eye.
b. That of testimony.
    "Witness": where is the witness?
a. 7:3 is the witness of eternality.
b. No ending is recorded for Melchizedek.

and, so to say, through Abraham even Levi, who receiveth tithes, hath paid tithes

> Through Abraham, Levi paid tithes to Melchizedek. Abraham, by paying tithes, made himself and his posterity inferior to the priesthood of Melchizedek. (Calvin, p. 163.) This is to establish greatness in the type of Christ's priesthood. "Who receiveth tithes" refers to the Levites.
> a. Should the preacher tithe when he has been paid in tithes?
> b. Certainly, for he is as much a steward of God as others.
> The superiority of the ancient order cannot be escaped by verses nine and ten.

For he was yet in the loins of his father, when Melchizedek met him

> Milligan says Levi then actually paid tithes to Melchizedek through the principle of federal representation.
> a. In a corporation, individuals pay, make obligations which bind on others.
> b. If we took our tithes and handed it to our children it would be quite a gift. This is not done, so my children are tithing. Would this also include Jesus, since Judah also was in the loins?
> a. Christ is not of the same order. Matt. 22:45: "If he is the son of David, how does David call Him his Lord?"
> b. Christ did not serve as priest on earth. He could not, for He was not of the Levitical tribe. 8:4.

Study Questions

1136. What is the significance of, "without father without mother"?
1137. Explain "without genealogy". Does this rule out Shem as being Melchizedek?
1138. Explain "neither beginning of days nor end of life".
1139. How was he like unto the Son of God?
1140. How could this be true when Christ has lineage?
1141. Explain "abideth a priest continually".
1142. Does "forever" always mean from the dawn of history until the extremity of the future?
1143. Why does he want us to consider how great Melchizedek was?
1144. Define "patriarch".

HELPS FROM HEBREWS

1145. Why does he say "chief spoils"?
1146. Did God ever require the chief spoils again?
1147. What can be said in this regard concerning Jericho and Ai?
1148. How were the Levites supported?
1149. How were the priests supported?
1150. What function was performed by Levites who were not priests? Cf. Num. 18:2-6.
1151. What is the significance of "tithes from brethren"?
1152. What law were the Levites under?
1153. What is the significance of saying that they, the Levites, came out of the loins of Abraham?
1154. Does this make Melchizedek superior to the Levite?
1155. Who is the "them" referred to in verse six?
1156. Who has the promise?
1157. Who has the blessing?
1158. What does he mean by, "without dispute"?
1159. Give illustrations of greater men blessing the lesser.
1160. Did Jesus ever bless His disciples? Cf. Luke 24:50.
1161. What is meant by, "here men that die receive tithes"?
1162. Was he speaking of the law, or the present church?
1163. What does the word "there" refer to in v. 8?
1164. If it referred to Christ, would it say "there" or "here"?
1165. Who is living in verse 8?
1166. How could it be said that Melchizedek "liveth"?
1167. Who is witnessed as living — Christ or Melchizedek?
1168. What witness is there that Melchizedek lives?
1169. Where is the witness that Melchizedek lives? Cf. 7:3.
1170. Is 7:3 the witness?
1171. From whom did the Levites receive tithes?
1172. Explain verse 9.
1173. Does he mean that Abraham made his posterity inferior to Melchizedek by payment of tithes to Melchizedek?
1174. May we infer that the preacher who receives tithes therefore ought to tithe?
1175. To whom did the Levites pay tithes as argued by verse 9?
1176. How many years before the Levitical priesthood did the Levites tithe through Abraham?

3. *As seen in the imperfection of the Levitical priesthood.* 7:11-19.

7:11-19

Text
7:11-19

11 Now if there was perfection through the Levitical priesthood (for under it hath the people received the law), what further need was there that another priest should arise after the order of Melchizedek, and not be reckoned after the order of Aaron? 12 For the priesthood being changed, there is made of necessity a change also of the law. 13 For He of Whom these things are said belongeth to another tribe, from which no man hath given attendance at the altar.

14 For it is evident that our Lord hath sprung out of Judah; as to which tribe Moses spake nothing concerning priests. 15 And what we say is yet more abundantly evident, if after the likeness of Melchizedek there ariseth another Priest, 16 Who hath been made, not after the law of a carnal commandment, but after the power of an endless life: 17 for it is witnessed of Him,
    Thou art a priest for ever
    After the order of Melchizedek.

18 For there is a disannulling of a foregoing commandment because of its weakness and unprofitableness 19 (for the law made nothing perfect), and a bringing in thereupon of a better hope, through which we draw nigh unto God.

Paraphrase

11 Moreover, to show you the inferiority of the Levitical priesthood to the priesthood of Christ, I ask, If the pardon of sin were really to be obtained through the ministrations of the Levitical priesthood, because on account of establishing that priesthood the Israelites received the law; what farther need was there that a different priest should arise according to the order of Melchizedek, and not to be called according to the order of Aaron? Is not the prediction, of the raising up of a priest of a different order from that of Aaron, a declaration of the inefficacy of the Levitical priesthood, and of God's intention to change it?

12 Wherefore, the priesthood, on account of which the law was given, being changed, of necessity there must be a change also of the law itself.

13 Now, God certainly intended to change the priesthood from the tribe of Levi: For He to Whom He said, Thou art a priest,

was of a different tribe, of which no one ever officiated as a priest at the altar; nor by the law could officiate.

14 For it is very plain from the scriptures, that our Lord Messiah, called by David, (Psalm cx. 1.) his Lord, and to Whom God said, 'Thou art a priest,' was to spring up from Judah; to which tribe Moses spake nothing concerning their obtaining the priesthood.

15 Moreover, it is still more exceedingly plain from God's oath, that, according to the similitude of Melchizedek, a different kind of Priest from the Levitical ariseth, Who, like Melchizedek, will be also a King;— wherefore, since the law was given for the purpose of establishing the priesthood, (ver. 11.), the priesthood being changed, the law must be changed likewise, ver. 12.:—

16 Who is made, not according to the law, whose commandment concerning the priests hath a respect only to their bodily strength, but according to the power of that endless life which He possesses, and by which He can minister as a priest for ever.

17 For God testifieth concerning Him, Thou art a priest for ever according to the order of Melchizedek. Like Melchizedek, thou art a Priest and a King, and shalt continue the only Priest of the people of God, so long as they have any need of the Priest's office.

18 Well, then, the priesthood being changed, there is a total abrogation of the precedent commandment, the law of Moses, because of its weakness in reforming mankind, and its unprofitableness in procuring for sinners;

19 For the law by its priesthood made no one perfect in respect of pardon and access to God: But the after introduction of a better priesthood, as the foundation of a better hope, maketh men perfect in these respects; by which priesthood we worship God acceptably. (See Eph. ii. 18.)

Comment

Now if there was perfection through the Levitical priesthood

> God's full benevolent and saving purpose was not in it. Frail, sinful man, acting as priests, could not be perfect. The Greek word for "perfection" means "properly completed, consummated".

for under it hath the people received the law

This is to say that the law was annexed to the priesthood. It was to show that the priesthood was foundational.
a. With it the law stood or fell.
b. The law then was no ultimate end at which we ought to stop.
c. When the priesthood was changed, naturally the law would go with it.

what further need was there that another Priest arise after the order of Melchizedek, and not be reckoned after the order of Aaron?

If the old system could bring perfection, then why did God speak through David of a change? Cf. Psalms 110:4. The blood of Jesus, not after the order of Aaron, would not have been required if perfection could be gained otherwise.

for the priesthood being changed, there is made of necessity a change also of the law

The Seventh Day Adventists cannot escape this.
a. Gal. 3:21: "If there had been a law given which could have given life, then verily righteousness would have been of law."
b. Gal. 3:23-29.
c. Col. 2:14 states that the law was nailed to the cross.
d. We are not obligated under law to tithe, but we are under love to do more.
1. The law of the tithe is changed, for that is the portion of the law he has dealt with in the tithe.
2. We cannot worship with a tithe, which is already God's, only as we sacrifice beyond the tithe.

For He of whom these things are said

Ps. 110:4: "Jehovah hath sworn and will not repent. Thou art a priest forever, after the order of Melchizedek." All of this discussion is centered upon Christ.

belongeth to another tribe

Jesus came from the house of David, of the tribe of Judah. Jer. 23:5 is the prophecy: "Behold the days cometh, saith Jehovah, that I will raise unto David a righteous branch and he shall reign as King and deal wisely." This shows the completeness of the change. The tribe of Judah was not allowed in the Old Testament to fill the priestly office.

a. II Chron. 26:19: King Uzziah of the tribe of Judah tried it, and became leprous.

from which no man hath given attendance at the altar
The tribe of Judah could not serve at the altar. Christ is a priest contrary to the law.

For it is evident that our Lord hath sprung out of Judah, as to which tribe Moses spake nothing concerning priests
"It is evident that our Lord sprang out of Judah" refers to the geneologies and prophecies. "Which tribe Moses spake nothing concerning priests" indicates the silence.

And what we say is yet more abundantly evident
The argument of silence, he says, is not all of the matter. The author is interested in giving unanswerable argument, and such is found only in the scriptures.

if after the likeness of Melchizedek there ariseth another priest
How was Melchizedek's and Christ's priesthood different from the Levitical?

a. *The Levitical Priesthood*
Many priests
Yearly, repeated sacrifices
Sinful
Final death

b. *Christ's priesthood*
One priest
Once
Sinless
The likeness is in the character of the office.

Who hath been made
The Levites were made priests, not because of superiority, but by carnal descent. Priests were made, appointed, and no one could take the office upon himself.

not after the law of a carnal commandment
Law was added as a temporary thing.
Law was given because of their hardness.
a. Matt. 19:8.
b. Mark 10:5.
Carnality is used here to suggest temporariness.

but after the power of an endless life

Christ is greater than the Levitical priests.
a. Those priests had no power, but our Priest does. Matt. 28:18.
b. Those priests were not kings, but Christ is.
c. Those priests did not have full sympathy, but Christ is touched with our infirmities. Heb. 4:15.
Newell says: "Endlessness is not the best word here, for it is the undying character of the risen Lord that is meant rather than its mere endlessness."

For it is witnessed of Him, Thou art a Priest forever after the order of Melchizedek

"It is witnessed of Him" refers to a testimony.
a. Also translated "it is testified". See Psalm 110:4.
b. The scriptures are the best interpreters of the scriptures. This ought to settle the question with the Jew, for David spoke of it.

for there is a disannulling

The old covenant is done away. It was for the children of Israel only.
a. Lev. 27:34: "These are the commandments which the Lord commanded Moses for the children of Israel on Mount Sinai." "Disannulling is the Greek *athetesis* — the same word as in 9:26 where we have "putting away sin". The disappearance is thorough.

The disannulling is discussed in several books of the New Testament:
a. Rom. 6:14.
b. Rom. 7:4-6.
c. Col. 2:14.
d. Eph. 2:15.

of a foregoing commandment

This refers to the old covenant. The inferiority of the old foregoing commandments is evident.
a. They were never given to the entire human race.
b. The law was given to Israel — to no other. Psalms 147:19-20.
c. The object was to reveal sin, not to save.
d. Its principle was law; the new law is love.

because of its weakness

It could not make alive. I Cor. 15:22: "In Christ all are made alive." It could not take away sin.

a. Heb. 10:4: "For it is impossible that the blood of bulls and goats should take away sins."
b. Only one life could show the real love of God.
  1. Not of cattle.
  2. Not of angels.
  3. Not of men, but Christ's life.
c. Christ's blood is able to take away sins, where other blood was unable to do so.
d. Rom. 3:25: Once for all. Cp. Heb. 9:28.
e. Gal. 3:21: "If there had been a law given which could make alive, verily righteousness would have been of the law."

and unprofitableness

Does this disagree with Gal. 3:24?
a. It brought us to that which is profitable.
b. It was unprofitable in its ability to take away sin.
It must mean that within itself it was unprofitable.

for the law made nothing perfect

It was not sufficient to meet and accomplish God's purpose.
a. Gal. 3:21: "Is the law against the promises of God? God forbid; for if there had been a law given which could make alive, verily righteousness would have been of the law."
b. Rom. 8:3: "For what the law could not do, in that it was weak through the flesh, God, sending His Own Son in the likeness of sinful flesh and for sin, condemned sin in the flesh."
Milligan argues that "Owing to the weakness and imperfection of the flesh (Rom. 8:3) the law perfected nothing."

and a bringing in thereupon of a better hope

All can see the superior hope of the Christian as seen in the power of Christ.
a. Rom. 8:11: "But if the Spirit of Him that raised up Jesus from the dead, dwelleth in you, He that raised up Christ Jesus from the dead shall give life also to your mortal bodies through His Spirit that dwelleth in you."
The wise person should always take the better when it is offered.

through which we draw nigh unto God

It is Christ, John 14:6, the Way, our Hope, which brings us nigh unto God. We may define our Hope in particulars, such as new body, new home, etc., but the fact remains that Christ is our Hope.

Study Questions

1177. Does verse 11 indicate that the law that contained the Levitical priesthood was not adequate?
1178. In what way did it lack perfection?
1179. What is actually meant by the word "perfect" here?
1180. Does this verse say that the law was affixed to an already existing priesthood?
1181. Who did Jacob and his sons pay tithes to?
1182. Jacob vowed to tithe. Who received it?
1183. The inability of the law called for what?
1184. Why couldn't it have been that God would improve the Aaronic priesthood instead of reckoning it after Melchizedek?
1185. When God changed priesthoods, what else did he also change?
1186. What does this do to the Seventh Day Adventist doctrine?
1187. Why did the law have to be changed? Cf. Gal. 3:21.
1188. What does this verse do to the law of tithe?
1189. Are we obligated more since we are under a greater priesthood?
1190. Can it be said that Jesus is a Priest contrary to the law of Moses?
1191. Is this an argument from silence — nothing said, nothing condemned?
1192. Of what tribe did Jesus come?
1193. What is the evidence?
1194. What did Moses have to say?
1195. What did the prophets say?
1196. If Christ had been of the tribe of Levi, would it have been as complete a change?
1197. What happened to King Uzziah of Judah when he tried to act as priest? Cf. II Chron. 26:19.
1198. Is the author through arguing the case according to v. 15?

1199. What is the more abundant argument? Is all of it found in v. 15?
1200. Name the differences in Christ's priesthood and the Levitical one.
1201. How is Christ's like that of Melchizedek?
1202. How were the Levitical priests chosen?
1203. Was it because of superiority over the other tribes?
1204. What is meant by, "carnal commandment"?
1205. Why was the law given at all? Cf. Matt. 19:8 and Mark 10:5.
1206. Whose endless life is referred to here?
1207. Could it be said that Melchizedek's endless life had power?
1208. What is meant by endless life?
1209. Is the word "after" a period of time?
1210. Describe the power that Christ had that these priests did not have.
1211. A witness is referred to here. What is witnessed? v. 17.
1212. What is the witness? Could it be Psalm 110:4?
1213. What word could be used in place of "witness"?
1214. Define the word "disannulling."
1215. Was the law a universal law? Cf. Psalm 147:19, 20; Lev. 27:34.
1216. If it was for the Jews only, how much was there a need for a universal law?
1217. Compare the disannulling expression with Rom. 6:14; 7:4-6; Col. 2:14; Eph. 2:15.
1218. What does the "foregoing commandment" refer to?
1219. If there were ten, why is it singular here?
1220. In what ways was the earlier commandment inferior to Christ's covenant?
1221. In what way was it weak?
1222. Could it make man alive? Cf. I Cor. 15:22.
1223. Could it take away sin? Cf. Heb. 10:4.
1224. Could anything less than Christ demonstrate so great a love?
1225. Was the law of no value when he says that it was unprofitable?
1226. Gal. 3:24 says something was a "tutor". What was it?
1227. In what realm was the law unprofitable?

1228. He says that the law made nothing perfect? Is this the fault of the law or of the men to whom it was directed? Cf. Rom. 8:3; Gal. 3:21.
1229. Was there ever a perfect person under the law?
1230. What brought in a better hope — the law?
1231. Was it the law of Moses, or the new priestly system?
1232. Why do you think so?
1233. Read the 18th and 19th verses as one sentence to give the true exegesis.
1234. Should we not always take the better of two ways?
1235. Name the ways in which our better hope works.
1236. What is it in this verse that helps us to draw nigh unto God?
1237. Is he saying that Christ is our Hope, and it is through Him that we draw nigh unto God?

B. *He is a priest made with an oath.* 7:20-22.

Text
7:20-22

20 And inasmuch as it is not without the taking of an oath 21 (for they indeed have been made priests without an oath; but He with an oath by Him that saith of Him,

The Lord sware and will not repent Himself,

Thou art a priest forever);

22 by so much also hath Jesus become the surety of a better covenant.

Paraphrase

20 Moreover, that the Gospel is a better and more effectual covenant than the law, is evident; for in as much as not without an oath Jesus the Mediator of the Gospel covenant was made a Priest:

21 For Aaron and his sons verily were made priests without an oath; but Jesus was made a Priest with an oath, in which an unchangeable priesthood was conferred on Him by God, Who said to Him, The Lord hath sworn, and will not repent of the appointment, Thou art a Priest forever, according to the order of Melchizedek:

22 I say, inasmuch as by the oath of God an unchangeable priesthood was conferred on Him, by so much was Jesus made the Mediator of a more permanent and effectual covenant than the Sinaitic.

Comment

And inasmuch as it is not without the taking of an oath

Psalm 110:4 expresses this oath. This is more of the abundant evidence.
a. God's oath is to show the certainty and immutability of the thing sworn.
1. He swore to Abraham. Gen. 22:16-18.
2. He swore that Israel would not enter his rest. Deut. 1:35.
3. He swore that Moses would not enter Canaan. Deut. 4:21.
4. He swore that David and his seed would endure. Psa. 89.4.
b. Now Christ's priesthood is sworn to, to show its unchangeableness. The Levitical priesthood not being sworn to indicates that it was temporary.

For they indeed have been made priests without an oath, but He with an oath by Him that saith of Him, The Lord sware and will not repent Himself, Thou art a Priest forever

"For they indeed have been made priest without an oath" indicates a contract.
a. Their priesthood came by natural descent.
b. The value of the covenant is determined by the presence or absence of an oath.

An oath is something final and determinative in nature. "But He with an oath" shows the superiority of Christ's priesthood. This is found in Psalm 110:4. "By him that saith of Him" indicates God's oath. "The Lord sware and will not repent Himself, Thou art a Priest forever, indicates the unchangeable priesthood.

by so much also hath Jesus become the surety of a better covenant

"By so much" — a term of measurement.
a. Heb. 1:4: A fuller revelation.
b. Heb. 3:3: "More honor."
c. Heb. 7:22: Better covenant.
d. Heb. 8:6: Better ministry.
e. Heb. 9:14: Complete cleansing.

"... hath Jesus become the surety" has the idea of "binding."
a. The Greek word for "surety" is *egguos,* and appears only here.
1. It means a sponsor or bondswoman.
2. Acts 17:30-31: It gives the idea of final evidence.

"Of a better covenant" ought to be of interest to all:

a. See Heb. 8:6, which says it is better because of better promises involved.
b. Most people realize the superiority of anything new over the old, except those who deal with antiques.
1. Too many are interested in religious antiques.
2. The new covenant with a superior priest and promises should be preferred.

Study Questions

1238. What was without an oath, or is this what the author says?
1239. Where is the oath recorded? Cf. Psalm 110:4.
1240. Is this more of the abundant evidence of v. 15?
1241. What other times did God swear? Cf. Gen. 22:16-18; Deut. 4:21; 8:1.
1242. If the Levitical priesthood was not sworn to, what can be assumed?
1243. What was the content of the oath?
1244. If the Levitical priests were not appointed by an oath, how were they appointed?
1245. Is the value of a priesthood determined by the oath?
1246. What is meant by "will not repent Himself"?
1247. What is meant by the expression, "by so much"?
1248. What is implied by the word "surety"?
1249. What is the surety of?
1250. How is it a better covenant? Cf. Heb. 1:4; 3:3; 7:22; 8:6; 9:14.

C. *He is an unchangeable priest.* 7:23-25.

Text
7:23-25

23 And they indeed have been made priests many in number, because that by death they are hindered from continuing: 24 but He, because He abideth forever, hath His priesthood unchangeable. 25 Wherefore also He is able to save to the uttermost them that draw near unto God through Him, seeing He ever liveth to make intercession for them.

Paraphrase

23 Besides, Jesus our High Priest is more powerful than the Levitical high priests in this respect, that they indeed are many priests, because they are hindered by death from continuing;

24 But He, because He liveth forever in the body, (see v. 25. note), hath a priesthood which shall never pass from Him to any other person on account of incapacity.

25 On which account He is even forever able to save all who approach to God through His mediation; always living an High Priest (v. 8, 24.) to make affectionate intercession with God for them.

And they indeed have been made priests many in number, because that by death they are hindered from continuing

> The old law had to have many priests because they were subject to death, and successors had to be trained. The new covenant has one eternal Priest since He is not subject to death.

but He, because He abideth forever, hath His priesthood unchangeable

> With early priests you might have a sympathetic priest today, and a different one tomorrow. Christ is the same always, perfection always. What a consolation this is!

Wherefore also He is able to save to the uttermost

> Christ is able to save, without doubt.
> a. We have One Who is able; all others are unable.
> b. "Uttermost" means "to the extreme, completely".
> This is a contrast to the feebleness of the old covenant.
> a. No sinner is too deep in sin to be gone.
> b. No condition of man is too far away for God through Christ to save.

them that draw near unto God

> This job is never done. We must always draw near. I Cor. 9:26. Christianity is a growth; we keep on drawing near. Phil. 3:14.

Study Questions

1251. What is the purpose of pointing out the many priests of the old system?
1252. How is Christ's priesthood superior in relationship to time?
1253. What value is there in having Christ as an eternal priest?

1254. If Christ was perfect on earth, what consolation have we about Him now?
1255. What assurance do we have that His priesthood will be changeless?
1256. What is Christ able to do?
1257. How does the ability of Christ compare to that of the false saviors of men?
1258. "Unto the uttermost" has what significance?
1259. Is the idea of "uttermost" in contrast to the feebleness of the Jewish covenant?
1260. Where does salvation take place — here or hereafter?
1261. What qualification is there to salvation?
1262. How about the people who never draw nigh?
1263. Do we ever actually get so close to God that we do not need to keep drawing near? Cf. I Cor. 9:26.

D. *He is a sinless priest.* 7:26-28.

Text
7:26-28

26 For such High Priest became us, holy, guileless, undefiled, separated from sinners, and made higher than the heavens; 27 Who needeth not daily, like those high priests, to offer up sacrifices, first for His Own sins, and then for the sins of the people: for this He did once for all, when He offered up Himself. 28 For the law appointeth men high priests, having infirmity; but the word of the oath, which was after the law, appointeth a Son, perfected for evermore.

Paraphrase

26 Now such an High Priest as Christ was suited to our exigencies, who being holy in affection, harmless in conduct, undefiled by those with whom He conversed, separated from sinners, and higher than all the inhabitants of the heavens, the angels;

27 He hath not, like the Levitical high priests, need from time to time to offer sacrifices, first for His Own sins, and then for the sins of the people. For Himself He offered no sacrifice; and for the sins of the people He offered sacrifice only once, when He offered up Himself.

28 The sons of Aaron needed to offer sacrifice for themselves, because the law constituteth men high priests who are sinners;

but the declaration of the oath, which happened after the law was given, constituted the Son an High Priest, Who is perfectly fitted for executing the office for evermore, by His absolute freedom from sin, and by His endless life.

Comment

For such a high priest became us

The writer says we ourselves needed such a high priest, and he became all that we needed. "Became us" probably refers to the partaking of Christ's human flesh with us in order that we might partake of his salvation.

holy

The word "holy" means "godlike, pious, devout".
The Levitical priesthood was sometimes corrupt.
a. Greedy. I Sam. 2:13-17.
b. Drunken. Isaiah 28:7.
c. Profane and wicked. I Sam. 2:22-24.
d. Unjust. Jeremiah 6:13.
e. Corruptors of the law. Isaiah 28:7; Mal. 2:8.
f. Slow to sanctify themselves for God's service. II Chron. 29:34.
Christ offered himself without spot or blemish. Heb. 9:14.

guileless

It is also translated "harmless".
a. The cleansing of the temple at first seems an exception, but note that He did no one harm.
b. No evil intent was intended.
"Guileless" means "without malice or ill will to anyone".
a. The prayer on the cross proved it.
b. His compassion on earth proved it also.
"Guile" means "deceitfulness, cunning". "Guileless" means that one is without these traits.

undefiled

Priests could be disqualified for sin or some blemish, but Christ was not defiled. The devil tried to defile Him with sin, but He refused.

separated from sinners

He ate with them, which brought criticism, but He was separate. Matt. 9:10-13; Matt. 11:19.

Heb. 4:15: He was tempted in all points like as we are, yet without sin.
a. Although He ate with sinners, yet He cannot be named among them.
b. His flesh did not see corruption as does that of sinners.
At the right hand of God, He is separated from sinners.

and made higher than the heavens

Other expressions that are similar:
a. Eph. 4:10: He is exalted far above all heavens.
b. Eph. 1:20-21.
The idea is to show His supremacy over all creation. This exaltation does not change His affections.

who needeth not daily like those high priests

The high priest was officially the head of the priesthood, and was responsible for the daily sacrifices. The contrast is found between "daily" and "one" sacrifice.

to offer up sacrifices first for His Own sins

The method of sacrifice:
a. The victim was brought to the north side of the altar of burnt offering, and there the sinner was required to lay his hand upon its head and kill it. Lev. 1:4-5; 3:2, 8, 13; 4:4.
b. If the whole congregation sinned, the elders were required to act as their representatives. Lev. 4:15.
c. On the day of Atonement, the high priest performed this. First he offered a young bullock for himself and his house. Lev. 16:11-16.
The earthly priest had his own sins to concern him as well as the people's sins who were under him.

for this He did once for all

Christ's sacrifice reaches out to all men everywhere. This sacrifice is so complete that it needs no repetition.

when He offered up Himself.

Here is the superiority of Christ over every high priest. This is only a part of it. God delivered up Christ.
Acts 2:23: "Him being delivered up by the determinate counsel and foreknowledge of God, ye by the hand of lawless men did crucify and slay."

Christ's sacrifice of self was sufficient. Remember, Christ laid down His life.
a. John 10:15-18.
b. John 13:37.

For the law appointeth men high priests
Their place was not assumed, but came by appointment. Ex. 29:44; Num. 3:3. The tribe of Levi and the house of Aaron, of course, were men of human frailty.

having infirmity
The priests were not always ideal, but wicked, proud and ambitious.
Aaron, the first priest, made a golden calf and encouraged the people to worship idols. Ex. 32:1-19.
They were to be perfect physical specimens, however.

but the word of the oath which was after the law
David spoke after the law, being second king of Israel, which dispensation followed the judges. This oath is found in Psalm 110:4.

appointeth a Son perfected forevermore
Although Christ was compassed by trial, temptation and difficulties, we see no infirmity in Him. He now accomplishes the will of God forevermore.

Study Questions

1264. Is drawing near equivalent to Christian growth? Phil. 3:14.
1265. If we cease to grow, are we failing to draw nigh?
1266. In verses 26-28 what is Paul's main discussion?
1267. How do you explain "became us"?
1268. Would it refer to Christ's partaking of human flesh?
1269. Does it mean that He became *like* us or *for* us?
1270. Define this first attribute of Christ.
1271. Was this true of the priests of Christ's day?
1272. What sins were the priests guilty of in Old Testament times? II Chron. 29:34. Cf. I Sam. 2:13-17; Isaiah 28:7; Jer. 6:13; I Sam. 2:22-24; Mal. 2:8.
1273. What can be said of Christ's sacrifice in regard to holiness? Cf. Heb. 9:14.

1274. What is meant by "guile"?
1275. Define "guileless".
1276. What other word is found in some versions?
1277. If it means harmless", was His cleansing of the temple an exception?
1278. Did Christ ever prove that He was without ill will?
1279. What did His compassion show?
1280. What did His prayer on the cross reveal?
1281. What attempts were made to defile Him?
1282. How did the Jews try to defile Him?
1283. How did the apostles unconsciously try to do it?
1284. With what is man defiled?
1285. When did this separation take place?
1286. Did He separate Himself from sinners while on earth?
1287. Did men misunderstand Him for associating with sinful people? Cf. Matt. 9:10-13; 11:19.
1288. Do we face such situations today?
1289. What is meant by "heavens"?
1290. Is this verse referring to location or rank?
1291. See what Eph. 4:10 and Eph. 1:20-21 have to say.
1292. Quote Peter on Pentecost when he dealt with a similar thought.
1293. In what way is Christ higher?
1294. Does this exaltation show His supremacy over the earth and heavens?
1295. What contrast is there with the word "daily"?
1296. What, officially, was the duty of high priests of men?
1297. How did the high priests go about making sacrifices for themselves?
1298. How did the high priest go about making sacrifices for other individuals?
1299. How did they make the sacrifices for a congregation?
1300. Did Jesus have to sacrifice for Himself? If not, why not?
1301. What is the significance of "He did once"?
1302. How universal is His sacrifice?
1303. Does "all" mean all men of all races?
1304. Why did man's sacrifice need repetition?
1305. When he offered himself, was this in contrast to Old Testament priestly sacrifices?
1306. It says that he "offered up himself". Do all the scriptures speak thus? Cf. Acts 2:23.

1307. Did Christ lay down His life, according to other verses? John 10:15-18; 13:37.
1308. What did Jesus say to Peter that would prove that Christ was laying down His life when Peter had a sword?
1309. What did Jesus say to His disciples who tried to keep Him from Jerusalem?
1310. What is the significance of the word "law"? What law? How did men get to be priests? Cf. Ex. 29:44; Num. 3:3.
1311. How may we explain priests having infirmities, when they were to be perfect specimens?
1312. Do you think that preachers ought today to be good specimens physically, mentally, spiritually?
1313. What does the word "infirmity" mean?
1314. Did Aaron ever show a lack of strength of character?
1315. What is meant by "the oath which was after the law"?
1316. Where is the oath found?
1317. Who spoke it? What is the date for David?
1318. Did Jesus ever show any weakness of resolution?
1319. Was His prayer in the garden an indication of infirmity?
1320. What shows Him to have been above weakness in resolution in His prayer on the cross?
1321. What is His appointment in this verse?
1322. How could He be appointed a Son?

Multiple Choice Over Chapter Seven

1. Melchizedek:
   1. Was king of Judah.
   2. King of love.
   3. King of Abraham.
   4. King of Salem.
2. Melchizedek:
   1. Was without mother and father.
   2. Without subjects.
   3. Without the plan of God.
3. Abraham gave to Melchizedek:
   1. A vow to be at peace with him.
   2. Tithe.
   3. A warning that God would destroy him.
4. In speaking of blessings in regard to Abraham and Melchizedek, it is stated:
   1. That the less is blessed by the greater.

2. Melchizedek was blessed more.
   3. Together they blessed God.
5. King of Salem means:
   1. King of war.
   2. King of peace.
   3. King of solemn things.
6. Melchizedek met a famous person returning from the slaughter of kings named:
   1. Saul.
   2. David.
   3. Abraham.
7. Melchizedek is a type of:
   1. Moses.
   2. John the Baptist.
   3. Christ.
8. Melchizedek gave of the spoils:
   1. One-tenth.
   2. One-fifth.
   3. He didn't give any.
9. The priesthood of Christ:
   1. Is unchangeable.
   2. Is to be followed by one of the Holy Spirit.
   3. Is of Jews only.
10. The name Melchizedek means:
    1. Father of truth.
    2. King of righteousness.
    3. High priest.
11. Levi who received tithes also paid tithes:
    1. In Abraham.
    2. To set a good example.
    3. Which was more than God demanded.
12. The priesthood on earth had men having infirmity; the priesthood of Christ was a person who:
    1. Had much time to sacrifice.
    2. No longer had any responsibility to man.
    3. Was perfected for evermore.
13. Jesus became the surety:
    1. Of a better covenant.
    2. For the good moral man.
    3. Of the Mosiac law.

14. This chapter teaches that since the priesthood has been changed, it necessitates a change of:
    1. God's heart.
    2. Gentile relationship.
    3. The law.
15. Christ sprang out of Judah, as to which tribe Moses spoke nothing:
    1. Concerning conquest of Canaan.
    2. Concerning perishing in the wilderness.
    3. Concerning priests.
16. Christ is made priest, not after the law of a carnal commandment, but:
    1. After Adam's failure.
    2. After the church failed to win all men to Christ.
    3. After the power of an endless life.
17. There was a disannulling of a foregoing commandment because of:
    1. Its weakness and unprofitableness.
    2. The fact that variety is the spice of life.
    3. The fact that Jesus was different from Moses.
18. In the old priestly system, the priests were made so:
    1. Without preparation.
    2. Without education.
    3. Without an oath.
19. Christ is able to save:
    1. To the uttermost them that draw nigh unto God.
    2. In spite of the doctrine of predestination.
    3. The angels that will repent.
20. Jesus ever liveth:
    1. Because someone must be in charge of the angelic host.
    2. To control the devil.
    3. To make intercession for our sins.

SUMMARY OF CHAPTER SEVEN

The argument in Chapter Seven is for the superiority of Christ's priesthood because He is Priest after the order of Melchizedek.

In verses 1-3 this is shown, together with some of the interesting characteristics of Melchizedek, by the fact that Abraham paid tithes to Melchizedek.

In 4-10 Christ's superiority to the Levitical priesthood is indicated by the fact that Levi through Abraham paid tithes to Melchizedek, who in turn blessed Abraham. Since the greater blesses the lesser, Melchizedek is superior to Abraham and his descendants who, in a figure, paid tithes to Melchizedek through Abraham. This makes Christ priesthood superior to the Levitical priesthood, since he is Priest after the order of Melchizedek.

But why is a change of priesthood necessary? The answer is given in verses 11-19 where Levitical priesthood is compared with Christ Who is Priest after the order of Melchizedek. It is a matter of "perfection". If the worshipper had been perfected under the law and the Levitical priesthood, then there would have been no need for a new kind of priest. But this glaring weakness of the law necessitated a new kind of priest after the order of Melchizedek. With the change of priesthood, there had to be a change of law, too; this point is more fully developed in Chapter Eight.

Verses 20-28 show how Christ received the appointment confirmed by God's oath to be Priest forever after the order of Melchizedek. For that reason He is able to save unto the uttermost those who come to Him.

E. *He is a priest of a better covenant.* 8:1-13.
1. *Officiates in the true tabernacle, of which the earthly was a type.* 8:1-5.

Text
8:1-5

1 Now in the things which we are saying the chief point is this: We have such a High Priest, Who sat down on the right hand of the throne of the Majesty in the heavens, 2 a Minister of the sanctuary, and of the true tabernacle, which the Lord pitched, not man.

3 For every high priest is appointed to offer both gifts and sacrifices: wherefore it is necessary that this High Priest also have somewhat to offer. 4 Now if He were on earth, he would not be a priest at all, seeing there are those who offer the gifts according to the law; 5 who serve that which is a copy and shadow of the heavenly things, even as Moses is warned of God when he is about to make the tabernacle: for, See, saith He, that thou make all things according to the pattern that was showed thee in the mount.

Paraphrase

1 Now, of the things spoken concerning the priesthood of Christ, the chief is, That in Him we have such an High Priest as described chap. vii. 26., Who, after offering the sacrifice of Himself for us in the true tabernacle, sat down at the right hand of the manifestation of the Divine Presence in the heavens, (chap. ix 5. note), as having by that sacrifice made a complete atonement,

2 And as an abiding Minister' of the real places, namely, of the heavenly tabernacle, which, being erected by the Lord and not by man, must be unspeakably more magnificent than the Mosaic tabernacle.

3 The sitting down of Christ at the right hand of God, as the Minister of the true holy places, is a demonstration that He offered an acceptable sacrifice for sin in heaven: For every high priest being constituted to offer both free-will offerings and propitiatory sacrifices, it was necessary that this High Priest, Who was constituted by an oath, should have some sacrifice which He might offer in heaven, the only place where He could officiate.

4 For verily if He were by the oath of God constituted a Priest on earth to offer sacrifice, He, Who was of the tribe of Judah, could not be a Priest, there being, in the only temple of God on earth, priests who offer sacrifices according to the law, which limits the priest's office to the sons of Aaron.

5 Farther, that Christ exercises His priesthood in heaven appears from this also, that these priests perform the service of the tabernacles with sacrifices which are a representation and shadow of the sacrifice and intercession of Christ in heaven; as is plain from this, that Moses, when about to construct the tabernacle, and appoint its services, was admonished of God: See now, saith He that thou make all things according to the pattern which was showed thee in the mount.

The chief point is this, we have such a high priest

    Everything said builds up to this one great point. All the discussion is to show the great superiority of Christ over all.

Who sat down on the right hand of the throne

    The authors are agreed.

a. This is where Peter said He was on Pentecost, Acts 2.

8:1, 2 HELPS FROM HEBREWS

b. This is where Stephen saw Him, Acts 7:55.
c. John saw Him there, Rev. 4.
   When did He sit down?
a. Heb. 10:11-13 answers: "But this Man after He had offered one sacrifice for sins, forever sat down on the right hand of God."

of the majesty in the heavens

The "majesty" refers to God. The "heavens" would refer to the holy of holies where Christ now serves as Priest.

a minister of the sanctuary

The word "minister" usually means a public office of high and honorable rank.
a. This can be civil, or military, or religious.
b. Christ ministers in the sanctuary, indicating a spiritual service. The word "sanctuary" is also translated "holy things". Milligan believes the word in the Greek means heaven itself. He says the word is used in that sense in 9:8, 12, 24, 25; 10:19; 13:11. The word "sanctuary" probably refers to the heavens but the holy of holies and the tabernacle, to the church.

and of the true tabernacle

Here he means the substantial one — the perfect as in contrast with the imperfect.
Milligan has a lengthy discussion at this point (p. 219.)
a. Some try to say that the sanctuary and the tabernacle are different, others that they are the same.
b. "... and of" indicates a different subject is referred to than the sanctuary.
   The church must be referred to here, for many scriptures teach that the church is a building. Acts 15:16-17; I Cor. 3:16; I Cor. 6; II Cor. 6:16; Eph. 2:19-22; I Tim. 3:15; I Peter 2:5; Heb. 3:6 and 10:21.

which the Lord pitched, not man

This is a temple not made with hands.
a. Stephen said so. Acts 7:48.
b. Paul said so. Acts 17:24.
   Matt. 16:18: "I will build My church," was a claim of Christ.
a. If the Lord pitched it, then we have no right to build otherwise.
b. The pattern is pitched; let us build accordingly.

For every high priest is appointed to offer both gifts and sacrifices
"Gifts" would refer to the free-will offerings. "Sacrifices" refers to those specifically commanded of God.

wherefore it is necessary that this High Priest also have somewhat to offer
What could He offer but Himself? This offering does not need to be repeated — Heb. 7:27; 9:12; 9:26; 9:28; 10:12. Jesus told what the greatest love was: " — to lay down a life for a friend." John 15:13.
a. Christ was therefore obligated to die for man.
b. If He gave anything less, He could not show His love as marvelously.

Now if He were on earth, He would not be a priest at all
He could not lawfully do it.
a. He was not of the house of Aaron; therefore, He was not qualified. Num. 18:1-7.
Severe punishment was provided for one who invaded the office. Num. 16:1-35; 18:3-7; II Chr. 26:16-21. Observe that even Levites were killed if they encroached upon the office. Num. 18:3.

who serve that which is a copy
"Serve" means "the performance of sacred rites".
a. The old covenant with its ordinances and priests pictured to us a priesthood to come.
b. "Serve" as used here means to "portray".
"Copy" means "an example".
a. The Levitical priests were serving as an example of what later was to come.
b. This made it very important that all things be made and done according to the pattern.

and shadow of the heavenly things
This is true typology. Too many endeavor to stretch typology over all the Old Testament, and they make some strange lessons. We can best understand heavenly things when God illustrates on earth as He did with this type.

Even as Moses is warned of God when he is about to make the tabernacle
The warning is Ex. 25:40. This is stronger than just being informed how to build.

that thou make all things according to the pattern that was showed thee in the mount

Moses was not allowed to change — add or substitute. Observe three things:
a. The ancient rituals were appointed for a purpose.
b. All modes of worship are false which are not invented by the hand of God.
c. There are no true symbols except those which the Lord gives. We have similar warnings today. Gal. 1:8-9; Rev. 22:18-19; I Cor. 11:2.

What would the church be like if it were built according to the pattern?
a. The modernist says there is no pattern.
b. How can we find fault with Protestantism and Catholicism if there is no pattern?
c. God has a pattern for His church, and we must build accordingly.

Study Questions

1323. In verse one Paul speaks of a "chief point". What is it?
1324. Where is this High Priest?
1325. Is there significance in the statement, "right hand"?
1326. Did other preachers and writers locate Him differently?
1327. What verse of the Bible tells us when He sat down there?
1328. What does the word "majesty" refer to?
1329. What does the word "heavens" refer to?
1330. What is the meaning of the word "minister"?
1331. What is the meaning of the word "sanctuary"?
1332. Could it mean "holy things"? Why?
1333. Could it mean heaven, or the holy of holies?
1334. What is the true tabernacle?
1335. Is the church ever spoken of as a building? Cf. Acts 15:16-17; I Cor. 3:16;(Heb. 3:6.
1336. Does Rev. 21:3, which says, "Behold the tabernacle of God is with men", have a bearing?
1337. Does Heb. 9:11 refer to the same tabernacle?
1338. Verse two says this tabernacle was pitched by God, not man. If it is not the church, then what has He built besides the church, and where is it recorded?
1339. What is meant by the name "Lord" — Christ or God?

1340. If the Lord pitched, what is meant by it?
1341. Do we have any right to build differently than the Lord commanded?
1342. In this verse two words are significant, "sacrifices" and "gifts". What is the difference?
1343. Would Christ be performing a priestly duty if He had nothing to offer?
1344. What did He offer?
1345. Is this offering repeated? Cf. Heb. 7:27; 9:12; 9:26, 28; 10:12.
1346. Verse four is a short one stating that Christ could not act as High Priest on earth. Why?
1347. Compare Num. 18:3 to see that Levites were limited in duties and privileges.
1348. What is the meaning of the word "serve"?
1349. What is the meaning of the word "copy"?
1350. If all the Old Testament ritual and service was a copy or example of something to follow, was it necessary for the copy to be right?
1351. What happens in a newspaper if the first copy has mistakes undetected or carelessly prepared?
1352. What is a warning? Is it generally accompanied by a threat?
1353. Of what was Moses warned? Exodus 25:40.
1354. Is this stronger than just telling him how to build?
1355. Would "according to the pattern" allow for substituting or alterations?
1356. Where did Moses get his pattern?
1357. Are there true symbols other than those of God?
1358. Do we have any warnings about the gospel being kept pure? Cf. Gal. 1:8-9; Rev. 22:18-19; I Cor. 11:2; II Tim. 3:16-17.
1359. If the modernist is correct that there is no pattern for the church, do we have any right to be critical of Catholicism or Protestantism?
1360. What would have been revealed about the character of Moses if he had dared to change the pattern, or was careless?
1361. Could the same charge be brought to us?

2. *He is a Mediator of a new covenant.* 8:6-13.

Text
8:6-13

6 But now hath He obtained a ministry the more excellent, by so much as He is also the Mediator of a better covenant, which hath been enacted upon better promises. 7 For if that first covenant had been faultless, then would no place have been sought for a second. 8 For finding with them, He saith,

Behold, the days come, saith the Lord,
That I will make a new covenant with the house of Israel and with the house of Judah;
9 Not according to the covenant that I made with their fathers
In the day that I took them by the hand to lead them forth out of the land of Egypt;
For they continued not in My covenant,
And I regarded them not, saith the Lord.
10 For this is the covenant that I will make with the house of Israel.
After those days, saith the Lord;
I will put My laws into their mind,
And on their heart also will I write them:
And I will be to them a God,
And they shall be to Me a people:
11 And they shall not teach every man his fellow-citizen,
And every man his brother, saying, Know the Lord:
For all shall know Me,
From the least to the greatest of them.
12 For I will be merciful to their iniquities,
And their sins will I remember no more.

13 In that He saith, A new covenant, He hath made the first old. But that which is becoming old and waxeth aged is nigh unto vanishing away.

Paraphrase

6 Besides, Jesus our High Priest hath now obtained a more excellent ministry, than the Levitical high priests, in as much as He is the mediator of a better covenant than the Sinaitic, of which they were the mediators; because it is established on better promises — promises better suited to our exigencies as sinners. See v. 7. note 1.

7 For if the Sinaitic covenant had been faultless; if sinners could have been sanctified and pardoned thereby; there would have been no need of introducing a second covenant:

8 But finding fault with the first covenant, and to show its inefficacy for sanctifying and pardoning sinners, God saith to the Israelites, Jerem. xxxi. 31. Behold the days come, saith the Lord, when I will complete a new covenant with the whole of the spiritual Israel among the Gentiles, and with believers among the Jews;

9 Even a covenant entirely different from the covenant which I made with their fathers, (chap. vii. 27. note) at the time of My taking them by the hand to lead them out of the land of Egypt into Canaan, when they did not abide in My covenant, but brake it repeatedly by their idolatries. Therefore I neglected them; I suffered them to be carried into captivity; saith the Lord.

10 For, agreeably to My promise that in Abraham's seed all nations shall be blessed, this is the covenant which I will make with believers of all nations in future times, saith the Lord: Under the gospel dispensation I will put My laws into their mind, and write them upon their hearts, instead of writing them on stones as under the former covenant; and I will be the object of their worship, and their Protector, and they who believe shall become My obedient people, whom I will bless through all eternity:

11 And, comparatively speaking, there shall be no occasion for what was commanded under the former covenant, in which no constant public instruction was provided: They shall not need to teach each other to know the Lord, (Deut. vi. 8.), for all shall know Me, from the lowest of them to the highest of them.

12 These things I will bring to pass, because I will pardon the unrighteousness of My people, and their sins and their iniquities I will remember no more, as I did under the former covenant, by appointing annual atonements for them.

13 By saying, I will make a new covenant, God hath declared the former covenant old. Now that which decayeth and waxeth old, is ready to be laid aside as useless. Wherefore, by promising a new covenant, God hath intimated the abrogation of the whole Mosiac dispensation.

Comment

But now hath He obtained a ministry

While on earth He ministered.
a. Acts 10:38: Jesus of Nazareth went about doing good.
b. Phil. 2:5-11.
This is not a contrast with His earthly ministry, but with the Levitical ministry. The context proves it.

the more excellent

It was a ministry "more excellent" than that of the Levitical priests. His ministry is that ministry in heaven. The way that it is more excellent is seen in this verse: it has better promises.

by so much as He is also the mediator of a better covenant

A mediator is one who intervenes or goes between two parties. Moses was a mediator. Ex. 20:19-21; 24; Gal. 3:19-20.
We have one and only one mediator. I Tim. 2:5: "For there is one God, one mediator also between God and men, himself man, Christ Jesus."
The high priest served on the day of Atonement. Lev. 16.

which hath been enacted upon better promises

The promises were largely physical in the old covenant.
a. Deut. 11:26.
b. Deut. 20:9-20.
c. Observe the promises of the tithe in Malachi.
The better promises of the new:
a. New home. John 14:1-6.
b. New body. I Cor. 15.
c. Eternal life. John 3:16.
d. Absolute forgiveness of sins.

for if that first covenant had been faultless, then would no place have been sought for a second.

See Gal. 3:21: "If there had been a law given which could make alive, verily righteousness would have been of the law." Rom. 3:20: "For through the law cometh the knowledge of sin." Many verses speak of the purity and righteousness of the law, but it was perfect insofar as its purpose was to bring men to Christ. Its purpose being limited, a second was needed.

for finding fault with them

    Finding fault with the people? Milligan says "yes".
a. Why? Because they had not kept the law.
b. Milligan interprets it to read, "finding fault, He saith to them." Finding fault with the covenant? Yes.
Rom. 8:3: "For what the law could not do in that it was weak through the flesh." Gal. 3:21.

Behold the days come, saith the Lord, that I will make a new covenant

    When was this?
a. The prophecy was given after the conquest of Jerusalem by the Chaldeans. Jeremiah 31:31.
b. Notice the order of covenants:
1. Gen. 12:1-3 to Abraham, repeated in 13:14-17; 15:1-6, 18-21; 17:1-8; 22:15-18.
a) This looked to the covenant with Israel, then to all men.
b) It looked to the covenant with all men, gentiles too.
2. The Mosaic covenant is referred to. This covenant was first physical, but Christ's is spiritual.
After the old had been tried, God prophesied of a new one.

with the house of Israel

    Israel means "praise with God". Notice to whom the term is applied:
a. Jacob, Gen. 32:28.
b. To all his descendants collectively, Ex. 4:22.
c. To the ten tribes that revolted from Rehoboam, I Kings 12:19-20.
d. To all believers in Christ, Rom. 9:6.
Newell says, "It isn't made yet."

and with the house of Judah

    Judah means "praise". Why is Judah singled out?
a. Because the tribe of Judah followed Rehoboam; thus all the Hebrews are to be included.
b. The tribe of Benjamin and some from the tribes of Simeon and Dan followed Rehoboam.
The gathering of the Jews will be into one body, under the new covenant.
a. Abraham's children had been divided; only Christ could unite.

    b. Too many are seeking a restoration of the Jews in Palestine. The restoration will be under Christ.
1. God is not interested in the place where the Jew's body is, but the condition of his heart.
2. If he is Christian, he can live anywhere.

Not according to the covenant that I made with their fathers, in the day that I took them out by the hand to lead them forth out of the land of Egypt.

    That was the Abrahamic promise being fulfilled to make them a mighty nation.
    The covenant with Moses had a very important carnal side.
a. God moved them out of law and order from Egypt; now they must have a new law.
b. The Mosaic covenant is largely carnal, in that it is a system of law that was given to make a nation.
    The day of this covenant is done and another covenant is established that is unlike the old one.

for they continued not in My covenant

    God promised them an abundance of everything, provided they would serve Him. They failed to keep their side.
a. The wilderness experience is one time they failed.
b. The sinfulness that led to the Babylonian captivity is another example.

and I regarded them not, saith the Lord

    He treated them as unfaithful people. He was Lord to them, so He could treat them as such. As Lord He could reject them. Since they did not abide faithful, God was free to let sin take its course with them.

for this is the covenant that I will make with the house of Israel after those days

    The time element should be noted here.
a. After the days of Israel's rebellion is noted in vs. 9.
b. God was free to make a new covenant, since Israel was so unfaithful.
1. They departed from God while Moses was in the mount.
2. They departed from God instead of conquering the land.
3. They departed from God and were carried away into captivity. In the light of Jewish history, God was under no obligation to continue the old covenant.

I will put my laws into their mind

> The old was engraved on stones, skins. These people were born into a Jewish environment and were to be obedient as a member of the nation.
> Th old was written on stone, two tables. Ex. 34:1, 28; Deut. 4:1-5; II Cor. 3:7.
> With the new covenant you cannot be a part of it unless you know in your mind what it is.

a. With the old it was accomplished by birth, and then teaching.
b. With the new law, it is accomplished by teaching and birth, "born again". Jn. 3:5.

and on their heart also I will write them

> The Christian has a born-again experience by which the Word lives in his heart. He belongs to God, not because of a fleshly birth which he could do nothing about, but because of a decision of life. The verse does not expressly deny that Old Testament characters did not have the law in their hearts, but a procedure is contrasted.

and I will be to them a God and they shall be to Me a people

> Sonship is a wonderful privilege. See Gal. 4:6: "And because ye are sons, God hath sent forth the Spirit of His Son into your hearts crying, Abba Father." Also Gal. 4:7. The privilege to pray, "Our Father" is an experience that only the Christian has.

And they shall not teach every man his fellow citizen and every man his brother

> Under the old, you were a member and had to be taught, but under the new you are taught, and thus you become a member.

a. The Jews had these multitudes of laws, and it was necessary for them to be taught constantly in order for the Jew to live up to them.
b. The new is spiritual. You were already obedient.
c. In the old you were a part of it by virtue of physical birth, but in the new you choose, and therefore know.
   No one ignorant of Jehovah can possible become a member of the new covenant. See 11:6: "He that cometh unto God." Jn. 1:13: "Born not of blood, nor of the will of the flesh, nor of the will of man, but of God."

We are fellow citizens in Christ. See Eph. 2:19. The brotherly relationship is obtained by the same method, teaching; hence, both know the Lord.

saying, know the Lord

We know the Lord already; that is why we are brothers. Brothers in Christ do not need to say, "Know the Lord," for knowing the Lord made them brothers.

for all shall know Me, from the least to the greatest of them

God's grace would be poured out upon all. This refers to people who are capable of knowing God.
a. Infants are not referred to here.
b. New babies in Christ would be the least, and mature Christians the greatest. God's grace would be poured out upon all ranks of men.

for I will be merciful to their iniquities

There was no mercy under the old like God's mercy now.
a. The elders could stone a wayward individual at once; there was no room for repentance.
b. This is one of the better promises referred to in v. 6.
Calvin passes over this verse, but his editor makes a note.
a. He says the verse differs in words, though not in substance, both from the Hebrew, and from the Septuagint version.
b. In Hebrew, "remission" or "forgiveness" is its meaning, but here, the idea expressed is mercy.

and their sins will I remember no more

The people of earth say, "I will forgive, but I will not forget." The Lord will not hold forgiven sins against us. See these verses:
a. Rom. 8:33: "Who shall lay anything to the charge of God's elect? It is God that justifieth."
b. Ps. 103:12: expresses the fact of sins hidden from God as far as the east is from the west.
In the Old Testament there was a covering temporarily from God's sight by the blood of offerings.
a. In those sacrifices there was a remembrance of sin year by year on the great day of Atonement. Heb. 10:3.
b. Now the blood of the eternal covenant offered by the Lamb of God takes away sin completely.

in that He saith a new covenant He hath made the first old

    How could He call something "new" without implying something old? As the new is substituted, it must be that the former has come to an end. When the dispensation of Moses was gone, so were the ceremonies to cease.

but that which is becoming old and waxeth aged is nigh unto vanishing away.

    It ended actually with Christ's death.
a. Col. 2:14 — nailing it to the cross.
    It ended practically with the destruction of Jerusalem, A.D. 10.
a. As long as the Jews' city stood, they would insist on the sacrifices and ceremonies, not realizing that the hope of Israel had been crucified and raised.
b. Hebrews was likely written before the destruction of the city, so this is then prophetic.

Study Questions

1362. Verse 5 speaks of Moses. Does verse 6 say that he now has a better ministry?
1363. Who obtained a beter ministry?
1364. In what way is it more excellent?
1365. In what way did Jesus minister on earth? Acts 10:38.
1366. What would happen if all members of the church did good?
1367. Is this a contrast to Christ's earthly ministry, or a contrast to the Levitical priesthood ministry?
1368. Is it Christ's earthly ministry or His heavenly one alluded to here?
1369. What is the "ministry the more excellent"?
1370. Why is it superior?
1371. Was Moses a mediator? Cf. Gal. 3:19-20; Ex. 20:19-21, 24.
1372. Did the Jews have others? Cf. Lev. 16:1.
1373. Does the Christian have more than one? Cf. I Tim. 2:5.
1374. What is a mediator?
1375. In what ways is our new covenant better?
1376. What does verse six say that makes it better?
1377. Name some of the promises.

HELPS FROM HEBREWS

1378. Why are the new promises better?
1379. Can we say that most of the promises of God in the Old Testament were physical?
1380. Is there an allusion to spiritual promises in God's promise to Abraham?
1381. Can we say that we were blessed more than Abraham?
1382. What was the nature of the blessings in Mal. 4?
1383. Does it seem that people are more interested in physical than spiritual blessings?
1384. What does the author find wrong with the first covenant? Does he name any faults?
1385. Compare Gal. 3:17-21 for the fault of the law.
1386. If it had no fault, why did God give it? Cf. Rom. 3:20.
1387. God found fault with what or whom? v. 8.
1388. How does Milligan translate verse eight?
1389. How do you feel toward the alternate reading in the American Standard Version of verse eight?
1390. Could it be that He found fault with the law and the people too?
1391. Where is the quotation of what God said found in the Old Testament?
1392. What did He say?
1393. When did He say it?
1394. With whom was it to be made?
1395. What does the word "Israel" mean?
1396. To whom is the term applied? Cf. Gen. 32:28; Ex. 4:22; I Kings 12:19-20; Rom. 9:6.
1397. Why does he say "Israel and Judah"?
1398. What do some interpreters say concerning this prophecy?
1399. Is God likely to be more interested in locating the Jews in Palestine than in saving the Gentiles?
1400. Are the Jews to be gathered in a place or under a covenant?
1401. What one thing will unite all of Abraham's seed?
1402. What "fathers" are referred to, Moses or Abraham? Could Moses be called their father?
1403. What part of Abraham's promise was being fulfilled?
1404. What was God planning when he led them out?
1405. Was the repeated covenant with Moses mostly carnal?
1406. What fault did God find with them?
1407. Was God obligated to keep His side, when they failed to keep theirs?

1408. What happened to them to prove they disobeyed?
1409. What is meant by "I regarded them not"? Could it mean that He would not protect them?
1410. After what "days" are referred to here?
1411. Where were the laws to be put under the new covenant?
1412. What is the difference here from the Old Testament laws?
1413. Can you be a part of the new covenant without having the law in your mind?
1414. Discuss the processes of birth and teaching in relationship to the two covenants.
1415. What is the method of God's "writing" on their heart?
1416 Did not the old covenant people have it on their heart?
1417. Were they under the covenant before it was on their mind?
1418. Are the procedures or methods of becoming a part of the two covenants contrasted here?
1419. Is the Christian in the covenant before it is written in his heart?
1420. What relationship does God have to those under the new covenant?
1421. Who are "they"? How inclusive is it? v. 11.
1422. What kind of condition is referred to where no teaching is necessary?
1423. Did "brother" and "citizen" have a system of institution under the old covenant?
1424. What eliminates the teaching of the old covenant? Is it the spiritual birth?
      Old — born, then taught.
      New — taught, then born.
1425. Brotherhood is obtained by all by the same method. Is that why some do not have to teach others?
1426. Who would be considered the "least" and "greatest"?
1427. Are these ranks in the new covenant?
1428. What can be said of mercy in the two covenants? v. 12.
1429. Did the Jews of Jesus' day seem merciful?
1430. Give an example of Christ's superior mercy.
1431. Show some instances of severity in the Old Testament.
1432. How superior to man's forgiveness is God's forgiveness?
1433. How can God remember sins no more? Can He forget them?
1434. What will cover them?

1435. How often was their remembrance under the old covenant? Cf. Heb. 10:3.
1436. Is this true of the New Testament?
1437. Can you have something called "new" without inferring something "old"?
1438. Is there any significance to the continuous action, indicated by the word "becoming"? v. 13b.
1439. Did man consider it old as soon as God did?
1440. If the law is a tutor, should we feel that it is a good thing for the Jew to be faithful in its observance?
1441. Does the continuous action indicated by the phrase, "becoming old", infer that Jerusalem had not been destroyed?

Multiple Choice Over Chapter Eight

1. We do not offer sacrifices today as did the Jew:
   1. Because it is not customary.
   2. We do not need to think of sin.
   3. Christ was our sacrifice once for all.
2. The covenant which we follow today is:
   1. The Mosaic covenant.
   2. The Abrahamic covenant.
   3. The new covenant.
3. Jesus became the mediator:
   1. Of a better covenant.
   2. To solve the problems of Jews and Gentiles.
   3. To bring back together the devil and God.
4. If Christ were on the earth He could not serve as a Priest because:
   1. He died on the cross.
   2. There was already an established priesthood.
   3. Because He offered only one sacrifice.
5. The second covenant is established on better:
   1. Laws.
   2. Promises.
   3. People.
6. Moses made all things according:
   1. To his wisdom counseled by Aaron.
   2. To the best in society.
   3. To the pattern.

7. The new covenant is written:
   1. In the hearts of the people.
   2. In the temple at Jerusalem.
   3. On tablets of stone because they are more permanent.
8. The high priest was appointed:
   1. To rule the people.
   2. To offer up gifts and sacrifices.
   3. To translate the scriptures.
9. Our High Priest:
   1. Is pleading for the souls in purgatory.
   2. Preaching to the spirits in prison.
   3. Seated at the right hand of the Father.
10. In the new covenant plan:
    1. Children are to be taught before they can come under it.
    2. Children are to be taught it after they have come under it.
    3. Faith of parents is to be imputed unto them.

True and False

_____1. The old covenant is spoken of as becoming old and nigh unto vanishing away.
_____2. A time when evangelism will not be needed is prophesied.
_____3. God found fault with the first covenant and the people under it.
_____4. Christ was different from the first priests in that He didn't need any sacrifice.
_____5. A fault of Israel was that they did not continue in the covenant of God.
_____6. The promise of God is that He will forgive our sins even though He will not forget.
_____7. The true tabernacle is the one the Lord pitched.
_____8. The new covenant was to be made with the house of Israel, and the house of Judah is specifically named.

SUMMARY OF CHAPTER EIGHT

The main issue of Hebrews is the fact that we do have a High Priest who serves in connection with the real worship of God. But He is also sitting at the right hand of the throne of God, a fact that emphasizes the peculiar nature of His priesthood — He is both Priest and King.

His is a more excellent ministry although on earth he wouldn't even be a priest. The Old Testament priests served a system copied from the model shown to Moses in Mount Sinai. Christ's priesthood is the more excellent because He is also Mediator of a better covenant than the one given at Sinai, for it has better promises.

In proof of the claim for a more excellent ministry, the quotation from Jer. 31:31-34 is given. It points out the fact that the new covenant was to be given because Israel broke the one given at Sinai. That covenant had been written on tables of stone, but God was going to make a new one by putting it into their minds and writing it on their hearts.

The essential elements of the new covenant is: "I will be to them a God, and they shall be to me a people". As a striking difference between the two covenants, all connected with the new shall know the Lord. The blessing of the new covenant is the fact that the merciful God promises to remember the sins of the people no more.

A closing word explains the use of the terms "new" and "old." The one given at Sinai was the old covenant. It had grown old and was near to vanishing away.

Special Study On The Priest And The Temple

Priest:

A priest is one who is duly authorized to minister in sacred things, especially to offer the sacrifices at the altar and to act as mediator between man and God.

I. In the New Testament the term is applied to four groups.
   A. Priests of Gentiles. Acts 14:13.
   B. Priests of Jews. Matt. 8:4.
   C. Christ. Heb. 5:5, 6.
   D. Christians. I Peter 2:9; Rev. 1:6.

II. The priestly office was of high rank.
   A. He stood next to the monarch in influence and dignity.
   B. Aaron, the head of the priestly system, was closely associated with Moses and shared with him the guidance of the nation.
   C. Through him, the people were instructed in the doctrine of sin, and its expiation in forgiveness and worship.
   D. He was indispensable as a source of religious knowledge for the people.

III. The nature of the priestly office.
   A. It was one of divine choice.
      1. It was one of appointment. Heb. 5:4.
         a. The priest was not elected by the people.
         b. Divine selection severed him from the people.
      2. Jesus was likewise divinely sent. Luke 4:18.
   B. It was one of representation.
      1. He appeared before God on behalf of the people. Heb. 2:17.
      2. He was the mediator for the guilty.
      3. There were two physical indications that he represented all the people.
         a. He wore the names of the tribes on his shoulders in the onyx stones.
         b. The names of the tribes were engraved in the twelve gems of the breastplate. See Ex. 28:12-21.
      4. What he did as a priest in an official capacity as prescribed by the Lord was reckoned as being done by the whole congregation. Heb. 5:1.
   C. It was one of offering a sacrifice for the people.
      1. His chief duty was to reconcile man to God by making atonement for their sins.
         a. This was done by sacrifice. See Heb. 5:1; 8:3.
         b. He carried the blood of the sin offering into the most holy place.
         c. Here he sprinkled it seven times on and before the mercy seat.
         d. This symbolized the covering of the sins from the eyes of God who dwelt between the cherubim. Ps. 80.
         e. He also marked the blood on the horns of the altar of burnt offerings in the court of the tabernacle.
         f. It was also done on the golden altar, that the red sign of propitiation might there be lifted up in the sight of God.
   D. It was a service of intercession.
      1. As the sacrifice was made, it was an appeal to the Righteous Judge to forgive.

2. After this sacrifice was completed the high priest came forth and blessed the people. See Lev. 9:22-24; Num. 6:22-27.
E. Special privileges of the high priest.
 1. He alone could wear the high priestly garment.
 2. He alone could enter the holy of holies to sprinkle the blood.
F. Qualifications.
 1. He was to be physically fit — perfect. Defects could disqualify. Lev. 21:17-21.
 2. His marriage must be with a pure virgin of pure Hebrew extraction.
  a. Couldn't marry a widow.
  b. Couldn't marry a divorced woman.
  c. Couldn't marry a polluted one or a harlot. Cf. Lev. 20:10-11.

IV. The consecrations.
 A. Both the high priest and his sons were washed with water. Exodus 29:4.
 B. The high priest was arrayed in a special garb.
  1. They were beautiful, with a breastplate over the heart.
  2. A holy crown was on his head.
  3. He had a turban with a golden plate bearing the inscription, "Holy to Jehovah".
 C. Then he was anointed with precious oil.
 Moses poured it on his head — He sprinkled the furniture with oil.
 D. Then the sacrifices were made. Ex. 29:10. Up to this point the sons have no work to do, but now they take a prominent part.
 E. The blood of the offering was applied to the father and sons. Ex. 29:20-21.
  1. Blood was put on the tip of the right ear — this brought his ear into subjection to God — to hear and do God's will.
  2. Blood was put on the thumb of the right hand. This consecrated his hand to the will of God.
  3. Blood was placed on the big toe — this consecrated his foot to walk in the statutes and commandments of the Lord.

V. The similarity of Christ's priesthood with that of the old covenant.
   A. Christ was appointed of God. Heb. 5:5.
   B. Christ was consecrated with an oath. Heb. 7:20-22.
   C. Christ was sinless. Heb. 7:26.
   D. Christ's priesthood is unchangeable. Heb. 7:23-24.
   E. Christ's offering is final. Heb. 9:25-28; 10:12.
   F. His intercession is all-prevailing. Heb. 7:25.
   G. As God and man in one Person, He is a perfect Mediator.

Temple:

The Temple Plans — The tabernacle lasted from the Exodus until the commencement of the monarchy.

David concluded that the ark of God ought not to dwell in ark of the covenant overlaid round about with gold, wherein was curtains. II Samuel 6:17.

The organized nation could have a tabernacle that need not be portable. It was to be beautiful. I Chron. 22:5.

David was not permitted to build because he was a man of war. II Sam. 7; I Chron. 22:8; I Kings 5:3.
   1. Solomon was to do it.
   2. David busied himself in making great and costly preparations, gathering wood, stone, gold, silver, etc., for the future sanctuary and its vessels.
   3. David left very minute plans. I Chron. 22:2; I Chron. 28:11.

The Character of the Building:
   1. The general outline of the structure was based upon that of the tabernacle.
   2. The dimensions are twice in size, with some exceptions.

F. *He is a Priest in a better tabernacle.* 9:1-28.
   1. *The old tabernacle and its imperfect services.* 9:1-10.

Text
9:1-10

1. Now even the first covenant had ordinances of divine service, and its sanctuary, a sanctuary of this world. 2 For there was a tabernacle prepared, the first, wherein were the candlestick, and the table, and the showbread; which is called the Holy place.

3 And after the second veil, the tabernacle which is called the Holy of holies; 4 having a golden altar of incense, and the ark of the covenant overlaid round about with gold, wherein was

9:1-10

a golden pot holding the manna, and Aaron's rod that budded, and the tables of the covenant; 5 and above it cherubim of glory overshadowing the mercy-seat; of which things we cannot now speak severally. 6 Now these things having been thus prepared, the priests go in continually into the first tabernacle, accomplishing the services; 7 but into the second the high priest alone, once in the year, not without blood, which he offereth for himself, and for the errors of the people: 8 the Holy Spirit this signifying, that the way into the holy place hath not yet been made manifest, while the first tabernacle is yet standing; 9 which is a figure for the time present; according to which are offered both gifts and sacrifices that cannot, as touching the conscience, make the worshipper perfect, 10 being only (with meats and drinks and divers washings) carnal ordinances, imposed until a time of reformation.

Paraphrase

1 Now verily, although the first covenant is to be laid aside, I acknowledge it had both ordinances of worship, and a worldly Holy place appointed by God. But the former being merely an emblem of the services of Christ in heaven, and the latter a shadow of the world or universe, the covenant of which they are the ordinances is become useless, now that Christ hath performed the services of heaven.

2 For the outward tabernacle, which is called Holy, was built and furnished so as to represent the earth and the visible heavens, having both the golden candlestick towards the south, and the table with the show-bread towards the north, Exod. xxvi. 35.

3 And behind the innermost veil, the tabernacle, which is called the Most Holy Place, was in like manner built and furnished according to a pattern formed by God, so as to be a representation of heaven, the invisible habitation of the Deity;

4 Having the golden censer, on which the high priest burned incense when he entered the Most Holy place, and the ark of the covenant, which was covered both on the inside and the out with gold; in which were the golden pot, having an omer of the manna wherewith the Israelites were fed in the wilderness, and Aaron's rod which blossomed and bare almonds, and the tables of the covenant from which the ark had its name;

5 And above the ark the cherubim of glory, overshadowing the mercy-seat, and forming a magnificent throne for the glory of the Lord, which rested between them, (Exod. xxv. 22.); con-

cerning the meaning of which things I have not time at present to speak particularly, my design being to explain what was signified by the services of the tabernacles.

6 Now the tabernacles with their utensils being thus constructed and arranged, the ordinary priests go at all times indeed into the first tabernacle, performing the services; of which the chief is their sprinkling the blood of the sin-offerings before the veil which concealed the symbol of the Divine Presence from their view:

7 But into the inward tabernacle, which represents heaven, the high priest and no one else goeth; and he only one day in the year; not however without the blood of different sacrifices, which he offereth for his own, and for the people's sins of ignorance.

8 By the absolute exclusion of the priests and people from the inward tabernacle, the Holy Ghost, who formed the pattern of the tabernacles and of their services, showed this, that the way into the true holy places, represented by the inward tabernacle, was not yet laid open to men, while this world, represented by the outward tabernacle, still subsisteth;

9 Which tabernacle with its services, whereby the worshipper was not brought into the immediate presence of the Deity, was a parabolical instruction concerning the time which is present, during which both gifts and sacrifices are offered, which cannot, by banishing the fear of punishment, make him perfect, with respect to conscience, who worshippeth God.

10 With nothing but meats and drinks, and divers immersions and ordinances respecting the purifying of the body, imposed only until the time of the reformation of the worship of God by Christ, who was to abolish the Levitical services, and to introduce a worship in spirit and in truth, which may be performed in every place.

Comment

Now even the first covenant had ordinances of divine service

The point he is making is this:

a. The whole form of worshipping God was annexed to the old covenant.
b. It had sacrifices, ablutions and symbols connected with the sanctuary.

9:1, 2   HELPS FROM HEBREWS

    c. They were divine services, for God planned them.
        Ex. 31:1-10 states that Bezalel was given the Spirit of God in order to construct the tabernacle and design the clothes.

Ordinances: (Services)

a. Milligan says that "services" is a verbal noun and means:
1. A righteous *action,* an act by which righteousness is fulfilled. Rom. 5:18.
2. A righteous *judgment,* indicating that a sinner is made righteous through the righteousness of Christ. Rom. 5:16.
3. A righteous *decree, or appointment, ordinance, law, rule.*
b. Milligan feels that the latter one (No. 3) is preferable here.

and its sanctuary a sanctuary of this world

    These words are stated to draw a contrast between the earthly tabernacle services with the Holy of holies in heaven. The Holy of holies in heaven has a Priest who has finished the sacrifice and is seated at the right hand of God.

for there was a tabernacle prepared, the first, wherein were

    "The first" is inserted, perhaps, to distinguish between the tabernacle and the temple, say some. The context indicates that the Holy place is referred to. Most authorities agree that this is the tabernacle, for the temple did not possess the tablets of stone after the captivity.

the candlestick

    It was made of a talent of gold. Exodus 25:31-40. Rabbis say that it was four cubits high, had six branches. It stood on the south side.

and the table

    This stood on the north opposite the candlestick. It was made of acacia wood overlaid with gold. On it was placed the twelve loaves, changed each sabbath. The setting of the table with bread, once a week, is a type of the Lord's table.

and the showbread

    Also called "the bread of the face", so-called because it was in the presence of God. On the table were placed every sabbath day by the high priest twelve cakes made of fine flour, six in a row, and on each row a cup of frankincense. Lev. 24:5-9.

which is called the Holy Place

The word "first" must refer to this place. In this section of the tabernacle, the priests worked continually.

and after the second veil, the tabernacle which is called the Holy of Holies

"After the second veil" refers to the veil that separated the Holy of Holies.
a. The first was at the entrance to the Holy Place.
b. The second refers to the one separating the Holy Place from the Holy of Holies.
1. The temple in Jerusalem at the time of Christ had a veil, for it was torn from the top to the bottom. Matt. **27**:51.
2. The temple of Solomon had wooden doors. I Kings 6:31-33. Into this second veil the priest entered but once a year. 9:7.

having a golden altar of incense

This is not mentioned by Moses as to location, some say. The high priest went in once a year to burn incense. Some think it was left just inside all year. This verse seems to locate it in the Holy of Holies.

McKnight says it was left in the Holy of Holies close enough so the priest could reach beneath the veil and pull it out. Newell says it was placed close to the veil in the holy place but is regarded by the Spirit of God, in Heb. 9:4, as belonging to the Holy of Holies. He says see Exodus 30:1, 6, 7, 10; Exodus 40:5. Solomon's building was like it. I Kings 6:19-22. The altars of incense represent prayer in the study of types.

and the ark of the covenant

The instructions for the building of this container: Deut. 10:1-5.
It was a sort of chest overlaid with gold.
a. In it were the two tables of the law. I Kings 8:9.
b. The things it contained are named in this verse, but the word "wherein" may not mean in the ark, but rather in the Holy of Holies.
c. It was made of shittim wood (acacia) 2½ cubits long and 1½ cubits broad and deep.

overlaid round about with gold

God has always used beautiful things in worship to impress

the people with its importance. God also makes wonderful use of simple things likewise, as seen in the emblems of the Lord's Supper.

wherein was a golden pot holding the manna

See Exodus 16:32-34. Manna was kept from the wilderness journey.
a. It contained an omer (seven pints).
Was the pot in the ark?
a. No, says I Kings 8:9, only the tables of stone.
b. By the time of Solomon, perhaps other contents had been lost, and so the time element enters into the problem here.
c. McKnight suggests that the words may mean "nigh to" the pot, and the rod may have been a part of the ark, but not actually in it.

and Aaron's rod that budded

See Num. 17:1-11 — It blossomed and bore ripe almonds. Clarke says that this was in the ark. However the reading may be understood to mean in the Holy of Holies. See I Kings 8:9 which says only the tables were in the ark. The time element should be considered.

and the tables of the covenant

Deut. 10:1-5 gives the account of the construction of it. I Kings 8:9 indicates that the pot of manna and Aaron's rod had been removed from the ark and likely lost before the temple.

and above it cherubim of glory

"Cherubim" is plural of "cherub". It means "keeper, guardian". See Ezek. 1:5-11, 13, 14 for their physical appearance. Ezek. 1:24; Ezek. 10:5: "The sound of their wings was as the voice of God."
These were of gold, and were at each end of the mercy seat. Ex. 25:18-20. The cherubim seem to be an order of angels. Gen. 3:24. The word "glory" may be understood in the light that these angels surround God, so between them would be the peace of God's glory.

overshadowing the mercy seat

They were at each end, facing each other, but looking down

on the cover or the mercy seat. The presence of the angels abiding in figure form renders a fit image of heaven.

of which things we cannot now speak severally

Christ can be seen in each. He is the Light, Bread, Ark, the Word. Examination of details is not necessary to perceive the lesson gained. Detail is not desired, but contrast is the author's purpose.

Now these things having been thus prepared the priests go in continually into the first tabernacle accomplishing the services

The priest went into the Holy Place twice daily.
a. There was the incense to burn in the morning.
b. There was the evening sacrifice.
There was a continued task. Lev. 4:6.
Observe the contrasts that can be made:
a. The high priest of Israel dared not go in at all times. Lev. 16:2.
b. He went in only once a year. Lev. 16:12-15.
c. He went in with blood; blood of animals, not his own.
d. He had to repeat the sacrifice yearly. It was never finished.
e. He had to pass through a veil that shut out all the people.
f. He was subject to death, and his office passed to another. 7:23. Christ's priesthood is forever. 7:24.
g. The sacrifices of the priest made a remembrance of sins. Christ takes them away.

but into the second the high priest alone

Only the high priest entered, and once a year, but he could enter several times on that day. Lev. 16. He alone had this privilege.

once in the year

This was a day prescribed by law. It was the tenth of the month Tisri, perhaps the 1st of October, for Tisri corresponds to our September and October.
Some say Lev. 16:12-15 shows he went in three times on that day. Jewish tradition says four times. One time may be for the purpose of bringing out the golden censor.
He brought in the incense and some say he placed it on the golden censor. Some say it was brought in too.

a. If it were placed just inside, it could be reached from beneath the veil.
b. Wherever the censor was placed, it was a part of the Holy of Holies.

not without blood

He brought the blood of a bullock.
a. He sprinkled some portion of it seven times before the ark and the veil. Lev. 16:14.
b. The blood was sprinkled in the inward tabernacle before the symbol of the divine presence.

Milligan says that this doesn't mean that he took blood all four times.

which he offereth for himself

Offered animal blood for himself since he was a sinner. It was not his own blood. See 9:25. Christ offered His own blood for all, but there was no need for offering blood for His sin, since He had none. Heb. 4:15.

and for the errors of the people

Clarke says, "For the sins of which they were not conscious — sins done in ignorance". See Num. 15:28-29. Of course no sacrifice existed for sin of "high hand," in open defiance, contempt. See Num. 15:30-31. By this the people were absolved of all sin of the past year and now had access to the mercy seat.

the Holy Spirit this signifying

The Holy Spirit designed, but also served as an interpreter.
a. We see in Heb. 10:14-22 the lesson that entrance has been made into heaven.
b. While the old covenant was in existence, entrance had not been made.

The Holy Spirit could signify a new message after the temple veil was ripped at the time of Christ's crucifixion.

that the way into the Holy Place hath not yet been made manifest

The fact that the priest could go in only once a year and then only if he had blood demonstrated that the way into heaven was not yet revealed.
a. They in a sense had salvation.

1. Ex. 3:6.
2. II Kings 2:1, 11.
3. Daniel 12:13.

   But all of it looked forward to Christ, which they did not understand. This suggests that it all was temporary; something better was in the future.

while the first tabernacle is yet standing

   The Old Testament is a closed way; the heavens were not opened by it. The New Testament is an open way.
a. Open veil — The old one was rent in twain.
b. Open tomb.
c. Open church.
d. Open heavens.

which is a figure for the time present; according to which are offered both gifts and sacrifices that cannot, as touching the conscience, make the worshipper perfect

   Even when the sacrifices were done and performed perfectly, yet now man knew he was a sinner.
   It took the torn flesh of Christ to reveal the mercy seat of God.
a. The temple veil being torn (Matt. 27:51) shows that God had now opened the Holy of Holies for man.
b. These sacrifices reminded men of sin, but could not cleanse the conscience.
   "As touching the conscience":
a. The law was to point out sin and to make men conscious of sin.
b. These caused the sinner to be concerned. 10:3: "But in those sacrifices there is a remembrance made of sins year by year."
c. We can have a cleansed conscience.
1. Heb. 9:14: "Cleanse your conscience from dead works."
2. Heb. 10:22: ". . . having our hearts sprinkled from an evil conscience."
3. I Tim. 3:9: ". . . holding the mystery of the faith in a pure conscience."
4. I Pet. 3:21: ". . . but the answer of a good conscience toward God".

being only with meats

Commentators have practically nothing to say here except Milligan, who feels the language is difficult. The point is that all of this is carnal, and Milligan feels that man's conscience was clear only in respect to meats and drinks and washings. The gifts and sacrifices could not clear his conscience, says Milligan.

It seems to me that Hebrews says man's conscience could not be cleared with gifts and sacrifices, since it was done only with meats, drinks, etc.

and drinks

This refers to the drink offerings that accompanied the other offerings. See Exodus 29:40-41.
a. According to Peloubet, this was excluded from the sin and trespass offering.
b. At all set feasts the drink offering was presented. Lev. 23:13, 18, 37.

Other verses are: Num. 15:4-7; 10-21: Num. 28:7-8; 9-10; 14-31; and Num. 29:6-39. We see in Lev. 10:9 that Aaron was forbidden the right to drink wine throughout his generations.

and divers washings

The washings were immersion in type. Here are some of them:
a. Whole body was washed.
1. The priest's whole body was washed at the time of his consecration. Lev. 16:4.
2. High priest on day of Atonement. Lev. 16:4, 24.
3. Priest defiled with uncleanness. Lev. 22:6.
4. Priest who officiated at the services of the red heifer. Num. 19:7.
5. Man who burned the red heifer. Num. 19:8.
b. Washing of hands and feet.
c. Washing of garments.
d. Washing of inwards and legs of burnt offerings.
e. Washing of wooden vessels.
f. Washing of spoils of war as could not pass through fire. Num. 31:21-23.

carnal ordinances
> Some would depend upon them today.
> I Tim. 4:1-3: "Forbidding to marry and commanding to abstain from meats."
> These things made the flesh clean, not the spirit righteous.

imposed until a time of reformation
> This may refer to the prophecy of Jeremiah 31:37, says one commentator. It is also translated "time of rectifying". This refers to the coming of Christ and the new covenant.

Study Questions

1442. What is referred to as the "first covenant"?
1443. What was included in the divine services?
1444. What is meant by "ordinances"?
1445. What is meant by "ablutions"?
1446. Who was instructed to construct the tabernacle and to make the priestly garments?
1447. What was the sanctuary?
1448. Why is it called "of this world"?
1449. What other names did it have?
1450. How was its construction financed? See Ex. 25:1-8; 35:4-29; 36:5-7.
1451. Is there any significance to the word "first"?
1452. Do other translations have the word?
1453. Why could it not refer to Solomon's temple?
1454. Where was the location of the candlestick, table, and showbread?
1455. Describe the tabernacle — the whole situation.
1456. Where did one enter?
1457. What was the size?
1458. How many parts did it have?
1459. As you enter, what did you see first? Next? What next?
1460. What was on the right side of it?
1461. What was on the left side of it?
1462. What was in the center?
1463. What is seen next as you proceed?
1464. What was in the Holy of Holies?
1465. What was in the ark?
1466. Which way did the tabernacle face?
1467. How large was the tent of meeting, or the Holy Place?

1468. Name the materials involved in construction of the whole tabernacle.
1469. What were the walls of the court made of?
1470. What were the walls of the Holy Place made of?
1471. How were they held together?
1472. We have a second veil mentioned. Where is it? Where was the first veil?
1473. Did the temple at Jerusalem have a veil?
1474. What was done to it? Matt. 27:51.
1475. Did Solomon's temple have a veil? See I Kings 6:31-33.
1476. How often and who had the privilege to enter this second veil? See Heb. 9:7.
1477. Where was the altar of incense located?
1478. What had a golden altar of incense?
1479. What are the opinions as to its location?
1480. What does Ex. 30:1, 6, 7, 10 and Ex. 40:5 says? Cf. Ex. 16:33; Num. 17:10; Lev. 16:12, 15.
1481. Was it an expensive thing?
1482. Does God always use beautiful and expensive things?
1483. Describe the ark of the covenant.
1484. Why do I Kings 8:9 and II Chron. 5:10 differ in regard to the content of the ark of the covenant?
1485. What did it contain?
1486. How large was it?
1487. Does the word "wherein" mean that the pot was in the ark or in the Holy of Holies?
1488. What does I Kings 8:9 say?
1489. Could the pot have been lost by the time of I Kings 8:9?
1490. What do you think of McKnight's explanation, saying, "nigh to"? Is this not the way the denominations deny water baptism?
1491. Describe Aaron's rod that budded.
1492. Does I Kings 8:9 affect this?
1493. Observe the Catholic Bible translation.
1494. What did it bud with? Num. 17:1-11.
1495. What is referred to by "the tables of the covenant"? Would this require the ark to be of sturdy construction to hold heavy tablets of stone?
1496. What appears above the ark?
1497. What is the meaning of the word "seraphim"?
1498. Is there more than one?

1499. Who were they? See Gen. 3:24.
1500. What do we know about their appearance? See Ezekiel 1:5-11, 13, 14.
1501. Were the cherubim silent? Cf. Ezek. 1:24; 10:5.
1502. Were they alive above the ark? See Ex. 25:18-20.
1503. If they had been alive, is it possible the interpretation of I Kings 8:9 means that articles were lost by the time of the temple?
1504. Does the author feel that he has gone into the subject thoroughly according to verse 5?
1505. What is meant by the expression that "the priest go in continually"?
1506. How many times daily did they go in, and what did they do?
1507. What continual task did they have? Lev. 4:6.
1508. Where was this done?
1509. Was the author of Hebrews speaking of the temple in Jerusalem, or the original tabernacle?
1510. What is meant by the word "second"?
1511. Contrast the work of the priest with that of the high priest.
1512. Contrast his work with that of Christ.
1513. What day was it that allowed the high priest to go into the Holy of Holies?
1514. Did he go in more than once on this day? Cf. Lev. 16:12-15.
1515. What did he have to possess when he went in?
1516. Does this mean he took blood all four times, if he went in that many?
1517. What persons were in need of the blood?
1518. Compare Hebrews 9:25 here.
1519. Does Heb. 4:15 tell why Jesus didn't offer blood for Himself?
1520. What does "the errors of the people" refer to?
1521. Was it for sins of which they were ignorant? Cf. Num. 15:28-29.
1522. Was there a sacrifice for deliberate sin? Cf. Num. 15:30-31.
1523. What fringe was worn as a memorial to the breaking of one of the ten commandments? Cf. Num. 15:37-41.
1524. What did the Holy Spirit signify?

HELPS FROM HEBREWS

1525. Did these old covenant people realize that heaven was not open yet to man?
1526. How long was heaven closed?
1527. What did God do to show that heaven was open and that the old covenant no longer had a closed Holy of Holies?
1528. What is meant by the word "figure"?
1529. What did it prefigure?
1530. What is meant by "both gifts and sacrifices"?
1531. What effect did the sacrifices have on the conscience?
1532. Could they make the conscience clear?
1533. Read Heb. 10:3 for a discussion of the cleansing of sin.
1534. Can the Christian have a clear conscience? Cf. 9:14; 10:22; I Tim. 3:9; I Peter 3:21.
1535. What kinds of attempts at reconcilation are mentioned in verse 10?
1536. What does "meats" refer to?
1537. What is referred to by "drinks"?
1538. Was it an offering? Cf. Ex. 29:40-41.
1539. What material was used in the drink offering? Lev. 23:13, 18, 37.
1540. Does it accompany all the offerings?
1541. Were all the priests allowed to drink wine in the drink offerings? Cf. Lev. 10:9.
1542. What is meant by "divers washings"?
1543. What things and persons were washed?
1544. Were the priests washed after each sacrifice?
1545. Were all sacrifices washed?
1546. Define the meaning of "carnal ordinances".
1547. Do people depend upon carnal ordinances today for salvation? Cf. I Tim. 4:1-3.
1548. How long were these things to last?
1549. What is meant by the word "reformation"?
1550. Is this Luther's reformation or Campbell's restoration?
1551. What other word is used by translators?
1552. How do we know what is meant?
1553. Are these commandments ordained this side of the cross?

2. *The superiority of Christ's ministry in the heavenly tabernacle. 9:11-14.*

Text
9:11-14

11 But Christ having come a High Priest of the good things to come, through the greater and more perfect tabernacle, not made with hands, that is to say, not of this creation, 12 nor yet through the blood of goats and calves, but through His own blood, entered in once for all into the holy place, having obtained eternal redemption. 13 For if the blood of goats and bulls, and the ashes of a heifer sprinkling them that have been defiled, sanctify unto the cleanness of the flesh: 14 how much more shall the blood of Christ, Who through the eternal Spirit offered Himself without blemish unto God, cleanse your conscience from dead works to serve the living God?

Paraphrase

11 But Christ being come, who is made an High Priest or Mediator of the blessings which are to be bestowed through the services of the greater and more excellent tabernacle, not made like the Mosaic tabernacle, with the hands of men, that is to say, a tabernacle not in this lower world,

12 Hath entered once for all into the holy places where God resides, (see Heb. ix. 5. note), not indeed by the blood of goats and of calves, but by His own blood, or death, as a sacrifice for sin; having thereby obtained for us, not redemption for a year, as the high priest did by entering the holy places on earth, but everlasting redemption; so did not need to offer Himself a second time.

13 That Jesus, by His death, should procure an eternal pardon for sinners is reasonable; for if the blood of bulls and of goats, offered by the high priest, and the ashes of an heifer, sprinkling the polluted, did, by the appointment of God, sanctify to the cleansing of the flesh, so as to fit the offender for joining in the tabernacle worship,

14 How much more reasonable is it that the blood of Christ, Who in obedience to God suffered death, and through the eternal Spirit, being raised from the dead, offered himself a victim without fault to God, should have merit sufficient to cleanse your conscience from the guilt of works which deserve death; that is, banish from your mind the fear of punishment, that ye may be fit to worship the living God with the hope of acceptance?

Comment

But Christ having come a High Priest of the good things to come

    Our blessings are future; the old was present.
a. Human priests were busy obtaining divine favor, but Jesus has obtained it.
b. The good things to come are those things obtained by His blood — pardon, access, heaven, etc.
    Some say "blessings to come" may refer to those promised in the Old Testament.

sanctify unto the cleanness of the flesh

    God has always had a meeting place for His people.
a. The altar has been that place in the past.
b. Now God comes where men are gathered in His name. Samaritan woman: John 4:21.
    God will some day have all who love Him around the throne.

not made with hands, that is to say, not of this creation

    The new tabernacle is eternal, not made with the feeble hands of men. Compare Rev. 11:19; 15:5.

nor yet through the blood of goats and calves

    Christ's blood was of more value than that of beasts. The old priests entered with the blood of a calf or a young bullock. Lev. 16:3.

but through His Own blood

    The death of Christ was discussed at the transfiguration. Luke 9:28-36.
    His death was foretold: Gen. 3:15; Isaiah 53.

entered in once for all into the Holy Place

    One entrance was sufficient.
    When did He enter? Between the statements to Mary and to Thomas?
a. He told Mary not to touch Him, for He had not yet ascended. John 20:17.
b. He told Thomas to touch Him. John 20:27.
c. Until greater light is thrown on these verses, we may assume the entrance was made after His commission was given and He made the ascension.

having obtained eternal redemption

> Milligan: The word "entered" is a verb, *Aorish,* and the word "obtaining" is a participle, *Aorists* and these are contemporaneous acts.

A redemption price that would stand good forever.

For if the blood of goats and bulls and the ashes of a heifer

Is this different from verse 12? Bulls and calves are named.
a. Calves are young bullocks, so there is no difference.
b. It was by the blood of these that the priest was able to enter heaven with his own blood.
c. This blood of goats and bulls also served to cleanse the flesh ceremonially.

"The ashes of a heifer" also had an important part.
a. The heifer was red. Num. 19:2.
1. The heifer was burned outside the camp, together with cedar wood, hyssop and scarlet.
2. The ashes were then prepared in water of purification to cleanse all who had touched a dead body or who had been in the tent with one.
b. Christ had no defilement, so this was never needed for Him.

sprinkling

It had to be applied to the people or else it was not sufficient. Num. 19:11-13.
a. Calvin, the Presbyterian, in his commentary does not deal with the word "sprinkling", so he does not advocate that it is a type of baptism by sprinkling.
b. To dip all the people in blood would have been an impossibility. Blood must be applied today.
a. Baptism is into the death of Christ.
b. The Lord's Supper is a partaking of His blood.

them that have been defiled

This water of purification was sprinkled upon anyone who had touched a dead body. Num. 19:11-12.

Observe the whole chapter for the process. Num. 19.

sanctify unto the cleanness of the flesh

If the blood of beasts was a true symbol of purgation, how much more shall the Christ purify man.

It is not cleanness of flesh that we must seek, but cleanness of the spirit.
a. Peter says baptism is not a physical bath but a cleansing of the conscience. I Pet. 3:21.
b. John 3:5 speaks of a "new birth".

how much more shall the blood of Christ

The blood of Christ is of singular importance.
a. John 1:29: "Behold the Lamb of God, That taketh away the sin of the world."
b. I John 3:5: "Ye know that He was manifested to take away sin."
c. I John 1:9: "If we confess our sins, He is faithful and righteous to forgive us our sins and to cleanse us from all unrighteousness."
If the blood of animals had some value, of course Christ's blood would have much more.

Who through the Eternal Spirit

Note the place of the Spirit in Jesus' life:
a. Jesus was conceived by the Holy Spirit. Matt. 1:18-20.
b. His commission was given by the Holy Spirit. Acts 1:2.
c. Jesus performed His miracles by the Spirit.
1. Matt. 12:28: "But if I by the spirit of God cast out demons, then is the kingdom of God come upon you."
2. Acts 10:38: God anointed Him with the Holy Spirit.
d. His death was done through the Spirit. Heb. 9:14.
e. By the Spirit He was raised from the dead. I Pet. 3:18.
There are different opinions as to what Spirit is referred to.
a. Some manuscripts read. "His Eternal Spirit."
b. Some suggest the thought that the trinity concurred in the salvation of the world.
c. Others think "Eternal Spirit" refers to His endless life.

offered himself

Does John 3:16 not say, "God *gave*"? Yes, but that is not all. Christ *came* voluntarily.
a. Phil. 2:5-11.
b. John 10:18 and 13:37-38.
No one can find sin in Jesus.

without blemish unto God
   a. Heb. 4:15: He was tempted in all points, yet without sin.
   b. Threefold temptation endured without sin. Matt. 4.
   c. Pilate said at His trial, "I find no fault in Him."
   The old sacrifices that were, without spot or blemish, were a type of Jesus.
   a. They were examined outwardly and inwardly to be sure of perfection.
   b. The life of Jesus was thoroughly examined, but no guile was found in Him.

cleanse your conscience
   "Purify" and purge" are also words used for "cleanse".
   The final step of entrance into the kingdom is to cleanse the conscience. I Peter 3:21.
   a. Baptism is not for cleansing the flesh, but to cleanse the conscience.
   b. When absolute forgiveness is assured, then the conscience is at rest.

from dead works
   General acts which bring the penalty of death.
   If it is not God's work, then it is a dead work. The conscience drives the heart of one who knows sin, to find relief. "Dead works", therefore, are the vain attempts to relieve a troubled conscience.

to serve the living God
   This is the purpose of being purged. We are not to plunge again into sin.
   a. II Pet. 2:21: "It were better for them not to have known —" Conversion has a high aim. Every convert should be converted to serve God.

Study Questions

1554. Of what is Christ a High Priest?
1555. Do the "things to come" refer to our blessings in the future or those looked forward to by the old?
1556. What good things do we expect?
1557. What tabernacle is referred to?
1558. Are hands involved in its making?

1559. Do we have to have a building in which to meet God? Cf. John 4:21.
1560. How does Revelation describe the new tabernacle? Rev. 11:19; 15:5.
1561. Translate verse 12 in your own words.
1562. Does it mean that Christ entered without blood?
1563. What blood did He take with Him to enter?
1564. Does this mean that Jesus ascended to heaven with His earthly crucified body?
1565. Can we infer that Jesus did not enter heaven after His resurrection until His final disappearance? Cf. John 20:17; John 20:27.
1566. What was obtained by Christ's entrance?
1567. Is there a difference in sacrifices here, since bulls are mentioned?
1568. How were the ashes of the heifer used?
1569. What were the ashes mixed with? See Num. 19.
1570. Who was cleansed by this mixture?
1571. What was sprinkled?
1572. Who was sprinkled?
1573. Why were the people sprinkled with blood, rather than being dipped in it?
1574. Is there anything significant now about cleansing the flesh?
1575. Is man in the New Testament to have a cleansed flesh or a cleansed spirit? Cf. I Peter 3:21; John 3:5.
1576. What contrast is seen in verse 13 and verse 14?
1577. What does the blood of Christ do? Cf. John 1:29; I John 3:5; 1:9.
1578. If blood of animals served a purpose, may we expect Christ's blood to be more effective?
1579. What adjective describes Christ's Spirit?
1580. Is it His Spirit or the Holy Spirit referred to?
1581. What has Christ accomplished by the Spirit?
1582. Does "offered Himself" conflict with John 3:16? Cf. Phil. 2:5-11; John 10:18; 13:37-38.
1583. "Without blemish unto God" is not a new idea. What other verses teach His sinlessness?
1584. Were the Old Testament sacrifices to be perfect?
1585. How did they insure a perfect sacrifice?
1586. Was the life of Jesus thoroughly examined?

1587. Of what is man's conscience cleansed?
1588. What could be classified as "dead works"?
1589. Are all things that are not God's works "dead works"?
1590. What is the final act that cleanses a man's conscience as he is obedient to God?
1591. After the cleansing, what is expected of man?
1592. What is involved in service?
1593. Do all understand that cleansing is for consecration?

3. *The effectiveness of the new covenant based upon the death of Christ. 9:15-22.*

Text
9:15-22

15 And for this cause He is the Mediator of a new covenant, that a death having taken place for the redemption of the transgressions that were under the first covenant, they that have been called may receive the promise of the eternal inheritance. 16 For where a testament is, there must of necessity be the death of him that made it. 17 For a testament is of force where there hath been death: for it doth never avail while he that made it liveth. 18 Wherefore even the first covenant hath not been dedicated without blood. 19 For when every commandment had been spoken by Moses unto all the people according to the law, he took the blood of the calves and the goats, with water and scarlet wool and hyssop, and sprinkled both the book itself and all the people, 20 saying, This is the blood of the covenant which God commanded to you-ward. 21 Moreover the tabernacle and all the vessels of the ministry he sprinkled in like manner with the blood. 22 And according to the law, I may almost say, all things are cleansed with blood, and apart from shedding of blood there is no remission.

Paraphrase

15 And for this reason, that the death of Christ is so efficacious, of the new covenant He is the Mediator or High Priest, by Whom its blessings are dispensed; and also the Sacrifice by which it is procured and ratified; that His death being accomplished for obtaining the pardon of the transgressions of the first covenant, believers of all ages and nations, as the called seed of Abraham, (Rom. viii. 48. note), may receive the promised eternal inheritance.

16 For, to show the propriety of Christ's dying to ratify the new covenant, I observe, that where a covenant is made by sacrifice, there is a necessity that the death of the appointed sacrifice be produced.

17 For, according to the practice both of God and man, a covenant is made firm over dead sacrifices; seeing it never hath force whilst the goat, calf, or bullock, appointed as the sacrifice of ratification, liveth.

18 Because from the beginning God ratified His covenant by sacrifice, to preserve among men the expectation of the sacrifice of His Son, hence not even the covenant of Sinai was made without sacrifice.

19 For when Moses had read every precept in the book of the law to all the people, taking the blood of the calves and goats which had been offered as the sacrifices of ratification, with water, and scarlet wool, and hyssop, he sprinkled both the book of the law itself as representing God, and all the people, in token of the consent of both parties to the covenant,

20 Saying, while he sprinkled the people, This is the blood whereby the covenant which God hath commanded me to make with you is ratified, both on his part and on yours. (See ver. 15, note 1.)

21. Moreover, to prefigure the efficacy of the sacrifice of Christ to render our acts of worship acceptable, both the tabernacle, and the altar, and mercy-seat, and all the vessels used in the worship of God, Moses in like manner sprinkled with blood, after they were made and set in order.

22 And, for the same reason, almost all things, according to the law, are annually fitted for the worship of God by sprinkling them with blood. (See Lev. xvi. 16. 19. 33.) In short, to show that pardon is procured through the blood of Christ, without the shedding of blood there is no remission of sin granted by the law.

Comment

And for this cause
    It means "on account of this" (blood). It may also be translated, "therefore", or "wherefore".

He is the mediator
Jesus is the Mediator for man. Note that he does not call Him "testament".
    No need for any other is felt if we know Christ in His purity.

new covenant

"Testament" is also used for "covenant". "Covenant" is better. It is the new contract between God and man.

The word means both "covenant" and "testament" F.N. of American Standard Bible.

Milligan: It means covenant. McKnight: If it is testament, who died for it to be in force?

that a death having taken place for the redemption of the transgressions

That by means of death all men could have forgiveness.
Heb. 10:4 says that the blood of bulls and goats could not take away sin.
a. We would ask then, "Are the Jews who were faithful in their sacrifices lost?"
b. This verse surely answers the question, saying that those under the first covenant are taken care of by the sacrifice of Jesus.

that were under the first covenant

Does this mean all the dead Jews, or does it mean simply those who were living under the first covenant? Milligan: "The death of Christ was necessary in order to accomplish the redemption of the transgressions which were committed under the old covenant during the Jewish age." p. 257. The exception Milligan states would be those who were justified by faith — Abraham, Isaac, Jacob. Rom. 4:2 3, James 2:21-23. Where did these men go? Milligan, 251:
a. If not immediately to heaven, at least to a place and state of high spiritual enjoyment.
1. Exodus 3:6.
2. Dan. 12:13.
3. Luke 10:23-24.
b. This is what Paul refers to in Rom. 3:25-26.

they that have been called

Milligan: The blood was a necessity before the called of any age could have an absolute right to the free and full enjoyment of the eternal inheritance. This is not merely a promised land calling, but for eternal life for all the called of all generations.

```
                Blood of bulls and goats   Christ
Adam — X..........................X...........X — Eternity
                Hebrews 10:4              Blood
```

may receive the promise of the eternal inheritance

This is not a physical land inheritance, but an eternal one in the presence of God.
a. I Pet. 1:4: "An inheritance incorruptible, undefiled that fadeth not away reserved in heaven for you".
b. Jesus said: "Lay up for yourselves treasures in heaven."
Our inheritance is with Christ as a joint heir. Rom. 8:17.

for where a testament is

Newell says to translate the word "testament" is confusing and incorrect.
a. A covenant has a mediator but not a testament, he says.
b. A testament has someone to execute it; so Newell is strained here.
Milligan: The word means both covenant and testament, and here he uses the second meaning.
Calvin: The Greek means both. p. 208.

there must of necessity

Death is necessary to the culmination of a testament. Inheritance follows the death of the testator.

be the death of him that made it

The testament, or will, goes into effect after the death of the testator. As long as the testator lives, he can change that will, but death fixes its points.

for a testament is of force, where there hath been a death: for it doth never avail while he that made it liveth

Legal language is used here. The testament is generally kept in a safety deposit box until the death of the testator. A division of the inheritance follows the death of the testator.

wherefore even the first covenant hath not been dedicated without blood

God has always emphasized sacrifice.
a. Their sacrifices were to keep alive the knowledge of the fact of sin and the need of forgiveness.

b. We have baptism, and the Lord's Supper, to remind us today. See Exodus 24:4-8 for the dedication.

for when every commandment had been spoken

This refers to Exodus 24:4-8. When they were recited the people said, "This we will do." He then wrote them and reread them. Verse 7. The people responded again. Then they were ratified by the blood.

He took the blood of calves and goats with water

The blood was put in basins and mingled with water to keep it from coagulating. He then took hyssop bound together with hyssop and dipped this in the basin and sprinkled it upon the people nearest him.
a. They represented all the people.
b. It was impossible to have blood enough for all.
Milligan says Moses doesn't mention all the details. Paul adds here that the water, blood of bulls and goats, scarlet wool, hyssop, sprinkling of the book of the covenant were part of the ceremony.

and scarlet wool

The wool was to help absorb the water and blood. It was scarlet, no doubt, for symbolism.

and hyssop

Occasions for the use of it are found in Ex. 12:22; Lev. 14:4-7; Num. 19:18-19. Usually the bunch of hyssop was fastened to a stick of cedar wood by means of a scarlet band and then wrapped round with scarlet wool for the purpose of absorbing the blood and water that were to be sprinkled. (Milligan, p. 260.)

and sprinkled both the book itself and all the people

Upon the book — why?
a. To show that it was ratified by blood.
b. The book was then sanctified for their obedience.
The people were sanctified to obey the words of the book.
saying, (Ex. 24:8) *This is the blood of the covenant which God commanded to you-ward*

This is the blood by which the covenant is ratified. This was not a covenant of equals, but words sanctified from one who had the right to command.

moreover the tabernacle and all the vessels of the ministry be sprinkled in like manner with the blood

This is not the same occasion as in Exodus 24:1-8 referred to, but later when it was constructed. The tabernacle was not constructed in Exodus 24:1-8 so it must refer to Ex. 40:9-11.

and according to the law I may almost say all things are cleansed with blood

"Almost": the law required that almost everything defiled should be purified by blood. In some cases it was done with water:
a. Lev. 16:26-28.
b. Num. 31:24.
Sometimes it was done by fire and water:
a. Num. 31:22, 23.

and apart from the shedding of blood there is no remission

Blood is spoken of as being essential to atonement.
a. Lev. 17:11: "I have given it (the blood) to you upon the altar to make atonement for your souls, for it is the blood that maketh atonement for the soul."
The poorest people who could not afford a sacrifice no doubt had theirs made by public expense. (Milligan, p. 261.)
a. Lev. 5:11-13: Those too poor to bring two turtledoves or two young pigeons for a sin offering were to bring seven pints of an ephah of fine flour, without oil or frankincense, a handful of which the priest was to burn as a memorial upon the altar.
b. Note, however, verse 13. The priest made atonement for him, which was very likely a blood sacrifice at public expense.
c. The memorial was made with flour, but the atonement was with blood.

Study Questions

1594. What is meant by "for this cause"?
1595. What is the work of a mediator?
1596. Is there room for Christ's mother here in forgiving sin?
1597. What kind of a covenant does Jesus serve?

1598. Is God obligated to keep His part of the covenant if man fails to keep his?
1599. Does the blood of Christ act backwards as well as forwards?
1600. For whom was Christ's blood shed?
1601. Can we say then that the Jews under the old covenant are saved?
1602. Were all saved by the blood of Christ?
1603. Who was excepted, according to Milligan?
1604. Compare Romans 4:3-4 and James 2:21-23 for his proof texts.
1605. Does Rom. 3:25-26 teach that Christ's blood was retroactive?
1606. What is meant by "passing over" in Rom. 3:25? Does it mean rolled forward?
1607. What does the calling refer to here?
1608. Is it the Hebrew promised land or eternal life?
1609. How is the inheritance described?
1610. How does I Peter 1:4 describe it?
1611. With whom is our inheritance? Rom. 8:17.
1612. What is meant by "testament"?
1613. Is it as good a word as covenant?
1614. What are the differences between "testament" and "covenant"?
1615. What is necessary for the fulfillment of a testament?
1616. When do we inherit from a testament?
1617. Whose death is necessary?
1618. Does death fix the terms with finality?
1619. Is it logical to say that Jesus was the dead Testator of the New Testament?
1620. What kind of language is used here in regard to the testament.
1621. Then do we have the right to be legalistic in our preaching?
1622. What is necessary to set a will in force?
1623. How was the first covenant dedicated?
1624. Why did God require the constant sacrifices?
1625. What do we have today to remind us of sin?
1626. What commandments are referred to here? Cf. Ex. 24:4-8.
1627. Did the people approve?
1628. Where is this occasion discussed in the Old Testament?
1629. Why was water mixed with the blood?

1630. Why was wool used?
1631. Why was it scarlet wool?
1632. What is hyssop?
1633. How was it used?
1635. Why was the book sprinkled?
1636. Why were the people sprinkled?
1637. Is this a covenant between equals?
1638. Have we the right to question the one who has the right to command?
1639. What is the significance of the tabernacle and vessels being sanctified by blood? Was it done frequently? Cf. Ex. 24:1-8; Ex. 40:9-11.
1640. Is the church sprinkled with blood? Cf. Eph. 5:25-26.
1641. Is the author in doubt when he says, "I may almost say"?
1642. What does he mean by "almost"?
1643. Do you think that you can express a better translation of this verse?
1644. What things were not purified by blood?
1645. What other element was used? Cf. Lev. 16:26-28; Num. 31:24.
1646. What other cleanser was used? Cf. Num. 31:22, 23.
1647. What was the purpose of blood being shed, as expressed in this verse? Cf. Lev. 17:11.
1648. How could sin be atoned if one could not afford a blood sacrifice? Cf. Lev. 5:11-13.
1649. What is meant by "memorial"?
1650. Did the priest offer blood for the poor people?
1651. If so, how were these offerings financed?

4. *Necessity and Adequancy of the Better Sacrifice.* 9:23-28

Text
9:23-28

23 It was necessary therefore that the copies of the things in the heavens should be cleansed with these; but the heavenly things themselves with better sacrifices than these. 24 For Christ entered not into a Holy Place made with hands, like in pattern to the true; but into heaven itself, now to appear before the face of God for us: 25 nor yet that He should offer Himself often, as the high priest entereth into the Holy Place year by year with

blood not His own; 26 else must He often have suffered since the foundation of the world: but now once at the end of the ages hath He been manifested to put away sin by the sacrifice of Himself. 27 And inasmuch as it is appointed unto men once to die, and after this cometh judgment; 28 so Christ also, having been once offered to bear the sins of many, shall appear a second time, apart from sin, to them that wait for Him, unto salvation.

Paraphrase

23 Seeing God would admit sinners into heaven without shedding the blood of His Son, to make the Israelites sensible of this, it was necessary that the tabernacles, the representations of the holy places in the heavens, (see chap. ix. 1. note 2.), should be annually cleansed, that is, opened to the priests and people, by the sacrifices of bulls and goats, as types of the sacrifice of Christ; but the heavenly holy places themselves, by a sacrifice more effectual than these.

24 Therefore Christ, our High Priest, hath not entered with the sacrifice of His crucified body (Heb. x. 10.) into the holy places made with the hands of men, the images of the true holy places; but into heaven itself, now to appear with that sacrifice before the manifestation of the Divine Presence, to officiate as the High Priest of these holy places on our account.

25 Though it was necessary that Christ should open heaven to us by offering the sacrifice of Himself, it was not necessary that He should offer Himself often in the heavenly holy places for that purpose, as the high priest entereth into the earthly holy places every year with other blood than His own;

26 For He must often have suffered death on earth, since the beginning of the world: But that this was not necessary, appeareth from the fact itself, for now once, at the conclusion of the Mosiac dispensation, Christ hath been manifested in the flesh, to abolish the Levitical sin-offering by the sacrifice of Himself.

27 And, for as much as it is appointed by God, that men shall die but once as the punishment of the sin of the first man, and that, after death, every one shall be judged and punished but once for his own sins.

28 Even so Christ, being once offered in order to carry away the guilt of the sins of many, justice required no more sin-offering for them: and therefore He will, to them who wait for Him,

appear a second time on earth, without dying as a sin-offering, in order, as their King and Judge, to bestow on them salvation.

Comment

It was necessary therefore
   The necessity is found only in the type. If the old is to picture the new, then cleansing is necessary.

that the copies of the things in the heavens
   Perhaps the church is referred to. It was bought with blood. Acts 20:28: ". . . feed the church of the Lord which He purchased with His own blood".
a. If the church is not meant here, then heaven is, and heaven then is cleansed.
b. If the tabernacle is a picture of the church, then the church may be referred to.
   The heavenly pattern was to be cleansed in a different way than the old.
   Milligan: "Copy" is also translated "pattern".

should be cleansed with these
   McKnight says this refers to the cleansing of the tabernacle.
a. See Lev. 16:16-18 where atonement is made for the Holy Place.
b. This made it ceremonially prepared for the worship services. The copies, or pattern, were made ceremonially clean to picture a pure church and a pure heaven.

but the heavenly things themselves with better sacrifices than these
   Milligan says perhaps because of the sins of angels, Heaven itself must be cleansed.
   "Heavenly things" do not necessarily have to be in heaven. Milligan: The "heavenly things" refers to both the church on earth and heaven itself. The church is a heavenly thing, the kingdom of heaven, so why believe he is talking about heaven itself?
   Why would heaven need to be cleansed?
a. Milligan says: "Take this as a matter of faith", for we cannot give a satisfying answer.

For Christ entered not into a holy place made with hands, like in pattern to the true, but into heaven itself now to appear before the face of God for us
   Does heaven have a tabernacle?

a. Yes, according to Rev. 11:19.
   So verse 23 may refer to heaven.
   Is heaven in need of cleansing?
a. We would first answer no, for God does not dwell where sin is.
b. Our answer is to be qualified, however. See Job 15:15 and 25:5.
   The important part of the verse for us is expressed in "now to appear before the face of God for us."
a. The cleansing of heaven may not be clear, but this surely is.
b. Christ is before God for us.

nor yet that He should offer Himself often, as the high priest entereth into the holy place year by year with blood not of his own

>   Christ's one sacrifice is contrasted with old covenant " often." Christ entered once with His own blood. That one time is sufficient.

else must He often have suffered

>   The sacrifice of Jesus is necessary for atonement, but it comes in the midst of the generations of man. A constant sacrifice of Jesus is not needful when one brings absolute forgiveness

since the foundation of the world.

>   He was the Lamb. Rev. 13:8. His blood is still considered as in the act of being continually poured out.

but now once at the end of the ages

>   The conclusion of the Jewish dispensation is referred to. At the end of an age is sufficient, as much so as if it had taken place before or during the age. Some understand this to be future.

hath He been manifested to put away sin

>   Clarke says he was manifested to abolish sin offerings. This ended the Mosaic laws. The sin offering ceased, as foretold by Dan. 9:24.
>   Others' opinion:
a. It refers to the putting away of the guilt, power, and being of sins from the souls of believers.
b. Of course, sin offerings are ended, but to put away sin was the real purpose.

by the sacrifice of Himself

No blood of animals is involved here. God gave, but Christ came to offer Himself. Compare Heb. 2:14 for the importance of this verse.

it is appointed unto man once to die

All are under the decree, "Dust thou are and unto dust shalt thou return." Gen. 3:19. Death and judgment are the appointments which the ungodly ought to dread.
a. There are exceptions to the sentence of death: Enoch, Elijah, those persons who are alive at His coming. See I Thess. 4:13-18.
Man makes the second-death appointment by his choice to live in sin.

and after this cometh judgment - see p 291

It is death once and judgment once, no second chance and no transmigration of the soul. No purgatory is alluded to here.
a. A person's true character has been revealed while on this earth, and nothing can be done to change it after death.
b. The rich man found out that nothing could be done, for a gulf is fixed. Judgment discussed: John 5:28-29; Rev. 20:11-15.

so Christ also, having been once offered to bear the sins of many

Isaiah 53:4-6: "Jehovah hath laid on Him the iniquity of us all."
Our sin is borne by the Christ.
a. This gives us peace.
b. This gives us remission of sins.

shall appear a second time

He shall come out of the Holy of Holies
a. I Thess. 4:16.
b. Acts 1:11.
Christ's appearance this time will be that of a victor, and not a slain lamb.

apart from sin

He will not come then bearing the sins of the people. He will come as Saviour and Judge. All men shall then see. He is the **Way, Truth, and Life.**

to them that wait for Him

This is one difference between the godly and the unsaved.
a. I Thess. 1:9: "How ye turned unto God from idols to serve a living and **true** God."
b. I Thess. 1:10: "And to wait for His Son from heaven, Whom He raised from the dead, even Jesus, Who delivereth us from the wrath to come."
"Them that wait" — For what do we wait?
a. II Pet. 3:13: "We look for new heavens and a new earth."

unto salvation

b. II Tim. 4:8: "Unto all them that love His appearing."
c. II Pet. 3:17.
This will be the final experience of the Christian. We talked about being saved now, but at His coming, salvation will be ours. The experience of the reward is referred to here.

Study Questions

1652. What was necessary as expressed in verse 23?
1653. What is meant by "copies of the things in the heavens"?
1654. Is "copies" referring to sacrifice or tabernacle or both?
1655. Was the tabernacle a copy of something in heaven?
1656. Was heaven cleansed? If so, how?
1657. Could it mean that He simply entered heaven with His blood?
1658. What is referred to by the word "these"?
1659. If the tabernacle was a type of the church, and it was cleansed, what should we expect of the church?
1660. Do you know of any "dirty" churches?
1661. What will cleanse the church?
1662. Does heaven have to be cleansed? Cf. Job 15:15 and Job 25:5.
1663. Does "heavenly" refer to a place or a kind of things?
1664. If the church and the kingdom of God are the same, could it be considered the "heavenly things" referred to?
1665. If heaven had to be cleansed, how could it have been cleansed by Christ's blood when it was shed on earth?
1666. This verse teaches that Christ entered a holy place. Does heaven have a tabernacle? Cf. Rev. 11:19.
1667. What is meant by "appear before the face of God"?
1668. Why is He before the face of God?

HELPS FROM HEBREWS

1669. How may we harmonize this with other passages where Christ is seated at the right hand of God?
1670. How often does Christ offer Himself?
1671. How often does Christ enter the Holy Place?
1672. What is meant by "blood not of His own"?
1673. Why did other priests have to offer blood often?
1674. Why does Jesus not need other blood?
1675. What is meant by "Since the foundation of the world"? Cf. Matt. 13:35; Matt. 25:34; Rev. 13:8.
1676. Compare Rev. 13:8 in various translations.
1677. Can it be true that Jesus was slain "from the foundation of the world"?
1678. What is meant by "end of the ages"?
1679. Discuss the word "manifested".
1680. What is meant by "put away sin"?
1681. How did Jesus put sin away?
1682. What appointment is referred to?
1683. Does this mean that a date is set for us?
1684. Name some who escaped that appointment.
1685. Will others escape it? Cf. I Thess. 4:13-18.
1686. How soon comes judgment after death?
1687. Is there room for purgatory?
1688. Can anything be done according to the story of the rich man and Lazarus?
1689. What is meant by judgment?
1690. Compare John 5:28-29 and Rev. 20:11-15.
1691. Is the Christian judged? Cf. Rom. 14:10; II Cor. 5:10; Heb. 10:30.
1692. Does the next verse read as though we are judged?
1693. Discuss the expression, "*bear* the sins."
1694. Discuss this subject in comparison to Isaiah 53:4-6.
1695. What is meant by "appear a second time"?
1696. How will He appear in relationship to sin next time?
1697. To whom will He appear?
1698. What is meant by "wait for Him"?
1699. Is waiting the kind of thing some have done by selling everything, then watching for Him to come at a given time?

Special Study On Hebrews 9:27
Judgment: *Krisis*

Often in the New Testament the word "judgment" ethically means:

(1) To decide, give a verdict, declare an opinion: *Krino.* Luke 11:42; Acts 15:19.

(2) To investigate, scrutinize. *Anakrino*: I Cor. 2:15; I Cor. 4:3.

(3) To discriminate, distinguish: *Diakrino.* I Cor. 11:31; 14:29.

Since God's judgments are declarations of His divine justice with His own condemnations, justice, condemnation, and judgment sometimes are all the same. Cf. Rom. 5:16.

In John 5:29 we read of the resurrection of judgment, which is also translated "damnation."

The last judgment may be thought of as an act when God interposes into human history directly to bring this present course of the world to an end, and determines the eternal fate of human beings and places them in surroundings which fit their spiritual condition.

We have a different idea in Rom. 14:10 and II Cor. 5:10, where we are told that we must appear before the judgment seat (*bema*) of Christ. In Heb. 10:30 we read that God will "judge" His people — the word is *Krino* — meaning to give a verdict. He will do the same for the adulterers, according to 13:4.

The word *krisis,* translated "judgment", is often used in the Word of God.

Matthew uses the word often in speaking of judgment, such as, "the men of Ninevah will rise up in the day of judgment;" "the queen of the south rising up in judgment." Matt. 12:41-42.

The same word is used in Heb. 9:27, ". . . once to die, and after this cometh judgment." Also 10:27.

I John 4:17 speaks of having boldness in the day of judgment.

In I Peter 4:17, we read that judgment must begin at the house of God. The word is *Krima.* It is the same word as in Matthew 7:2, "With what judgment ye judge, ye shall be judged."

In I Cor. 4:4, Paul says, "He that judgeth me is the Lord." — *Anakrino.*

This verse, Heb. 9:27, does not leave room for transmigration of the soul, purgatory, or repentance.

When the body returns to dust and man has his appointment, his death sentence or his commendation is fixed.

Questions On Chapter Nine
True and False

_____ 1. The first covenant was of no consequence since God did not swear by Himself.
_____ 2. The tabernacle contained a Holy of Holies in which the candlesticks and table of show bread were placed. Verses 2-3.
_____ 3. Within the veil of the Holy of Holies were placed the golden censer, ark of the covenant, golden pot of manna.
_____ 4. The priests, who never commited sins, were very faithful to God in their duties.
_____ 5. The new covenant could not be established except by the death of Jesus.
_____ 6. Remission of sins is obtained only by the shedding of blood.
_____ 7. It is appointed unto angels once to die and after that the judgment.
_____ 8. The altar of burnt offerings was placed in the Holy of Holies.
_____ 9. The high priest went into the Holy of Holies twice each year to offer blood for his errors and those of the people. Verse 7.
_____10. Only the high priest was allowed in the Holy of Holies.
_____11. After Christ's crucifixion He entered in once and for all into the Holy Place. Verse 12.
_____12. A difference between the two covenants was that the first was not dedicated with blood. Verse 18.
_____13. Christ entered not into a holy place made by hands. Verse 24.
_____14. According to the law, no blood was to touch any of the sacred vessels in the temple or tabernacle.
_____15. A testament is of no strength while the testator lives. Verses 16-17.
_____16. Christ is coming another time to give the world a second chance to accept Him.
_____17. In the tabernacle was Elisha's rod that budded.

_____18. In the tabernacle the cherubim represented the Presence of God or the Spirit.
_____19. In this chapter the High Priest of man appears before the face of God.
_____20. The priests on earth rarely had any duties to perform.

Multiple Choice Questions Over Chapter Nine

1. The old covenant was:
   1. Dedicated with blood.
   2. First given just before entrance to Canaan.
   3. Repeated by the prophets.
2. Aaron's rod that budded:
   1. Was a limb off the tree of life from Eden.
   2. Probably a cutting from a willow tree that grew in that area.
   3. Was placed in the Holy of Holies.
3. Where a testament is, there must be:
   1. Witnesses to the first drafting of it.
   2. A parallel agreement.
   3. The death of him that made it.
4. Sprinkling in the old covenant was upon:
   1. The infants too young to believe.
   2. The book and the people.
   3. Those who were diseased.
5. Old Testament sacrifices were offered without blemishes. Since Christ was made in human flesh:
   1. His sacrifice was not without blemish.
   2. He was in spite of it a Sacrifice without blemish.
   3. He has yet to sacrifice for Himself.
6. The tabernacle and all the vessels of the ministry:
   1. Were replaced year by year.
   2. Burned after each high priest died.
   3. Were sprinkled with blood.
7. Christ became a High Priest:
   1. Of good things to come.
   2. Of the tribe of Judah from which He came.
   3. Of those too young to make their own sacrifice.
8. The ark of the covenant was overlaid:
   1. With gems.
   2. In later years with silver by loving hands.
   3. With gold.

9. The blood of goats and bulls and ashes of a heifer sprinkled upon the people:
   1. Sanctified unto the cleanness of the flesh.
   2. Was one sacrifice repulsive to the people.
   3. Was the most difficult to perform.
10. The blood of Jesus is:
    1. To cleanse the conscience from dead works.
    2. To be applied immediately upon the person who has faith.
11. Christ's death took place for the redemption:
    1. Of those under the first covenant.
    2. For only those who have been predestined to be saved.
12. In the old priestly system the high priest was privileged once a year to enter into the Holy of Holies:
    1. To go in with all his assistants.
    2. To take the janitor in with him.
    3. To go in alone.
13. The old priestly system with its meats, drinks, divers washings, and carnal ordinances was imposed:
    1. Until a new tribe of priests could serve.
    2. Until Melchizedek should return from the dead.
    3. Until a time of reformation.
14. Christ shall appear a second time apart from sin:
    1. Because He is ceremonially clean.
    2. To set up a priesthood for angels.
    3. To them that wait for Him.
15. It is appointed unto man once to die and:
    1. After that the judgment.
    2. He goes immediately to his reward.
    3. He then must sleep for a millennium.

SUMMARY OF CHAPTER NINE

Having reached the main point of the discussion in Chapter Eight which tells of Jesus' ministry in connection with the new covenant, the ninth chapter explains the contrast between Christ's ministry in the "greater and more perfect tabernacle" with the work of the Old Testament priests in the earthly tabernacle which was built at Sinai.

The chapter begins with a brief description of the tabernacle and its furniture and proceeds to show something of its purpose and limitation. Its gifts and sacrifices could not cleanse the conscience of the worshipper.

But Christ's ministry in the tabernacle which was not of this creation did obtain eternal redemption through His own blood. This was in connection with His work as Mediator of the new covenant. His death provided redemption for those under the first covenant as well as for those under the new covenant. The shedding of His blood is explained by the example of the dedication of the first covenant — dedicated with blood which Moses sprinkled on both the book and the people and on everything connected with the tabernacle.

The meaning of Christ's sacrifice is explained over against the ceremony pertaining to atonement in connection with the first tabernacle.

The chapter closes with the warning that Christ, Who has gone into heaven to appear before the face of God, will appear again to those who wait for Him for salvation.

G. *He is a Priest of a better sacrifice.* 10:1-39.
1. *The impossibility of the Mosaic sacrifice to take away sins.* 10:1-4.

Text
10:1-4

1 For the law having a shadow of the good things to come, not the very image of the things, can never with the same sacrifices year by year, which they offer continually, make perfect them that draw nigh. 2 Else would they not have ceased to be offered? because the worshippers, having been once cleansed, would have had no more consciousness of sins.

3 But in those sacrifices there is a remembrance made of sins year by year. 4 For it is impossible that the blood of bulls and goats should take away sins.

Paraphrase

1 Wherefore, since the law, in the services of the high priests in the inward tabernacle, contains a shadow only of the blessings which were to come through the services of Christ in the heavenly tabernacle, and not the very substance of these blessings, it never can, with the same kind of sacrifices which the high priests offer yearly forever, make those who come to these sacrifices perfect in respect of pardon.

2 Since, if these sacrifices could have made the worshippers perfect in respect of pardon, being once offered, would they not have

ceased from being again offered? because the worshippers, being once pardoned, should have had no longer any uneasiness in their conscience on account of the sins for which the atonement was made.

3 Nevertheless, in these sacrifices annually repeated, and in the confession of sins made over the scape goat, a remembrance of all the sins of the people is made yearly, as not pardoned. Lev. xvi. 21.

4 Besides, it is impossible, in the nature of things, that the blood of bulls and of goats should procure the pardon of sins, either in the way of substitution or by example.

Comment

For the law having a shadow of the good things to come

> Law shadowed the gospel. Aaron shadowed the Christ. Levitical sacrifices shadowed the Lamb of God.
> Purification in the Old Testament pictured complete redemption in Christ.
> Earthly Canaan pictured the heavenly rest.
> The tabernacle pictured the church.

not the very image of the things

> It was a simple representation. The gospel is the image or thing itself. An artist first draws a shadowy picture, then fills in with color. So, the law is a foreshadow of the gospel age.

can never with the same sacrifices year by year

> There were yearly sacrifices, Lev. 23, and these were performed in the same manner by priests who were subject to death and had to be succeeded.
> The blood of Christ had been shed, which the old sacrifices pictured, but the Jews did not see that they were done away.

which they offer continually make perfect them that draw nigh

> No perfection existed in the old, yet the Jews accept these sacrifices in place of the perfect sacrifice. The Jews must quit drawing nigh unto the old, and must approach the new.

a. Heb. 10:22 tells how to draw nigh.
b. James 4:8 holds a promise to those who draw nigh.
c. Heb. 10:38-39 shows danger in not drawing nigh.

else would they not have ceased to be offered? because the worshippers, having been once cleansed would have had no more consciousness of sins

Repetition would not have been necessary if results were obtained. A debt cancelled does not need a repeated payment. Sacrifices made them conscious of sin, not free from it.

A person needs cleansing in order to escape a consciousness of sin.
a. It can be done. Acts 22:16.
b. Rom. 6:1-6 pictures death to old sins and the sinner.

but in those sacrifices there is a rememberance made of sins year by year

Note the word is "remembrance" — not remission.
a. There were special offerings: Num. 15:27-28; Lev. 4:3, 14, 23, 28.
b. There were daily ones: Ex. 29:38-46.
c. Weekly ones: Num. 28:9-10.
d. Monthly: Num. 28:11-15.
e. Yearly at three great festivals.

With the Christian there is forgiveness immediately upon repentance because of the one great sacrifice.

for it is impossible that the blood of bulls and goats should take away sins.

Let this verse answer the question, "Were the sacrifices able to cleanse from sin?"
a. They were to make atonement, yes, but only as performed by faith, at last to be made final in the blood offering of Jesus.
b. See Rom. 4:25: " — delivered up for our trespasses — " This shows that Christ's sacrifice is the one great sacrifice. Let the Jew turn from the impossible sacrifices to the possible sacrifice.

Study Questions

1700. What is the law likened to? Would your explanation please a Seventh Day Adventist?
1701. Was "shadow" a general word or a specific one?
1702. What is meant by " shadow"?
1703. It was to foreshadow good things. What were the good things?

1704. What did the law shadow?
1705. What did Aaron foreshadow?
1706. What did purification precede?
1707. What did the earthly Canaan represent?
1708. What did the tabernacle picture?
1709. How can you best define or explain "shadow"?
1710. Is it the same idea as "image" in the next phrase?
1711. Do you think that a good illustration of "shadow" would be the artist's first sketch before the actual oil painting?
1712. What does verse one say about the futility of the old law?
1713. Why did God have them do it, if year after year it could not remove sin?
1714. What is meant by "which they offer continually"?
1715. Who is referred to as drawing nigh?
1716. What did they draw nigh to?
1717. How can we draw nigh to the "good things"? Cf. Heb. 10:22; James 4:8; Heb. 10:38.
1718. Is this first phrase an affirmation or a question?
1719. What is the implied answer?
1720. Would repetition have been necessary if they could have achieved perfection?
1721. Did their sacrifices free their conscience?
1722. Does the Lord's Supper also disturb our conscience?
1723. How do the Lord's Supper and the Jewish sacrifice compare in this respect?
1724. How does baptism into Christ compare with Jewish sacrifices in regard to conscience? See Acts 22:16; Rom. 6:1-6.
1725. This verse uses the expression "once cleansed." If they were cleansed by one sacrifice, why did their conscience trouble them?
1726. Is it answered in verse 3?
1727. Is the word "remembrance synonymous with "remission"?
1728. Does "year by year" refer to the three great yearly sacrifices?
1729. How often did they have sacrifices?
1730. What were the daily sacrifices for? See Ex. 29:38-46.
1731. **Were there** sacrifices of a less frequent nature? See Num. 28:9-10.
1732. **Were there** sacrifices less frequent than weekly ones? See "monthly" — Num. 28:11-15.
1733. What advantage does the Christian have?

1734. If we have to observe communion each week for forgiveness, is our condition the same?
1735. What sins do we remember at communion time?

2. *The efficacious and final sacrifice of Christ. 10:5-10.*

Text
10:5-10

5 Wherefore when He cometh into the world, He saith,
Sacrifice and offering Thou wouldest not,
But a body didst Thou prepare for Me;
6 In whole burnt offerings and sacrifices for sin Thou hadst no pleasure:
7 Then said I, Lo, I am come
(In the roll of the book it is written of Me)
To do Thy will, O God.
8 Saying above, Sacrifices and offerings and whole burnt offerings and sacrifices for sin Thou wouldest not, neither hadst pleasure therein (the which are offered according to the law), 9 then hath He said, Lo, I am come to do Thy will. He taketh away the first, that He may establish the second.
10 By which will we have been sanctified through the offering of the body of Jesus Christ once for all.

Paraphrase

5 Wherefore, to show this, when coming into our world, Messiah saith to God, The sacrifice of bulls and of goats, and the offering of the fruits of the earth, Thou dost not now command, but a body Thou has prepared Me, that by dying I might make the atonement prefigured by these sacrifices.

6 The whole burnt-offerings, and the sin-offerings, appointed in the law, having become the occasion of superstition, Thou are not pleased with them.

7 Then I said, Behold I come into the world to do, O God, Thy will with respect to the bruising of the head of the serpent, by dying as a sin-offering, which is written concerning Me in the volume of the book of the law. Gen. iii. 15.

8 On the foregoing remarkable passage I reason thus. — The only begotten, Who knew the will of His Father, (John i. 18.), on coming into the world, first having said, Certainly sacrifice, and offering, and whole burnt-offerings, and sin-offerings, notwith-

standing they are offered according to the law. Thou dost not now will, neither art pleased with, being abused to the purpose of superstition:

9 Next, seeing He hath said, Behold I come into the world, to do, O God, Thy will, by offering Myself a Sacrifice for sin; He hath showed, that God hath abolished His former will or command concerning the Levitical sacrifice, that He may establish His second will or command **concerning** the sacrifice of His Son.

10 By establishing which second will of God, we are persons who being pardoned are fitted for worshipping God here, and for entering heaven hereafter, through the offering of the body of Jesus Christ once; that being sufficient to procure us an eternal pardon. (See Heb. ix. 26. note 1.)

Comment

Wherefore when He cometh into the world

Since the Levitical sacrifices had no power to take away sin, therefore a better sacrifice was needed. Christ came therefore to give a sacrifice that could redeem the world.

He saith (Ps. 40:6)

Calvin says this Psalm is improperly applied to Christ, for look at the contrast. It says, "My iniquities have laid hold on me." (Verse 12.)

Christ could quote part of the verse and **apply it to Himself** without applying all of it to Himself.

sacrifice and offering Thou wouldest not

We would expect Christ to have some things to say on the matter of sacrifice, and this is it. Christ says God was not satisfied with the old covenant **atonement**.

but a body didst Thou prepare for Me

This is New Testament doctrine.
a. John 1:14: "**The Word became flesh.**"
b. Phil. 2:5-11.
   Observe how the Psalm reads in the original language:
   "An ear Thou hast opened for Me."
   "An ear Thou hast bored for Me."
a. This alludes to an ancient custom: A man's ear was bored, then he was a servant forever. Ex. 21:5-6.

b. It was in this spirit that Christ submitted.
Evidently the author quoted thought, and not verbatum, says Milligan. It seems the quotation was from the Septuagint — the Greek.
Changes in words are sometimes necessary in translation into other languages for illustration.
a. The verse in Matt. 7:10, "Will he give him a serpent?" if translated into Hindu would not be the meaning that Jesus portrays, because of local Indian custom.

in whole burnt offerings and sacrifices for sin Thou hadst no pleasure

This is an echo of the former verse. Burnt offerings are discussed in Lev. 1:1-17.
a. This offering is so named because it was consumed upon the altar.
b. Milligan says this was the offering instituted immediately after the fall.
The sin offering is discussed in Lev. 4:1 to 5:13.
a. This was an important part of the sacrifices in that it had special reference to sin.
b. It is first mentioned in Ex. 29:14.

then said I, Lo I am come

The New Testament says that Jesus came.
a. John said so: John 1:11: "He came unto His own."
b. Jesus said so: John 6:38, 41, Matt. 20:28.
An interesting study is made when we examine the scriptures where Jesus said, "I come," "come," etc.

in the roll of the book it is written of me

Also translated "volume" or "chapter," and the word "book" refers to the Old Testament. The psalmist doesn't say where, but note Jesus' own words in Luke 24:44. See Gen. 3:15; 22:17; 49:10; Deut. 18:18; also Old Testament prophecies. "Roll" refers to the scroll type of preservation of manuscripts.

to do Thy will, O God

Others tried, but only Christ could actually do the will of God. Luke 24:44: All will be fulfilled concerning Christ.
In Gethsemane Christ prayed to do God's will.

John 4:23-34: "I have meat to eat that ye know not of. My meat is to do the will of Him that sent Me, and to accomplish His work." The devil made a supreme effort to turn Jesus from the will of God as he tempted Him after Jesus' baptism.
a. Fortunately for the world, the devil failed.
b. Only as we do the will of God will the obedience of Christ avail in our life.

saying above, Sacrifices and offerings and whole burnt offerings and sacrifices for sin Thou wouldest not, neither hadst pleasure therein (the which are offered according to the law)

Here he names all the sacrifices to indicate the inability of all of them. Four classes are named, with the amazing statement that God had no pleasure in any of those offered according to law.
"Neither hadst pleasure therein" is suggestive.
a. Of course, if done in hypocrisy God would not be pleased.
1. David realized the futility of the old sacrifices. See Ps. 51:16: "For Thou desirest not sacrifice; else would I give it. Thou delightest not in burnt offering."
2. The prophets cried out against the Jews for unsatisfactory sacrifices. See Amos 5:21-24.
b. Here he refers no doubt to those that are done correctly, but still there is no pleasure in them, for they are offered according to law.

then hath He said, Lo I am come to do thy will

While this expression is found in verse 9, it is really a conclusion to verse 8. Since God has no pleasure in the old sacrifices, Christ came to make a sacrifice that would please God. Christ made it plain that He was doing the Father's will. John 4:34; 5:30.

He taketh away the first

The whole arrangement under which these sacrifices were made is taken away. The whole plan is now removed; not just the scaffolding, but all. This checks with 7:18-19 where we learn the foregoing commandment is disannulled. It is taken away through the sacrifice of Jesus.
a. He fulfilled Matt. 5:17, so it could be taken away.
b. It was nailed to the cross. Col. 2:14.

that He may establish the second

    The new covenant is the second. The second is discussed in the next verse.

    Wise is the person that lives under the covenant that is established.

a. We cannot expect salvation upon something that God does not recognize.
b. This is the rock upon which we are to establish our lives.
Milligan says the first was not the will of God, but the second is His will.

by which will

a. This sounds a little dangerous.
b. Gal. 3:24 shows that God had a purpose in the law.
If the law had value, then it must have been God's will.
a. Of course, certain marriage laws were added, because of their hardness of heart, Mark 10:4, but the law was of God.
b. The law was His will for that dispensation.

we have been sanctified

    Observe Newell, page 339, for a foolish point.

a. He says the character of the object is not changed, but its relation to God is changed.
b. "Sanctified" here does not refer to our consecration or action of the Holy Spirit within us. He quotes the following:
I Thess. 5:23: "And the God of peace Himself sanctify you."
II Thess. 2:13: "Unto salvation in sanctification of the Spirit."
I Peter 1:2.
Surely we are changed when we are sanctified by the new will, for we have a new birth, a new will.

through the offering of the body of Jesus Christ.

    See what happens by reading 10:14. "Perfection" is the word. The word "sanctified" is not the whole truth, for we are perfected.

a. This must refer to the absoluteness of the effect of Christ's work on the cross in respect to cleansing and saving from sin.
b. The offering, of course, does not make us live perfectly. I Jn. 1:10.

once for all

The old sacrifices were numerous, various and repeated often, and brought no perfection. Christ's sacrifice was offered once and sanctifies unto perfection.

Study Questions

1736. Does this verse answer the question concerning the remission of sins under the old covenant?
1737. The Jew had the impossible, but the Christian has the possible. Is this true?
1738. What did "atonement" mean if it did not mean "cleansing from sin"?
1739. Could we use the word "appeasement" for "atonement"?
1740. Who is speaking in verse 5?
1741. Can this Psalm refer to Christ when verse 12 speaks of iniquities?
1742. Observe different translations. Do all translations say "He", or do some say "Christ" as though it appears this way in the original? What does one of the new versions say?
1743. Where did Christ say it? Is there any New Testament verse in the four gospels where it is recorded?
1744. Could Christ quote only a part of a verse and apply it to Himself?
1745. What is meant by "wouldest not"?
1746. What is meant by "the body Thou didst prepare for Me"?
1747. Is this New Testament doctrine?
1748. Quote some verses that show that Christ had a body.
1749. Can you read this in the Psalm?
1750. How may we explain the difference?
1751. Does the author quote thought or verbatum?
1752. What is meant by ear boring? See Ex. 21:5-6.
1753. What does "whole burnt offering" refer to? Cf. Lev. 1:11-17. Why is it thus called?
1754. Where was the sin offering made? Cf. Ex. 29:14.
1755. What was the sin offering like? Lev. 4:1 to 5:13.
1756. Could the two offerings be the same? If not, what is the whole burnt offering for? Cf. Lev. 1:13.
1757. What material was used? Cf. Ex. 29:14.
1758. Where in the New Testament do we find the expression, "I come"? Cf. John 6:38, 41; Matt. 20:28.

HELPS FROM HEBREWS

1759. Does it make any difference whether we believe that Jesus came or not?
1760. What is meant by "roll of the book"? What would "roll" suggest in reference to the shape of Old Testament scriptures?
1761. Did Jesus ever refer to the Psalms as referring to Him? Cf. Luke 24:44.
1762. Could Jesus refer to God as "O God"?
1763. Is the expression "to do Thy will" significant? Did others try to do it? Did Christ succeed?
1764. Was it an easy thing for Jesus to do the will of God?
1765. How early did He announce that He intended to do it?
1766. Was age twelve the first? Cf. John 4:32, 34; 5:30.
1767. Did the devil ever try to keep Him from it?
1768. What was actually God's will for Christ?
1769. What does the expression, "saying above," refer to?
1770. How many classes of sacrifices are named here?
1771. This verse says that God had "no pleasure in them." Does this refer to hypocritical sacrifices and offerings? Cf. Psalm 51:16; Amos 5:21-24.
1772. Can we assume that good sacrifices performed correctly are referred to here?
1773. Does the expression "according to the law" verify it?
1774. What is the inference in verse 9?
1775. Does it mean that He would make a sacrifice that would please God?
1776. What is taken away?
1777. Is it the sacrifices taken away or the whole law?
1778. Is this the same as 7:18, 19 says?
1779. Is this what Col. 2:14 means?
1780. How could He take it away? Cf. Matt. 5:17.
1781. What is the second thing referred to?
1782. What is meant by "establish"?
1783. Do you base your hope on something established or something taken away?
1784. How is the second established?
1785. What is established in this second covenant? How?
1786. "By which will" — does this refer to the will of the covenant or the will of God?
1787. Did God have purpose in the old? Cf. Gal. 3:24.

1788. Was everything that the Jew observed as law the actual will of God? Cf. Mark 10:4.
1789. What is it that sanctifies?
1790. Does the sanctification refer to our character, or our state, or both?
1791. What part does Jesus have in this sanctification?
1792. Compare this word "offering" with the power of the offering in verse 14.
1793. Does the expression "once for all" speak of a sacrifice in contrast to others?
1794. Is it for all people in this verse, or is it a statement of finality?

3. *Finality of Christ's priestly ministration.* 10:11-14.

Text
10:11-14

11 And every priest indeed standeth day by day ministering and offering oftentimes the same sacrifices, the which can never take away sins: 12 but He, when He had offered one sacrifice for sins for ever, sat down on the right hand of God; 13 henceforth expecting till His enemies be made the footstool of His feet. 14 For by one offering He hath perfected forever them that are sanctified.

Paraphrase

11 And indeed every ordinary priest standeth morning and evening ministering and offering the same sacrifices, which showeth that these sacrifices never can take away sins.

12 Whereas Christ, having offered only one sacrifice for sins through His whole life, sat down at the right hand of God, a Priest in heaven, that of royal dignity and certain conquest was added;

13 Thence waiting till His ministry as High Priest upon His throne, Zech. vi. 13. to Whose glory as High Priest, and government as King, shall issue, according to God's promise. Psal. cx. 1. in the utter destruction of His enemies.

14 Wherefore it is evident, that, by one offering of Himself, Christ hath procured an everlasting pardon for them who by faith and repentance are sanctified; that is, prepared to receive the benefit of that offering.

Comment

And every high priest indeed standeth day by day

In Exodus 29:38-46 are found recorded the daily sacrifices. The wearisome, continuous, ineffectual sacrifices are contrasted here with the one effectual sacrifice.

ministering and offering oftentimes the same sacrifices the which can never take away sins

This idea is expressed often, so evidently we are to understand that no sin was taken away by the Old Testament sacrifices.

a. However, it was essential that they be done.
b. For us, confession of faith, repentance, baptism, and belief are essential, although actually it is the blood of Christ that cleanses.
c. If they had failed to act in good faith, they could not have the blood of Christ applied, just as we today cannot if we fail to act upon the steps of salvation.

For them it was a sacrifice that could "never" take away sin. With Christ it is a sacrifice that "can ever" take away sin.

but He, when He had offered one sacrifice for sins forever

One sacrifice forever effectual was done by Christ. "Forever" goes with one sacrifice, not "sat down".
Christ is to leave heaven to receive those that wait for Him. 9:28.

sat down at the right hand of God

The priest had to hasten out of the Holy of Holies, for it was a place where he had no free access. He could never feel at home there. Christ sits down with God in the glory of His work accomplished.

henceforth expecting

This is Christ waiting for the fulfillment of a promise.
Milligan says He is calmly and patiently waiting, but surely Christ must be greatly sorrowed at the slow progress of His church with its indifference, coldness, and stinginess.

till His enemies be made the footstool of His feet

Ps. 110:1 is referred to here. His sacrificial work is over, but *for by one offering He hath perfected forever*

It does not mean that the believer is perfected immediately into a full-grown person in Christ. The sacrifice does take away all sin so that the person stands perfectly cleansed before God and a new creature in Christ. Rom. 6:1-4. It is perfection in standing, not actual perfection, which makes one faultless and sinless in life. One sacrifice forever perfects forever; therefore Christ does not have to stand and daily repeat His sacrifices.

them that are sanctified

Who are the sanctified?
a. His brethren, in verse 2:11, must be the answer.
b. Those baptized into Christ. Gal. 3:27.
c. Those who walk in a newness of life. Rom. 6:4; Col. 2:12; Col. 3:1; II Peter 1:3.

Does this mean that we are perfected, and therefore have no danger of falling?
a. We must abide in Christ as a branch.
b. We must not shrink back. 10:39.

Study Questions

1795. Describe the day-by-day sacrifices of the priest. Ex. 24:38-46.
1796. What is the author's purpose in mentioning it?
1797. Why did they do it if it couldn't cleanse?
1798. Can we say that it is a contrast of "never" and "ever"?
1799. Contrast the number of sacrifices under the old with the new.
1800. How soon did Jesus sit down?
1801. Where is He seated?
1802. What does this signify?
1803. Is Jesus seated forever, or is it a sacrifice forever?
1804. What word could express the thought "expecting"?
1805. What work is yet to be done?
1806. What Psalm is quoted?
1807. Enemies are named. What or who are they?
1808. What is the last enemy according to I Cor. 15:26?

1809. What enemies are named in Rev. 19:11-12?
1810. Is the Christian perfected forever?
1811. Does the verse teach that all who are sanctified have no sin? Cf. I John 1:10.
1812. Is it perfection in standing that he is describing?
1813. Who is included in the words, "them that are sanctified"?
1814. Could it be those of 2:11? Cf. Gal. 3:27; Col. 2:12.
1815. What does the word "sanctify" mean?
1816. Is it a condition over which we have no control?
1817. If believers cannot fall, why does he close the chapter warning against shrinking back? Cf. Heb. 10:39.

4. *Finality of Christ's sacrifice confirmed by prophecy.* 10:15-18.

Text
10:15-18

15 And the Holy Spirit also beareth witness to us; for after He hath said,
　16 This is the covenant that I will make with them
　After those days, saith the Lord:
　I will put My laws on their heart,
　And upon their mind also will I write them;
then saith He,
　17 And their sins and their iniquities will I remember no more.
　18 Now where remission of these is, there is no more offering for sin.

Paraphrase

15 And even the Holy Ghost testifieth this to us, according indeed to what was before cited, chap. viii. 10. 12.,; namely,

16 This is the covenant which I will make with My people the spiritual Israel of all nations, in the latter days, saith the Lord: I will give them a strong love to My laws, and a clear knowledge of them; (see Heb. viii. 10-12. notes.)

17 And their sins and their iniquities I will nevermore call to remembrance, as I did under My former covenant, by the repetition of the annual expiation.

18 Now, where God forgives iniquities, so as never to remember them more, no further atonement is needed; Thus hath the Holy Ghost testified, that, by one offering, Jesus has perfected forever the sanctified, ver. 14.

Comment

And the Holy Spirit also beareth witness to us; for after He hath said

> Paul calls attention to Jeremiah 31:33-34. This is given to show that God planned that through one offering, the obedient may have absolute forgiveness.

This is the covenant that I will make with them after those days, saith the Lord: and I will put My laws on their heart and upon their mind also will I write them

> These words are quoted from Jeremiah and are found in Hebrews, chapters 8, 10, 12 as directed inspiration of the Holy Spirit to Hebrew believers. How wonderful that God's laws may be found within the heart of man!

and their sins and their iniquities will I remember no more

> "Remember no more" is a contrast to "remembrance year by year." Man remembers, but God forgets when He forgives.

now where remission of these is, there is no more offering for sin

> We need no other offering. John 14:6; Acts 4:12; "In none other is there salvation."
> When sin is forgiven under the new covenant, there just isn't any other sacrifice necessary.

Study Questions

1818. Beginning with verse 15 and ending with verse 18, what evidence does he use to establish and confirm the finality of God's sacrifice?
1819. What prophet confirms it?
1820. What writing material is contrasted here?
1821. Does it infer that the new covenant would not be written except in the heart and mind?
1822. In what other chapters does he quote from Jeremiah?
1823. What is the difference between sin and iniquities?
1824. Can sin be defined as breaking divine will?
1825. Is iniquity that which lacks justice, hence is unrighteous, etc.?
1826. How thorough is God's ability to forget?
1827. Is "no more" a contrast to anything inferior in the old?
1828. Why do we not need sacrifices according to this verse?

1829. Define "remission."
1830. How does Acts 4:12 apply here?

5. *Exhortation based on the priesthood of Christ.* 10:19-39.

Text
10:19-39

19 Having therefore, brethren, boldness to enter into the Holy Place by the blood of Jesus, 20 by the Way which He dedicated for us, a new and living Way, through the veil, that is to say, His flesh; 21 and having a great Priest over the house of God; 22 let us draw near with a true heart in fulness of faith, having our hearts sprinkled from an evil conscience: and having our body washed with pure water, 23 let us hold fast the confession of our hope that it waver not; for He is faithful that promised: 24 and let us consider one another to provoke unto love and good works; 25 not forsaking our own assembling together, as the custom of some is, but exhorting one another; and so much the more, as ye see the day drawing nigh.

26 For if we sin wilfully after that we have received the knowledge of the truth, there remaineth no more a sacrifice for sins, 27 but a certain fearful expectation of judgment and a fierceness of fire which shall devour the adversaries. 28 A man that hath set at nought Moses' law dieth without compassion on the word of two or three witnesses: 29 of how much sorer punishment, think ye, shall he be judged worthy, who hath trodden under foot the Son of God, and hath counted the blood of the covenant wherewith He was sanctified an unholy thing, and hath done despite unto the Spirit of grace? 30 For we know Him that said, Vengeance belongeth unto Me, I will recompense. And again, The Lord shall judge His people.

31 It is a fearful thing to fall into the hands of the living God.

32 But call to rememberance the former days, in which, after ye were enlightened, ye endured a great conflict of sufferings; 33 partly, being made a gazingstock both by reproaches and afflictions; and partly, becoming partakers with them that were so used. 34 For we both had compassion on them that were in bonds, and took joyfully the spoiling of your possessions, knowing that ye have for yourselves a better possession and an abiding one. 35 Cast not away therefore your boldness, which hath great

recompense of reward. 36 For ye have need of patience, that, having done the will of God, ye may receive the promise.

37 For yet a very little while,
He that cometh shall come, and shall not tarry.

38 But My righteous one shall live by faith:
And if he shrink back, my soul hath no pleasure in him.

39 But we are not of them that shrink back unto perdition; but of them that have faith unto the saving of the soul.

Paraphrase

19 Well then, brethren, as the improvement of the doctrine of Christ's priesthood, all believers having boldness in death, the entrance into the habitation of God, by the blood of Jesus;

20 Which entrance Christ hath dedicated for us Jews and Gentiles, by making it a way new and life-giving, into the true Holy Place, through the veil, that is, through His flesh, by the rending of which He hath opened to us this new way;

21 Also, having a great Priest officiating in heaven, the true house of God, Who presents our addresses to the Father, and is able to help us when tempted;

22 Let us worship God with a sincere heart, in full assurance of acceptance through faith in Christ's death as an effectual sin-offering; being cleansed, not in the body by the legal sprinklings, but in hearts from the terrors of an evil conscience, by repentance and by the blood of Christ;

23 And being washed in body with the clean water of baptism, whereby we professed our faith in Christ as our only High Priest, let us hold fast the confession of our hope of salvation through His ministrations, unmoved by the threats of our persecutors; for faithful is He who hath promised us pardon through Christ.

24 And, when in danger of being seduced, by the arguments, examples, and threatenings of unbelievers, let us attentively consider one another's virtues, and failings, and circumstances, that by proper motives we may excite one another to love and good works;

25 Not leaving off the assembling of ourselves together for worshipping God, as the custom of some is who are afraid of persecution from unbelievers, but exhorting one another; and this so much the more, as from the signs of the times ye see the day approaching, in which the power of your unbelieving brethren will be broken.

26 For if, terrified by the evils which attend the profession of the gospel, we renounce it contrary to our conscience, after having attained to the knowledge and belief of the gospel, there remaineth to such persons no more sacrifice for sins;

27 But some dreadful apprehension of the judgment remaineth, and a punishment by fire, the effect of God's anger, to devour all the adversaries of God, whether secret or open.

28 The justice of never pardoning them who wilfully apostatize from the gospel, will appear to you, Hebrews, from this, That any one who presumptuously disregarded the law of Moses, though but a political law, was put to death without mercy, if convicted by two or three witnesses.

29 If so, of how much sorer punishment, think ye, shall he be counted worthy, who, by wilfully renouncing the gospel, hath trampled under foot the Son of God as an impostor, and reckoned His blood, whereby the new covenant was ratified, and the apostate himself was separated to the worship of God, the blood of One justly crucified; and hath maliciously opposed the Spirit, the Author of the miraculous gifts.

30 The character of God makes the punishment of apostates certain: For we Jews know how powerful and terrible He is Who hath said, Punishment belongs to Me, I will repay, saith the Lord. And again, The Lord will avenge His people of their oppressors. If so, will He not avenge His Son, and Spirit, and the disciples of His Son, of those who insult them?

31 To fall into the hands of an enraged enemy is dreadful; but it is far more dreadful to fall into the hands of the living God, Whose power no enemy can resist.

32 Be not terrified by your persecutors; but, to encourage yourselves, call to remembrance the former days, in which, being newly enlightened with the Gospel, ye courageously sustained, with God's assistance, a grievous persecution from your unbelieving brethren;

33 Partly, indeed, whilst ye were made a public spectacle, as malefactors in a theatre, both by the reproaches cast on you as atheists for deserting the institutions of Moses, and by the afflictions which befell you on that account; and partly, whilst ye kept company with and comforted them who were treated in the same cruel manner.

34 For ye even suffered with me in my bonds, both at Jerusalem and at Caesarea, and the loss of your goods ye took with joy,

because ye were inwardly persuaded that ye have better substance laid up for you in heaven, even a permanent substance, which cannot be taken from you either by force or by fraud.

35 Wherefore, having formerly behaved so bravely, cast not away your boldness now, as cowardly soldiers cast away their shields, and run in the day of battle; which courage, maintained to the end, will have a great reward in heaven.

36 Ye must however have perserverance as well as courage, that when ye have done the will of God, by enduring to the end, ye may receive the accomplishment of Christ's promise, Matt. xxiv. 13, to save you from your enemies.

37 The persecution will not last long: For, to use the words of Habakkuk, ii. 3, in a very short time He Who is coming will come, and destroy the Jewish state, and will not tarry; and then your brethren shall cease from persecuting you.

38 Live in the firm belief of these things, for (Hab. ii. 4.) the just by faith shall live. But if he draw back, if he loseth his faith, God's soul will not be well pleased with him.

39 But I am persuaded we are not of the number of those who draw back from Christ, unto their own destruction; but of those who live by faith, so as to obtain the salvation of the soul.

Comment

Having therefore, brethren, boldness

> We need not be fearful, trembling souls, with an inferiority complex, before a forgiving Christ. Salvation has been planned; let us accept it at once. Come with confidence.
>
> I John 3:21: "Beloved, if our heart condemn us not, we have boldness toward God."
>
> The high priest of old entered with fear and trembling because if he neglected a small item he could expect death, but we may enter with assurance of life.

to enter into the Holy Place

> Does he mean heaven or the church?

a. McKnight says, "Heaven itself where Deity dwells."
b. Milligan agrees that the "holiest of places" is referred to. We only enter heaven as we have entered the kingdom of heaven, the church.

by the blood of Jesus Christ
>The priest could enter only with blood, so there is now no other way. Jesus is the Door (John 10:9) of the church, of heaven itself.

by the way which He dedicated for us a new and living Way, through the veil, that is to say, His flesh.
>We have a dedicated Way dedicated by Jesus.
>a. John 14:6 — speaks of Christ as the Way.
>b. Christ's Way became a persecuted Way, Acts 9:2.
>c. The word "Christianity" does not appear. It was spoken of as The Way. Acts 19:9: "But spoke evil of The Way." 19:23: "Arose no small stir about The Way." 24:14: "After The Way, which they call a sect."
>
>The new and living Way is in contrast to the old way.
>a. It is a Way prepared by a living Saviour, in contrast to the lifeless pavement trodden by the high priest.
>b. We attain it by a living sacrifice. Rom. 12:1.
>c. "New" means "freshly slain, newly slain". Newell, p. 344.
>1. Thayer is quoted: "Properly, lately slaughtered."
>2. Vincent: "Later the word was weakened into 'new.'"
>d. It is as though He were just now slain for us.
>
>"Through the veil, that is to say, His flesh," contrasts the old veil with the new.
>a. The Jew could not enter the tabernacle's Holy of Holies, but we shall have the privilege to pass through the veil into heaven.
>b. Christ's way is so superior to the old covenant that a Jew is foolish to fail to see it.
>c. Christ's flesh is the veil here in figure, but it is spoken of in another sense by Jesus. John 6:54: "Whoso eateth My flesh, and drinketh My blood hath eternal life and I will raise him up at the last day." Also verses 55, 56.

and having a great High Priest
>Newell says we do not serve Him as Priest; He serves us. But of course Christ has other relationships with His people which demand service. "Great" is probably used to indicate His personal dignity and royal highness. We Christians "have Him." What a glorious privilege!

over the house of God

The place where people dwell is meant by the word "house." He must mean the church if "house" is meant.
a. McKnight says this was meant by the translators.
b. McKnight disagrees, however, and feels heaven is meant. Milligan feels that both the church and heaven are meant.
a. See I Tim. 3:15: The church is the house of God.
b. See 8:2: Christ is a minister of the heavenly sanctuary. "Things pertaining to God" may be meant.

let us draw near

Here we have the approach of man to his God.
a. It must be done, and done correctly.
b. Proper attitudes are symbolized in the Old Testament.
1. Without washing, the priests **were not allowed to minister, and were** threatened with death. Ex. 30:19-21.
2. This symbolized the washing of the inward heart.
We cannot come to God unrepentant and unclean in heart.

with a true heart

Absence of hypocrisy, deceit, guile, not with **a** heart that trusts in sacrifices of animals, but in God. There is nothing in Christ but truth, so we must make our lives correspond with His.

in fulness of faith

Being fully persuaded, full of conviction. Hebrews speaks of "shrinking back", 10:39, which is the opposite of fulness of faith.

having our hearts sprinkled

This is symbolism; you can't actually **sprinkle your heart**.
a. You can't run it through a grinder and sprinkle it.
b. You can't open up the heart and sprinkle on it a substance. "Sprinkled" means cleansed. Observe the many related verses: I John 1:7: "The blood of His Son cleanseth us from all sin." Num. 19:2-10: The Hebrews were sprinkled.
Heb. 12:24: "We are come to the blood of sprinkling that speaketh better than Abel."
Note in **9th** chapter — sprinkling with hyssop.

I Pet. 1:2: "Unto obedience and sprinkling of the blood of Jesus Christ."

Newell observes that beginning with Ex. 29:16 the word "sprinkle" appears forty times.

from an evil conscience

Compare I John 1:9: "If we confess our sins, He is faithful and righteous to forgive our sins and to cleanse us from all unrighteousness." The Christian can never forget his sin and be free, but he can feel that his conscience is cleansed.

and having our body washed

Observe these similar New Testament verses:

Titus 3:5: "Both of regeneration — according to His mercy He saved us through the washing of regeneration and renewing of the Holy Spirit."

Eph. 5:26: "That He might sanctify it, having cleansed it by the washing of water with the Word."

Acts 22:16 "And now why tarriest thou? arise and be baptized and wash away thy sins calling on His name."

The Old Testament parallel:

a. The high priest was to wash his flesh before putting on the garments. Lev. 16:4.
b. Levites were cleansed the same way.
c. See Lev. 8:6, 24. Both sprinkling and washing with water are illustrated in the consecration of Aaron and his sons.
d. Ex. 30:19-21: Priests were to wash before serving, and were threatened with death if they failed to do so.

Calvin, page 237, should be noted here:

1. "(This scripture) is generally understood of baptism, but it seems to me more probable that the apostle alludes to the ancient ceremonies of the law; and so by water he designates the Spirit of God, according to what is said by Ezekiel: 'I will sprinkle clean water upon you.' Ezek. 36:25."

If sprinkling is figurative, then washing must be likewise.

a. The subject of immersion is not so destitute of proof that this verse is needful to prove it.
b. Milligan challenges this and says it refers to the bath of regeneration as found in Titus 3:5.

with pure water

Observe Newell, page 350: "It doesn't refer to baptism for it is just as effective with muddy water as with pure water." Does he mean purified water? There is no insrtuction as to purification in the New Testament.

a. In the case of Philip and the eunuch, no purification of the water took place.
b. On Pentecost, no purification of water is suggested.

If actual clean water is meant here literally, then at times the Jordan and many streams would delay baptism until the muddy season expired.

let us hold fast the

Man's job, not God's, is stated here.
a. I Thess. 5:21 "Prove all things, hold fast that which is good."
b. II Tim. 1:13: "Hold fast the pattern of sound words."
c. Heb. 3:6: "Whose house we are, if we hold fast our boldness and the glory of our hope firm unto the end."
d. Heb. 4:14: "Having a great High Priest, let us hold fast our confession."
e. Rev. 2:25: "Nevertheless that which ye have, hold fast till I come."
f. Rev. 3:3: "Hold fast and repent."
g. Rev. 3:11: "Hold fast which thou hast."

Too many exhortations to "hold fast" are found to believe that God will do all of it.

confession of our hope

The word "profession" probably is the meaning. Confession's importance is stated frequently in the New Testament:
a. Luke 12:8-9.
b. Rom. 10:9-10.
c. Heb. 13:15.
d. Matt. 10:32.

We confess the Person in Whom is our hope.

that it waver not

Small faith, wavering faith, is condemned.
James 1:6: "But let him ask in faith, nothing doubting, for he that doubteth is like the surge of the sea, driven by the wind and tossed."

Matt. 14:31, to Peter who was sinking: "O thou of little faith, wherefore didst thou doubt?"

As a wavering S. O. S. is fatal for men and ships, so a wavering faith often fails to bring God to the rescue.

for He is faithful Who promised

Since Christ and God are so faithful, there is no need for an occasion of doubt.

a. Christ did all that He said He would do on earth, so proving His faithfulness.
b. He said He would rise from the dead, and He proved it, so no more evidence is needed.

Christ's faithful life ought to make us steadfast in His promises.

and let us consider one another

We are our brother's keeper, although Cain inferred otherwise. We can't live the Christian life alone, and we must be considerate of others.

to provoke

Means "to excite, to stir up." Our lives are to be salt, light, leaven and provocation. Matt. 5:16.

unto love and good works

Too many Christians have people mad and disgusted instead of encouraged to good work. Love for one another, love for the Lord, the church, good works, must be encouraged by our lives.

not forsaking our own assembling together

Nothing is accomplished without assembling.

a. Political rallies depend upon assemblies for victories.
b. Education, for sharing of knowledge, depends on regular attendance.

We have definite reasons for assembling.

a. To worship God.
b. To fellowship with His people.
c. To commemorate Christ's death.
   Observe "assembling" in the scripture:
   Acts 2:42: "They continued."

Acts 2:44-46: "And all that believed were together — continuing stedfastly with one accord."
Acts 4:23: "Being let go they came to their own company."
Acts 4:32; 5:12-14; 11:26; 12:12.

as the custom of some is

Perhaps because of persecution some were neglectful. What excuse is there for people who have such a custom today?
a. Freedom of worship has come to mean "free not to worship."
b. Those who neglect to worship are those who neglect to encourage, to pray and to pay.

but exhorting one another

Some say to exhort one another of the coming day of judgment, but we don't exhort to assemble for this. Some say the day of death, but this isn't a day to exhort. The day of assembling to worship is what he means when he tells us to exhort.
a. A day of worship approaching is a day for us to exhort brethren to anticipate.
b. He is talking about assembling, and we must exhort brethren to get ready to assemble as the day for assembling around the table of the Lord approaches.

so much the more

It should cause us to be more zealous, more diligent as time hastens. Exhortation should be more intense as the time factor becomes more prominent.

as ye see the day drawing nigh

The Lord's Day must be referred to, the day for assembling to remember the Lord.
Milligan, page 284, also McKnight, have a conviction here:
  "It refers to the day of Jerusalem's overthrow."
  "If not the above, then it refers to Christ's coming."
It is true that the expression, "the day," refers to future events connected with the coming of the Lord, but not in this verse.
a. The text speaks of assembling that can be forsaken.
b. Those who were forsaking assembling were not forsaking an assembly in judgment time, but regular assembly privileges afforded to them then each Lord's Day.

for if we sin wilfully

    Observe he has been talking about absentees.
a. Deliberately absenting oneself from the Lord's Supper is wilful sin.
b. Church members should examine their hearts to see if it is an excuse or a reason that kept them from the table.

Sinning wilfully is producing sin

c. Producing sin is not in the nature of the Christian.
    II Peter 1:4: "Become partakers of the divine nature, having escaped from the corruption that is in the world by lust."
2) I John 2:1: "These things I write unto you that you may not sin."
3) I John 3:9: "Whosoever is begotten of God doeth no sin because His seed abideth in him and he cannot sin, because he is begotten of God."
d. Note the Greek word for "sin wilfully", *poion — poiei,* in I John.
1) The verb is *poico*: "to make, to form, to construct."
2) The unregenerate man lives in sin and loves it; the regenerate man may lapse into sin, but he loathes it.
e. The Christian does not practice or form sin.

after that we have received the knowledge of the truth

    A knowledge of the truth should make us produce fruit of the Spirit, instead wilful sin. A return to sin is a worse state than the first, according to II Pet. 2:20-22.

there remaineth no more a sacrifice for sin

    The Jews had none for the sin of the high hand.
a. Num. 15:30: "But the soul that doeth aught with a high hand, whether he be home born or a sojourner, the same blasphemeth Jehovah and that soul shall be cut off from among the people."
b. See Isaiah 1:10-15; 59:1-2.
c. Also Jeremiah 6:19-20; 7:9-16.
    God hates sin deeply, and for those enlightened ones who know better and have the power to escape and refuse it, there is no sacrifice to cover it.
    With the power of God, there is no excuse for wilful sin. See Phil. 4:13; I Cor. 10:13.

The Christian Life

Not willful Sin	Not unto Death
Sacrifice for sin	Renewed unto Repentance
With Christ	Exhorts Christ
Faith in Blood	Honor to Holy Spirit
Holy	

The Willful Sinner

Contrast the above with Heb. 10:29

Sin of High Hand	Willful Sin
Cp. Num. 15:30	Death

No sacrifice for sin

Falling away; impossible to renew without Christ

Trodden underfoot the Son of God

Counted the blood an unholy thing

Done despite unto the Spirit of Grace

but a certain fearful expectation of judgment

Those who go out from the blood of Christ have not only an evil conscience to feel but also the wrath of God to face.
a. Heb. 10:31 expresses fearfulness of God's wrath.
b. II Peter 3:8-13 describes the method of God's destruction. Nahum expressed that God's judgment grows out of the fact that He is a jealous God. See Nahum 1:2, 6-7.

and a fierceness of fire

Of course this is not a new doctrine.
a. Fire destroyed Sodom and Gomorrah.
b. Fire destroyed Korah and his rebellious company. Num. 16:35.
c. John preached about fire. Matt. 3.
d. Peter preached about fire. II Pet. 3:8-14.
e. Hebrews 10:27 says God is a consuming Fire.
f. Christ will come as a flaming Fire. II Thess. 1:8.
This Greek word *Luxos* does not always mean fire.
a. In Acts 13:45 it is translated "envy, jealously".
b. Acts 5:7 — "wrath, indignation".
c. Rom. 10:2. It is translated "zeal".
d. Heb. 10:27. The American Standard Version footnotes it as "jealousy".

which shall devour the adversaries

Whether the above word is "fire," "jealousy," or "indignation," the result is the same.
a. The backward-treading individual is to be counted as an enemy.
b. Those not for Him are adversaries. Matt. 12:30.
Paul, in I Cor. 16:9, says that there are many adversaries.

a man that hath set at naught Moses' law dieth without compassion on the word of two or three witnesses

"Setting aside" amounted to apostasy and was a capital offense. Deut. 17:3-6. "Without compassion" shows the strictness of an absolute God.
a. Num. 15:32-36 is an example.
b. Sentiment cannot enforce the law. Enforcement calls for all sentiment to be aside.
Two or three witnesses was required to establish the fact.

a. See Deut. 17:6.
b. Note the fact that an elder must likewise have a plurality of accusers before being condemned. I Tim. 5:19.

of how much sorer punishment

Such offenses were trifling in comparison to turning against Christ after once being for Him. The word "sorer" carries the idea of severity.

think ye, shall he be judged worthy

Deserving the worst for deserting the best is suggested. Cf. Luke 12:47-48.

a. Jesus suggested that the one who knew that he was sinning, but did not cease from it, deserved many stripes.
b. How undeserving of forgiveness is the one who turns his back on Christ after knowing Him.

Note the three charges against such a one:
a. Treading upon Christ.
b. Discounting the blood of Christ.
c. Insulting the Spirit.

who hath trodden under foot the Son of God

"Who has treated Christ with contempt" is meant here. It is an utter disregard of the King of our lives, tramping upon Him as though we were king and He a lowly conquered creature.

and hath counted the blood of the covenant

Note the ways it is spoken of:
Heb. 10:19: "The blood of Jesus."
Heb. 9:14: "The blood of Christ."
I Pet. 1:2: "The blood of Jesus Christ."
I Pet. 1:19: "The precious blood of Christ."
I John 1:7: "The blood of Jesus, his Son."
Rev. 7:14: "White in the blood of the Lamb."
The blood is to take away the errors of repentant people, not wilful sinners.

wherewith he was sanctified an unholy thing

"Unholy" in Greek means "common," in contrast to "sacred." He has treated it as though no power or atonement, were in it.

and hath done despite

Insult, defiance is meant here. We see people who try to hurt loved ones; this is spite.

Despite is an intensified form of the word, translated, "to treat shamefully" in Matt. 22:6; "to insult" in Luke 18:32; Acts 14:5; I Thess. 2:2.

unto the Spirit of grace

The Spirit that bestowed upon them such wonderful blessings is meant. When we turn from the path of the fruit of the Spirit to produce evil fruit, we endanger our soul.

How important is the Spirit?

Matt. 12:28: By Him Christ worked miracles.

John 16:8: By Him God convinces the world of righteousness and judgment.

John 7:39 and Rom. 8:26: He comforts the saints and helps their infirmities.

When we insult Him there is no forgiveness. Matt 12:32; also Mark 3:29; Luke 12:10.

for we know Him that said

Deut. 32:35-36: God is speaking. The Hebrews knew the God that stated this. The Hebrews knew the faithful God Who in times past punished men for sin. They no doubt knew the severity of God in His dealing with Ananias and Sapphira.

vengeance belongeth unto Me

God has certain rights, and vengeance is one of them.
a. Lev. 19:18: "Thou shalt not avenge."
b. Rom. 12:19: "Avenge not yourselves."
c. I Thess. 4:6: "The Lord is the avenger."

A discussion of vengeance should consider three things:
a. God delegated the power to execute apostates of the nation of Israel to the rulers of the people.
b. Now He has resumed the power, and He reserves apostates for an everlasting destruction.

Justice demands vengeance.

I will recompense

God can do an adequate job.
a. Rom. 1:27: "Receiving in themselves that recompense of their error which was due."

b. Heb. 2:2: "Every transgression received a just recompense of reward." How shall we escape?
c. I Pet. 4:18: "For if the righteous are scarcely saved." Man's judgment is feeble in comparison to God's.
a. Observe these scriptures:
Matt. 25:46: "These shall go into everlasting punishment."
II Thess. 1:9: "Everlasting destruction from the presence of the Lord."
II Pet. 3:10-13.
b. Compare this with our one-to-five year imprisonments with good food, libraries, recreation, etc., furnished to the criminal. And again, Deut. 32:36.

the Lord shall judge His people

"Judge" here means "govern."
a. God will divide the godly from the hypocrites.
See Ps. 1:5: "Therefore the wicked shall not stand in the judgment." Also Matt. 25:46.
b. The hypocrites may grow as tares, but their doom is certain. I am glad God governs His people and that He will judge us, rather than men who judge by the outward appearance.

it is a fearful thing to fall into the hands of the living God

Examples of it — Old Testament characters:
a. Adam and Eve.
b. Cain.
c. People of Noah's day.
d. Sodom and Gomorrah.
e. Korah.
An example of it in the New Testament is that of Ananias and Sapphira. The destruction pictured by Peter, and by the Book of Revelation, is the worst yet.

but call to remembrance the former days

They had had days of strife, battle and victory over sin, and these should be remembered.
Early days of Christian experience, a reminder of past faithfulness, should encourage me to strive again.

in which after ye were enlightened
> Enlightment is of Christ.
> John 8:12: "I am the Light of the world, He that followeth Me shall not walk in the darkness, but shall have the Light of life."
> God's word casts the light for men to follow.

ye endured a great conflict of sufferings
> Probably the persecution that broke out after Stephen's death.
> Acts 8:1; 12:3.
> The persecution by brethren of loved ones is the most severe. Jesus prophesied that brethren would deliver up brethren. Matt. 10:21-22.

partly being made a gazingstock
> "Exposed to public shame" is meant. The meaning or use of the word "partly" should be considered.
> a. Some suggest: "This suffering took place partly while they were being made a gazingstock."
> b. Likely not all had endured the same suffering.
> In Greek and Roman theaters, criminals were often publicly abused and insulted. Acts 19:29 and I Cor. 4:9.

both by reproaches and afflictions
> "Reproaches" were the unkind words heaped upon the Christians. The unbelievers treated the Christians as they treated Christ.
> "Afflictions" refers to those various sufferings and calamities which they endured.

and partly becoming partakers with them that were so used
> If they as individuals had not suffered, they had helped financially those that had been persecuted. This may be alluded in Heb. 6:10.

for ye both had compassion on them that were in bonds
> King James version: "For ye had compassion of me in my bonds," makes it personal.
> a. The difference appears in some manuscripts.
> b. The difference doesn't affect the meaning.

1. In either case he praises them for their faithfulness.
2. Paul had endured all that is named, so if they had helped Paul only, they had shared.
    This is the commendable thing about the Hebrews, as seen in Heb. 6.

and took joyfully the spoiling of your possessions

The early church was scattered, Acts 8, which no doubt meant possessions were taken from them. Those whose treasures are in heaven do not sorrow for earthly losses.

knowing that ye yourselves have a better possession and an abiding one

Our possessions cannot be spoiled.
Matt. 6:19: "lay not up for yourselves treasures upon the earth, where moth and rust consume"; I Cor. 9:25: "They do it to obtain a corruptible crown"; I Pet. 1:4.
Everything here is temporary, while in heaven everything is abiding.

cast not away therefore your boldness

The cowards in battle would throw aside their weapons and flee, and of course this meant defeat. The Christian is to gird on, to be strong, to be confident, with the shield of faith. Eph. 6:13-18.
The word "boldness" here is not "cockiness" nor haughtiness, but confidence.
a. This is gained in Christ. See Eph. 3:12.
b. Only the confident have the confidence of God.

which hath great recompense of reward

The faithful know that their labor is not vain in the Lord.
a. I Cor. 15:58: Eternal life will be ours.
b. Gal. 6:9: "We shall" expresses certainty.
c. John 6:27: Some labor for that which perishes.
    If we cast away our confidence, we throw away our chances for eternal life.

for ye have need of patience

The author's analysis of their specific need is patience. We win our own salvation by patience, and also win the souls of others. See Luke 21:19.

that having done the will of God ye may receive the promise

Patience in spite of discouragement leads one on to do the will of God. When God's will is done, then God's promise is assured and received.
a. Abraham found it to be true. Heb. 6:15.
b. The children of Abraham by faith will someday obtain the promise.
Eternal life and all its joys is meant here.

for yet a very little while

This suggests that a short time remains. Milligan and the American Standard Version editors feel that this language is from Habakkuk 2:3.

He that cometh shall come and shall not tarry

Milligan: "Obviously it is Christ." He says not the second coming, but the providential coming to save them from Jerusalem. Newell thinks Christ's coming is the promise found in verse 36.
The Christian does not look to death but to the coming of Christ.

but My righteous one

Footnote: "the righteous one." If the expression, "My righteous," is allowed, we see the ground on which God claims us, the principle of faith. We ought to live so that God will say to us, "My righteous one."

shall live by faith

This is a quotation from Hab. 2:3-4. It appears three times in the New Testament, and each time in an interesting light.
a. Rom. 1:17: Connected with the "just" or "righteous."
b. Gal. 3:3: Connected with the subject of being perfected.
c. Heb. 10:38: Set in the midst of conflict of sufferings.

and if he shrink back

The words "any man" appear in the King James version, but not in the original.
a. It is not "any man" that he is speaking of, but the just man.
b. We are to live by faith, in spite of all that the devil sends against us.
With God by our side let us not shrink back like Saul's army,

but like David live by faith, and we are a match for any enemy. The danger lies in living by appearance rather than by faith. See II Cor. 5:7.

My soul hath no pleasure in him

Shrinking back puts us in the class with Cain, wilderness wandering Israel, Ahab and the others. God loves the persevering, like Joshua, Abraham, David, Paul and others named in the following chapter.

but we are not of them that shrink back

It may seem a little thing to yield to sin, but how terrible are the results.
a. It is a turning from glory to doom.
b. The Christian is to "keep on keeping on."

unto perdition

This sets forth damnation; and note that it is a place of bad company.
a. The false Christ, antichrist, and false prophets are doomed to perdition. Rev. 17:8-11.
b. II Thess. 2:3: The same word is applied to this evil one.
c. Judas was the "son of perdition." John 17:12.
d. I Tim. 6:9 speaks of destruction and perdition together.
e. II Pet. 3:7: Perdition of ungodly men.
"Shrinking back" then must be a condition in danger of being permanent.

but them that have faith unto the saving of the soul

It is a joy to be on the salvation side of faith.
a. The author no doubt expresses this to give them courage.
b. We are on the road to eternal life, whereas the shrinkers-back are on the road to perdition.
There is a faith that will not save us.
a. The wavering faith will not. Heb. 10:39.
b. The faith without works. See James 2:17-26.

Study Questions

1831. Who is blessed with boldness? v. 19.
1832. Did the high priest of old have fear?
1833. What is the Holy Place referred to here — heaven, or the church, or the Presence of God?

HELPS FROM HEBREWS

1834. With what do we enter as we do it with boldness?
1835. What adjectives describe the Way?
1836. Is the word "Way" a familiar one in the New Testament?
1837. A road, a building is generally dedicated. How about Christ's Way?
1838. Can it be now considered a new Way? What did the idea express in the beginning?
1839. In what way can it be considered a living Way?
1840. What kind of a sacrifice must we make to attain?
1841. What is the veil to our Holy of Holies?
1842. How important is the blood atonement of Christ as seen by this chapter?
1843. What does John 6:54-56 say concerning His flesh?
1844. Is blood conditional with us as it was with the priest?
1845. What does the Christian possess in verse twenty?
1846. Has the Hebrew author given any pre-eminence to Jesus' mother, Mary, the blessed virgin?
1847. Has he mentioned her?
1848. What is suggested by the word "great"? v. 21.
1849. What is meant by "the house of God"?
1850. Compare I Tim. 3:15 for a similar expression.
1851. Compare Heb. 8:2.
1852. Is it actually a house, or "things pertaining to God's house"?
1853. Do we use the word "house" to mean other than a dwelling?
1854. What would cause us to draw near to the house of God?
1855. Would we be so bold if we had not such a great Priest?
1856. What must be the condition of our heart?
1857. What would characterize a true heart?
1858. Describe "fulness." v. 22.
1859. Is it the opposite of a shrinking faith?
1860. Does this verse teach sprinkling?
1861. Is it figurative or literal sprinkling?
1862. Can you literally sprinkle the heart?
1863. What is the significance of the term?
1864. What were the occasions for sprinkling in the Old Testament?
1865. What word could be used in place of the word "sprinkle"?
1866. What other verses in the Bible use the word "sprinkle"?

1867. Is there any place where it speaks of using sprinkled water as a substitute for immersion?
1868. Does the word "water" appear with the word "sprinkle"? What word does appear with it?
1869. What is the sprinkling to do for us?
1870. How can a person have a free conscience when he can't forget his sin even though God does?
1871. A washing is referred to here. Is this an isolated teaching? Cf. Titus 3:5; Eph. 5:26; Acts 22:16.
1872. Is it fair to say that sprinkling is figurative and that this is literal?
1873. What Old Testament practices do we have as an example of washing? Cf. Lev. 16:4; Lev. 8:6, 24; Ex. 30:19-21.
1874. Does Ezekiel 36:25 bear on the subject?
1875. Who was the prophecy concerning?
1876. What is meant by "pure water"? Is it holy water or purified water?
1877. Do we have any example in the New Testament of purifying water?
1878. Would this eliminate baptizing in the Jordan during the muddy season?
1879. When is a water pure — to the heathen, to the farmer drinking from a well, to the scientist, or to the health nurse?
1880. If this verse does not refer to our immersion, then what does it refer to?
1881. Does it read "having had our body washed"?
1882. Is it something that the Christian experiences, or is it something that we have had done in the past?
1883. God has prepared the sacrifice. Whose job is named here? v. 23.
1884. Is the expression "hold fast" a familiar one?
1885. If God will not let us go, then are these not unnecessary admonitions?
1886. How can one "hold fast"?
1887. What are we to hold to?
1888. Does the word "confession" carry the idea of "profession"?
1889. Do we confess hope or confess a Person in Whom is our hope?
1890. Is the word "hope" personalized?

1891. What must not waver? Did Simon waver while walking on the water?
1892. What will the sailor do in a lifeboat when he loses hope?
1893. What will the wavering Christian do?
1894. What does this verse teach that will bolster our hope? v. 23.
1895. Did Christ keep His word on earth?
1896. What great declaration did He make that was established so that our hope could be a reality?
1897. Does this verse teach that we are our brother's keeper?
1898. Did Cain infer otherwise?
1899. Do we consider one another as we ought?
1900. What is the meaning of the word "provoke"?
1901. Are we "provoking" people, thereby causing dissension in the church?
1902. If we provoke people to love, what should they love?
1903. How can we encourage people in good works?
1904. How can we do it through our work as a minister, elder, Bible School teacher?
1905. What could be included in good works?
1906. Can you name anything great accomplished with people, without having assemblies?
1907. Can you have an army without assemblies for drill and instruction?
1908. What definite reasons may be given for the Christian assembly?
1909. What examples do we have in the Bible?
1910. Is the day of assembly the day that draweth nigh?
1911. How can we see any other day drawing nigh?
1912. If it is not the day of worship, what are we to encourage — to exhort?
1913. If it is not a day of worship, what is violated? What does the willful sin refer to?
1914. If neglect of worship was a serious transgression in the Old Testament, is it not a sorer sin under the new covenant?
1915. If absenteeism is condemned, is it the same as willful sin?
1916. What was the custom of some? Who do you suppose they were?
1917. Why do you suppose that they were neglectful?
1918. Why do people neglect attending church today?

1919. Can 30% to 50% of a church in assembly be as effective as it should be?
1920. Do we have a responsibility to our brethren in this matter?
1921. If church people exhorted, would the preacher be so occupied with non-assembling Christians that he does not have time to call on the non-professing ones?
1922. What do you say when you exhort?
1923. What is meant by "so much the more"?
1924. This verse suggests a time element. What ought consideration of it do to us?
1925. What is the day referred to here?
1926. What day do some think it is?
1927. Does it not refer to a day of assembly, which men were neglecting by failure to assemble?
1928. Is there anything to suggest that it refers to the overthrow of Jerusalem?
1929. Could it refer to Christ's coming?
1930. Could this day be forsaken by us?
1931. Is it possible to neglect a day if you do not know that it is a day drawing nigh?
1932. If absenteeism is discussed in the previous verse, then what is the willful sin here?
1933. Ought we to be very much alarmed at the small percentage of a membership gathered around Christ's table?
1934. What percent of your members were present last Lord's Day?
1935. What if a company tried to manufacture with such **absenteeism**?
1936. What truth have we received? v. 26.
1937. What should truth produce in us — neglect or diligence?
1938. Should the Christian be a willful exhorter or neglectful assembler?
1939. What was the willful sin in the Old Testament called? Cf. Num. 15:30.
1940. What does Peter say concerning the Christian who returns to evil? Cf. II Peter 2:20-22.
1941. Was there a sacrifice for sin of the high hand in the Old Testament? Cf. Num. 15:30; Isaiah 1:10-15; 59:1-2; Jer. 6:19-20; 7:9-16.
1942. Does God hate the sin of the enlightened ones more than the sin of those living in sin?

1943. What is meant by "no more sacrifice for sin"?
1944. With the power of God at our disposal, is there any excuse for our falling? Cf. Phil. 4:13; I Cor. 10:13.
1945. Does this verse mean that such a one can't return and repent?
1946. What may the backslider expect? v. 26.
1947. What is Paul's adjective to describe the expectation of judgment?
1948. What does 10:31 say about it?
1949. What is the cause for God's ability to be fierce according to Nahum 1:2, 6, 7?
1950. What will accompany the judgment?
1951. Has God ever used fire to destroy people? See Gen. 19:28; Num. 16:35.
1952. Is the expression "fierceness of fire" a new doctrine?
1953. Did John preach about fire? Cf. Matt. 3.
1954. Did Paul? Cf. II Thess. 1:8; Heb. 10:27.
1955. Did Peter? Cf. II Pet. 3:8-14.
1956. Does the word translated "fire" always mean "fire"?
1957. What other meanings has it? Is it ever so translated?
1958. Is the result the same, as seen by the word "devour"?
1959. Is the indifferent person an adversary? Cf. Matt. 12:30.
1960. Was it a great sin to set aside the law of Moses?
1961. Was it a capital offense? Cf. Deut. 17:3-6.
1962. Do we have an example of the lack of compassion? See Num. 15:32-36.
1963. Why did God insist on a multiplicity of witnesses?
1964. Does God require witnesses against an elder? Cf. I Tim. 5:19.
1965. Is God sentimental when His laws are concerned?
1966. What does the word "sorer" mean?
1967. Do we deserve the worst when we have broken the best? Cf. Luke 12:47-48.
1968. How deserving of forgiveness is the one who turns his back on it?
1969. What are the sins named in this verse as deserving of punishment?
1970. How can we tread upon Christ?
1971. Do we walk on Him when we neglect His table for visiting, fishing, picnicking, etc.?
1972. In what relationship does he speak of the blood here?

1973. How is it expressed in other verses? Cf. Heb. 10:19; 9:14; I Pet. 1:2, 19; I John 1:7; Rev. 7:14.
1974. What is meant by the expression "unholy thing"?
1975. How can the backslider by his life make the sacrifice seem unholy?
1976. Define "done despite."
1977. See other verses for examples. Cf. Matt. 22:6; Luke 18:32; Acts 14:5; I Thess. 2:2.
1978. If the Spirit produces the blessings in our lives, what may we expect if we treat Him shamefully?
1979. If He is the Comforter, may we expect comfort by insulting Him?
1980. What did Jesus say concerning sin against the Holy Spirit? Matt. 12:32; Mark 3:29; Luke 12:10.
1981. Who is known in verse 30?
1982. What verse is quoted?
1983. Did these people know God?
1984. Do you suppose that they knew Ananias and Sapphira?
1985. What is meant by "vengeance"?
1986. Was this an old doctrine carried over into the New Testament? Cf. Lev. 19:18; Rom. 12:19; I Thess. 4:6.
1987. Does justice demand vengeance?
1988. Is a law of value if God does not enforce it and punish for it?
1989. Does God mean by "recompense" that He can do an adequate job?
1990. Will He give a just recompense? Cf. Heb. 2:2; Rom. 1:27.
1991. How does God's judgment compare with our modern penal systems, with libraries, food, recreation, etc.?
1992. Did Jesus teach the judgment of God? Cf. Matt. 25:46.
1993. What is meant by God judging His people?
1994. Does God exercise His absolute power now?
1995. How does God's judgment differ from man's?
1996. If man judges by outward appearance, ought we to be the more careful?
1997. Give examples of the fearfulness of God's judgment in the Old Testament. In the New Testament.
1998. Is that pictured in Revelation and by Peter worse?
1999. What former days are to be recalled?
2000. What pleasant and worthwhile memories should they recall?

HELPS FROM HEBREWS

2001. What would "enlightened" refer to? v. 32.
2002. What had they endured in suffering?
2003. Could it be the persecution after Stephen's death?
2004. What kind of good could come from such a memory?
2005. Does easy living make for careless religion?
2006. What is meant by "gazingstock"?
2007. What does the word "partly" refer to?
2008. Could it mean that some of them had been gazingstocks, and others had not?
2009. Was it common for people to be publicly abused? Cf. Acts 19:29; I Cor. 4:9.
2010. What is the difference between reproaches and afflictions?
2011. Does verse 34 give a clue?
2012. How could they "partly" be partakers with abused people?
2013. Could Heb. 6:10 be a reference to this?
2014. What two things were commendable in their life according to this verse?
2015. Does the King James Version read differently here?
2016. Is the commendation in order in either case?
2017. What is meant by spoiling of possessions? v. 33.
2018. What possessions cannot be spoiled by man?
2019. What is inferred by the word "abiding"?
2020. "Cast away" would be the sign of what?
2021. The Christian should be girding for battle. What kind of a soldier would he be if he lost his courage?
2022. Is boldness the same as cocksureness?
2023. Is there room for haughtiness in this boldness?
2024. What apostle had boldness?
2025. What is meant by "recompense"?
2026. Is it evident that the Christian will be rewarded?
2027. Did Jesus ever warn concerning working for a losing cause?
2028. If we lose our boldness, what hope have we?
2029. Has the author analyzed the need of the Hebrews?
2030. What did he conclude that they needed? Cf. Luke 21:19.
2031. What is an alternate translation of the word "patience"?
2032. Name some Old Testament characters who exemplified patience.
2033. What will patience lead one to do according to verse thirty-six?
2034. What is the promise mentioned here?

HELPS FROM HEBREWS

2035. Why is it singular when we have so many promises?
2036. What does he say concerning time?
2037. Is this a quotation?
2038. Who is the One coming?
2039. Is it the actual coming or a providential coming?
2040. What do the scholars mean by the "providential" coming?
2041. Could the promise of verse 36 be the coming referred to in verse 37?
2042. If it referred to the actual coming of Christ, then is this false hope in verses 36 and 37?
2043. What is meant by "righteous one"?
2044. How can we be considered righteous when we have sin?
2045. Does it say "My righteous one" or "the righteous one"?
2046. Is this an original statement by the Hebrew author?
2047. Is living by faith peculiar to God's people, or does the principle of faith act in other relationships?
2048. How does the King James Version differ here?
2049. Is it any man, or the righteous man referred to here?
2050. What is meant by "shrink back"? Shrink from what?
2051. Is the believer a shrinker — a coward?
2052. Does God have a soul?
2053. In whose class would we be if we shrink back?
2054. Name some courageous people in whom God was pleased.
2055. Does the author identify himself with the shrinkers or perseverers?
2056. What is meant by "perdition"?
2057. The Christian keeps on for what?
2058. The shrinker shrinks back to what?
2059. In whose company would we be if we shrank back? Cf. Rev. 17:8-11; II Thess. 2:3; I Tim. 6:9; II Pet. 3:7.
2060. If perdition is so serious, can we take backsliding lightly?
2061. In what class are those who keep on keeping on?
2062. Is this a statement to give courage?
2063. Does this verse infer two kinds of faith, one that saves and one that cannot?
2064. Who has a faith that will not save?
2065. What does James 2:17-26 say about faith?

HELPS FROM HEBREWS

Questions On Chapter Ten
True and False

_____ 1. The law being a shadow of the good things to come can make perfect them that draw nigh.
_____ 2. We have been sanctified through the offering of the body of Christ.
_____ 3. It is the custom of some to forsake the assembling together according to Hebrews.
_____ 4. This chapter speaks of a wilful sin, and there is no sacrifice for it.
_____ 5. Under the law of Moses, seven witnesses were required before a person could be put to death.
_____ 6. Because we are sensitive, vengeance is a privilege extended to each of us.
_____ 7. Christ is spoken of as being seated at the left hand of God after He had offered sacrifice for our sins.
_____ 8. Our hearts are to be sprinkled from an evil conscience.
_____ 9. God is pictured as a God of love, yet it is said that "it is a fearful thing to fall into the hands of the living God"
_____ 10. Christ is to be at the right hand of God until His enemies are made to be His footstool.
_____ 11. The first sacrifices were ended in order to establish the second sacrifice.
_____ 12. Day by day sacrifices were essential in the task of the priests under the old covenant.
_____ 13. The one Sacrifice perfected forever the sanctified ones.
_____ 14. A warning suggests that men may shrink back, but it is not unto perdition.
_____ 15. The persons who were the objects of this epistle must have had a very easy Christian life.
_____ 16. Men may be guilty of treading under foot the Son of God.
_____ 17. This chapter does not refer to fire as a means of God's punishment.
_____ 18. Christ dedicated a Way for us through the veil.
_____ 19. We are to hold fast our confession of hope and to keep it from wavering.
_____ 20. The sanctified can never count the blood of the covenant unholy.

HELPS FROM HEBREWS

Multiple Choice Over Chapter Ten

1. Our bodies are to be:
   1. Washed.
   2. Covered entirely.
   3. Purged.
   4. Sprinkled.
2. Each priest stands day by day making sacrifices which can:
   1. Never be viewed by God.
   2. Never take the place of Christ.
   3. Never take away sins.
3. We shall enter the Holy Place:
   1. By study.
   2. Goodness of God.
   3. Blood of Christ.
4. The sacrifices in the Old Testament were:
   1. A remembrance made of sins every year.
   2. Were to be made semi-annually.
5. If a righteous one shrinks back:
   1. God will overlook it since once we are saved we are always saved.
   2. It is proof that he never was saved in the first place.
   3. God will have no pleasure in him.

SUMMARY OF CHAPTER TEN

The first eighteen verses of Chapter Ten conclude the teaching on the ministry of Jesus as High Priest which began in 8:1 and according to that verse is the main point in the book.

The weakness of the continual offering of the Old Testament system is again pointed out, for they could not cleanse the conscience from sin. But the offering of the body of Jesus, in harmony with the will of God as the scripture indicated, did what all the animal sacrifices could not do. So when Christ had made the one Offering with its permanent effect He assumed His position at the right hand of the throne of God as King and Priest.

The rest of the chapter as suggested in the outline begins the application of this doctrinal issue in the form of a final appeal to faithfulness. In the light of the efficacy of the offering of Christ, why should one forsake Him as High Priest and King for the weak things of the former life under the Levitical priesthood? Considering the privileges enjoyed under Christ, the appeal is made to patiently endure the trial that may come and ultimately receive the reward of faithfulness.

Special Study On Faith
What Faith Will Cause A Person To Do

I. Please God.
   A. In a sacrifice. Abel, 11:4.
   B. Enoch, v. 5.
II. Defy kings.
   A. Moses' parents, v. 23, hid him.
   B. Moses, v. 27, didn't fear the wrath of king.
   C. Rahab, v. 31.
III. Become great warriors.
   A. Gideon, v. 32, defeated enemies.
   B. Barak, v. 32, defeated Sisera.
   C. David, v. 32, slew Goliath, slew tens of thousands.
   D. Abraham, v. 8.
   E. Moses, v. 27.
   F. Samson, v. 32.
   G. Jephthah, v. 32, victory over Ammonites and Ephraimites.
IV. Suffer for righteousness.
   A. Moses, v. 25, rather to enjoy pleasure.
   B. Daniel, v. 33, wrought righteousness.
   C. Trials of mockings, scourging, bonds, imprisonment, v. 36.
   D. Stoned, v. 37, sawn asunder, tempted, slain with sword.
   E. Wore animal skins in destitution, v. 38.
   F. Afflicted, ill treated, v. 37.
   G. Wandered, lived in caves, v. 38. Abraham did, v. 9; Elijah, II Kings.
V. Looked for something better.
   A. Abraham, v. 10, "city whose Maker is God."
   B. Abraham's seed, vs. 12-16, "heavenly country."
   C. Moses, v. 26, "recompense of reward."
   D. "Better resurrection," v. 35.
   E. Chose death for better resurrection, v. 35.
VI. Had narrow escapes.
   A. Rahab, v. 31.
   B. Daniel, v. 34.

HELPS FROM HEBREWS

      C. Hebrew children.
      D. Lot.
   From Animals
      A. Samson, v. 33.
      B. Daniel.
      C. David, I Sam. 17:34.

VII. Offered sacrifices.
      A. Abel, v. 4.
      B. Abraham, v. 17.
      C. Moses, v. 28, kept Passover, sprinkling of blood.
      D. Noah.
   What women did by faith
      A. Sarah conceived, v. 11.
      B. Rahab escaped, v. 31.
      C. Received dead by resurrection.
          1. I Kings 17:22 — Widow of Zarephath had son raised by Elijah.
          2. II Kings 4:34 — Elisha raised Shunamite woman's son.
          3. Mary, Martha.
          4. Widow of Nain.

VIII. Pronounced blessings.
      A. Isaac, v. 20, blessed Jacob and Esau.
      B. Jacob, v. 21, blessed his twelve sons.
      C. Joseph, v. 22.

IX. Faced mental anguish.
      A. Moses, v. 26, reproach of Christ.
      B. Mockings, v. 36.
      C. Samson mocked by Philistines, Judges 16:25.
      D. Micaiah, I Kings 22:27, mocked by Ahab.
      E. Jeremiah, Jer. 22:2-7.
      F. Isaac was mocked by Ishmael.
      G. Elisha was mocked by the children.
      H. Noah.
      I. Sarah.
      J. Abraham.
      K. Joseph, sold into slavery.
      L. Daniel, v. 33.

X. Obeyed unusual commands.
      A. Noah built an ark, v. 7
      B. Abraham to slay Isaac, v. 7

C. Abraham to leave country, v. 8.
D. Rahab, red cord.

Nation
A. Israel crossed Red Sea.
B. Israel caused Jericho to fall, v. 30.
C. Kept Passover.
D. Left Egypt.
E. Wilderness.

PART THREE

THE NATURE, DEVELOPMENT AND DUTIES OF FAITH. 11:1-13: 25

I. *The nature of faith.* 11:1-3

Text
11:1-3

1 Now faith is assurance of things hoped for, a conviction of things not seen. 2 For therein the elders had witness borne to them. 3 By faith we understand that the worlds have been framed by the Word of God, so that what is seen hath not been made out of things which appear.

Paraphrase

1 Now the faith of the just who shall live, is the firm persuasion of the reality of the blessings hoped for in consequence of God's promise, and the evidence of the matters of fact not seen, which revelation informs us have happened, or are yet to happen in the world.

2 And for this faith the ancients, namely Abel, Enoch, Noah, Abraham, and the rest were borne witness to by God, as justified and accepted persons.

3 By faith in the divine revelations, we understand that the worlds were produced by the command of God from nothing; so that the things which are seen, the things which compose this visible world, were not made of things which then did exist, but without any pre-existent matter to form them of.

Comment

Now faith is assurance of things hoped for, a conviction of things not seen

"Faith" in the original languages:
a. The Greek is *pistis* — in its forms means "steady, faithful."
b. In the Hebrew several words are used, also with the idea of stability, steadiness.

The world of men lives by faith in all realms.
a. An auto is driven by faith, or else we would stay off the highway. We have a faith in the machine, faith in self, faith in others.
b. We travel by train, bus, airplane, and ship, by faith in these respects: in pilot, navigator, engineer and on the signal system.
c. We marry on faith. Faith is important for true love.
d. History is accepted by faith.

Some of the questions about faith:
a. The importance of faith. How important is it?
1. Heb. 11:6: Without faith it is impossible to please God.
2. Abraham's life illustrates it to be a basis of friendship with God.
b. What is faith?
1. Heb. 11:1 defines it.
2. Belief that God exists.
3. Belief in Christ.
4. Belief in the unseen or the spiritual.
5. The substantiating of things hoped for.
c. How do we get faith?
1. Rom. 10:17: It comes by hearing.
Illustrations of it: Pentecost; Phillipian Jailor; Ethiopian eunuch.
2. John 7:17: It comes by doing.
a) John 14:1-4:
Two things about God: — He exists and, He is a rewarder. Christ is the Son of God. John 20:31.
b) Heb. 11:1: "Things hoped for."
d. How is this faith stated?
Matt. 16:16: "Thou art the Christ."
e. What part does the Bible have in faith?
John 20:31: "These are written."
f. Does faith alone save us?
James 2:24: "Ye see then how that by works a man is justified and not by faith only."

g. What is the end of your faith?
   I Pet. 1:9: "Receiving the end of your faith, even the salvation of your souls."
   1. We have a new body every seven years, but it slowly wears out.
   2. Through it all the real person endures.
h. What is the end of one who does not believe?
   1. John 8:24: "If ye believe not that I am He, ye shall die in your sins."
   2. Rev. 21:8: "But for the fearful and unbelieving, their part shall be in the lake that burneth with fire and brimstone, which is the second death."
   3. Mark 16:16: " — he that disbelieveth shall be condemned."

is assurance

King James Version — "evidence."
Alternate — "giving substance, essence, confidence."
Greek — *Hyportasia*, "title deeds" — Rimmer.
Other appearances of the word *hypostasis:*
a. Heb. 1:3: "The very image of His substance."
b. Heb. 3:14: "If we hold fast the beginning of your confidence."
Faith is the substantiating or giving substance of these things hoped for. Faith precedes prayer. Prayer is not working at God's reluctance, but taking hold of His willingness.

of things hoped for

He is only defining; he does not give the things hoped for, but we see them in this eleventh chapter — what faith was to others.
a. To Abraham, a new city.
b. To Daniel: Mouths of lions to be stopped.
Our faith becomes hope when it expects, anticipates.

a conviction

Also translated "test, evidence." It is full persuasion wrought in the mind. Noah could have conviction without ever looking at the sky if he had faith.
Some Christians are so pessimistic and faithless that they blow out their candles to see how dark it is. Too many are like Peter, who was afraid and began to sink. Matt. 14:30.

11:1, 2 HELPS FROM HEBREWS

Faith is

*F*orsaking
*A*ll
I
*T*ake
*H*im.

of things not seen

This is spiritual.
a. God, Christ, divine power, heaven are not seen, but by faith we believe in Their existence.
b. Reward, reunion are unseen, but are nonetheless real to the person.
c. Faith therefore becomes a power in our lives when it launches us out beyond the physical.
things are nonetheless real in other realms.
a. Wind is unseen, yet we believe it exists.
b. Force of gravity exists.
c. Tracks of an unseen person convince us of his existence, so does God's handiwork convince us of His existence.
Illustration. 11:2-3.

For therein

He now illustrates what faith has accomplished. In their faith they were conquerors.

the elders

"Elders" ordinarily refers to those in authority. Milligan says here it refers to all the heroes of the faith.

had witness born to them

Approved of God, by His blessings perhaps.
a. Enoch had witness born to him that he had been well pleasing. v. 4.
b. Abel had witness born to him that he had been well pleasing. Disapproval of God by His curses was manifested.
a. Cain was sent out.
b. God turned the Israelites free to wander for forty years. Note the King James Version: "Obtained a good report."
a. This is misleading if you think of it in the light that an elder is to be of good report.

b. Their report was not good to those of the outside, for note in verses 25-28 they were tortured, etc.
  c. It was an approval on the divine side.

by faith we understand

Things that seem impossible are understood when faith takes hold. Faith puts meaning in life.
a. Atheists are always chronic complainers.
b. The atheists build no hospitals, orphanages, or charitable organizations, but condemn the faith of those who do.
c. If this is a mechanistic world, then it is meaningless; but we see too much of God to believe in atheism.

that the worlds have been framed

"Worlds" — the literal meaning is from the Greek *aieves,* ages." May mean the world that is seen — the physical world, universe.

The same word is rendered "world" in verse 30 and in I Cor. 10:11. Here he affirms what Moses has stated.
a. Look at the theories suggested by men who have no faith.
b. The Java man, "missing link" theories, are promoted by those missing faith.

Ages began with creation:
a. Eph. 1:4: "Before the foundation of the world."
b. II Tim. 1:9: Before times eternal.
c. Titus 1:2: Before time eternal.

"Framed" is translated by others in such language as this: "Compacted, adjusted, produced, formed"; and Calvin says, "Fitted or joined together."

by the Word of God

Genesis says that God spoke things into existence with the words, "Let there be . . . " The "Word" takes on new meaning when we come to the New Testament:
a. John 1:1 says Christ was the Word.
b. Heb. 1:2: "By Whom also He made the worlds."
c. Heb. 11:3: Framed by the Word.

so that what is seen hath not been made out of things which appear

Calvin says, "as that they become the visible of things not visible, or not apparent."

Heathens, infidels, atheists have their ideas, but all are more difficult to believe than Genesis. Genesis uses the word *bara*, "to create," generally understood to mean to make something out of nothing.
a. The use of the word in other places does not bear this out, however.
b. God did not make them out of material which we see.

Study Questions

2066. In the original language, what idea does the word "faith" convey?
2067. Are shrinking and shirking compatible?
2068. Is faith limited only to religion?
2069. If you had no faith in men, what would be eliminated in your life?
    Could you eat a loaf of bread?
    Could you travel by bus, airplane?
    Could you be treated by a physician?
    Could you accept any history?
    Could you believe in Washington, Lincoln?
2070. What is Paul's definition of faith?
2071. What part of the definition includes belief in God?
2072. What would be included in "things hoped for"?
2073. How is Abraham an illustration of faith?
2074. Is faith more valuable than knowledge?
2075. How do we get faith? Cf. Rom. 10:17.
2076. Give an illustration of the method.
2077. Can you name one who received faith otherwise?
2078. What objects are required in faith?
2079. What two things are we to believe about God?
2080. What are we to believe about Christ?
2081. How is faith stated?
2082. Dare we ask men to confess more?
2083. Do we require unwritten confessionals, while condemning written ones?
2084. What part does the Bible have in faith? Cf. John 20:30-31.
2085. Is faith alone sufficient? Cf. James 2:24.
2086. What is the end of our faith? I Pet. 1:9.
2087. What is the end of the disbeliever? Cf. John 8:24; Rev 21:8; Mark 16:16.
2088. What does he mean that faith is "assurance"?

HELPS FROM HEBREWS

2089. Which is the better translation — "evidence" or "assurance"?
2090. What other words may be used?
2091. What things might be included in the "things hoped for"?
2092. Tell what the following people hoped for: Abraham, Daniel, David.
2093. Does this not sound like hope rather than faith?
2094. Could you have hope without faith?
2095. What is meant by the word "conviction"?
2096. What evidence did Noah have that it would rain?
2097. What evidence do you have of your faith in God? Christ?
2098. Is it things *yet to be* seen or *not* seen?
2099. Is it something seen by the eye of faith?
2100. What are the "things not seen"?
2101. How do you know unseen things exist?
2102. Are the unseen things less real?
2103. How do you know there is gravity, wind, electricity?
2104. "The elders" would refer to whom?
2105. "Witness borne to them" could be differently expressed. How?
2106. Hod did Enoch have witness borne? Abel?
2107. What does he mean by saying, "by faith we understand"?
2108. Can faith understand?
2109. Does infidelity render purpose and meaning to life?
2110. What does the word "world" mean?
2111. What does the word "framed" mean?
2112. How does this compare with the theory of evolution?
2113. What brought everything into existence according to the Word of God?
2114. What method was used?
2115. Identify the word used in verse three.
2116. What is included in the expression, "what is seen"?
2117. Does this help to solve what the "world" is in the first part of the verse?
2118. Does he mean that the present things are not remolded old things?
2119. Does this fit the pre-creation theory?
2120. Could the expression "had become waste and void" taught by pre-creation theorists have any substantiation here?

II. *Progressive development of faith during patriarchal and Mosaic dispensations.* 11:4-40.
A. *The antediluvian: faith in God.* 11:4-7.

Text
11:4-7

4 By faith Abel offered unto God a more excellent sacrifice than Cain, through which he had witness borne to him that he was righteous, God bearing witness in respect of his gifts: and through it he being dead yet speaketh. 5 By faith Enoch was translated that he should not see death; and he was not found, because God translated him: for he hath had witness borne to him that before his translation he had been well-pleasing unto God: 6 and without faith it is impossible to be well-pleasing unto Him; for he that cometh to God must believe that He is, and that He is a rewarder of them that seek after Him. 7 By faith Noah, being warned of God concerning things not seen as yet, moved with godly fear, prepared an ark to the saving of his house; through which he condemned the world and became heir of the righteousness which is according to faith.

Paraphrase

4 By faith, by rightly understanding and believing what was said concerning the seed of the woman's bruising the head of the serpent, Abel offered to God more sacrifice than Cain: For with an humble penitent heart he offered a sin-offering, on account of which he was declared to be righteous; God testifying this upon his gifts: and so by that sacrifice, though dead, Abel still speaketh, recommending to us repentance, humility, and faith.

5 By faith Enoch, having lived in a continued course of piety, was translated in the body from this earth, the habitation of sinners, to heaven, that he might not see death, and was not found, because God had translated him on account of his singular virtue. For before his translation it was testified by Moses, that he walked with God.

6 But without faith it is impossible, in any dispensation of religion, to please God. For he who worshippeth God acceptably, must believe that He exists, and that He will reward all them who sincerely worship and obey Him, and who persevere in piety and obedience to the end of their life.

7 By faith Noah, when he received a revelation concerning the destruction of the world by a deluge, a thing which no man had ever seen, being seized with religious fear, prepared an ark, according to God's command, for the saving of his family: by which religious fear he condemned the inhabitants of the old world, to whom, without success, he preached the revelation which had been made to himself, (2 Pet. ii. 5.), and became an heir of the righteousness of faith; of which his temporal deliverance was a pledge.

Comment

By faith Abel offered unto God

How did he get his faith? He received it like all do, by hearing. Rom. 10:17. God spoke to men directly in that day and Abel knew, just as we know — by hearing.

a more excellent sacrifice than Cain

How was it more excellent? It was offered by faith — that made the difference.

a. The conditions of offering, some blemish, the wrong kind of offering — whatever was wrong, it indicated a failure in faith on the part of Cain.
b. Most people feel Cain's offering was vegetable, in place of a blood offering.
Newell, p. 377: "Cain forgot that the ground was cursed."
a. However, animals live off the ground just as much as plants do.
b. Besides, animals were also cursed; they became wild and uncontrollable.
Of course, only a blood sacrifice could be a type of the coming sacrifice of Christ. "More" carries the idea of number, quality, or excellency.

through which he had witness borne to him that he was righteous

How it was done, no one knows, but God showed pleasure. Perhaps the sacrifice was consumed by fire, as seen in other instances.

a. Lev. 9:24: "And there came forth fire."
b. I Kings 18:38.
c. II Chr. 7:1.
Faithlessness, then, must be equivalent to unrighteousness.

God bearing witness in respect of his gifts

Gifts generally refer to free will.
a. Perhaps Cain was not sincere, and offered a substitute.
b. It may have been a small offering as the word "more" allows. How did God bear witness?
a. Perhaps He consumed it, like He did Elijah's. I Kings 18:38.
b. God has no respect for sacrifices that are not made in faith. John discusses it.
a. I John 3:12: "Wherefore slew he him? because his works were evil, and his brother's righteous."

and through it he being dead, yet speaketh

What speaks, the offering or Abel? Note that the pronoun shows that Abel speaks, although dead these many centuries. He speaks: "Work, serve, offer, by faith."

by faith Enoch was translated that he should not see death

Little is known of him.
a. Gen. 5:24: "And Enoch walked with God and he was not because God took him."
b. Jude 14 says that he was a prophet, and warned the people.
c. Gen. 5:18: He was the son of Jared.
This great character named after Cain's first son surely doesn't help the theory of original sin. Gen. 4:17.
a. Cain's child must have been good, or else Enoch would not have been named after him.
b. No one names their child "Cain" or "Judas."
c. If Cain had such an awful nature, we might expect this to be passed on directly.

for he had witness borne of him that before his translation

What a joy it must have been to have had the smile of God upon him. Unless we have witness we shall not be translated or received of God.
a. Rom. 8:16 has a special meaning in the light of Enoch's translation.
b. If we do not measure up to the word, we have no witness.

he had been well pleasing unto God.

Heb. 11:6: This is done by faith, and without faith it can't be done. These characters represent phases of faith:

a. Abel represents the *path of salvation* by faith.
b. Enoch represents one *walking with God,* who declared him righteous.
c. Noah represents the next result of faith — *testimony of coming judgment.*
d. Abraham, a tent-dwelling pilgrim, *living on divine promises.*

and without faith it is impossible to be well pleasing unto him

An earthly parent wants the confidence of his children, as does God.

Look what unbelief does:
a. It breaks God's word.
   Adam and Eve, Gen. 3:11.
   Korah, Jude 11.
b. It makes men fearful, fear then becomes the ruling motive of life.
   Adam: "I was afraid." Gen. 3:10.
   Cain: "They will kill me." Gen. 4:14.
   Israel: "We are grasshoppers." Num. 13:33.
   Peter was afraid and began to sink. Matt. 14:30.
c. It breaks God's fellowship.
   Adam and Eve hid in the garden.
   Gen. 4:16: Cain went out from the Presence of God. I John 3:12: "Not as Cain was of the evil one and slew his brother . . . because his works were evil, and his brother's righteous."
d. It leads to sin.
   How impossible then it is for the faithless one to please God.

for he that cometh to God must believe that He is and that He is

There is a way to God. We must come that way.
a. John 14:6: "The Way."
b. John 10:1: One is a thief and robber if he enters not by the door.
c. Prov. 28:26: A fool trusts in his own heart.
   Things to believe about God are suggested here.
a. That He is — He exists.
1. Ps. 14:1 calls the atheist a fool.
2. If there is no God, then let us quit saying, "Everything has a cause."

3. If God does not exist who made the world, then I can believe that there was no builder of this building.

a rewarder of them that seek after Him
b. He is a rewarder to seekers.
1. God is benevolent, and will balance the accounts.
2. Right may seem to be on the scaffold, and wrong on the throne, but above is God who keepeth watch over His own.

by faith Noah being warned of God concerning things not seen as yet, moved with godly fear
Noah alone paid regard to God's words, though deferred for 120 years. Look what his faith caused him to do:
a. Prepared the ark.
b. Condemned the world.
c. Became an heir of righteousness.
Disbelief makes one fearful, but faith builds a godly fear.
a. Disbelief makes one inactive.
b. Faith makes one active.

prepared the ark to the saving of his house
Look how often faith saves the house:
a. Noah, Heb. 11:7.
b. Joshua, Josh. 24:15.
c. Cornelius, Acts 10.
d. Lydia, Acts 16:14-15.
e. Phillipian Jaior, Acts 16:34; 18:8.
Pitiful are the stories of lost families where the father did not have faith.

through which he condemned the world
What condemned the world, Noah's deliverance, his faith or the ark?
a. Calvin says: "By the ark he condemned the world, for by being so long occupied in building it, he took away every excuse from the wicked."
b. Newell: "This faith had the double effect of condemning the world. (1) Noah's warning as a preacher of righteousness; (2) the effect of making Noah heir of righteousness."
Milligan feels that his faith condemned the world.

and became heir of the righteousness which is by faith
Moses records that he was a righteous man.

a. Noah had sin, yes, but the long, laborious work of Noah in the building of the ark must not be shoved aside.
b. Man has a tendency to condemn a man for one sin and categorize him unjustly.

Study Questions

2121. How did Abel get his faith?
2122. If he acted by faith, was he acting upon a command?
2123. If he had not been given directions, could it have been by faith?
2124. How was his sacrifice more excellent?
2125. What made the difference?
2126. Was Cain's less excellent or just plain unsatisfactory?
2127. What must have been the nature of Cain's offering?
2128. Could a vegetable sacrifice be unsatisfactory because the ground had been cursed after Eden?
2129. Could Abel have offered animals, but less worthy ones?
2130. How did Abel know that his sacrifice was acceptable?
2131. How did God manifest it?
2132. What did God show Cain to be?
2133. If obedience makes one righteous, what does failure to obey do?
2134. Define the word "gifts".
2135. Could this mean that the sacrifices were not done by command, but were free gifts?
2136. What does Abel speak? What words or message?
2137. Could we say that Cain also speaks? What?
2138. What is meant, "Enoch was translated"?
2139. Did he have faith that he would be translated?
2140. What did his faith do for him?
2141. What do we know about Enoch from other texts?
2142. Who had the same name?
2143. What witness had he received of God's pleasure?
2144. Does Rom. 8:16 throw any light on the subject?
2145. Enoch was well pleasing. Can we be too? How?
2146. Can we be pleasing otherwise?
2147. What would characterize a person without faith?
2148. Does an earthly parent want his child to have faith in him?
2149. What does unbelief do?
2150. What does it do in relationship to God's Word?
2151. What does it do in relationship to courage?

2152. Give illustrations of fearful people in the scriptures.
2153. What does it do in relationship to fellowship with God?
2154. What is essential in order to come to God?
2155. What approach must be the Christian method?
2156. What two things must be believed about God?
2157. If a man does not believe in God's existence, what is he called?
2158. Is expectation of reward evil in the light of this verse?
2159. Are God's rewards here and now?
2160. Why did God give a message to Noah?
2161. What three things did his faith do?
2162. Can we say that belief makes one active?
2163. Then what does disbelief do?
2164. Give the example of Christ's warning of Jerusalem's destruction.
2165. A "house" was saved by the ark. What is meant?
2166. Name some other houses that were saved.
2167. What condemned the world — deliverance, faith, the ark or preaching?
2168. Could it mean that his faith caused him to preach, thus condemning the world?
2169. What was he an heir to?
2170. Is the life of a righteous one a very long one?
2171. How can we be an heir of righteousness?

B. *The patriarchal: faith in God plus faith in His promises.* 11:8-27.

Text
11:8-27

8 By faith Abraham, when he was called, obeyed to go out unto a place which he was to receive for an inheritance; and he went out, not knowing whither he went. 9 By faith he became a sojourner in the land of promise, and in a land not his own, dwelling in tents, with Isaac and Jacob, the heirs with him of the same promise: 10 for he looked for the city which hath the foundations, whose Builder and Maker is God. 11 By faith even Sarah herself received power to conceive seed when she was past age, since she counted Him faithful Who had promised; 12 wherefore also there sprang of one, and him as good as dead, so many as the stars of heaven in multitude, and as the sand, which is by the sea-shore, innumerable.

13 These all died in faith, not having received the promises, but having seen them and greeted them from afar, and having confessed that they were strangers and pilgrims on the earth. 14 For they that say such things make it manifest that they are seeking after a country of their own. 15 And if indeed they had been mindful of that country from which they went out, they would have had opportunity to return. 16 But now they desire a better country, that is, a heavenly; wherefore God is not ashamed of them, to be called their God; for He hath prepared for them a city.

17 By faith Abraham, being tried, offered up Isaac: yea, he that had gladly received the promises was offering up his only begotten son; 18 even he to whom it was said, In Isaac shall thy seed be called: 19 accounting that God is able to raise up, even from the dead; from whence he did also in a figure receive him back. 20 By faith Isaac blessed Jacob and Esau, even concerning things to come. 21 By faith Jacob, when he was dying, blessed each of the sons of Joseph; and worshipped, leaning upon the top of his staff. 22 By faith Joseph, when his end was nigh, made mention of the departure of the children of Israel; and gave commandment concerning his bones. 23 By faith Moses, when he was born, was hid three months by his parents, because they saw he was a goodly child; and they were not afraid of the king's commandment. 24 By faith Moses, when he was grown up, refused to be called the son of Pharaoh's daughter; 25 choosing rather to share ill treatment with the people of God, than to enjoy the pleasures of sin for a season; 26 accounting the reproach of Christ greater riches than the treasures of Egypt: for he looked unto the recompense of reward. 27 By faith he forsook Egypt, not fearing the wrath of the king; for he endured, as seeing Him Who is invisible.

Paraphrase

8 By faith in the divine promises Abraham, when called to go out from his kindred and country, namely, Ur of the Chaldees, into a land which he should afterwards receive as an inheritance, obeyed, and relying on the power and veracity of God, went out, although he did not know the country to which he was going; nor whether it was a good or bad country.

9 By believing that Canaan was promised to him and to his seed only as the type of a better country, he acquired no pos-

sessions in Canaan except a burying-place, and built no houses there, but sojourned in the land which was promised to him as in a country belonging to others, dwelling in moveable tents with Isaac and Jacob, the joint heirs of the same promise:

10 For he expected the city having firm foundations, of which city the Builder and Lawgiver is God; consequently a city more magnificent and happy than any city on earth.

11 By faith in God's promise, even Sarah herself, though at first she thought the matter impossible, received strength for the conception of seed, and brought forth a son when past the age of child-bearing; because she at length attained the strongest persuasion of the faithfulness and power of Him who had promised her a son.

12 And therefore, by her, there sprang from one, namely Abraham, who on account of his great age was absolutely unfit for procreating children, a race as the stars of heaven in multitude, and as the sand upon the sea-shore, which is innumerable, agreeably to God's promises to him, recorded Gen. xv. 5. xxii. 17.

13 All these died in faith, though they did not receive the blessings promised: For, descrying them afar off, and being persuaded of their certainty, and embracing them with ardent desire, they confessed that they were strangers and pilgrims in the land of Canaan, and on the earth itself. (See Gen. xxiii. 4. xlvii. 9.)

14 Now persons who spake in this manner plainly declared, that they did not consider Canaan as the country principally meant in God's promise, but that they earnestly sought to go to their father's country; the country which God promised to their fathers.

15 And they by no means wished to go back to Chaldea: For truly if they had longed after that country from which they came out, they might have had an opportunity to have returned to it.

16 But indeed they longed after a better country than Chaldea, even an heavenly country, which God had promised to them: Therefore God was not ashamed of them (Abraham, Isaac, and Jacob) to be called their God, long after they were dead, notwithstanding He gave them no possession in Canaan, because He hath prepared for them a city, even the new Jerusalem.

17 By a great exercise of faith, Abraham, when tried, offered up Isaac; laid him on the altar to sacrifice him: He who had received the promises, that his seed should be as the sand on the

sea-shore innumerable, and should inherit Canaan, and that the nations should be blessed in his seed, offered up even his only begotten.

18 Concerning whom it was expressly said, Surely by Isaac a seed shall be to thee, in whom all the promises which I have made to thy seed shall be fulfilled.

19 Yet, notwithstanding the apparent contradiction in the divine revelations, Abraham laid Isaac on the altar, reasoning that, although he were burnt to ashes, God was able to raise him, and would raise him even from the dead: from whence on this occasion he received him, by being hindered from slaying him, even in order to his being a type of Christ.

20 By faith in the divine revelation, Isaac foretold to Jacob and Esau the blessings which were to be bestowed on them and their posterity.

21 By the like faith, Jacob, when near his death, Gen. xlvii. 20 blessed each of the sons of Joseph; and, in token of his faith in the promises concerning their possessing Canaan, worshipped God leaning on the top of his staff.

22 By faith in God's promise of giving Canaan to Abraham and to his seed, Joseph, when ending his life, made mention of the departing of the children of Israel out of Egypt, as a thing certain; and to preserve the knowledge and expectation thereof among the Israelites, he commanded them to carry his bones with them into Canaan.

23 By faith in the promises of God, Moses, when born, being circumcised, was hid three months by his parents till he was recovered, because they saw the child beautiful, and presaged he might be the person appointed to deliver them; and were not afraid of the king's commandment to give up their children to be killed. Exod. i. 22.

24 By faith in the promises of God, made known to him by his brethren, Moses, when he was grown up, resolving to join himself to his people, refused to be called any longer the son of Pharaoh's daughter;

25 Choosing rather to suffer persecution with the people of God, than, as the son of Pharaoh's daughter, to have the temporary fruition of the pleasures of sin in the court of Egypt;

26 Esteeming the scoffs cast on the Israelites for expecting the Christ to arise among them, in whom all the nations of the earth

should be blessed, greater riches than the treasures of Egypt; for he looked off from them to the reward which he expected in the life to come.

27 By believing that God would deliver His people, notwithstanding the number and power of their oppressors, Moses left Egypt with the Israelites, not being afraid of the wrath of Pharaoh, who he knew would pursue them: For he courageously persevered in his purpose, as expecting aid from the invisible God.

Comment

By faith Abraham when he was called

This man is so great as to be recognized by the three theistic religions in the world.
a. His grave at Hebron is the common shrine for Judaism, Islam and Christianity.
b. His name occurs more than three hundred times in twenty-seven books of the Bible.

He was called of God in the midst of idolatry, for Ur was the center of moon worship.
a. Abraham worshipped God, for otherwise he would not have obeyed God.
b. The faithful receive the call of God, for they hear His voice.

obeyed to go out unto a place which he was to receive as an inheritance and he went out, not knowing whither he went

Gen. 12:1-3 gives us his call in substance. This land to be given to his posterity was unknown to him at the time. To leave home and loved ones shows a strong faith.

He went out to Haran where he remained five years. Where his father died, and then he went on to Canaan at the age of seventy-five. (Gen. 12:4). Compare Gal. 3:17; Ex. 12:40-41. He died at age one hundred seventy-five. See Gen. 25:7.

by faith he became a sojourner in the land of promise, as in a land not his own

Milligan makes much of the word "sojourner," saying that he never really possessed the land.

Round about were the walled cities, over which he was not King, but he made an impression. The Hittites said, "Thou art a prince." See Gen. 23:6.

dwelling in tents with Isaac and Jacob

They lived in fragile homes, moving here and there. From the birth of Isaac to the Exodus was four hundred years. Gen. 15:13. There were walled cities, property everywhere, but still Abraham had to purchase a burying place. Gen. 23:3-20.

the heirs with him of the same promise

The promise of Abraham was theirs likewise. They sojourned in the same promise by faith as did Abraham.

for he looked for the city which hath the foundations, whose Builder and Maker is God

This accounts for their stedfastness.
a. They did not worry about living in tents when cities abounded, for their eyes penetrated heaven.
b. "Foundations" suggests perpetuity rather than something transitory and fading.
Milligan thinks that they had revelations which have never been transmitted to us.
a. He feels this "city" is the heavenly Jerusalem, Gal. 4:26; Heb.12:22; 13:14, which is for the present located in heaven.
b. He says, "It will descend to the earth after it shall be renovated by fire." Rev. 21.
c. Then will be fulfilled in its proper and full sense that Abraham and his seed be the "heirs of the world." Rom. 4.
Regardless of the location, God is the Architect and Builder.
a. He will locate it where it ought to be.
b. It will be a permanent place for the people of God.

by faith even Sarah herself received power to conceive seed when she was past age

The introduction of Sarah shows that this truth belongs to women also.
a. She is mentioned since she is the mother of the faithful.
b. She was openly charged with unbelief, so it may seem strange for her to be included. Gen. 18:12-13.
c. Remember Abraham also laughed at first. Gen. 17:17.

since she counted Him faithful who had promised

God promised; that made the difference.
a. Rom. 10:17: Faith comes by hearing.

11:11-14

b. True faith then is that which hears God speaking and rests on His promise.

She was about ninety years of age, Gen. 17:17, past the natural period of child-bearing, but faith brought to her power to do it.

wherefore also there sprang of one, and him as good as dead

This refers to dead Abraham — dead as to the power of begetting children. This accounts for his attitude in Gen. 17:17, where he named his age and laughed.

so many as the stars of heaven in multitude and as the sand which is by the seashore innumerable

Whatever pride the Jews may have, everything must be ascribed to the faith of Abraham and Isaac. This reference to the faith of this great man ought to serve to encourage the hearts of the despondent.

these all died in faith, not having received the promises

What promises are meant?
a. He never saw his posterity in such numbers.
b. He never saw his seed receive an everlasting inheritance. Gen. 12:7; 13:15; 15:18-21; 17:8.
c. He never saw the earth blessed through his seed. Gen. 12:3; 22:18.

but having seen them and greeted them from afar

Jesus may throw light on this expression.
John 8:56: "Abraham rejoiced to see My day, and he saw it and was glad."
"Them" must refer to promises and not to people. A distant view was had, but that was all.

having confessed that they were strangers and pilgrims on the earth

Abraham could say, "I see a new city, but I am a stranger here."
This confession Jacob made to Pharaoh. Gen. 47:9.

for they that say such things make it manifest that they are seeking after a country of their own

The confession made in verse 13 is referred to.

a. This shows that they had faith in a better country.
b. If they in spirit, amid dark clouds, took a flight into the celestial country, how much more ought we, as Christ beckons. "Where I am, there you may be also."
The promise of Christ should be more real to us than the promise to them.

if indeed they have been mindful of that country from which they went out

These could have returned to their native land if they had desired to do so.
a. Abraham could have returned to Ur of the Chaldees, for he was not banished.
b. Eliezer, Abraham's steward, was sworn to never carry Isaac into Chaldea. Gen. 24:5-8.
"They would have had opportunity" suggests that nothing stood in their way.

but now they desire a better country, that is a heavenly

The fact that Abraham didn't return to Chaldea showed his disinterest in earthly land. He looked for a country better than Canaan or Chaldea.

wherefore God is not ashamed of them, to be called their God

God showed this in Exodus 3:6 when God said He was God of Abraham, Isaac and Jacob.
a. It is a singular honor for God to attach His name to men.
b. When they renounced the world, considered themselves pilgrims, then God claimed them.
We must do the same if God would claim us.
a. Gal. 3:26 indicates that we are sons of God through faith.
b. Gen. 17:7 shows that God promised this relationship to Abraham's seed.

for He hath prepared for them a city

God is able to give life to their bodies and to make it possible for them to live in their city. Why would God allow man to be outlived by trees, turtles, and elephants, if it were not for the fact that man will live again?

Abraham, being tried, offered up Isaac

    This was a proving of Abraham.
a. Archeologists show that child sacrifices were common among the people of that day.
b. The heathens loved their gods enough to sacrifice a child. Here was a greater God asking Abraham to do it.
c. Would Abraham do it? He would by faith.
    His resolution to obey was then the same as though he had actually sacrificed his son.

offering up his only begotten son

    This shows how severe the trial was.
a. Abraham had gladly received promises, and Isaac was the only hope of their being fulfilled. See Gen. 17:2; 21:12.
b. Now in taking away Isaac, it was the same as taking away the promises.
    Isaac is called the "only begotten," for Ishmael had been driven from the family and was not considered a part of the promise.

accounting that God is able to raise up, even from the dead

    According to this verse, Abraham surely concluded that God would restore Isaac to life. This was further strengthened by Abraham's words to his servants, "We will worship."
a. "Come again." Gen. 22:5.
b. In the Hebrew it is in the plural, "We will return."

from whence he did also in a figure receive him back

    Some think this refers to Isaac's supernatural birth, but this is poor exegesis. Abraham received him back from the altar as one raised from the dead.
a. Abraham's obedience until God stayed his hand caused Isaac to be the same as dead.
b. He was figuratively raised from the dead.
    God said Isaac had not been withheld, so he was sacrificed as far as God was concerned. Gen. 22:12-18.

by faith Isaac blessed Jacob and Esau, even concerning things to come

    The ability to bless was, in a sense, a prophecy.
a. Isaac had nothing in the land, except the right of burial, yet

he could say, "Let peoples serve thee and nations bow down to thee." Gen. 27:29.
b. Isaac had nothing to bestow but the Word of God.
The unusual thing about this blessing is that he distinguished between the twins.
a. He gave first place to the younger, which meant taking away the rights of the firstborn.
b. Isaac by faith spoke the thing that God desired.
c. Isaac refused to change the blessing, saying, Gen. 27:33: "I have blessed him, yea, and he shall be blessed."
A comparison of the history of Esau's people, the Edomites, with the blessing of Isaac shows that Isaac made a prophetic outline of the fortunes of the two races.
a. Edom was quite a nation before Israel had kings. Gen. 36:31.
b. Edom was independent while Israel was in bondage in Egypt.
c. Saul and David finally conquered the Edomites. Compare I Sam. 14:47; II Sam. 8:14.

by faith Jacob, when he was dying, blessed each of the sons of Joseph

Joseph's sons were Ephraim and Manasseh, and were blessed by their grandfather. Gen. 48:1-22.
a. This occurred when Joseph took the sons to see their sick grandfather.
b. They were adopted as sons and made the honored heads of separate and distinct tribes.
c. He put his right hand on Ephraim and his left hand on Manasseh as he made the blessing.
Ephraim became so superior as a tribe that often the ten tribes were included under his name, so that in a manner they did lie down under its shade.
a. Ephraim was the younger, yet Jacob in his dimness of eyes crossed his hands so that Ephraim received the greater blessing.
b. Jacob sounded as though he were lord of the land from which he was driven by famine.
Faith is the only explanation for such a prophecy.

and worshipped, leaning upon the top of his staff

Here is a dramatic picture, an old man dying, blessing, worshipping, leaning. The act of worshipping that we know from

Genesis occurred prior to this blessing when Joseph promised not to bury his father in Egypt. Gen. 47:31.

Some make a great deal out of the fact that in some versions it reads, "Israel bowed himself upon the bed's head."

a. Several suggestions are made to clarify the issue, one of which suggests the Hebrew word may mean either a bed or a staff, depending upon the vowel pointing in the Hebrew language.

b. Some suggest Paul quoted from an incorrect text, but this view destroys inspiration. An inspired writer would select an inspired text, or would know the truth.

Both can be right in my judgment. Here is an old man dying, and he would need support, and so his staff and bed were both used.

Joseph, when his end was nigh, made mention of the departure of Israel and gave command concerning his bones

Here is one of the finest characters in the Old Testament.

a. His conception of sin stands out. "How can I do this great wickedness and sin against God?" Gen. 39:9.

b. He is one of the few of which no evil is recorded of him. His prophecy is found in Gen. 50:24.

a. His faith is seen in that he requested that they carry his bones in a box with them into the promised land. Gen. 50:25.

b. Genesis ends with him in a coffin in Egypt, but his bones were carried into the promised land, for Moses remembered. Ex. 13:19.

By faith Moses, when he was born, was hid three months

Pharaoh commanded every son to be cast into the river. Ex. 1:22.

a. Moses was cast into the river, but an ark was under him. Ex. 2:3.

b. Amram and Jochebed had faith, and it was wonderfully rewarded by Pharaoh's daughter's care and devotion.

The description "a goodly child" is no doubt the same as Acts 7:20: "Fair unto God." (alternate reading).

a. The parents were not just charmed by his beauty, but saw in him a person destined to serve God.

b. Putting him in the river was not a wavering of their faith as some suggest, but another attempt to preserve him.

by faith, Moses, when he was grown up refused to be called the son of Pharaoh's daughter

    How did he go about it formally?
a. Very likely he just showed a preference for his own people. Ex. 2:11-12; Acts 7:24.
b. His mother no doubt had taught him very early about his true identity.
    Being about forty years old, Acts 7:24 shows that this was not a hasty, headstrong decision of a youth.

choosing rather to share ill treatment with the people of God

    The Egyptians were learned, powerful, and influential in the world; the Hebrews were oppressed and degraded.
a. The world would say, "What a poor choice!"
b. It was a choice between temporary vanity and eternal glory, and Moses chose rightly.
    Man begins to live when he connects his life with a great cause, and Moses became the great lawgiver of Israel.

than to enjoy the pleasures of sin for a season

    Faith in God causes one to see the folly, pleasures of sin, and glitter of wickedness that soon fades. A season or an eternity must be our choice, and faith makes the difference.
a. It was not pleasures in Canaan, for ill treatment would be too much of a price for earthly pleasures in that land.
b. It was the joys of a heavenly Canaan which Moses could see by the eyes of faith.

accounting the reproach of Christ greater riches than the treasures of Egypt

    Did Moses know that he was to suffer the reproach of Christ? Did he know Christ?
a. Some answer, "It was such reproach as Christ Himself endured."
b. Some say, "Reproach suffered on account of Christ."
c. Others, "It was reproach on Moses as a type of Christ."
d. It is the reproach which Christ had to bear and also the reproach that all true believers have to bear.
e. It is the reproach of Christ's people.
    I believe that it is a reproach like Christ's. As He, though rich, became poor to redeem mankind, so Moses despised the treasurers of Egypt to deliver Israel.

for he looked unto the recompense of reward
  a. Calvin says, "It corresponds to what he did; his retribution was his success."
  b. Milligan says "the great and final recompense."
  c. McKnight says it was nothing earthly, for he could have had more and in greater perfection by staying in the palace.
  A man like Moses doesn't have to hear specific offers of remuneration before he works for God. To please God would be enough.

by faith he forsook Egypt, not fearing the wrath of the king: for he endured as seeing Him who is invisible
  This does not refer to his departure into Midian, for he left them in great fear. Ex. 2:14-15.
  When did he forsake Egypt?
  a. Perhaps when he made his choice to be among the Israelites.
  b. Many suggest when he led Israel out.
  c. Milligan holds to the flight to Midian.
  1. Because it fits the chronology, the Passover was instituted after his return from Midian but not after the Exodus.
  2. The departure was in opposition to the will of Pharaoh.
  3. If the Exodus were meant, all Israel would have been named.
  There are some glaring weaknesses to Milligan's view:
  a. The author is not interested in chronology in this chapter, for the men are named out of order.
  b. He doesn't necessarily say, "instituted the Passover" although the Greek allows it and the context suggests it.
  c. He is not talking about Israel, but Moses.
  d. Leaving Pharaoh, quitting, would no doubt provoke wrath. "Him who is invisible" suggests the true God.
  a. Perhaps Christ could be included, for Christ was on the journey. I Cor. 10:4.
  b. The main point to gain is his faith in One unseen that made him endure.

Study Questions

2172. Abraham is the chief character for discussion. What three religions honor him?
2173. Does his name appear frequently in the scriptures?
2174. Name the New Testament books that refer to him.
2175. How did God call him in Ur?

HELPS FROM HEBREWS

2176. What did the call include?
2177. Where was he living? What do we know about the place?
2178. Show how faith and obedience are connected in his life.
2179. Do you think his call was challenging to faith?
2180. Does the word "inheritance" mean that he was to own a great land?
2181. Did he ever seem to possess it?
2182. What is meant, "he became a sojourner"? v. 9.
2183. Did he ever make much of an impact on their civilization?
2184. In his battle with the kings, what may we judge about him?
2185. How did the Hittites feel about him?
2186. What kind of home did he live in?
2187. Does this show that he had a permanent home?
2188. Does the size of the herds indicate that, in a sense, he owned a great amount of land?
2189. How do Isaac and Jacob figure in the promise?
2190. Was Abraham hoping for one of the cities which he saw?
2191. What is the significance of the word "foundations"? v. 10.
2192. Who would make this city?
2193. Is it possible that we do not have recorded the complete revelation to Abraham?
2194. Will it be a city limited to the descendants of Abraham?
2195. Could it be the same city referred to in Revelation?
2196. Is the heavenly Jerusalem to be moved?
2197. Who is the first woman of faith mentioned in the text?
2198. How could she be considered of faith when she laughed at the promise of God?
2199. Did Abraham laugh as she did? Cf. Gen. 17:17.
2200. What attribute of God did Sarah rest upon?
2201. Who is referred to in verse 12?
2202. What is meant by, "as good as dead"?
2203. How many sprang from Abraham?
2204. Are the Jews a numerous people today?
2205. Who is referred to by the expression, "These all died"? v. 13.
2206. What promises are meant?
2207. What all did Abraham fail to see?
2208. Did he ever see his descendants possessing the earth?
2209. Did he ever see his seed blessing the earth?

2210. What is referred to by the expression, "having seen them"?
2211. Does it refer to people, or days, or promises? Cf. John 8:56.
2212. When was a confession made that the Hebrews were strangers and pilgrims? Cf. Gen. 47:9.
2213. What are the "such things" of verse 14?
2214. Are we looking for a country?
2215. Should our promise be more real to us?
2216. What did Jesus say about our abiding place?
2217. Did they concern themselves over the land they had left?
2218. Could Abraham have returned to Chaldea? Cf. Gen. 24:5-8.
2219. Was Abraham's desire for an earthly home?
2220. What was the "better country"? v. 16.
2221. Did God ever exhibit pride in these patriarchs?
2222. When did He confess their name? Cf. Ex. 3:6.
2223. What was required of them in order to be claimed by God?
2224. Compare Gal. 3:26 and Gen. 17:7 to see if this can be our experience.
2225. If they did not inherit the promise, when will they receive it?
2226. Why does he speak of it as a city sometimes, and a country in other places?
2227. What was Abraham's greatest trial?
2228. Was the offering of a son a common thing?
2229. Was the resolution to sacrifice Isaac the same as obedience?
2230. How could Isaac be considered "only begotten"?
2231. Where else does this phrase appear?
2232. If Isaac had been taken, what else would have been taken away?
2233. What may we judge that Abraham believed God would do if he killed Isaac?
2234. Compare the statement in Gen. 22:5.
2235. What is the figure described here?
2236. Was it a figurative resurrection?
2237. Was it a figurative sacrifice?
2238. What was the nature of a blessing in the Old Testament?
2239. Were these Old Testament characters so influential with God that they could promise, and God had to fulfill?

2240. What was the blessing in Gen. 27:29?
2241. Was this unusual?
2242. Can we say that Isaac by faith spoke what God desired?
2243. Who were Esau's descendants?
2244. How great were the Edomites?
2245. Who finally conquered them? Cf. I Sam. 14:47; II Sam. 8:14.
2246. Tell of the blessing of Jacob on his death bed. Cf. Gen. 48:1-22.
2247. Upon whom was it pronounced?
2248. What did he pronounce?
2249. What did he do when he pronounced the blessing?
2250. Was this blessing unusual?
2251. Did the younger or the elder receive the greater blessing?
2252. Did Ephraim become great?
2253. How may we explain that Jacob seemed to be lord of a land from which he had been driven by famine?
2254. What four words describe Jacob in this experience?
2255. How did Joseph reveal his faith in the fact of a new country being promised? Cf. Gen. 50:24-25.
2256. Did Moses obey this request which Joseph made? Cf. Ex. 13:19.
2257. How does Genesis end? Is the coffin mentioned at the end?
2258. How did faith involve Moses early in his life?
2259. Was he cast into the river as Pharaoh commanded?
2260. What was under him?
2261. How was his parents' faith rewarded?
2262. What is meant, "a goodly child"?
2263. Compare Acts 7:20 for a description of him.
2264. Was it good appearance that saved him?
2265. If not, what does the description, "a goodly child" mean?
2266. How did Moses refuse to be called the son of Pharaoh's daughter? Compare Ex. 2:11-12 and Acts 7:24.
2267. How old was he when he took his stand?
2268. How did he learn of his true identity?
2269. What was the object of his faith that would cause him to reject Pharaoh's house?
2270. Show the contrast of what he rejected and what he accepted as a Jew.
2271. Did he make a wise choice in the eyes of the world?

2272. Does the world choose temporary vanity in place of eternal glory?
2273. Would he have been an historical character if he had stayed with the Egyptians?
2274. Is it a great cause that makes the man, or the man who makes a cause great?
2275. Does faith still cause men to see the folly of sin?
2276. What is meant by the word "season"? v. 25.
2277. Is a season's pleasure worth the loss of eternity with God?
2278. Did Moses know Christ?
2279. Was it a reproach like Christ's?
2280. Could Moses be considered a type of Christ in suffering?
2281. Did Jesus empty Himself of treasure to be poor? Cf. Phil. 2:5-11.
2282. What was Moses' expected reward — earthly or heavenly?
2283. Could pleasing God be enough to challenge a man like Moses?
2284. What is meant by, "he forsook Egypt"?
2285. Could it be referring to the time he left for Midian? Why not?
2286. Does Exodus 2:14-15 answer the above question?
2287. When did he forsake Egypt? Is it the same time as referred to in verse 25?
2288. Why does Milligan feel that the flight to Midian is meant?
2289. Is the chronology a good reason for believing it?
2290. If the Exodus is meant, would he have necessarily have included all Israel?
2291. Would leaving Pharaoh make Pharaoh wrathful?
2292. Do people become angry when you refuse their so-called "social graces"?
2293. Are people offended when you refuse to drink with them?
2294. What is meant by, "Him Who is invisible"?
2295. Could Moses have seen Christ?
2296. Compare I Cor. 10:4.
2297. Is spiritual sight more foresighted than that of the physical eye?

C. *Israelitish nation: faith in God's promises of the coming Messiah.* 11:28-40.

Text
11:28-40

28 By faith he kept the passover, and the sprinkling of the blood, that the destroyer of the firstborn should not touch them.
29 By faith they passed through the Red sea as by dry land: which the Egyptians assaying to do were swallowed up. 30 By faith the walls of Jericho fell down, after they had been compassed about for seven days. 31 By faith Rahab the harlot perished not with them that were disobedient, having received the spies with peace.
32 And what shall I more say? for the time will fail me if I tell of Gideon, Barak, Samson, Jephthah; of David and Samuel and the prophets: 33 who through faith subdued kingdoms; wrought righteousness, obtained promises, stopped the mouths of lions, 34 quenched the power of fire, escaped the edge of the sword, from weakness were made strong, waxed mighty in war, turned to flight armies of aliens.
35 Women received their dead by a resurrection: and others were tortured, not accepting their deliverance; that they might obtain a better resurrection: 36 and others had trial of mockings and scourgings, yea, moreover of bonds and imprisonment: 37 they were stoned, they were sawn asunder, they were tempted, they were slain with the sword: they went about in sheepskins, in goatskins; being destitute, afflicted, ill-treated 38 (of whom the world was not worthy), wandering in deserts and mountains and caves, and the holes of the earth. 39 And these all, having had witness borne to them through their faith, received not the promise, 40 God having provided some better thing concerning us, that apart from us they should not be made perfect.

Paraphrase

28 By faith in the promise of God, that the first-born of the Egyptians should be destroyed, but those of the Israelites spared, Moses appointed the passover, and the dashing of the blood of the paschal lamb on the door-posts of the Israelites, Exod. xii. 7. that the angel who destroyed the first-born of the Egyptians might not touch theirs.
29 And although the Israelites were terrified by the pursuit of the Egyptians, and spake against Moses before they came

to the sea, (Exod. xiv. 10.), yet on his exhortation they went forward and when the waters of the sea were miraculously divided, by faith they passed through the Red Sea as by dry land, which the Egyptians essaying to do were drowned.

30 By faith in God's promise, the walls of Jericho fell down agreeably to that promise, after having been encompassed seven days by the Israelites in obedience to God's command.

31 By faith in the true God, of Whose miracles she had heard, (Josh. ii. 10.), Rahab the harlot was not destroyed at the sacking of Jericho, with the unbelieving inhabitants, having entertained and concealed the spies in a friendly manner.

32 And what need is there to produce more examples of the power and efficacy of faith? for the time would fail me to speak of the great actions performed by Joshua and those who came after him, namely Gideon, and Barak, and Samson, and Jephthah, and David also, and Samuel, and the prophets Elijah, Elisha, Daniel, and the rest;

33 Who, firmly believing that God would maintain the Israelites in the possession of Canaan, subdued the neighboring idolatrous kingdoms, performed the righteous actions commanded them by God, and in reward, obtained promises, and stopped the mouths of lions,

34 Were unhurt by the strongest fire, — he means Shadrach and his companions, whose faith is recorded Dan. iii. 17.; — escaped the edges of the sword; — Moses escaped the sword of Pharaoh, Exod. xviii. 4. Elijah that of Jezebel, and David that of Saul; — waxed strong from sickness, as did Hezekiah, Isa. xxxviii. 17.; — became valiant in battle, and overturned the camps of the enemies; — Gideon overturned the camp of the Midianites, and Jonathan that of the Philistines.

35 Women received their dead children alive by a resurrection, as did the widow of Zarephath, I Kings xvii. 21, and the Shunamite, 2 Kings iv. 34.; — others were beaten to death, not accepting deliverance on the condition offered, that they might obtain a better resurrection.

36 And others, like Jeremiah, (Jer. xx. 7.), had experience of mockings, and scourgings, and moreover they were fettered, and imprisoned in filthy dungeons.

37 Others were stoned to death, as Zechariah, (2 Chron. xxiv. 21.); they were sawn asunder, they were tempted, they died by the slaughter of the sword, (1 Sam. xxii. 18. I Kings xix. 10.):

They wandered about in sheep's skins, and in goats' skins, being destitute, afflicted, maltreated by those to whom they delivered the messages of God;

38 Of these the world was not worthy: Yet they wandered by day in deserts and mountains, and by night lodged in caves and holes of the earth; as Elijah, and the hundred prophets hid by Obadiah, and David, I Sam. xxiv. 3.

39 Now all these, though they have justly obtained the highest renown among men, along with the better approbation of God on account of their faith and great actions, have not yet received the heavenly country promised to Abraham and to his seed.

40 The reason is, God having forseen, that by the gospel He would bestow some better means of faith on us, in order to our becoming Abraham's spiritual seed, resolved, that the ancients without us should not be made perfect by receiving the promised heavenly country. For He determined that the whole spiritual seed of Abraham, raised from the dead, shall be introduced into that country in a body at one and the same time, namely, after the general judgment.

Comment

By faith he kept the passover, and the sprinkling of the blood

>The Greek language allows also "instituted" or "hath made" for "kept." The passover, rather than the feast later instituted, is no doubt meant by the "sprinkling" and the reference to "the destroyer."

that the destroyer of the firstborn should not touch them

>The passover was instituted by God through Moses in that Moses gave direction for the sprinkling. Faith caused Moses to deliver the message, and faith caused Israel to be obedient.

by faith they passed through the Red sea

>The Egyptians also tried to pass through, but faith was lacking there. Reliance upon God was the measure of faith here, for the pursuing Egyptians could easily have swallowed them up.

by faith the walls of Jerico fell down

>The city of Jericho stood in the way of a conquest of the land. The command to march around once a day, and seven

times on the seventh day may have seemed unnecessary to the unbelieving, but it marked victory for the faithful.

by faith Rahab the harlot perished not with them that were disobedient, having received the spies with peace

Seven things about Rahab by Newell, p. 387: (Compare Joshua 2:1-22; 6:22-25; James 2:25. See Joshua 2:1-22; 6:22-25; James 2:25.)

a. She was a sinner, even a harlot. Rom. 3:23: All have sinned.
b. Rahab's faith was confessed; and so must ours be. Matt. 10:32.
   Joshua 2:8-11: "I know that Jehovah hath given you the land and that the fear of you is fallen upon us, and that all the inhabitants of the land melt away before you."
c. Faith meant turning against her people; the believer must also be willing if necessary.
d. Faith included the belief that Jericho would be destroyed, and it brought concern for her people. 2:13.
e. It brought the typical scarlet cord tied in her window, by which the spies escaped. 2:15-21. We have the blood of Christ.
f. By her faith all her kindred were saved. 2:19; 6:22-25.
g. She became the mother of Boaz (Matt. 1:5); great grandfather of David, the king. Ruth 4:21-22.

Was she a harlot?

a. Milligan: Many Jews erroneously interpret the word so as to make it mean a seller of food or an innkeeper.
b. Calvin: The word is *zune*. Some render it "hostess" as though she kept a public house, but as the word is rendered "harlot" for everyone else, so it must be here. The Jews think it disgraceful to their nation, so they render it otherwise.
c. Calvin: She is mentioned as a harlot to amplify the grace of God.

Faith in God made her hazard her life in receiving and concealing the spies, so she is named among the faithful.

time will fail me if I tell of Gideon

Here the author names a number of people drawn from the exploits, deliverances, and heroic endurance of faithful men and women.

Gideon stands chronologically after Barak. Gideon was the

son of Joash of the tribe of Manasseh, and was the fifth judge of Israel. Two things perhaps make him worthy of being named here.
a. His fight against Baal.
b. He used only 300 men out of an army of 32,000 men. Judges 6:11-8:32.

Barak

He was a leader of Israel of the tribe of Naphtali. The Israelites were oppressed by Jabin, king of Canaan, and Sisera, the captain of the host. The enemy had 900 chariots, and for twenty years oppressed Israel. Judges 4:23.
Deborah, the prophetess, called Barak and gave him a plan for victory. 4:6-7. With Deborah and 10,000 men he led Israel to a complete victory. Judges 4:1-5:31.

Samson

Samson, in the scripture, appears after Jephthah.
Zwemer in his book, *Sons of Adam,* says that his career is put into the record anonymously, for who but Samson did these things in verses 33-34?
a. Moses was the "brain," learned in the wisdom of Egypt; Samson was a man of brawn, up to all the tricks and sports of a giant.
b. Moses' life is a long epic; Samson's, a brief tragedy.
c. Moses was the man of God; Samson, the man of the people. The above offers the contrast between Moses and Samson. These feats of muscular power are of course the chief things about him.

Jephthah

He was the son of Gilead by a concubine, and became the ninth judge of Israel. His victories over the Ammonites and the Ephraimites, Judges 11:1-12:7, with faith in God, ranks him a name among the faithful. He made a hasty foolish vow, and the finest victory was marred by the cruel death of his own daughter.
a. In all the faithful ones, we find imperfection, yet they attained much by faith.
b. Perhaps we should see that faults should not break us down or dishearten us. We must go on in the race of our calling.

David

Calvin says: "Under David's name he included all the pious kings." He was the second king of Israel, and is known for his faith in God.
a. This is established by the Psalms that express it. Cf. Ps. 18:6-17.
b. It is shown in his many victories for the Lord, one of which was his slaying of Goliath.

Samuel and the prophets

Samuel is placed after David, most likely in order to connect him with the prophets, says Milligan. The prophets are to be greatly admired, for they had to preach in such wicked and wayward days.
a. Their patience was sorely tried, but their faithful messages are recorded for the ages.
b. They are lessons in faith and faithfulness for us today.

who through faith subdued kingdoms

Some of them did some of the things that are named here.
a. David is probably chief here, but definitely Joshua's work should be noted as he led in the conquest.
b. Asa, Jehoshaphat, Hezekiah, and Josiah are others who could be named. This work is similiar to verse 34 — "turned to flight armies of aliens."

wrought righteousness

This work was the main concern of the prophets who cried out against sin and for the establishment of justice. The work of Elijah and Elisha stands out.
King Josiah's work, II Kings 22:1-23:30, is an outstanding work among the kings. Compare David, II Sam. 8:15.
Samuel's work as a judge is outstanding in the field of righteousness. See I Sam. 12:4.

obtained promises

The one great promise of the Messiah they did not obtain, but some promises were fulfilled in their lives.
a. Joshua and Caleb obtained the promised land after 40 years. Josh. 14:6-14.
b. Isaiah saw Jerusalem delivered from the invasion of Sennacherib.

c. Daniel saw the end of the Babylonian captivity.
   d. Nehemiah lived to see the wall of Jerusalem rebuilt.
   e. Abraham received the promised son.
   f. David was promised the kingdom, and received it.
   Some feel that it only means verbal promises, but this is far less meaningful.

stopped the mouths of lions

   Several people accomplished this.
   a. Daniel is the greatest example. Dan. 6:22: " — saying, My God hath shut the lion's mouth."
   b. David had victory over the lion and the bear. I Sam. 17:34.
   c. Samson, Judges 14:6, on the road to Timnah.
   d. David's mighty man Benaiah: I Chr. 11:22. " — slew a lion in the midst of a pit in time of snow."
   The examples are given to show the importance and power of faith.

quenched the power of fire

   This indicates that the flames were not stopped, but their power and violence were taken away.
   a. The great example is that of the three Hebrews recorded in Dan. 3.
   1. The fiery furnace was likely the new type of place of sacrifices designed by Nebuchadnezzar.
   2. He desired a place where the work of priests could be observed, according to the archeologists.
   b. No other persons are suggested from the Bible, but of course many martyrs experienced the flames.
   Rudelback tells of a martyr at Brussels who said that the flames felt like roses as they covered him.

escaped the edge of the sword

   Many are such instances as this one.
   a. David escaped the sword many times, from the hand of King Saul, as well as Goliath. Cf. I Sam. 18:11; 19:10-12.
   b. Elijah did. I Kings 19:1-16.
   c. Elisha is included. II Kings 6:14-23; 31-33.
   d. Jeremiah. Jer. 36:26. Compare Jer. 39.
   Milligan likes to include the Maccabean movement, which is a thrilling history.

11:34, 35   HELPS FROM HEBREWS

from weakness were made strong

This power may be seen in several ways.
a. Sarah had power to conceive. Heb. 11:11.
b. Gideon trembled when he was called.
c. Jeremiah said he was like a child. He couldn't speak, but he was made to speak.
d. Isaiah said, "Woe is me."
Remember how the enemies talked about Nehemiah's effort to rebuild the walls, saying, "Feeble Jews."

waxed mighty in war, turned to flight armies of aliens

The history of God's people is a mighty war epic.
a. Gideon with 300 men conquered the hosts of Midian.
b. Abraham with 318 men rescued Lot.
c. Joshua had many victories.
1. Defeated Amalek. Ex. 17.
2. Defeated the Amorites in a long day. Josh. 10:12-13.
"Aliens" probably refers to all who opposed the government of Israel.

women received their dead by a resurrection

The widow of Zarephath, I Kings 17:21. Elijah dwelt there, and Elijah raised up her dead son.
II Kings 4:34. The Shumanite woman's son raised by Elisha.

and others were tortured

This also may be translated, "beaten to death." Torture is not always done by heathens, but has been done in the name of God.

not accepting their deliverance

"Deliverance" may be also translated "redemption." This may refer to a mother and her seven sons mentioned in II Maccabees 7:1. (In the *Apocrypha*)
a. They would not submit to eating swine's flesh and other heathen customs.
b. Few more heroic stories appear than that of the Maccabeans. Elizar, a Jewish scribe, was also killed.
a. He died on the *typamum,* a large wheel on which they were stretched in order to beat them to death with clubs.
b. Such cruelty could not persuade him to be delivered.
Polycarp — ("80 and 6 years") would be an example but

380

not included here, since his death came after Hebrews was written.

that they might obtain a better resurrection

Torture seemed a small thing when they were seeking a resurrection that God could give. When men have a faith, hope, and a love for God, man cannot touch it.
a. Riches, popularity, etc., can be taken, but not our hope.
b. Faith gives strength to endure and the spirit to rejoice in it.

others had trials of mockings

Instances of mocking are recorded in the Old Testament.
a. Philistines mocked Samson. Judges 16:25.
b. Ahab imprisoned Micaiah. I Kings 22:27.
c. Jeremiah was cruelly treated and mocked by Pashar and others. Jer. 22:2-7; 33:2-3.
d. Isaac was mocked by Ishmael.
e. Elisha was mocked by the children.
Mocking is severe in that it makes one angry and causes him to lose self-control.

scourgings, yea moreover of bonds and imprisonments

Scourging in the synagogue was common.
Several instances of imprisonments are mentioned.
a. Joseph was cast into prison.
b. Jeremiah was lowered into a dungeon of mire. 37:16; 38:6.
"Bonds" refers to being bound in fetters and shackles. This was a common experience for the apostles.

they were stoned

An example is Zechariah.
a. He was the son of Jehoiada.
b. Joash, king of Judah, had him stoned. II Chr. 24:20-22.
Stephen, the first New Testament martyr, experienced this.

they were sawn asunder

The Talmud says that this happened to Isaiah by the order of Manasseh, king of Judah. An Apocryphal book, *The Ascension of Isaiah,* (5:11) gives this tradition about Isaiah.

they were tempted

This probably refers to the offers of life, wealth, honor, etc., that the faithful received in exchange for their faith. Temptations like Jesus faced are no doubt meant.

they were slain with the sword

   Elijah made this charge in a complaint to God. I Kings 19:10.
   Jehoiakim slew the prophet Uriah. Jer. 26:23.
   Ahab's reign was characterized by slaughter.
   Herod slew James. Acts 12.

they went about in sheepskins, in goatskins being destitute, afflicted, ill treated

   This was a type of garment worn by the prophets.
a. See Elisha and Elijah, II Kings 2:8-13; I Kings 17:3-9; 19:3-14.
b. Elijah is called "a hairy man" in II Kings 1:8, most likely because of his garb.
   False prophets wore these clothes in order to deceive. Zech. 13:4.

of whom the world was not worthy

   Such cruel men as persecuted these prophets and martyrs did not deserve such good examples of faithful men. You do not hear men like Paul, a saint, ever saying that he was too good for the world.

wandering in deserts and mountains and caves and holes of the earth

   These places were places of refuge for persecuted men and women.
   God's great outdoors is a safer place for man than in the presence of the unbeliever.

these all having had witness borne to them through their faith received not the promise

   If these had the light of grace and were faithful, how much more should we be. We have the full sunlight of God's grace upon us. If a spark led them to seek the promise, the full light should enable us to attain.

the promise

   What is it? There is in the future a promise to be fulfilled, in the future to us and to the ancient saints.

The better thing, Heb. 10:40. Cf. 9:15, the atonement.
The ancients died without obtaining either.
a. We may experience both.
b. This may express the idea that they are not yet in possession of the inheritance promised them.
c. Then all saints, whether before or after the coming of Christ, will at the same time come into the inheritance.

God, having provided some better thing concerning us

This must refer to the atonement through Christ. Newell expresses it as "our heavenly calling."

that apart from us

What God has planned for all mankind, He will do for all mankind at the same time. When it is done, whatever it is, I have faith that it will be done right.

they should not be made perfect.

This is done through Christ. Heb. 12:23: "We are come to the spirits of just men made perfect."
This perfecting looks forward to that salvation consummated at the coming of Christ. 9:28: "To them that wait for Him unto salvation."
It includes the redemption of the body. Rom. 13:11.
Newell: Enoch has already been made perfect. Heb. 12:23 refers to him: "Ye are come unto the spirits of just men made perfect." Spirits are made perfect, but bodies are not. Someday, however, we will have a glorious new body. I Cor. 15.

Study Questions

2298. What is meant by "Passover"? Was it the passing over of the death angel, or the feast?
2299. Does the reference to sprinkling of blood settle the question?
2300. What did Moses have to do with the passover?
2301. What all was involved in the Red Sea experience?
2302. Does the Modernist have enough faith to believe in Israel's faith, or the Biblical record of the account?
2303. Tell of the faith involved in the destruction of Jericho.
2304. Was the command that took a week to complete, a test of faith?
2305. In what was Rahab's faith?
2306. If it was in God, how did she get it?

HELPS FROM HEBREWS

2307. How were Jericho's people disobedient?
2308. Was she a believer in God, thus accounting for her receiving the spies in peace?
2309. What did faith cost her?
2310. What did faith gain for her?
2311. Name the things which she did.
2312. Does she fit into God's scheme of future events? Cf. Matt. 1:5; Ruth 4:21-22.
2313. Was she a harlot in the modern meaning of the word?
2314. Could she have been a woman of faith, and also an evil woman?
2315. Is it likely that the spies would have sought the help of such a person?
2316. Why is Gideon listed in the roll of faithful ones?
2317. What was Gideon's responsibility?
2318. Was it customary for a judge of Israel to be also a warrior?
2319. How does Barak fit into the listing of Hebrews? When did he live?
2320. What single event may have earned him this place?
2321. What woman helped him? What was her duty?
2322. How did Samson earn his place?
2323. Could he be the one the author had in mind for a portion of v. 33?
2324. Compare Moses and Samson in length of service.
2325. Tell of the work of Jephthah.
2326. What race or tribe troubled Israel in his day?
2327. Was he without criticism?
2328. Was his background good?
2329. Were any kings named among the faithful?
2330. Why was David singled out?
2331. Is there any single accomplishment that would gain him recognition in Hebrews?
2332. Were his victories numerous ones?
2333. Have these men been named in chronological order?
2334. Who was first, Samuel or David?
2335. What was Samuel?
2336. What was so discouraging about a prophet's work?
2337. Name some men who might be included in the expression, "subdued kingdoms."
2338. What class of men is most likely included?

HELPS FROM HEBREWS

2339. Were any kingdoms subdued by prophetic preaching?
2340. Who among the Hebrews that subdued many kingdoms is not mentioned?
2341. Could Joshua be considered a man of faith?
2342. What group wrought righteousness?
2343. Were the prophets the only ones?
2344. Name some outstanding prophets.
2345. Name some outstanding kings.
2346. What judge was successful in reforms?
2347. What promises were obtained by Joshua, Isaiah, Daniel, Nehemiah, Abraham, David, etc.?
2348. What great promise did they miss?
2349. Name some who stopped the mouths of lions.
2350. How does Benaiah resemble David?
2351. Were flames quenched, or was it their power that was quenched?
2352. These men could not be considered God's firemen, could they?
2353. Who may be referred to here? Were there many?
2354. Could the author have in mind any New Testament martyrs?
2355. Name some who escaped the sword.
2356. Did David escape many times?
2357. What prophets were in danger of the sword?
2358. What is meant by "made strong"?
2359. Was it always physical strength?
2360. Have great men of God felt weak on occasion?
2361. Did Nehemiah, rebuilding walls, look feeble?
2362. Could Samson be included in this?
2363. Discuss the idea, "waxed mighty in war."
2364. Did they always depend upon a mighty army?
2365. How many did various warriors use?
2366. Tell of one great battle where the time element was involved.
2367. What is meant by "aliens"?
2368. What Old Testament women received their dead alive?
2369. Did Jesus raise the dead for any women?
2370. Could the resurrection of dead saints that accompanied Jesus' death be included?
2371. What methods of torture have been used?
2372. Name some instances.

2373. Has cruelty been used only by heathen?
2374. What is meant by, "not accepting their deliverance"?
2375. Which is easier, to die in battle or to suffer for righteousness?
2376. What period of history do the commentators think may have been included here?
2377. Could Moses be included?
2378. Could the three Hebrew children be included?
2379. What was the deliverance they could have accepted?
2380. Why was it rejected?
2381. How did faith help?
2382. Name some mockers and some mocked ones.
2383. Was it always heathenism against God's men?
2384. Was it ever brother mocking brother?
2385. How is mocking a hard trial?
2386. What is "scourging"?
2387. What are "bonds"?
2388. Name some Old Testament imprisonments.
2389. Was imprisonment a common experience for the apostles?
2390. Do we have an example of one being stoned?
2391. Was it a common practice?
2392. Who was subject to stoning?
2393. Do we know of anyone being sawn asunder?
2394. How do we know Isaiah suffered this kind of death?
2395. What all may be included in the word "tempted"?
2396. Name some men who experienced these.
2397. Name some who were slain with the sword.
2398. Who was Jehoiakim?
2399. Who was Uriah?
2400. Is dying a common way to escape duty?
2401. Who may have gone about in sheepskins, etc.?
2402. Was this a characteristic garb?
2403. Did others ever wear them? Cf. Zech. 13:4.
2404. What is meant by, "of whom the world was not worthy"?
2405. What is the significance of verse 39?
2406. What witness was borne?
2407. What promise is referred to?
2408. Can we infer by these verses that they have not yet gained eternal life — that they are still in the tombs?
2409. What "better thing" is referred to in verse 40?

2410. Is God going to bless all, the faithful of the past, and us at the same time?
2411. What is meant by perfect? Cf. Heb. 12:23.
2412. Was Enoch made perfect. Will we be coming to him and others?
2413. What form will we have when we are perfected? Cf. I Cor. 15.

True Or False Over Chapter Eleven

_____ 1. By faith Cain offered a more excellent sacrifice than Abel.
_____ 2. It is impossible to please God without faith.
_____ 3. Abraham proved his faith by his willingness to offer up Jacob to God.
_____ 4. Faith is a factor in the tumbling of the walls of Jericho.
_____ 5. Noah by faith looked for a city whose Builder and Maker is God.
_____ 6. Faith is the substance of things hoped for.
_____ 7. The elders obtained a good report by faith.
_____ 8. By faith Noah was translated that he should not see death.
_____ 9. This chapter offers an explanation for the existence of the universe.
_____10. Isaac was an adopted son of Abraham because Sarah, his wife, could not bear children.
_____11. Moses chose to spend his life in the court of Pharaoh, but God's call was so insistent that he was compelled to heed.
_____12. Abraham looked for a city whose Builder and Maker is God.
_____13. The walls of Jericho fell on the eighth day of marching around it.
_____14. Faith is based on something that we have seen for ourselves.
_____15. The Old Testament heroes of the faith escaped all affliction and hardship because of their faith.
_____16. Moses was hidden three months in the bullrushes.
_____17. By faith, the mouths of lions were stopped.
_____18. Everything that exists was made out of something that we can see.

_____19. We are to believe that God is a Rewarder of them that seek after Him.

_____20. Abraham went out to the place that he was to inherit, not knowing where it was.

_____21. It was a godly fear that Noah had while he prepared the ark.

_____22. Men who dwelled in tents nevertheless looked for a city which hath foundations whose Builder and Maker is God.

_____23. Moses' endurance is attributed to the fact that he was able to see Him Who is invisible.

_____24. The world was not worthy of those who suffered so greatly for God.

_____25. God has given men great strength when they were weak.

SUMMARY OF CHAPTER ELEVEN

This is the great chapter on faith. It shows what a man does who acts on faith. It illustrates, with examples from the Old Testament, the meaning of acting by faith; faith is obeying the commands and instructions of God. It shows the victories and rewards of faith.

This chapter continues the appeal which began in 10:19, and in particular it elaborates upon the last verse of Chapter Ten, which mentions the faith that preserves the soul. Throughout Hebrews, which discusses the high priesthood of Jesus Christ, the appeal has been for the Christian to remain faithful to Him. This chapter explains the nature of faith and shows why it is the basic cause of God's approval on the lives of those whose victories and triumphs are presented in the Old Testament.

It begins (1-3) with a statement about the nature of faith and the point to be developed in the chapter — God's approval of the faithful. The examples are taken from the Old Testament and follow the order of the Bible, beginning with Genesis and Exodus and closing with the summary of the historical books. So we read, as the order is given in Genesis, about Abel, Enoch, Noah, Abraham, etc.

The grand theme of the chapter, "by faith," is repeated with impressive force as it strengthens the Christian's determination to overcome trials and join the company of the faithful who attain to the reward of heaven.

III. *The perfect and final faith of the Christian dispensation.* 12:1-29.

A. *Jesus, the Author and Perfector of our faith.* 12:1-3.

Text
12:1-3

1 Therefore let us also, seeing we are compassed about with so great a cloud of witnesses, lay aside every weight, and the sin which doth so easily beset us, and let us run with patience the race that is set before us, 2 looking unto Jesus the Author and Perfecter of our faith, Who for the joy that was set before Him endured the cross, despising shame, and hath sat down at the right hand of the throne of God. 3 For consider Him that hath endured such gainsaying of sinners against Himself, that ye wax not weary, fainting in your souls.

Paraphrase

1 Wherefore, even we, like the combatants in the Grecian games, having so great an assembly of witnesses placed around us, laying aside every weight of worldly hopes and fears, and cares, and friendships, which encumber us in running, and the sin of apostasy which is so easily committed, let us run with perserverance the race appointed us;

2 Looking off from the ancients to Jesus, the Leader and Rewarder of the faithful, Who, for the joy of bringing many sons into glory which was set before Him, endured the lingering agonies of the cross, despising the shame of suffering as a malefactor, and sat down at the right hand of the throne of God. See Chap. viii. 1.

3 Wherefore, attentively consider the dignity of Jesus your Leader, Who, before He was thus rewarded, patiently endured such calumny, opposition, and persecution from sinners against Himself, that ye may not be weary, being dispirited in your minds through the continuance of the persecution.

Comment

Therefore let us also, seeing

> This is done with our spiritual sight. We have just gone through God's memory album to behold the monuments to the saints of God.

12:1   HELPS FROM HEBREWS

we are compassed about

Whatever way we are turned in trials or tribulations, there before us are people who had to suffer like experiences or more. As Israel was under a cloud on the way to Canaan, so are we surrounded by the breath of all time.

with so great a cloud of witnesses

"Cloud" is a classical metaphor used for a multitude.
a. Homer speaks of "a cloud of footmen,
                  a cloud of birds, and
                  a cloud of horsemen."
b. Tivy speaks of "a cloud of footmen."
"Witnesses" refers to those of Chapter Eleven.
a. It does not mean that this crowd is watching us.
1. Our feeble efforts surely would cause them too much anxiety.
2. A witness is used as a bit of evidence for us, but not necessarily a present observer of us.
b. We are surrounded by these great examples of faith. In the midst of such a company how can we shrink back?
Some feel that a grandstand of present people is meant, but I think the word "great" refers back to Chapter Eleven.

lay aside every weight and sin

The figure here is that of a race, which requires light equipment.
a. The "weight" would be burdens which delay or impede our progress.
b. An Olympic competitor strips himself of everything but essential equipment in order to run his best.
c. The weight carrier will be soon passed by the one who knows enough to lay aside weight and sin.
We hear people say, "What is the harm or sin in doing this or that?"
a. Is it a weight, a sin, or a wing?
b. "Does it help or hinder?" is a good question.

which doth so easily beset us

Some sins are besetting sins.
a. A Negro man once called this "upsetting" sin.
b. Sin so easily sets in our lives.
Newell believes unbelief is referred to here, but this is not

proved. Newell: Sin is as natural to the flesh as it is for animals to draw breath, and the moment you take your eye off Christ you have the certainty of the sin besetting you.

The sin will be different with individuals. Each one must lay aside his own peculiar weakness and sins, and run the race.

let us run with patience

"Patience" is also translated "stedfastness." Look at the examples of it.
a. Moses chose ill treatment with God's people rather than sin.
b. David proved true in great danger as Saul sought his life.
c. Paul says, I Cor. 9:24-26: "I therefore so run as not uncertainly." Phil. 3:12-14; Acts 20:24; II Tim. 4:7-8.
First we had the preparation for the race; now the running.
a. A race has three stages: preparation, patience and prize.
b. The figure is a race that requires endurance, for it pictures the Christian's life.
Sin will slow us down in the Christian race.

that is set before us

The course is set for us; we have to run under every condition that befalls us.
a. The runner does not prepare the course; he runs.
b. The runner prepares only himself, not the course.
We are not to complain about our race, but rejoice in the privilege to run because of the cloud of witnesses, the reward and the company who run with us.

looking unto Jesus

This is the Goal.
a. Keep your eye on Jesus as you run.
b. Many an athlete has lost a race by losing sight of the goal.
He is our Pacemaker. This gives us our strength, our second wind.
a. With eyes on Christ we see the perfect Example and Energy for the Way.
b. Thayer suggests "looking unto" in the Greek means "to fix the eyes on something."

the Author

"The leader" is a second translation.
a. Thayer: One who takes the lead.

b. In a great cloud of faithful people Christ is the Leader. Here is the great Chief Witness.

Perfecter of our faith

Christ is not only the beginning of our race but the Finisher likewise. This word, "perfecter," also rendered "finisher" occurs nowhere else in the New Testament.
a. It means a completer, perfecter, or finisher.
b. It carries the idea of one who brings any plan to its full and perfect consummation.

Who for the joy that was set before Him

Joy in spite of suffering.
a. Isaiah 53 pictures Him as a Man of sorrows and acquainted with grief, yet He was joyful to bring salvation to the world.
b. Phil. 3 pictures Christ's glad willingness to show the love of God to the world.

A bitter, cruel experience was endured by Him so that He might bring joy into the world.

McKnight says it was not a joy which He was in possession of, but one to be received.

endured the cross

Jesus' race required some endurance likewise. His race course was set for Him and He faced it.

Angels could have rescued Him. Matt. 26:53.

His disciples tried to change His course. Luke 9:51.

despising shame

He endured the awfulness of the cross, and the shame of sin. He did not rejoice in it, but despised it. This verse lends credence to a later phrase interpreted, "endured such contradiction."
a. Joy was in it, but shame was there, too.
b. It is impossible for us to understand how Christ was joyful in the saving of those who were His enemies.
c. While we were sinners Christ died for us.

and hath sat down at the right hand of the throne of God

He ran His course and this was His privilege, to be seated at the side of God. If we run our course, some day we will have the privilege to be where He is. John 14:1-4.

for consider Him

You have considered the sacrifice of the heroes of the faithful to obtain an inheritance. That is good. Now consider Jesus who endured for you.
a. How can we turn away from Him in despair?
b. How can we turn again unto sin?
Let us study Christ, His attitude in every trial, for He had all the trials.

that hath endured such gainsaying of sinners

"Gainsaying" is also translated "contradiction." The word in Greek is *antilogia*, "opposition."
Observe His opposition.
a. John 1:11: Came to His own, but they did not receive Him.
b. Chief priest, scribes. John 12:42-46.
c. Roman law put Him to death.
To consider Him is to endure. The interpretation, "endured such contradiction," is sometimes allowed to show that Christ had contradictions, such as "joy" and "despising shame."
a. "Of sinners" indicates that men contradicted and opposed Him.
b. He was opposed every way He turned.

against Himself

What did they say against Him?
a. Beelzebub was His power. Matt. 10:25; Matt. 12:24.
b. He is Joseph's Son. Luke 4:22.
c. He is a deceiver. Matt. 27:63.
All this may be forgiven. Matt. 12:32.
Some authorities allow it to be read "themselves" rather than "himself."

that ye wax not weary, fainting in your souls

Many are the exhortations to stedfastness:
a. Rom. 8:17: "If so be that we suffer with Him, that we may be also glorified with Him."
b. Gal. 6:9: "Be not weary in well doing."
c. Rev. 2:3: "Thou — hast not grown weary."
d. II Thess. 3:13: "Be not weary."
In times of distress just keep looking to the Lord, remembering His afflictions.

Study Questions

2414. Describe the nature of the 12th chapter.
2415. After the heroes of the faith are exalted in Chapter Eleven, what Person is exalted here?
2416. What conclusion is drawn to open the chapter?
2417. How does the Christian see?
2418. What are we to see in this chapter and in this verse?
2419. What is meant by, "compassed about"?
2420. Could we suffer anything not suffered already by someone in God's album?
2421. Enlarge on the idea of the "cloud."
2422. Has God used clouds in history?
2423. Discuss the word "witness."
What is the word in the original?
Does it mean that they are in the spirit world all about us watching us?
Could it refer to people around us who watch us?
Does the word "great" help to clarify who they are?
Would the patriarchs be pleased to watch us?
Could we use the word "example" in place of witness?
2424. What is the Christian to do with weight and sin?
2425. What is the difference between weight and sin?
2426. Do people become encumbered with good things that destroy their effectiveness, such as lodges, clubs, sports, etc.?
2427. Can good actually be evil in some instances?
2428. Define the idea of "beset us."
2429. Do we have our own "besetting sins"?
2430. Do athletes have problems that are peculiar to them in training that we might apply here?
2431. What figure of athletics is used here?
2432. What is inferred by "running"?
2433. What is an alternate translation of "patience"?
2434. Is the race a common figure in the Word of God?
2435. Will sin give us wings or weight?
2436. Are there stages of a race that can be lessons for us in the Christian life?
2437. What does "set before us" imply?
2438. Do runners prescribe the characteristics of the track?
2439. What does the runner prepare?
2440. Have we had great company in the race of life?

HELPS FROM HEBREWS

2441. How important is sight in a race?
2442. What is the Christian to look to?
2443. What is our danger if our eye is not on Christ?
2444. What are the figures used of Christ in this verse?
2445. What does author mean by Perfecter? Does he mean perfection?
2446. Can we say that He is the Alpha and Omega of the race?
2447. Who is the Chief Witness?
2448. How can He serve us in these capacities?
2449. Did Jesus enjoy the race?
2450. Compare Phil. 2:5-11 with this idea.
2451. In life did He have joy or sorrow?
2452. When is there joy involved in a race?
2453. Aren't the greatest joys being chosen to race, and the victory?
2454. Was the endurance of the cross joy?
2455. Wherein did He have joy?
2456. Was His course set for him?
2457. Did anyone try to get Him to look aside? Why?
2458. Does His endurance challenge you?
2459. How could he be "joyful," yet "enduring" and "despising"?
2460. What is meant by the expression, "despising shame"?
2461. Are these phrases examples of a great work that we may not like to do, but the joy of victory that makes up for it?
2462. What was at the end of the course for Christ?
2463. In the roll of faithful, who does the author want us to give special consideration to?
2464. Can we turn away from Him when we consider His love, sacrifice, concern and reward?
2465. What is the difference between the endurance of Christ and that of the heroes of the faith?
2466. What phase of Christ's life is to be considered?
2467. Can we ever face any trials that Jesus didn't face?
2468. What do you understand "gainsaying" to mean?
2469. From what source did His opposition come?
2470. Were there other sources of opposition to His purpose by persons who thought that they were helpful?
2471. What groups of men opposed Him who should have been followers?
2472. What did they say of Him?
2473. A consideration of Jesus should do what for us?

2474. Name some other verses that speak of weariness.
2475. Is there any promise of reward to those who wax weary?

B. *Perils threatening the life of faith.* 12:4-17.
1. *Failure to respond to chastening.* 12:4-13.

Text

4 Ye have not yet resisted unto blood, striving against sin: 5 and ye have forgotten the exhortation which reasoneth with you as with sons,

My son, regard not lightly the chastening of the Lord,
Nor faint when thou art reproved of Him;
6 For whom the Lord loveth He chasteneth,
And scourgeth every son whom He receiveth.

7 It is for chastening that ye endure; God dealeth with you as with sons; for what son is there whom his father chasteneth not? 8 But if ye are without chastening, whereof all have been made partakers, then are you bastards, and not sons. 9 Furthermore, we had the fathers of our flesh to chasten us, and we gave them reverence: shall we not much rather be in subjection unto the Father of spirits, and live? 10 For they indeed for a few days chastened us as seemed good to them; but He for our profit, that we may be partakers of His holiness. 11 All chastening seemeth for the present to be not joyous but grievous; yet afterward it yieldeth peaceable fruit unto them that have been exercised thereby, even the fruit of righteousness. 12 Wherefore lift up the hands that hang down, and the palsied knees; 13 and make straight paths for your feet, that which is lame be not turned out of the way, but rather be healed.

Paraphrase

4 Your sufferings are far short of those which Christ endured. For not yet hath the blood of any of you been shed in combating against your wicked persecutors.

5 Besides, have ye forgotten the exhortation in which God reasoneth with you as His children? My son, do not think lightly of the Lord's chastisement, as they do who regard affliction as things accidental; neither, through too quick a feeling of the chastisement, nor by considering it as a token of God's anger, fall into despair when thou are rebuked of Him.

6 Instead of being tokens of God's anger, afflictions are proofs of His love: For whom the Lord loveth He chastiseth, and

sharply corrects for his faults every son whom He adopteth.

7 If then ye endure affliction, know that God behaveth towards you as His children, giving you such correction as must be of great advantage to you. For what legitimate son is there whom his father never punishes for his faults?

8 But if ye live without that chastisement whereof all the sons of God are partakers, certainly ye are treated as bastards whose education is no object of their father's care, and not as the genuine sons of God.

9 Further, we have had fathers of our bodies, who chastised us for our faults, and yet we loved and obeyed them: shall we not much rather, from affection and gratitude, be in subjection to the Father of our spirits, when He corrects us for our faults, to fit us for living with Him for ever?

10 This submission is due to the Father of our spirits, because He corrects us with more prudence and affection than our earthly fathers. For they verily, during the few days of our childhood, chastised us according to their own will governed by passion, but He always for our advantage, that we might partake of His holiness; it being necessary to our living with Him eternally, that we be holy.

11 Now no chastisement, indeed, whether from God or man, at the time it is inflicted, is the cause of joy, but of sorrow to be chastised: Nevertheless, afterwards, it gives as a reward the peaceful fruits of righteousness to them who are properly disciplined by it.

12 Wherefore, bring into the posture of action your arms which hang down, and your weakened knees; that is, vigorously exert your whole faculties in the conflict with affliction:

13 And by removing every temptation, make smooth paths for your feet, that if ye are infirm in any part, that which is lame may not be wholly dislocated by your falling, but rather strengthened by proper exercise.

Comment

Ye have not yet resisted unto blood

This means they have not fought the limit.
a. Paul could say that he had.
1. Acts 16:33: The jailor washed Paul's stripes.
2. II Cor. 6:5.
3. II Cor. 11:23.

    4. II Cor. 11:24.
    b. Jesus could say that He had.
    1. Isaiah 53: "With His stripes we are healed."
    2. The cross meant shedding blood for Him, although He did not resist the cross, but sin.
    3. Christ's resistance was against those who would have changed His course.

    How simple are our hardships today in comparison to theirs.

unto blood

    An ancient figure of speech concerning boxers may be alluded to here.
    a. Leather thongs containing pieces of metal were fastened to arms, etc.
    b. Fighters were often very bloody after a battle.

    Many modern preachers are afraid of blood.
    a. They are afraid to preach against sin because it might make them unpopular.
    b. Some are afraid of loss of salary or loss of position.

    Churches do not want "bloody" preachers.
    a. They want him to be loved and respected by all the denominational brethren.
    b. It is time to "resist unto blood."

striving against sin

    We are to hate evil, Ps. 97:10. Sin, says Vincent, is personified here. Fighting evil brought blood upon Jesus. Striving against sin brought blood to Stephen and James, but not to those who would read Hebrews.

and ye have forgotten the exhortation which reasoneth with you as with sons

    The word for "sons" is "adult sons," not infants.
    a. Infants cannot reason.
    b. Paternal reasoning is here called "exhortation."

    It is a joy to see infants grow up and enter into the parental councils.
    a. Too much of our trouble in churches is a result of spiritual infancy rather than mature thinking on the part of Christians.
    b. God desires to reason with us as sons old enough to be reasonable.

Some question whether this statement is an affirmation or a question.
a. The American Standard Version expresses affirmation.
b. Verse 12 rather suggests that some had forgotten, so this may be understood as an affirmation.

My son

A quote from Proverbs 3:11-12. It is a free quotation but an accurate one.
a. It is to show a tender relationship that God has for us even though we are chastened.
b. If God calls us a son, we ought to bear anything that comes our way.

regard not lightly the chastening of the Lord

Love and responsibility prompt chastening.
a. Rev. 3:19: "As many as I love I reprove and chasten."
1. We do not ordinarily discipline other people's children.
2. We are most concerned with those we love most.
b. Eph. 6:4 teaches responsibility.
Chastening has wonderful value for us.
a. A "thorn" kept Paul humble. II Cor. 12:7-10.
b. Trials work patience. James 1:2-4; Rom. 5:3.
c. Enduring of temptation brings a crown of life. James 1:12.
d. It yields peaceable fruit. Heb. 12:11.
e. It brings eternal glory. II Cor. 4:17.

nor faint when thou art reproved of Him

We are not to cower like an abused dog. Reproof is for improvement.
a. II Tim. 3:16 "Every scripture is profitable — for correction."
b. Rom. 5:3: "We also rejoice in our tribulations."
c. II Cor. 4:17: "For our light affliction which is for the moment, worketh for us more and more exceedingly an eternal weight of glory."
Is all affliction of God?
a. It does not come directly. James 1:12-13 says God tempts no one.
b. Paul's "thorn" was spoken of as a messenger of Satan. II Cor. 12:7-10.
c. God allows the devil to tempt us and try us, as he did Job.

for whom the Lord loveth He chasteneth

    Does He not chasteneth the ungodly too?
a. There is a difference in punishment, for theirs will be eternal.
b. The sun shines on the just and the unjust, so the wicked receive chastening.

    How does He chasten the loved ones?
a. Peter answers, trial. I Pet. 1:6; I Pet. 4:6.
b. Paul found a thorn in the flesh. II Cor. 12:7-10.
c. Through enduring temptation, says James. James 1:12.
d. Through suffering, says Peter. I Pet. 5:10.

    God can turn it to good if we love Him. Rom. 8:28.
    God will not allow us to be tempted above what we are able to endure. I Cor. 10:13.
    Let us not be like Cain who said it was greater than he could bear. Gen. 4:13.

and scourgeth every son whom He receiveth

    No child of God should expect to enter heaven without passing through the furnace of affliction.

    Paul said, "With much tribulation," we enter the kingdom of God. Acts 14:22.

    God's afflictions are paternal in nature only when we submit to Him.
a. For the ungodly, it is fate or chance.
b. For the Christian, it is a lesson to be learned from God.

it is for chastening that ye endure

    Also translated "endure unto chastening," "if ye endure chastening." Alford says, "It is not for punishment, not for any evil purpose; you are under the attention and affection of the Father."

God dealeth with you as with sons for what son is there whom his father chasteneth not?

    He reasons from the common practice of men, that it is not right that God's children should be exempt. Proper discipline leads to proper conduct.

but if ye are without chastening whereof all have been made partakers, then are ye bastards and not sons

    This rather makes one tremble, who has such an easy time in life compared to those in Chapter Eleven.

a. Which of us has suffered?
b. How easy we Christian people live in these United States!
c. We begin to wonder whether we might be illegitimate offspring.
   Feel encouraged by chastening, for it is evidence of your true sonship.

furthermore, we had the fathers of our flesh to chasten us, and we gave them reverence; shall we not much rather be in subjection unto the Father of spirits and live?

We gave them reverence if we were trained properly.
a. Parents who allow their children to abuse them do the child an injustice.
b. No reverence exists if the child pouts and grouches.
   Observe how insistent God is on respect of children for parents.
   Eph. 6:1-2: "Obey your parents in the Lord."
a. It is a commandment, "which is the first commandment with promise."
b. Failure brought severe judgment. 6:3.
c. Compare the law of Moses. Deut. 21:20.
   The Father of spirits deserves reverence, and upon it we will deserve to live.
a. "Father of spirits" is also translated "Father of our Spirit."
b. The spirit comes from God and goes back to Him at death. See Ecc. 12:7.
c. Parental obedience was essential to life under the old covenant, and Heavenly Father reverence is essential to life now.

for they indeed for a few days chastened us as seemed good to them

Here temporary parental chastening is contrasted with loving discipline of God. At best, it is earthly chastening for a brief span of our life.

but He for our profit

Chastening does good. It is for our profit, not God's. Observe the many exhortations to endure chastening. Rom. 5:3; Rom. 12:12; II Cor. 7:4; I Pet. 4:13; I Pet. 4:19.

that we may be partakers of His holiness

God expects holiness, and this is the way He gets it.
a. I Pet. 3:13-17: "Be ye holy."
b. Rev. 22:11: "He that is holy, let him be made holy still."
True Christians are holy.
a. I Pet. 2:9: "Ye are an elect race, a royal priesthood."
b. Heb. 12:23: "Ye are come to the spirits of just men made perfect."
c. Heb. 3:1: "Wherefore, holy brethren."

all chastening seemeth for the present to be not joyous but grievous

At the time it is severe, but it brings a person to be obedient. We are like children. We shun the rod even when we need it, and know we deserve it.

yet afterward it yieldeth peaceable fruit

A person who is selfish is spoiled, cantankerous, and far from being peaceable.
Let us not be hard-hearted, but enter into the discipline with surrender and joy. This is the proper spirit for us to have.

unto them that have been exercised thereby

They were to be "trained" by it, is the Greek meaning.
Examples of it working in men's lives:
a. Paul — thorn in the flesh.
b. David — II Sam. 12:1-23; II Sam. 16:9-14.
c. Job — 42:7-8.
We should enter into chastening with surrender and joy.

even the fruit of righteousness

Gal. 5:22. The fruit of the spirit is meant here.
If we are disciplined right by our attitude, we will produce right.

wherefore, lift up the hands that hang down and the palsied knees

A quotation from Isaiah 35:3.
a. Here is the figure of weary travelers.
b. Perhaps one is worn with sickness, fatigue.
c. Weakness is pictured.
In the light of the good things concerning chastening, weak knees and powerless hands should be made strong.

a. The happiest people are sometimes invalids.
b. The most miserable are sometimes millionaires with money, health and prestige.
Extend hands of glad service, and walk joyfully in spite of all hardships.

and make straight paths for your feet

This sounds like John the Baptist. Matt. 3:3.
It sounds like Isaiah. 40:3.
Take the straight way, not the rough, crooked way. The person who has prepared himself to endure evils goes on in a straight way.

that they which are lame

The journey "out of the way" is so much more difficult for those who are strong. Elijah put up this proposition. I Kings 18:21. We can picture a group traveling on foot; some are weak and lame.
a. The strong and courageous ought to make a smooth, straight journey for the sake of the weak.
b. Many a church is defeated by some half-hearted elder who says, "I don't think we can do it."

be not turned out of the way

This may also be translated, "put out of joint," or "lest halting should grow worse."
Becoming feeble for awhile may result in a complete loss.
a. We do not go bad all at once, but by degrees.
b. When led into a diverse path, many remain entangled.

but rather be healed

What is the healing?
a. Renewed faith. Appreciation for chastening has healing power in it.
b. It is faith such as the old patriarchs had that gives strength. Why be feeble, wayward, and downcast when healing may be had?

Study Questions

2476. Who has resisted unto blood?
2477. How many of us suffer for Christ?
2478. Have we fought a bloody battle?

2479. Did Paul resist unto blood? How many times?
2480. Was it prophesied that Jesus would?
2481. "Unto blood" may refer to what ancient custom?
2482. What may the blood refer to? Is it literal or figurative?
2483. Are preachers afraid of blood today?
2484. Describe the bloody gladiators.
2485. Do churches want a "bloody" preacher or one popular with the denominations?
2486. What will make the striving preacher "bloody"?
2487. Where will we find sin personified as our opponent?
2488. Is all sin to be found in the world?
2489. Is the word "sons" inclusive of children in its idea?
2490. Can infants reason with the logic of this book?
2491. Is there some special exhortation forgotten by them? Where is it found?
2492. Who is doing the exhortation which is a reasoning one?
2493. If God calls us sons, what ought we to do?
2494. What degree of attention should we give to chastening?
2495. Does the Lord chasten us? Cf. Rev. 3:19.
2496. Who does a father chasten, his or the neighbors' children?
2497. What two things felt by a father in his heart cause him to be willing to chasten?
2498. Is there value in being chastened?
What did Paul hear from God?
What do trials work?
What will endurance bring, according to James 1:12?
What does it yield? Heb. 12:11.
What is its eternal reward? Cf. II Cor. 4:17.
2499. Should we cower before God like an abused animal?
2500. What is reproof for if not for improvement?
2501. Is the preacher to reprove?
2502. Is all affliction of God? Cf. James 1:12-13.
2503. Was Paul's thorn from God? Cf. II Cor. 12:7-10.
2504. Who afflicted Job?
2505. What is the difference between the chastening of the wicked and righteous?
2506. If God doesn't send it, how can it be said that He chastens us?
2507. Who in the early history of man complained of his chastening?
2508. Whom does God chasten?

2509. What is the difference in attitude of the chastened wicked ones, and righteous people?
2510. What does God do to those whom He loves?
2511. Does He chasten the evil ones too?
2512. What is the difference?
2513. Can God use evil for good purposes? Cf. Rom. 8:28.
2514. Should we expect to gain heaven without some chastening?
2515. Give a different translation of verse 7.
2516. Are we to endure chastening, or is it for chastening that we endure?
2517. In what relationship does God deal with us in verse 7?
2518. If earthly fathers need to discipline children, should we expect it from our divine Father?
2519. What is evidence of our true sonship?
2520. If you have had it easy, what questions might you ask?
2521. Who is meant by, "We"?
2522. What is meant, "father of our flesh"?
2523. Who is the Father of our spirits?
2524. Does God teach respect for earthly parents?
2525. How much emphasis does He give?
2526. What was a parent to do to a child that would not respond?
2527. Could much juvenile delinquency be ended if we practiced the teachings of the Old Testament?
2528. Is there a plan that is better?
2529. What conclusion is drawn after his discussion of reverence to earthly parents?
2530. What is his point in the time discussed?
2531. Who thinks discipline is good, the child or the parent?
2532. Can we act more mature than children?
2533. Is there to be something gained from chastening?
2534. What is to be developed in us by chastening?
2535. For what ought the Christian to suffer? Cf. I Pet. 4:13, 19.
2536. What is holiness?
2537. Were the Hebrews holy? Cf. 3:1.
2538. How can holiness be obtained by chastening?
2539. Do people shun the rod, according to verse 11?
2540. Is there danger in seeking discipline?
2541. How do people take chastening at the moment?
2542. Tell how heathens bring pain upon themselves?
2543. Did heathens chasten themselves at Mount Carmel?
2544. What does good discipline yield?

2545. Are spoiled people peaceable?
2546. Why is good spoken of as "fruit" while evil is spoken of as "works"?
2547. What is meant by "exercised thereby"?
2548. What does "hands that hang down" refer to?
2549. Where is the original expression found?
2550. What is the figure?
2551. Is this an exhortation to do good to others or an exhortation to self?
2552. Why do hands hang down? Is this not the place for them?
2553. Tell of Moses' tired hands.
2554. Define "palsied knees."
2555. Tell of others who used the same language as v. 13.
2556. What does "straight" mean?
2557. Can you turn aside to evil and still walk straight?
2558. Is this the same word as Matthew 3:3?
2559. Tell who the word "lame" refers to.
2560. What kind of a picture is to be represented by these figures?
2561. Is there any responsibility beyond self taught in this verse?
2562. What is the alternate translation of "turned out of the way"?
2563. What is the danger of feebleness and lameness?
2564. What is the method of healing?
2565. Does chastening help?
2566. Is there any need for being lame when we have healing available?
2567. Would you classify the members of your congregational fellowship as lame or strong?

2. *Falling short of the grace of God.* 12:14-17

Text
12:14-17

14 Follow after peace with all men, and the sanctification without which no man shall see the Lord: 15 looking carefully lest there be any man that falleth short of the grace of God; lest any root of bitterness springing up trouble you, and thereby the many be defiled; 16 lest there be any fornicator, or profane person, as Esau, who for one mess of meat sold his own birthright. 17 For ye know that even when he afterward desired to

inherit the blessing, he was rejected; for he found no place for a change of mind in his father, though he sought it diligently with tears.

Paraphrase

14 Earnestly cultivate peace with all men, with the Gentiles as well as with the Jews, and even with your enemies: But at the same time maintain holiness, without which no one shall see the Lord;

15 Carefully observing your own behaviour, and that of your brethren, lest any one, through gross sins continued in, come short of the reward God has graciously promised to the faithful, lest some apostate rising trouble you, and, by his errors and bad example, many of you be corrupted;

16 Also, lest there be among you any fornicator — any one addicted to his appetites; or any profane person, who, despising spiritual blessings, renounces them for the sake of present pleasures, as Esau did, who for one meat gave away his birthrights.

17 And his folly ye know from the scripture by this, that although afterwards he wished to inherit the blessing, he was reprobated by his father, who durst not retract words which he felt himself moved by inspiration to utter; for he found no place of repentance in his father, though he earnestly sought the blessing with tears. Instead of repenting, his father confirmed the blessing to Jacob, Gen. xxvii. 33.

Comment

Follow after peace with all men

    Christ set the example.
a. He taught turning the other cheek. Matt. 5:39.
b. He refused to let Peter defend him. Matt. 26:52.
c. He came as a lamb to the slaughter. Isaiah 53.
    The word "follow" is a strong word.
a. In Greek it is "to pursue, as in a chase or battle."
b. It is something to work at, for a warring world will do all it can to keep us from peace.
    We are exhorted to strive for peace.
a. Rom. 12:18: "As much as in you lieth be at peace."
b. Col. 3:15: "Let the peace of God rule."
c. I Thess. 5:13: "Be at peace."

d. Rom. 14:19: "Follow after the things which make for peace." It is a qualification for elders and deacons.
a. I Tim. 3:3: "No brawler."

and the sanctification

This is the experience of all. It does not encourage camp meetings, emotionalism, where "second blessings" are sought.
a. All in Christ are sanctified. I Cor. 1:2.
b. In Hebrews, "sanctified" means "separated unto God."
1. It does not refer to feelings, but to Christ's blood.
10:10: "We have been sanctified through the offering of the body of Jesus once for all."
2. When we become Christians we are then sanctified.
Sanctification is obtained by yielding once for all to God. It is not a second filling. The word "sanctification" is also translated "holiness."

without which no man shall see the Lord

There then is no salvation for any except by the blood. The moral man had better come under the blood if he would see God.

The denominationalist had better be sure of Christ's own Ways, for it is the Way of sanctification. This sanctified being of ours has many responsibilities, and these must be pursued if we would see the Lord.

looking carefully

Four kinds of troubles should be looked for.
a. Those who fall short.
b. Bitterness springing up.
c. Fornication.
d. Profane person.
This is not gossip-hunting, but a carefulness on the part of those who watch in behalf of souls.

lest there be any man that falleth

Observe the repeated warnings that show the possibility: II Cor. 6:1; Luke 8:18; Heb. 3:12, 4:1, 6:6, 10:31. Sometimes the least likely ones fall, so it requires a careful watch.

short of the grace of God

>One so great as Paul was afraid of this happening to himself, for he says, I Cor. 9:26: "So fight I."
>Compare I Tim. 4:1; Gal. 5:4; Rev. 2:5.
>If we fall short of God's grace, then we have missed everything. This the Christian can do.

lest any root of bitterness springing up trouble you

>Most every church has a few devilish members who set the tone for bitterness and strife. Calvin feels this alludes to Deut. 29:18.
>a. Moses warned the people to beware lest any root of germination should bear gall and wormwood among them.
>b. If we allow a wicked person to grow in the church, it will corrupt and defile many.

and thereby the many be defiled

>A few trouble-makers can bring reproach upon all. One bad apple soon causes the bushel of apples to be rotten. Israel allowed a few people to turn to idolatry, and soon ten tribes were carried away with it.

lest there be any fornicator

>This is an awful sin, for it undermines the home.
>a. I Cor. 5:9-13 says to put him out of the fellowship.
>b. Heb. 13:4 says God will judge him.
>c. Compare also I Cor. 6:9.
>This was a warning made by the Jerusalem counsel in Acts 15.

or profane person

>The Greek word is *bebelas*. It doesn't necessarily mean to blaspheme or do violence, evil.
>a. It refers literally to a threshold that anyone and everyone may trample over.
>b. It refers to something in which there is no special consciousness. Compare I Tim. 1:9; 4:7; 6:20; II Tim. 2:16.
>A "profane" man is one who has not thought of God.

as Esau who for one mess of meat sold his own birthright

>Sin can destroy one's birthright. Esau found it out.

12:16, 17 HELPS FROM HEBREWS

   a. Milligan says the tradition of the Jews is that Esau was also a fornicator.
   b. His profanity is seen in Gen. 25:34 where we read, "despised his birthright."
Sin is a selling out to the devil.

for ye know that even when he afterward desired to inherit the blessing he was rejected

A moment of pleasure may cause us to think that we shall never be disappointed, but we will be.
   a. In a time of soberness a person comes to desire all that he has lost.
   b. The prodigal son, when he came to himself, remembered his home and blessings.
Esau finally sought his birthright, but then it was too late.

for he found no place for a change of mind in his father

The father could not be wishy-washy because of the weakness of others. Why should a father undo all that was done for a careless son who had no respect for sacredness in a moment of hunger? Does this mean that man can repent to no avail, that God will never change?
   a. This section is a warning with Esau as an example, and that is as far as it should be pressed.
   b. We have no way of knowing whether Esau made a genuine repentance, so the illustration cannot be pressed.

though he sought it diligently with tears.

Stupid, ungodly persons, burning with lusts, plunge themselves into sins which bring tears, but often tears are too late. Tears are shed many times, not in repentance for sin, but in sorrow for what is lost.

Study Questions

2568. What is the significance of the word "follow"?
2569. Are we exhorted to follow a person in this verse?
2570. Is the world conducive to peace?
2571. Tell how Christ followed after peace.
2572. Can the Christian always be at peace?
2573. Was Jesus always at peace?

2574. What other verses of the Bible have a similar exhortation as v. 14? Cf. Rom. 12:18; 14:19.
2575. Is this virtue important in the life of an elder? Cf. I Tim. 3:3.
2576. What does "sanctification" mean in the Bible?
2577. What does it mean to the denominationalist?
2578. Is it a matter of feeling or a matter of fact?
2579. Are we sanctified after we are Christians by growth?
2580. Can spiritual growth enable us to be more sanctified?
2581. What does Hebrews 10:10 say sanctifies?
2582. Is sanctification a second blessing, or a state of the Christian?
2583. How important is sanctification to eternal life?
2584. Can "the good moral man" expect salvation without sanctification?
2585. If blood sanctifies, can we expect salvation without it?
2586. What is meant by "looking carefully"? v. 15
2587. What four things are we to look for?
2588. Does this encourage looking, like a gossip-hunter does?
2589. Is this an exhortation to an individual person or to the elders of the flock?
2590. Does this verse indicate that a person may fall?
2591. Why should we look carefully?
2592. Compare other verses on the subject of falling.
2593. According to this verse, can we fall from grace?
2594. Was Paul ever afraid it might happen to him? Cf. I Tim. 1:9; 4:7; 6:20; II Tim. 2:16.
2595. What is "the grace of God"?
2596. Does verse sixteen or verse seventeen tell us what would destroy God's grace toward us?
2597. What is the figure of speech used in verse 15?
2598. Could this be an allusion to Deut. 29:18?
2599. Is a bitter person dangerous to the flock?
2600. What could be back of bitterness? Could it be disappointment, jealousy?
2601. How extensive may the influence of the "root of bitterness" be?
2602. How extensively could the root do damage?
2603. Give illustrations in Israel's history.
2604. How are we to treat the fornicator in the church, according to I Cor. 5:9-13?

2605. What will God do with him? Cf. Heb. 13:4.
2606. What is meant by a "profane person"? Is it one who swears?
2607. What person is illustrative of profanity? How? Cf. Gen. 25:34.
2608. What is the significance of the expression, "profane person" in application to us?
2609. Compare I Tim. 1:9; 4:7; 6:20; II Tim. 2:16.
2610. How could Esau be an example of a profane person?
2611. Whom would we sell out in order to be profane?
2612. Is a person who curses unthoughtful of God?
2613. How permanent was Esau's profanity?
2614. Is there danger in bad mistakes as seen in the life of Esau?
2615. Can a moment of pleasure ruin our life?
2616. Name persons of the Bible whose life was ruined or blighted by selling out to the devil.
2617. Is repentance ever too late?
2618. Was Esau's father hard-hearted?
2619. Can God be "wishy-washy" because people are?
2620. Is law good when it does not have good enforcement?
2621. Does this verse mean that God cannot always be touched by our repentance?
2622. How true was Esau's repentance?
2623. Are tears always a sign of repentance?

C. *The nature of the old covenant in contrast with that of the new.* 12:18-24.
1. The terror of the old. 12:18-21.

Text
12:18-21

18 For ye are not come unto a mount that might be touched, and that burned with fire, and unto blackness, and darkness, and tempest, 19 and the sound of a trumpet, and the Voice of words; which Voice they that heard entreated that no word more should be spoken unto them; 20 for they could not endure that which was enjoined, If even a beast touch a mountain, it shall be stoned; 21 and so fearful was the appearance, that Moses said, I exceedingly fear and quake:

Paraphrase

18 Now, that ye may understand the value of your birthrights as Abraham's seed, (Gal. iii. 18.), which I am exhorting you not to throw away, know, that ye shall not, like your fathers, come to a tangible mountain which burned with fire, to show that God is a consuming fire to the impenitent; and to blackness, and to darkness, which was an emblem of the obscurity of the Mosiac dispensation, and to tempest,

19 And to the noise of a trumpet, like that by which the angels called the Israelites together to hear the law, and which, by waxing louder and louder, terrified the Israelites exceedingly; and to the sound of words uttered by God Himself, the hearers of which, strongly impressed with the holiness and power of their Lawgiver and Judge, earnestly entreated to hear not a word more, (Exod. xx. 18, 19.)

20 Although, before they were affrighted by the voice of God, they could not bear that which was strictly commanded, Even if a beast touch the mountain while the symbol of the Divine Presence rests on it, it shall be stoned or shot through with an arrow. It seems they expected, by drawing near, to see God without being terrified.

21 And so terrible was that manifestation of the Divine Presence which appeared, that Moses cried to God, I am exceedingly afraid and quake.

Comment

For ye are not come unto a mount that might be touched

> We have no sacred mount or place, as did the Jews. John 4:21. Adventist, you can't come to Mount Sinai and expect salvation. The mountain was not to be touched, although being a mount it might be touched. Ex. 19:12-13.

and that burned with fire

> This was the way God taught them reverence. Cf. Deut. 4:11 and Deut. 5:4-5. This was magnificent, but not to be compared with our mount.

and unto blackness and darkness

> We have the revelation of light. The "blackness" probably refers to a dark or thick cloud. Cf. Ex. 19:16.

12:18-21   HELPS FROM HEBREWS

and tempest

We have the one who stills the tempest. "Tempest" is not mentioned in Exodus or Deuteronomy, but it includes evidently the thunders and lightnings.

and the sound of a trumpet

Does this mean there is no musical instrument in the church or heaven?
a. No, he is including the trumpet as part of the frightening experience. See Ex. 19:16; 20:18.
b. Observe the use of musical instruments.
1. Joel 2 was quoted on Pentecost.
2. Joel 2:1: "Blow the trumpet."
3. Joel 2:15: "Blow the trumpet."
a) We may assume a musical instrument was used on the birthday of the church.
b) Ps. 49:4, "will open my — on the harp," suggests the use of instruments in relationship to the Gospel.

and the Voice of words

The whole group heard the voice. Deut. 5:22. Heb. 12:26 says this Voice shook the earth.

which Voice they heard and entreated that no word more should be spoken unto them

The giving of the law excited terror; the Gospel brings peace. In Ex. 20:19 the people requested that Moses speak to them in place of the Voice.

for they could not endure that which was enjoined

Ex. 19 speaks of the serious bounds put on the people. The frightening trumpet, voice, quaking, and all was more than they could stand without a mediator.

if even a beast touch the mountain it shall be stoned

This was enjoined in Ex. 19:12-13. Absolute reverence was demanded, even to the animals being required to be away.

and so fearful was the appearance that Moses said, I exceedingly fear and quake

Is this statement of Moses found here only?
a. Some suggest that Paul received it from Jewish tradition.

b. Some say the author inferred it.
c. Some suppose Ex. 19:16-17 is referred to where Moses stood with all the people.
  In Ex. 19:19 we read, "Moses spoke."
a. What he spoke is not recorded.
b. If Paul were inspired, he could have written what Moses said that day.
c. Jesus promised the disciples guidance into all truth. See John 16:13.

Study Questions

2624. What mountain is referred to in verse 18?
2625. Does the Christian have a sacred mountain?
2626. What did Jesus say about worship at a mountain? Cf. John 4:21.
2627. Why did the mount of Moses burn with fire? Cf. Deut. 4:11; 5:4-5.
2628. What was the name of the mountain?
2629. Could the mountain be touched — was there any danger? Cf. Ex. 19:12-13.
2630. What is meant by "blackness and darkness"?
2631. How does darkness compare with our "mountain"?
2632. What is meant by the word "tempest"?
2633. Is there any tempest described? What could it refer to?
2634. Was there a musical instrument at Mount Sinai?
2635. Does this infer that a musical instrument is not to be included in the church?
2636. Why is it mentioned? See Ex. 19:16; 20:18.
2637. What is the trumpet referred to in verse 19?
2638. Tell of the various uses of the trumpet in the Bible.
2639. What is referred to in the Voice of words? Cf. 12:26 and Deut. 5:22.
2640. What was Israel's reaction to the words heard first from the mount?
2641. Why did the Hebrews request the Voice to be silenced?
2642. Will men ever feel that way again?
2643. Does the Gospel strike terror to some?
2644. How did the scene at Sinai impress the Hebrews?
2645. What factors were frightening?
2646. Why were animals forbidden to be near the mountain?

2647. Should we be careless about the Lord's house today?
2648. Why was the mountain "out of bounds" for man and beast?
2649. Where did Moses make the statement found in v. 21?
2650. What explanations are made?
2651. Could Moses have spoken with others recorded in Ex. 19:16-17?
2652. In the giving of the law, what was Moses' first reaction?
2653. What did Moses speak in Ex. 19:19?
2654. How did the author of Hebrews get this information?
2655. Could John 16:13 be an answer?

2. *The mercy of the new.* 12:22-24.

Text
12:22-24

22 but ye are come unto mount Zion, and unto the city of the living God, the heavenly Jerusalem, and to innumerable hosts of angels, 23 to the general assembly and church of the Firstborn who are enrolled in heaven, and to God the Judge of all, and to the spirits of just men made perfect, 24 and to Jesus the Mediator of a new covenant, and to the blood of sprinkling that speaketh better than that of Abel.

Paraphrase

22 But ye shall come to a place which I call Mount Zion, because there God will appear to you, not in the terribleness of His Greatness as on Sinai, but in the beauties of His goodness; and instead of being brought to any earthly city to worship, ye shall be brought to the city of the living God, the heavenly Jerusalem, and in your worship shall associate with ten thousands of angels;

23 To the general assembly and church of the Firstborn, brought from the different parts of the universe to worship God. These are enrolled in heaven as citizens. And, instead of standing afar off, as your fathers did at Sinai, ye shall come near to God the supreme Ruler of the whole universe, and to the spirits of just men made perfect by their union with their glorified bodies, and their introduction into heaven,

24 And to Jesus the Mediator of the new covenant, and to His blood, which is the true blood of sprinkling typified by the

Levitical sprinklings, and which, by crying for mercy to penitents, speaketh better things than the blood of Abel, which cried for vengeance on his murderer.

Comment

But ye are come into Mount Zion

"Ye are come unto Mount Zion" is in contrast to Mount Sinai.
a. They had a mount that they had to avoid.
b. We have a mount that we can approach.
c. McKnight: "But ye shall come," making it future.
"Mount Zion."
a. Mount Zion stands for grace, and not a literal mountain.
b. Mount Zion is a part of the hill of Jerusalem, and being the seat of both the royal and sacerdotal authority it was properly called the "holy hill of Zion." Ps. 2:6.
c. No Gentile ever came before Mount Zion, except as he came as a Jewish proselyte or to plunder or to destroy.

and unto the city of the living God the heavenly Jerusalem

Zion is spoken of as being the habitation of God. Ps. 132:13. This is the celestial city that Abraham looked for. Heb. 11:10. This city is described in Rev. 21 and 22. I understand it to be the Jerusalem above as Paul taught in Gal. 4:26.

We are come unto it, but our bodies not yet redeemed. We have not seen the new city except by faith.

and to innumerable hosts of angels

The throne of God seems to have great numbers of angels present. See Rev. 5:11; the number was thousands of thousands. It is to such a place of praise that we shall some day come; not to praise the angels, but the object of the angels' praise.

to the general assembly

Milligan says: "Here it denotes the joyful and multitudinous assembly of angels around the throne of God, who there forever celebrate His praises." See Rev. 5:11; 7:11-12.
a. This makes it a festive assembly of angels.
b. This rules out that our assembly on earth is meant.
If all thus far is future, then let us assume that the general

assembly will someday be held, when Christ gathers His faithful from the ends of the earth.

church of the Firstborn

We, of course, have come to the church already, being members of it; but is this what he meant?
a. McKnight says this refers only to those pious Israelites of all ages who by faith deserve to be called God's firstborn.
b. Milligan says it refers to the church on earth.
1. He quotes James 1:18 to show we are first fruits.
2. All its members are honored with this title, he says.
c. Calvin says it refers to the patriarchs and renowned saints of the earthly church.
d. Newell says Irsael is the firstborn of earth, but the church is the first fruits of heaven.

I prefer to allow the church to mean the "called out" that will someday be called into the great assembly. This is church future, not church present.

Christ wears the title "Firstborn," Rom. 8:29, and the church is His.

who are enrolled in heaven

God does the writing, for we can't climb or fly to the book to do the writing. It is a source of joy to have the privilege of having our name there. Luke 10:20 and Phil. 4:3.

Some prefer to have their names in social registers, so-called churches, lodges, etc., than on the church of the firstborn.

and to God the Judge of all

Who does judge? This is a big subject.
a. God will judge the sinners.
1. Heb. 13:4: God will judge adulterers.
2. Rom. 2:16: God will judge the secrets of men.
b. The saints will likewise do some judging.
1. I Cor. 6:2: will judge the world.
2. I Cor. 6:3: will judge the angels.
3. Compare Rev. 20:4.

The problem of judgment is God's. It will be just how He planned it.
a. We have come to Him already, and He no longer is our Judge but our Saviour.
b. In a sense He is our Judge, so let this inspire fear on our part to do His will.

and to the spirit of just men made perfect
>This refers to our heavenly position. Are there any "spirits made perfect" there now?
a. What God does with a spirit after death is His business, and I am confident that it is fair and just. But I do not know.
b. I agree with I John 3:2: "It is not yet manifested."
1. John says, "What we shall be."
2. I add my own ignorance, *"When* it shall be."

and to Jesus the Mediator of a new covenant
>What covenant is this?
a. Newell says this is not the better covenant of Chapter Eight, but the new covenant with Israel which lies in the future with Israel.
b. Here Newell is in error.
1. The characteristics of the covenant are the same; they must be the same.
2. Jesus only spoke of one covenant, on the night of His betrayal, and He calls it a new covenant. Luke 22:19-20.
3. In 13:20 the covenant is spoken of as an eternal covenant, and surely he means the same covenant as in Chapter Eight.
4. In 8:7 he speaks of the old being replaced by the second, but does not mention a third covenant.
>The covenant is the one by which the blood of Jesus will save all men, and to Whom He acts as Mediator.

and to the blood of sprinkling that speaketh better than that of Abel
>Abel's sacrifice speaks, according to 11:4.
a. Abel's sacrifice by faith spoke, saying that it pays to be obedient. In a sense, it is a warning.
b. Abel's sacrifice is not meant here, but his blood.
>What does Abel's blood speak?
a. Gen. 4:10-11 says, "Brother's blood crieth."
b. The blood of Abel called for judgment.
>What does this blood speak that is greater?
a. Newell says it speaks of judgment past forever and of eternal peace.
b. The popular idea is that the blood of Abel speaks a call for mercy.
c. Milligan: "Abel's blood speaks well, but Christ's speaks better."

12:25 HELPS FROM HEBREWS

d. If the following verses are considered, we might say this blood speaks a greater warning — "refuse not." v. 25.
No one questions that the blood is that of Christ.
a. Christ's blood speaks better because it avails pardon for sin.
b. His blood cries out, "The atonement is made."

Study Questions

2656. Contrast the Christian's mountain with Moses' mountain.
2657. Is our mountain figurative or literal?
2658. What is the name of our mountain?
2659. What was the location of Mount Zion?
2660. What did it represent?
2661. What else does the Christian have a right to approach?
2662. Compare other verses that speak of Zion. Cf. Ps. 132:13; Heb. 11:10; Rev. 21, 22; Gal. 4:26.
2663. Is this verse to be interpreted as past tense, present, or future?
2664. How do we see the city? Like Abraham? Heb. 11:10.
2665. When does the heavenly Jerusalem take place, according to Revelation?
2666. If this is present, how may we explain that we are in the midst of angels?
2667. How numerous are God's angels? Rev. 5:11.
2668. Does it say *"into Mount Zion"* or *"unto"*?
2669. How many are 12 legions of angels?
2670. Is this general assembly that of angels or men?
2671. Is it an earthly assembly?
2672. What is the description of the church here?
2673. What is meant by "Firstborn"?
2674. Is this the church on earth?
2675. If all of the other expressions refer to future experiences, can we assume that the church on earth is referred to here?
2676. Does Christ wear the title "Firstborn"? Rom. 8:29.
2677. Who all will be in His church?
2678. Who enrolls men in heaven?
2679. Compare Luke 10:20 and Phil. 4:3.
2680. If God writes our name, what can we do to cause God to write it there?
2681. Do men seem to prefer other registers?
2682. If God is Judge, do we come to Him?

2683. Will the Christian come to Him?
2684. Do we come to Him to be judged? Do we come to Him as Judge or Savior?
2685. Will Christians do any judging?
2686. Compare I Cor. 6:2, 3; Rev. 20:4.
2687. What is meant by "spirits"?
2688. Could this refer to our heavenly position or to our state now as Christians?
2689. If we have already come to Mount Zion, the new Jerusalem, how may we explain, "and to the spirits of just men made perfect," in verse 23 when we know none are perfect?
2690. If none are perfect on earth now, can we interpret this whole message as present action?
2691. Is this covenant the one of which we are a part?
2692. How many new covenants are there? Is there one for Jews and one for Gentiles?
2693. Is the one in Chapter Eight the same here and in 13:20?
2694. How many covenants did Jesus teach? Cf. Luke 22:19-20.
2695. What is the purpose of the covenant? To save from sin or to get Jews back to Jerusalem?
2696. What did Abel's blood sacrifice speak?
2697. What adjectives are used to describe the covenant?
2698. What is meant by, "we are come to the blood of sprinkling"?
2699. Whose blood is sprinkled?
2700. Why is the word "sprinkled" used?
2701. Could it be figurative that Christ is our Passover?
2702. Is Abel's blood, or Abel's sacrifice, referred to here?
2703. If his sacrifice is meant, what does it speak?
2704. From where did Abel's blood speak?
2705. Could it be that Abel speaks, and not his blood or sacrifice?
2706. Which could do a better job of speaking, Abel's blood or Abel's sacrifice?

D. *Warning.* 12:25-29.

Text
12:25-29

25 See that ye refuse not Him that speaketh. For if they escaped not when they refused Him that warned them on earth, much more shall not we escape who turn away from Him that

warneth from heaven: 26 Whose Voice then shook the earth: but now He hath promised, saying, Yet once more will I make to tremble not the earth only, but also the heaven. 27 And this word, Yet once more, signifieth the removing of those things that are shaken, as of things that have been made, that those things which are not shaken may remain. 28 Wherefore, receiving a kingdom that cannot be shaken, let us have grace, whereby we may offer service well-pleasing to God with reverence and awe: 29 for our God is a consuming fire.

Paraphrase

25 Take care that ye disobey not God Who is now speaking to you from heaven by His Son. For, if the Israelites did not escape punishment who disobeyed God delivering an oracle on earth, by Moses, commanding them to go into Canaan, much more we shall not escape punishment, who turn away from God speaking to us the Gospel from heaven by His Son.

26 God's voice at the giving of the law shook the earth, in token that idolatry was to be shaken in Canaan by the law of Moses. But now concerning His speaking by His Son He hath promised, saying, Yet once I shall not shake the earth only — the heathen idolatry and the powers which support it— but also the heaven; the Mosaic worship and Jewish state.

27 Now this speech, Yet once, signifieth the removing of the things shaken; the abolition of the former religions, and the destruction of the powers which uphold them, as of things which were made with hands — things of an inferior and imperfect nature; that the things not to be shaken, the Gospel church and worship, may remain to the end of the world.

28 Wherefore we, the disciples of God's Son, having in the Gospel dispensation received the kingdom foretold by Daniel to be given to the saints, and which is never to be shaken, let us hold fast that gift, that excellent dispensation of religion by which we can worship God acceptably, if we do it with reverence and religious fear.

29 For, even under the gospel, our God is as much a consuming Fire to infidels and apostates, as under the law.

Comment

See that ye refuse not Him that speaketh

    Who speaks?

a. Evidently God, but there is an allusion to the shaking at Sinai.
b. Christ spoke not threats that He carried out as this verse suggests. Of course Christ is the Word of God, but only in this sense can this verse apply to Him.

for if they escaped not when they refused Him that warned them on earth

    What occasion is referred to?

a. Noah surely is a possibility.
b. Moses' warning is a better one, since it fits the context better. Does this infer that now there is a warning direct from God without the messenger, man?

a. No. Neglect for so great a salvation demands heavier judgment. Heb. 2:3.
b. No speaker of greater dignity speaks, but a greater message is delivered.

much more shall not we escape

    We should not expect to go free, just because Christ taught that God is a Father. We sin against a greater demonstration of love, and we should expect a greater demonstration of wrath if we trample upon Christ.

who turn away from Him that warneth from heaven

    Observe that "warneth" is in italics. Actually it reads "that is from heaven."

a. This clarifies the point perhaps. He is simply locating the Voice.
b. Of course Moses' message was from heaven, but it was more directly from a mountain that shook and trembled.
This atoning message is from heaven, and it must not be rejected. Mark 16:16.

Whose Voice then shook the earth

    This refers to Mount Sinai, described in Ex. 19:18. The Psalmist described it, Ps. 114:4: "the mountains skipped like rams."

but now He hath promised, saying,

Hagai 2:6 is the quotation though not literal, says Calvin. Milligan says it was spoken primarily to the building of the second temple by Zerubbabel and is therefore chronologically connected with the coming of the Messiah.

yet once more will I make to tremble not the earth only but also the heavens

Though God shook the earth when He published the law, yet now He speaks more gloriously, for He shakes both earth and heaven. Has this been fulfilled?

a. Calvin: "The voice of the gospel not only thunders through the earth, but also penetrates above the heavens."
b. The earth quaked at Jesus' crucifixion and resurrection, so this could have been fulfilled.

"The heavens," says McKnight, refers to the Jewish state and worship.

a. He says here it pictures an alteration which was to be made in the political and religious state of the world.
b. If "heavens" is literal, no explanation can be given unless it refers to the event of darkness that accompanied the shaking of the earth at the cross.

There is a possibility that this refers to the end of time.

and this word, Yet once more

Newell says this is the divine interpretation of the above verse, and three things are seen:

a. Heaven and earth are to be done away.
b. The reason is that their end is accomplished.
c. Things unshaken will remain.

McKnight feels that Hag. 2 proves that earthly kingdoms, the Levitical system, etc., are meant.

a. He feels that "yet once" means that the gospel will remain to the end of the world, as the only form of religion acceptable to God.
b. This means then that shaking will continue until God's will prevails. Milligan agrees to this and refers to II Pet. 1:11 and I Cor. 15:24-25.

The words of the prophet are these, "Yet a little while."

signifieth the removing of those things that are shaken

    The destruction of Jerusalem almost destroyed Judaism, but God is still shaking it, for Jews will not give up their faith. The kingdoms of the world are yet to surrender to Jesus, but they will. Rev. 11:15.

    If earth means idolatry, and heaven the Jewish economy, as McKnight suggests, much shaking needs to be done.

    Newell insists that "heavens" are included here, for sin began in heaven, and it too must be shaken.

as of things that have been made

    Some suggest that this means things made with hands of man. McKnight and Milligan agree. Some suggest the creation.

that those things which are not shaken may remain

    The kingdom of heaven was set up during the time when kingdoms and thrones were being shaken.

a. It will endure when the heavens shall have passed away as a scroll. Cf. I Cor. 15:24 and II Pet. 1:11.

b. This kingdom will not give way as did the old law. Dan. 2:44. Man has done everything that he can to shake the church, but it cannot be done.

1. He tried persecution, burning Bibles, creating division, false doctrines, modernism, and worldliness and yet the church grows.
2. The church will remain, for the gospel is to shake this world.

wherefore receiving a kingdom that cannot be shaken

    How wonderful it is to be a part of something eternal, victorious and with a destiny. Things created are subject to decay, to destruction, but not the church; for not even the gates of Hades can prevail against it.

let us have grace

    Grace has been given to us, in that salvation has been provided. Calvin says this expression is strained. It reads as an exhortation. It should read, "we have grace."

    I prefer to let it be an exhortation.

a. We will have more grace as we offer up service.

b. The Christian is to work at grace, not just rejoice in it. *Pulpit Commentary* says it means, "Let us show thankfulness."

whereby we may offer service well pleasing to God

"Well pleasing" is familiar. We read that without faith we cannot please God. 11:6.

"Service" is the watchword for those in the kingdom.

a. We were won to win, told to tell, saved to serve.
b. James makes it plain that faith without works is dead.

with reverence and awe

Reverence is also translated, "godly fear," We are to serve with promptness and delight, yet it must be united with humility and due reverence. If "let us have grace" means to give thanks, then with thankfulness, reverence, and fear we serve.

"Awe" is also translated "dread."

for our God is a consuming fire

This verse is from Deut.4:24. Here the Israelites were warned of forgetting the covenant. The Lord's nature is not changed; He is a consuming fire as He declared at Sinai. If we scorn this present dispensation of grace, the day of judgment will be to us a day of terror.

Study Questions

2707. Who is speaking in the reference of verse 25?
2708. Does this verse refer to one specific person's warning, or several warnings of men through one God?
2709. Name some warnings that went unheeded.
2710. Does this verse refer to one of them?
2711. Does this verse teach that God gave a warning that did not come through man as other warnings did?
2712. Why should we have less chance of escaping?
2713. Do we sin against a greater speaker?
2714. Do we sin against a greater demonstration of love?
2715. Is the word "warn" in the original?
2716. How does it actually read?
2717. Was Moses' message from heaven or from a mountain?
2718. Who warns from heaven and what warning is meant?
2719. Does the verse refer to Moses' warning in comparison to Christ's warning?
2720. Is the place the point of emphasis, or the person?

2721. Does verse 26 help to answer whether it is Christ or God referred to in verse 25?
2722. Whose voice shook the earth?
2723. How does Ps. 114:4 describe it?
2724. Where is the saying referred to here?
2725. What is the difference in the second shaking?
2726. Could it have been fulfilled when Christ was on the cross?
2727. How was heaven shaken at Christ's crucifixion?
2728. What does heavens refer to — that God will shake?
2729. Could this refer to the end of time? Why?
2730. Are "shaking" and "trembling" synonymous in ideas?
2731. Could it be a shaking of political and religious conditions?
2732. If the shaking is being done by the Gospel, what has been shaken?
2733. What is meant by "heavens"?
2734. Explain what is meant by "yet once more".
2735. What did God permit that was greatly responsible for breaking up organized Judaism?
2736. Could verse 27 be an interpretation of verse 26?
2737. How long will God shake heaven and earth?
2738. What bearing does I Peter 1:11 and I Cor. 15:24-25 have?
2739. What is signified?
2740. Will the kingdoms of the world ever be annihilated?
2741. What made things are referred to here?
2742. Are they of God's making or man's?
2743. Has the church been shaken?
2744. Can it be shaken down?
2745. What has man done to the church?
2746. What remains in the earth that cannot be shaken?
2747. Is there room for pessimism in verse 28?
2748. Does this suggest that evil will win and that the church will be impotent?
2749. What is meant by "let us have grace"?
2750. Is this an exhortation?
2751. Is there any way for grace to be increased?
2752. How can we offer service to God?
2753. What is a prerequisite to pleasing God?
2754. Will God always be pleased with things done in Christ's name?
2755. Is there any spur to labor when you realize God's grace and victory are to be had?

2756. What should be our attitude as we serve God?
2757. Define "reverence."
2758. Define "awe."
2759. Were the Pharisees of Jesus' day failing here?
2760. What is our attitude in service to please God?
2761. Where is the expression "consuming fire" found in the Old Testament?
2762. How did the author prove that we should be in awe?
2763. Will it be demonstrated again?
2764. If we are not in awe, how will we appear some day?

True Or False Over Chapter Twelve

_____ 1. The Christian life is compared with running a race.
_____ 2. The Author and Finisher of our faith is Christ.
_____ 3. The Lord chastens those whom He loves.
_____ 4. Esau bought his brother's birthright.
_____ 5. A term applied to the church is "the general assembly."
_____ 6. Our God is said to be a "consuming fire."
_____ 7. The "besetting sin" here referred to was unbelief.
_____ 8. The Christian is told to lay aside every weight and fleshly sin.
_____ 9. If a beast should touch the mountain where Moses was receiving the Commandments, it should turn to stone.
_____10. The law was given at Sinai, but the Gospel was to go forth from there, too.
_____11. Esau was a profane person.
_____12. At no time on the journey was Moses fearful.
_____13. The kingdom of which we belong is spoken of as one which cannot be shaken.
_____14. It was the joy set before Christ that enabled Him to go to the cross.
_____15. Harsh chastening that seems hard to bear will result in peaceable fruit in our lives.
_____16. God is so longsuffering that He will forgive people for overlooking warnings from heaven.
_____17. The earth and heaven will be shaken, but it is not true of the kingdom of heaven.
_____18. God chastens us, and in it He is dealing as a Father with a son.
_____19. A teaching in this chapter is that man can fall short of the grace of God.

_____20. Jesus said that His way was straight, but here we are told to make straight paths for our feet.
_____21. A few angels comprise witnesses to our Christian life.
_____22. God may be called Father, for He is the Father of spirits.
_____23. Sanctification is essential to see the Lord.
_____24. The blood of Jesus is a blood of sprinkling that speaks better than that of Abel.
_____25. Weariness is generally thought of as fleshly, but we are exhorted to not grow weary, fainting in our souls.

SUMMARY OF CHAPTER TWELVE

This chapter brings to a grand climax the final appeal to approach God with a true heart in a fully assured faith which began in 10:19. It was continued through Chapter Eleven, which shows God's approval on men whose faith was expressed in obedience, caused them to endure trials and enabled them to win victories.

Chapter Twelve opens with the well-known figure of the athletic games by which the relation of the Christian to the heroes of the faith is explained. It proceeds with an explanation of the purpose of chastisement, and appeals to the Christian to pursue peace and purity, without which no man shall see the Lord.

The climax of the appeal to approach God is given in the contrast between Israel's fearful experience at Sinai and the Christian's joyous relationship to God under the new covenant which began at Mount Zion.

The chapter closes with a final warning to those who have received the kingdom that cannot be shaken; to heed and serve Him, "for our God is a consuming fire."

IV. *Final exhortation regarding duties pertaining to the Truth.* 13:1-25.
A. *Social duties.* 13:1-7.

Text
13:1-7

1 Let love of the brethren continue. 2 Forget not to show love unto strangers: for thereby some have entertained angels unawares. 3 Remembering them that are in bonds, as bound with them; them that are ill-treated, as being yourselves also in

the body. 4 Let marriage be had in honor among all, and let the bed be undefiled: for fornicators and adulterers God will judge. 5 Be ye free from the love of money; content with such things as ye have: for himself hath said, I will in no wise fail thee, neither will I in any wise forsake thee. 6 So that with good courage we say,

> The Lord is my Helper; I will not fear:
> What shall man do unto me?

7 Remember them that had the rule over you, men that spake unto you the Word of God; and considering the issue of their life, imitate their faith.

Paraphrase

1 Let that brotherly love, for which I commended you, continue to be exercised by you to all the disciples of Christ, whether they be Jews or Gentiles.

2 Do not neglect to entertain strangers, though unacquainted with them, for thereby some have had the happiness to entertain angels, without knowing they entertained angels.

3 By your prayers and good offices assist them who are in bonds for their religion, as equally liable to be bound for that good cause; and them who suffer any kind of evil, as being yourselves also in the body, subject to adversity.

4. In opposition to the notions of the Essenes, let marriage be esteemed an honourable state among all ranks, and let adultery be avoided. For fornicators and adulterers, though not punished by men, God will severely punish, as invaders of their neighbour's dearest rights.

5 However poor ye may be, show no immoderate love of money in your dealings; being contented with what things ye have. In every difficulty rely on God. For, when he ordered Joshua to conduct the Israelites, He Himself said, (Josh. i. 5.), 'As I was with Moses, so I will be with thee, I will not fail thee, nor forsake thee.'

6 So that when afflicted, but especially when persecuted, taking courage, we may say with the Psalmist, (Psal. cxviii. 6. LXX.), The Lord is my Helper, and I will not be afraid of any evil that man can do to me in opposition to Him.

7 Remember your teachers who have preached to you the Word of God; of whose conversation attentively considering the

ending, imitate their faith in the doctrines, and precepts, and promises of the Gospel, that when ye end your conversation, ye may be supported as they were.

Comment

Let love of the brethren continue
   This sounds as though brotherly love characterized them.
a. This is true. See Heb. 6:10-11.
b. They must have been strong on the "social gospel" and weak in other ways.
1. In 5:11 they were dull of hearing, were in need of teaching.
2. The many exhortations to lay hold, press on, etc., are indications of a special need.
   This virtue characterized the early Hebrew church. See Acts 2:44-47; 12:5-12:15:22, 25.

forget not to show love unto strangers
   What does "love" mean if strangers are to receive it?
a. This was a command for Jews in the Old Testament. Lev. 19:34.
1. The Hebrews would therefore understand what was meant.
2. This just reminds them to not neglect it.
b. It probably meant the exercise of love which all owe to all men. II Pet. 1:7.
   There is no honor to us if we love only those that love us. See Matt. 5:43-46.
a. The church will grow when strangers, visitors, now Christians, are warmed with the friendly helpfulness of Christians.
b. The world needs love, for there is so much of bitterness and strife in the world.

for thereby some have entertained angels unawares
   Instances of it are found in the visit to Abraham and Lot.
a. Calvin and Milligan agree to this.
b. See Gen. 18:2-10; 19:1-3.
   Our guests may often be messengers sent to us from God for our special benefit.

remember them that are in bonds, as bound with them that are illtreated, as being yourselves also in the body
   The people had been in bonds themselves at one time. See 10:32-34.

13:3, 4   HELPS FROM HEBREWS

a. These people at that time had remembered one another. 10:34.
b. The possibility of them forgetting others in bonds must have been a possibility now that their days were easier.
c. Perhaps these people were the strangers, for to their own countrymen they had been so helpful in the past.

Ill treatment was often displayed in that day.

a. Romans were known for their cruelty to their children and to their slaves.
1. All slaves were slain if the master were slain by a slave.
2. A story is reported of a master who killed a slave so that a guest could see the spectacle of a dying man.
3. Another Roman fed his fish with the mutilated body of a slave.
b. The early church received severe persecutions.
1. The Jews were cruel, as seen by Stephen's treatment.
2. The Romans were severe, as seen by Nero and others.

"As being yourselves also in the body," suggests identifying one's self with them as the Golden Rule suggests. Luke 6:31.

Let marriage be had in honor among all, and let the bed be undefiled: for fornicators and adulterers God will judge.

"Let marriage be had in honor among all" suggests that is a state that should be revered.

a. God instituted marriage by providing Eve for Adam.
b. The conduct of married people to each other is suggested often in the New Testament.
1. Eph. 5:22-28: Subjection of the wife is in order.
2. I Cor. 7:1-5: A clean marriage state.
3. I Pet. 3:1-7: The wife is to be honored.
c. Celibacy is advocated by some as though marriage is not honorable.
1. If it is to be honored by all, it is honorable for all.
2. Fornication is a disregard for marriage, and adultery is a defilement of marriage.

God will judge those guilty of defiling the honorable marriage relationship with fornication and adultery.

a. It was a sin that brought capital punishment in the Old Testament. See Lev. 20:10.
b. The New Testament indicates that people guilty of this will be in hell. I Cor. 6:9; Rev. 2:22.

Be ye free from the love of money

It is "a root of all kinds of evil" when it is loved. I Tim. 6:10.
a. It causes people to lie, steal, cheat, commit murder.
b. It causes people to hope for the death of those leaving money to them as an inheritance.
c. It corrupted the temple in Jerusalem. John 2:14; Matt. 21:12.
d. It kept the rich young ruler from Jesus.
This section has an alternate translation.
a. "Let your conversation be without covetousness."
b. Let your mind be free.
The passage in all translations teaches us to avoid a covetous life.
a. Men with money are sometimes possessed of it.
b. Money only seems to bring contentment.

content with such things as ye have

Paul gave us an example of this in his own life.
a. In Phil. 4:12 he said he knew how to be abased.
b. Paul gave up everything for Christ.
It is not a destruction of ambition or legal endeavor as seen by other passages. See Rom. 12:11: "In diligence not slothful." Also Eph. 4:28; II Thess. 3:11. We are not to be like animals reaching across a fence for grass no greener than we deserve.

for Himself hath said, I will in no wise fail thee

Deut. 31:6 is probably the source of this quotation.
a. Similar expressions are found in Josh. 1:5; I Chr. 28:20.
b. This, says Milligan, became a proverbial saying among the Hebrews because of its consolation.
This is a sentiment expressed by Jesus in the Sermon on the Mount. Matt. 6:25-30.

neither will I in any wise forsake thee

This was conditional, however, for those who would not forsake God.
a. Israel found God forsaking them in the day of provocation.
b. We have no right to expect God to reward us for unfaithfulness. Jesus promised to be with us even unto the end of the world if we preach the Gospel. Matt. 28:18-20.

so that with good courage we say, The Lord is my Helper

We may speak confidently that the Lord is our Helper.
a. The word "we" appears often in this book.
b. We do not need to understand that Paul had an assistant author.
c. Anyone who has faith can make the statement.
"The Lord is my helper" is an expression of faith. Ps. 118:6 is quoted, but observe that in the original Psalm it is translated, "The Lord is on my side."
a. Milligan says this was one of the collection of hymns that was sung at the close of the feast of tabernacles.
b. Paul expressed the same thought: "If God be for us, who can be against us?" Rom. 8:31.

I will not fear: what shall man do unto me?

This verse does not suggest that man will never do man bodily harm.
a. David knew differently.
b. Paul knew differently; so did these brethren, for they had been afflicted.
The idea is, "What can man do that God cannot undo?"
a. Man can bring pain, but God will give us a body that knows no pain.
b. Man can kill, but God can make alive.

remember them that had the rule over you

This very likely refers to such men as Stephen, James, the brother of John, and other faithful preachers.
a. These men had preached the gospel to the Hebrews.
b. Actually it means "those leading you."
Newell suggests that the Greek word means "to go before," which suggests it was their work, not an office.
a. There were no bosses in the early church, such as Popes, etc.
b. These men were leaders because of work.

men that spake unto you the Word of God

Paul once was spoken of as the chief speaker, Acts 14:12, and the same Greek word appears here.
There were others who spoke. Acts 14:12
The elders also were responsible to speak. I Tim. 5:17; Acts 20:28-31.

and considering the issue of their life

In Greek, "the manner of their life."
a. Blessed is a people who have a leader whose good life is worthy of consideration.
b. These leaders had been unmoved in their hours of trial.
c. Their lives were like Abraham of old — lived in faith. Something was to be learned from their leaders.

imitate their faith

Faith — can it be imitated?
a. It is all that should be imitated.
b. Imitate faith, not mannerisms.
c. Imitate their method with God.
d. Imitate their reliance, confidence in God.
In all other respects we must imitate God. Eph. 5:1: Imitation of God as beloved children.

Study Questions

2765. Characterize the 13th chapter.
2766. What may we assume characterized the Hebrew brethren by v. 1?
2767. Does Hebrews 6:10-11 verify this?
2768. Did they major on the "social gospel" and fall short in other respects? Cf. 5:11.
2769. What verses in Acts show that the Hebrews loved one another?
2770. What did the Jerusalem church require of Paul at the Jerusalem Conference?
2771. What is meant by "show love unto strangers"? Is it possible?
2772. Were the Hebrews consistent in their love?
2773. Who would "strangers" be?
2774. How would the Jews know who was meant? Cf. Lev. 19:34.
2775. Compare II Pet. 1:7, as it includes "all men."
2776. Is there any honor in loving those who love us? Cf. Matt. 5:43-46.
2777. Explain "have entertained angels unawares."
2778. Who could be included in the word "some"?
2779. Compare Gen. 18:2-10; 19:1-3.
2780. Who could be referred to as being "in bonds"?

2781. Had the Hebrews ever been in bonds?
2782. What is meant by, "as bound with them"?
2783. What would such identification do?
2784. Was cruelty, ill treatment, common in that day?
2785. What does the author teach concerning marriage?
2786. How do we know marriage is to be revered?
2787. What is meant by the word "honor"?
2788. Give other verses of scripture that speak of married conduct. Cf. Eph. 5:22-27; I Cor. 7:1-5.
2789. Does celibacy teach that marriage is honorable for all?
2790. Were the apostles married?
2791. What is meant by, "God will judge"?
2792. How serious a sin was adultery in the Old Testament?
2793. What is the difference between fornication and adultery?
2794. Is it serious today? I Cor. 6:9; Rev. 2:22.
2795. How could Jesus allow remarriage in the case of adultery?
2796. If adulterers are not killed under our law, is it less serious with God now?
2797. Why are we exhorted to be free of the "love of money"?
2798. Show instances of corrupted people in the New Testament.
2799. What does love of money cause today?
2800. If it causes murder, jealousy, envy, thefts, kidnapping, etc., is it not a very dangerous sin?
2801. How is this verse translated by some?
2802. Is the meaning the same?
2803. Does contentment destroy ambition?
2804. What is our attitude to be toward our possessions or lack of them?
2805. Compare Paul in this regard. Phil. 4:12.
2806. Is this verse against ambition? Cf. Rom. 12:11; Eph. 4:28; II Thess. 3:11.
2807. Where is this verse quoted?
2808. Did Jesus express this sentiment?
2809. What consolation does he give for those in need?
2810. Did God place any condition on it?
2811. Did He ever forsake the Hebrews?
2812. Did Jesus promise to be with us? Cf. Matt. 28:18-20.
2813. Does verse 6 suggest a double authorship?
2814. How is the Lord our Helper?

2815. What may be the source of the expression, "The Lord is on my side"?
2816. Does this verse suggest that God will not allow man to suffer ill treatment?
2817. Can God undo everything that man does to the body?
2818. What is inferred by "remember"?
2819. Who had the rule over them?
2820. Who are the rulers referred to in verse 7?
2821. What seemed to constitute the rule?
2822. Were they leaders, or bosses?
2823. Who might they have seen?
2824. Who spoke the word in the early church?
2825. Besides remembering, what were they to consider?
2826. Define "issue of their life."
2827. What does he recommend to imitate?
2828. How can you imitate faith?

B. *Doctrine and worship.* 13:8-16.

Text
13:8-16

8 Jesus Christ is the same yesterday and today, yea and forever. 9 Be not carried away by divers and strange teachings: for it is good that the heart be established by grace; not by meats, wherein they that occupied themselves were not profited. 10 We have an altar, whereof they have no right to eat that serve the tabernacle. 11 For the bodies of those beasts whose blood is brought into the holy place by the high priest as an offering for sin, are burned without the camp. 12 Wherefore Jesus also, that He might sanctify the people through his own blood, suffered without the gate. 13 Let us therefore go forth unto Him without the camp, bearing His reproach. 14 For we have not here an abiding city, but we seek after the city which is to come. 15 Through Him then let us offer up a sacrifice of praise to God continually, that is, the fruit of lips which make confession to His name. 16 But to do good and to communicate forget not: for with such sacrifices God is well pleased.

Paraphrase

8 Jesus Christ, yesterday and today, is the same powerful, gracious, and faithful Saviour, and will continue to be so forever.
9 Be not tossed about with discordant and foreign doctrines,

taught by unauthorized teachers, concerning the efficacy of the Levitical sacrifices: For it is good that your courage in suffering and death be established on God's free pardon of sin through the sacrifice of Christ, and not on the Levitical sacrifices made of animals designed for meats, by which they have not been profited in respect of pardon who continually offer them.

10 That ye must not seek the pardon of sin through the sacrifices of animals appointed for meat, ye may know by this, that we have a sacrifice for sin of which they have no right to eat, who, to obtain pardon, worship in the tabernacle with the sacrifices of eatable animals appointed for sin-offerings.

11 This was showed figuratively in the law: For of those animals whose blood is brought as a sin-offering into the holy places by the high-priest, the bodies are burnt without the camp as things unclean, of which neither the priests nor the people were allowed to eat.

12 Therefore Jesus also, who was typified by these sin-offerings, that He might be known to sanctify the people of God with His own blood presented before the throne of God in heaven as a sin-offering, suffered without the gate of Jerusalem, as the bodies of the sin-offerings were burnt without the camp.

13 Well then, let us go forth, after His example, from the city of our habitation to the place of our punishment, bearing the reproach laid on Him; the reproach of being malefactors.

14 The leaving our habitation, kindred, and friends, need not distress us; for we have not here an abiding city, but we earnestly seek one to come; namely, the city of the living God, of which I spake to you, chap. xii. 22.

15 And though persecuted by our unbelieving brethren, through Him, as our High-priest, let us offer up the sacrifice of praise continually to God for His goodness in our redemption, namely the fruit of our lips, by confessing openly our hope of pardon through Christ, to the glory of God's perfections.

16 But, at the same time, to do good works, and to communicate of your substance to the poor, do not forget; for with such sacrifices God is especially delighted. See Phil. iv. 18.

Comment

Jesus Christ is the same yesterday and today, yea and forever

Jesus Christ is the same, for there is no need for him to change.

HELPS FROM HEBREWS 13:8, 9

a. He is the same in His love and His saving power.
b. The Christ that sits at God's right hand is as immutable as the Father Who promised Abraham.
Yesterday He came from the Father to do the will of God and finished it. Today He serves as Priest before God on man's behalf.
a. He has not changed in His attitude toward sin.
b. He hates evil and loves man as always.
c. Some try to define the time element, when today began, but this is beside the point.
"Yea and forever" refers to the ages.
a. This is for the eternity to come.
b. Change with us is constant, but our Lord is wonderfully perfect.
c. Perfection cannot change for the better.

Be not carried away by divers and strange teachings

The Christian has Christ Who is unchanging truth; therefore, He should avoid all other teachings.
a. Those who have latter day revelations always conflict with other latter day teachers as well as with the scripture.
b. God's revealed Word is able to furnish us completely, so what more can a strange teaching do? See II Tim. 3:15-17. If we are anchored in Christ we will not be carried like a ship into a sea of false doctrine, with waves of error. Paul warns about winds of doctrines. Eph. 4:14.

for it is good that the heart be established by grace

The heart of man by the grace of God may be established.
a. This is in contrast to the worldly ones who are drifting, shifting, to one pleasure, doctrine, etc.
b. Strange doctrines, foreign to the truth, will never establish one.
This verse suggests the anchoring of the soul, as seen in Chapter Six.

not by meats, wherein they that occupied themselves were not profited.

This refers to the meats used in sacrifices, which no longer is a method for atonement.
a. Christ was the perfect Sacrifice, made once and for all, so no other sacrifice is needed.

b. The kingdom of God is not meat and drink, says Paul in Rom. 14:17. Only one sacrifice profits the sinner, and that is Christ's.

We have an altar

What is our altar? Several opinions are listed here.
a. Some say that this is a general statement, and no particular thing is meant. It is only imagery.
b. Christ is the altar, some say.
c. Others suggest the Lord's table.
d. Some say the heavenly place where Christ offers the virtue of His own blood.
e. The cross on which Christ was crucified is suggested.
f. It signifies the divine nature of Christ on which the human nature is supposed to have been offered.
g. One suggests it refers to the one in the old tabernacle.
Christ is in no place called an altar, neither is the cross.
a. The altar was the place where the victim was placed, so what could be referred to but the cross?
b. It is the cross where blood was shed for the remission of our sins.
c. Very likely he does not refer to the Christian at all.
The author is referring to an Old Testament altar, for the next expression has no meaning otherwise.

whereof they have no right to eat that which serve the tabernacle.

If the altar was the Lord's table, this would be a good proof for closed communion. This is an allusion to the Old Testament custom.
a. Those who served the tabernacle could eat of the sacrifices.
b. The exception was on the Day of Atonement. The bodies which gave the blood carried into the Holy of holies were burned without the camp. See Lev. 6:26, 30; 4:7, 18, 21; 16:15, 27, 28.
These animals were not eaten for meat as were others.

For the bodies of those beasts whose blood is brought into the holy place by the high priest as an offering for sin are burned without the camp.

Other animals were consumed for food. See I Cor. 9:13; I Cor. 10:18. The great sacrifice on the Day of Atonement was burned outside the camp. Leviticus 16:27.

Wherefore Jesus also, that He might sanctify the people through His own blood, suffered without the gate

    Jesus was not offered in the temple at Jerusalem, but outside the city wall.

a. His blood was taken into the heavenly sanctuary, so He fits the type completely except for the burning.
b. The burning had nothing to do with the atonement, for it is the blood that atones.

    Those who retain the old sacrifice in preference to this of Christ lose the sanctification in Christ's blood.

Let us therefore go forth unto Him

    Going is our responsibility; the sacrifice awaits. We must leave the tabernacle to follow Jesus Christ.

a. If no atonement is in the blood of bulls and goats, why stay in the shadow of the tabernacle?
b. Out on the hill of Calvary is the place for the sinner to go.

without the camp.

    The types of Hebrews are those of the tabernacle, and this alludes to the sacrifice without the camp.
Newell says "it refers to all those religious developments by whatever name called. It reveals where Christ is and His followers are, as to this world and its religions."
Christ went out of the ctiy of Jerusalem to be sacrificed. This is nearer the truth than Newell's idea.

bearing His reproach

    The Christian is not promised an easy time, but reproach should be expected.

a. It is prophesied, II Tim. 3:12, by Paul.
b. Jesus said it would come to His disciples. John 16:2.

    The first Christian martyr suffered for the reproach of Christ outside the city.

for we have not here an abiding city

    If we stay in Jerusalem, it will be dissolved like all the world. II Pet. 3:8-13; Matt. 24. We must turn our eyes from our cities, for they are only temporary.
Something Paul had in mind, the destruction of Jerusalem, which came about nine years afterward.

but we seek after the city which is to come

    Revelation speaks of that city. Rev. 21.
    Peter speaks of it in II Pet. 3:8-13.
    The author has previously spoken of it in 11:10 and 16.

Through Him then let us offer up a sacrifice of praise to God continually

    Instead of frequent sacrifices like the Jew, let us offer our sacrifice through Jesus Christ.

a. We need no order of priests who blasphemously undertake to do that work for men which Christ has done.
b. This sacrifice is praise to God, not a begging for a forgiveness. Peter comments on the Christian's sacrifice, I Pet. 2:5. "Continually" is a good word. The kingdom of Christ has no sacred days or season, no special sanctuaries, for God is approached always through Christ.

    "Sacrifice of praise" most men feel alludes to the Levitical term for thank-offering. See Lev. 7:12, 15.

that is, the fruit of lips which make confession to His name

    Whose name?

a. We praise God continually, so a confession is surely in order.
b. Many verses suggest confessing Christ, so likely His name is meant here. Matt. 10:32; Rom. 10:9-10.

    In a world pressing on to judgment, glorying in men, let us rejoice, praise God, for who would want to neglect so great a salvation?

But to do good and to communicate forget not

    Doing good, helping others, will come naturally with a life of continual praise. See Rom. 12:13; Gal. 6:6; Heb. 6:10; Ps. 50:23. Jesus set the proper example before us, **for he went about doing good.** Acts 10:38.
    This is an essential factor in salvation. Matt. 25:34-46.

for with such sacrifices God is well pleased.

    There are three reasons why it is pleasing:

a. God works in harmony with God's nature.
b. It indicates a good state of mind.
c. It is beneficial to others.

    If we wish to sacrifice to God, we must pray to God and serve our fellow man.

Study Questions

2829. How can Jesus be considered the same always?
2830. Has He changed in character?
2831. Has His work changed?
2832. What are the three time elements named?
2833. Why is the author declaring this great truth?
2834. Were the changing Hebrews being challenged to follow the unchanging Christ?
2835. If perfection were changed, what would be its condition?
2836. If Christ is Truth, what results when people follow other teachers?
2837. What is meant by "carried away"?
2838. What is meant by "divers"?
2839. Why do people go to strange doctrines?
2840. Are such warnings few in the Word of God?
2841. What will keep a person from drifting into strange doctrines?
2842. What is meant by "established"?
2843. In what should we be established?
2844. How can grace do it?
2845. What is it that is to be established?
2846. Could the establishing idea be similar to the anchoring referred to in Chapter Six?
2847. What does the author say that cannot establish us?
2848. What is meant by meats?
2849. If Christ's sacrifice is sufficient, is there further need for sacrifices?
2850. What is meant by "occupied themselves"?
2851. Who may be referred to by the expression, "occupied themselves"?
2852. State some explanations for the expression, "we have an altar."
2853. What is our altar? Who is meant by "our"?
2854. Could he be pointing out the weakness of the Jewish altar rather than suggesting a Christian altar?
2855. Give weaknesses of each.
2856. Who could eat what?
2857. What tabernacle is referred to?
2858. Could the priests eat the sacrifices?
2859. When could they not eat?

HELPS FROM HEBREWS

2860. Could he be saying, "They who serve earthly tabernacles have no right to the Christian's altar"?
2861. What was done with animals sacrificed on the Day of Atonement that differed from sacrifices on other days?
2862. What is meant by, "without the camp"?
2863. Do we have any clue for this request?
2864. Is our sacrifice eaten?
2865. Show the similarities between the Old Testament sin offering and our sin offering.
2866. What is meant by, "suffered without the gate"?
2867. Where was Jesus offered?
2868. Where was His blood taken?
2869. Give scriptures that teach that His blood was considered to be taken into heaven.
2870. Does the burning of the Old Testament type serve as a type of Christ?
2871. Did the burning have anything to do with the sacrifice?
2872. Where does he exhort the Christians to go?
2873. Can we have the merit if we do not go?
2874. Do we go to the tabernacle or to the hill of Calvary?
2875. What camp is referred to?
2876. Explain "bearing His reproach."
2877. Can we ever bear reproaches?
2878. Did Jesus prophesy reproaches for His followers?
2879. What city is referred to?
2880. Do you think he refers specifically to the city of Jerusalem?
2881. Was he prophesying the destruction of Jerusalem?
2882. Is he speaking of Jews here as in 13:7 when he says we have an altar?
2883. What will happen to any city of the world according to II Peter?
2884. How soon was Jerusalem destroyed after this text?
2885. Identify the city to come. What do we know about it?
2886. Who is meant by the expression "by Him"?
2887. How can we offer up sacrifices?
2888. Do we need an earthly priest?
2889. What kind of a sacrifice are we to offer?
2890. Is this to be periodic?
2891. Is this room for complaint in this sacrifice?
2892. For what should we praise God?

2893. Could it allude to the Levitical thank offering? Lev. 7:12, 15
2894. What is to be the fruit of our lives?
2895. Whose Name is to be confessed?
2896. What part does confession have in the praise?
2897. Should we consider confession of faith as a step of salvation never to be taken again?
2898. Will we have time to glory in men if we are praising God as we should?
2899. Who is our great example in doing good?
2900. Will this be natural for us if we are Christ-like?
2901. Compare other verses, such as Rom. 12:13; Gal. 6:6; Heb. 6:10.
2902. Is it essential to salvation? See Matt. 25:34-46.
2903. What do you understand by "communicate"?
2904. What does he conclude about this kind of service?
2905. Has he stated that service is twofold — one to God and one to others?

C. *Obedience to elders.* 13:17.

Text
13:17

17 Obey them that have rule over you, and submit to them: for they watch in behalf of your souls, as they that shall give account; that they may do this with joy, and not with grief; for this were unprofitable for you.

Paraphrase

17 Follow the directions of your spiritual guides, and submit yourselves to their admonitions, for they watch over your behaviour for the good of your souls, as those who must give account to God. Obey them, therefore, that they may do this with joy, as having promoted your salvation, and not with mourning on account of your forwardness; for that would be unprofitable for you, ending in your condemnation.

Comment

Obey them that have the rule over you

Beyond any question, this is spiritual rule, for "watch over souls" suggests this.

a. Rulers no doubt refers to rulers in the church for it is unlikely that Christian magistrates existed in government.

    b. Good elders, no doubt, are meant, for elders are to rule. Acts 20:28-31; I Tim. 5:17; I Tim. 3:1-7; Titus 1:5-9; James 5:14-15; I Pet. 5:1-4.

    Verse 7 indicates former rulers had passed on, and now present rulers are to be obeyed. If elders are qualified, the members will be glad to obey.

and submit to them

    Submission rather than resistance, rebellion, and strife is enjoined.

    a. A church can't go forward with elders going in one direction and the membership trying to go another.

    b. Of course not every elder is qualified to rule.

    Many problems arise when churches carelessly elect unqualified leaders and then refuse to follow, or follow carelessly.

for they watch in behalf of your souls

    This pictures the ideal ruler. Paul told the Ephesian elders what to expect of false teachers who would seek to destroy the flock. Acts 20:29. The care of souls is a sacred trust.

as they shall give account

    This makes it serious.

    a. James 3:1: "Be not many of you teachers" is a serious warning.

    b. Ezek. 3:18-21 suggests the watchman must give account.

that they may do this with joy

    It is a joy to be a leader of a devoted church.

    a. **See III John 4.** John expressed it, "There is no greater joy."

    b. Paul urges the Thessalonians to be faithful, for they were his joy. I Thess. 2:19-20.

    There should be no joy in our heart if we stand in the way of joy in the heart of a righteous elder.

and not with grief

    Grief, sorrow, heartache should not be brought on by Christain people into the lives of men who have the care of souls. If the Jerusalem church had different sentiments about the efficacy of the Levitical sacrifices, no doubt much grief was had or would be experienced.

for this were unprofitable for you

This rather suggests that evil would come upon trouble-makers.

a. Note that strife, contention, etc., are named among the fruits of the flesh. Gal. 5:17-21.
b. Division is condemned in I Cor. 1:10.

It would no doubt be more unfortunate for the trouble-maker than the troubled one. No reward from God is in store for the troubler.

Study Questions

2906. What rulers are referred to in this verse? How do you know?
2907. If elders are of the right kind, should we not expect to obey them?
2908. Whose fault is it if rulers do not watch after souls?
2909. What verses teach us that elders are to rule?
2910. What would be the opposite of "submit"?
2911. Why should we submit to them?
2912. Would unqualified men watch over souls?
2913. Should elders take their work lightly? Cf. Ezek. 3:18-21.
2914. Is there joy for the faithful shepherd?
2915. How did John feel about it? III John 4.
2916. Did Paul have joy in his concern?
2917. Is much of the grief in a church brought on by believers who are not wholly consecrated?
2918. Are trouble-makers in the church condemned by scripture?
2919. Are there trouble-makers who do right? Is the Christian to keep silent under all circumstances?

D. *Request for prayers.* 13:18-19.

Text
13:18-19

18 Pray for us: for we are persuaded that we have a good conscience, desiring to live honorably in all things. 19 And I exhort you the more exceedingly to do this, that I may be restored to you the sooner.

Paraphrase

18 Pray for me: For, though ye may dislike my doctrine set forth in this letter, I am certain, in teaching it, I have maintained a good conscience, having delivered it to you faithfully; willing in all things to behave suitably to my character as an inspired teacher.

19 And I the more earnestly beseech you to pray for me, that through the help of God I may be restored to you the sooner.

Comment

Pray for us: for we

Who is "us"?
a. Many apostles and evangelists were known by the Hebrews, and they should pray for them.
b. With four commentaries before me, no one suggests who might be included, except Milligan who suggests the above.
A request for prayer is common with Paul. Eph. 6:18-19; I Thess. 5:25; II Thess. 3:1; Rom. 15:30; II Cor. 1:11; Philemon 22.

are persuaded that we have a good conscience, desiring to live honorably in all good things

The integrity of his own conscience is used to move them to feel an interest in him.
"Persuaded," Calvin feels, suggests modesty.
The author's desire to live righteously in all things called for their help.

And I exhort you the more exceedingly to do this

This is an urgent request by one who knew they knew his needs. The faith the man had in prayer here shows that he felt God was able to act providentially on behalf of man.

that I may be restored to you the sooner

This suggests that troubles, persecution, or perhaps imprisonment detained him. Timothy's difficulty, verse 23, may be the factor that kept the author from being in their midst.
Was Paul ever a part of the Hebrew brethren?
a. This verse suggesting "restoration" challenges Pauline authorship for me.
b. Paul generally is associated with Antioch and Gentiles.

Study Questions

2920. "Pray for us" refers to whom?
2921. How does this knock the authorship anonymous theory?
2922. Is it possible to live honorably in all evil things?
2923. How may we live righteously or honorably?
2924. How does the restoration of the author affect Pauline authorship?
2925. Was Paul ever a part of the fellowship of the Hebrew brethren?

E. Prayer for them. 13:20-21.

Text
13:20-21

20 Now the God of peace, who brought again from the dead the great shepherd of the sheep with the blood of an eternal covenant, even our Lord Jesus, 21 make you perfect in every good thing to do His will, working in us that which is well-pleasing in His sight, through Jesus Christ; to Whom be the glory for ever and ever. Amen.

Paraphrase

20 Now may God the Author of all happiness, who to save mankind brought back from the dead our Lord Jesus the great Shepherd of the sheep, may He, through the blessings procured by the blood whereby the new covenant, which is never to be changed, was ratified.

21 Prepare you for every good work, to do what He has commanded, producing in you every disposition acceptable in His sight, through the doctrine and assistance of Jesus Christ, to Whom be ascribed the glory of our salvation, forever and ever. Amen.

Comment

Now the God of peace

Isaiah 9:6 speaks of Christ as "Prince of Peace." All peace comes from God through Jesus Christ.
This expression comes only from Paul. See Phil. 4:9; I Cor. 14:33; Rom. 16:20; Rom. 15:33; II Cor. 13:11: I Thess. 5:23.

Who brought again from the dead

This is true of God, even though Jesus said He would raise

Himself up. John 10:18. The resurrection of Jesus was a bodily ressurection, for no proof can be given of any other kind. See Rom. 6:4; Acts 13:30.

the great shepherd of the sheep

We have a great shepherd. Are we great sheep?
This title is given for two reasons.
a. Ezekiel 34:23 prophesies him as such.
b. Jesus claimed this title. John 10:11.
Other shepherds who lay down their life for their sheep cannot be brought back alive to the sheep.

with the blood of an eternal covenant, even our Lord Jesus

The word "with" here is a problem.
a. It is translated "by," "in," and "through."
b. Calvin prefers "in," saying, "Christ so arose from the dead that his death was not yet abolished, but that it retains its efficacy forever, as though he had said, 'God raised up His Own Son,' but in such a way that the blood He shed once for all in His death is efficacious after His resurrection . . ." Commentators question whether this phrase goes with what appears before or after. The Lord is the great Shepherd by shedding His blood and yet being alive now to act.

make you perfect in every good thing

This is a benedictive prayer. God seeks to make us perfect in good things, and Christ is a perfect example. If we follow the great Shepherd, we will be led to perfection.

to do His will

Perfection cannot be attained in any other will. No work is acceptable unless it is in harmony with the will of God.

working in us

"Us is also translated "you."
Eph. 3:20 shows God able to work surprises in us.
God has no hands but our hands to do His work today, and through us He can accomplish His will.

that which is well pleasing in His sight

Phil. 2:13 is a good commentary here on God's part.
Rom. 12:2 suggests our part.

through Jesus Christ

Two senses are possible here:
a. Working through Jesus Christ.
b. Well-pleasing through Jesus Christ.
Nothing is acceptable unto God except that it be through Christ.

to Whom be the glory for ever and ever, Amen.

There is no room for bragging in the church, for all power is of God.

Grammatically, says Milligan, glory goes to God here; but doctrinally, it may refer to both God and Christ, as seen by Rom. 16:27 and II Pet. 3:18.

Study Questions

2926. What is "exhortation"?
2927. Who is the Great Shepherd of verse 20?
2928. Name some verses that identify God as a God of peace.
2929. Is the sacrifice of Christ an attempt of God to bring peace to men?
2930. Is Jesus ever spoken of as a "shepherd"?
2931. Whose blood is spoken of in verse 20?
2932. What is meant by, "eternal covenant"?
2933. Does Paul expect perfection on the part of the Hebrews?
2934. Do we have an example of perfection?
2935. Through what person is perfection accomplished?
2936. Is perfection possible if we disregard Christ's commands?
2937. How does God work in us?
2938. What is required to live pleasing in His sight?
2939. Who is to receive glory in this verse?

F. *Exhortation.* 13:22.

Text
13:22

22 But I exhort you, brethren, bear with the word of exhortation: for I have written unto you in few words.

Paraphrase

22 Now, fearing ye may be prejudiced against me, I beseech you, brethren, take in good part the instructions I have given you concerning the law and the Levitical institutions, and judge

candidly of them; the rather, because I have written to you but briefly concerning these subjects, considering their importance.

Comment

but I exhort you

Exhortation is not doctrine. They now have had doctrine; their need is to act. This book is doctrinal, but it is exhortation, for it holds up the greatness of God and His plan of salvation.

brethren, bear with the word of exhortation

Men are inclined to be slothful, so they should bear with stimulation. This great book of exhortation should keep them from shrinking back, from depending upon anything but Christ for salvation.

"Bear," translated "suffer," means to receive with feeling of kindness and forbearance.

for I have written unto you in few words

This book is quite lengthy, but for the scope of subject matter it is short. The length is about 10,000 words, but how brief in comparison with the "ten thousand things of the law." Hosea 8:12.

Study Questions

2940. How often does the author use the word "exhort" in Hebrews?
2941. Explain verse 22 when he says he has written in "few words"?
2942. What does his reference to Timothy do to the theory of authorship by Paul?
2943. Does it infer that Timothy's release may affect his own release?

G. *Information concerning Timothy* 13:23, 24.

Text
13:23, 24

23 Know ye that our brother Timothy hath been set at liberty; with whom, if he come shortly, I will see you.

24 Salute all them that have the rule over you, and all the saints. They of Italy salute you.

Paraphrase

23 Know that my much respected brother Timothy is sent away by me into Macedonia, with whom, if he come back soon, I will pay you a visit: For I have ordered him to return to this place.

24 In my name, wish health to all your spiritual guides, and to all the Christians in Judea. The Christians of Italy, in token of their communion with you, wish you health.

Comment

Know ye that our brother Timothy hath been set at liberty

"Know ye" or "ye know" is a problem of language here.
a. Calvin prefers the latter, feeling that Paul was informing them of Timothy's liberty.
b. Evidently he was not where the author was.
"Set at liberty" may suggest freedom from prison or sent away on an errand, says Milligan.
a. In Phil. 2:19-24 we see Paul sending him on an errand.
b. Timothy was never pictured in prison by Paul's writings.

with whom if he come shortly I will see you

This verse definitely encourages the theory of Pauline authorship, although Paul's freedom discourages it unless he had been set free. Calvin says if this Timothy was the renowned champion of Paul it is very probable that either Luke or Clement was the author of the epistle.

H. *Salutation*. 13:24.

Salute all them that have the rule over you and all the saints. They of Italy salute you.

What is "salute"?
a. Just as though he had said, "Give my kindest regards."
b. Christianity rejoins common and proper courtesies.
Were they to salute the rulers, or was Paul (the author) saluting them?
a. They were to salute their leaders for Paul.
b. Why didn't Paul salute them directly if this be the case?
c. Calvin thinks he has singled out the rulers as a mark of honor to conciliate them.

13:24, 25   HELPS FROM HEBREWS

All of Italy suggests that the author was there, and those who hold to Pauline authorship say that this proves it.
a. Observe, the footnote says, "the brethren of Italy."
b. Some hold that he was elsewhere and meant the brethren from Italy.

Study Questions

2944. What is meant by the word "salute" in verse 24?
2945. Why didn't Paul salute the rulers?
2946. Does verse 24 indicate where the author was?
2947. What does Paul mean by, "Grace be with you"?
2948. How can grace be with us?

I. *Benediction.* 13:25.

Text
13:25

25 Grace be with you all. Amen.

Paraphrase

25 May the favour of God, and the assistance of His Spirit, be with you all. And in testimony of my sincerity in this wish, and in all the doctrines delivered in this letter, I say Amen.

Comment

Grace be with you all, Amen

This is a conclusion that is like Paul's, if not his.
a. Compare these verses: Rom. 16:24; I Cor. 16:23; II Cor. 13:14; Gal. 6:18; Eph. 6:24; Phil. 4:23; Col. 4:18; I Thess. 5:28; II Thess. 3:18; I Tim. 6:21; II Tim. 4:22; Titus 3:15; Philemon 25.
Grace is a special favor; ill will is absent, and the author is free from all that is evil.

Multiple Choice Over Chapter Thirteen

1. We are told to not forget to show love to:
   1. The minister.
   2. Our friends.
   3. Strangers.

454

2. We are told to obey:
   1. Those that we love.
   2. Those whom we choose since we are free in Christ.
   3. Those who have the rule over us.
3. Marriage is:
   1. Not recommended for Christians.
   2. Honourable.
   3. A defiling thing.
4. One thing that we should let continue is:
   1. Brotherly love.
   2. Our conscience to our guide.
   3. The government.
5. Jesus sanctified the people:
   1. With His own blood.
   2. By His transfiguration.
   3. By His baptism.
6. Jesus Christ is:
   1. The same yesterday, today, and forever.
   2. No doubt growing, for on earth He increased in wisdom, stature, and in favor with God and man.
   3. Not to be expected soon.
7. We are warned to be not carried away with:
   1. Emotions.
   2. Strange doctrines.
   3. On a rocket ship.
   4. With everything we hear.
8. Let brotherly love:
   1. Be natural.
   2. Continue.
   3. Be practised only with brothers in Christ.
   4. Be shown toward those who love us.
9. The writer of the Hebrew letter states that Jesus was sacrificed:
   1. Without the camp or gate.
   2. Within the camp or gate.
   3. In the eternal city.
10. The experience of Timothy at the writing of this epistle was:
    1. He was set at liberty.
    2. About to be put to death.
    3. Was imprisoned.

11. Them that have the rule over you:
    1. Rebuke.
    2. Chasten.
    3. Obey.
12. The author states that he has written to them:
    1. In thirteen chapters.
    2. At great length.
    3. In few words.
13. Since a greeting from Italy is sent, we may assume:
    1. The book was written there.
    2. The Pope was anxious to include Hebrews.
    3. The author was a Roman.
14. The author says that he and those with him have:
    1. A good conscience.
    2. A right to demand an offering from them.
    3. A long ministry ahead.
15. The sacrifice suggested for us to make is the:
    1. Firstborn in our family.
    2. Our money.
    3. Our pride.
    4. The fruit of lips.
16. The chapter states that the heart be established by grace.
    1. Not by meats.
    2. For God gives faith.
    3. So we may be graceful.
17. The author states that:
    1. We have an altar.
    2. We have no need of an altar.
    3. The church is the altar.
18. The Great Shepherd of the sheep was:
    1. Brought forth as David, the shepherd boy.
    2. Brought forth from the dead.
    3. Nehemiah, who shepherded the Israelites back from Babylon.
    4. Moses, who shepherded the Israelites from Egypt.
19. The author believed in prayer, for he said pray for us that:
    1. I may go to Spain to preach.
    2. You may learn how to commune with God.
    3. I may be restored to you the sooner.
20. In showing love to strangers, some have:
    1. Gotten themselves into complications.

2. Had much money given to them.
3. Entertained angels unawares.

SUMMARY OF CHAPTER THIRTEEN

The Book of Hebrews was directed toward those who were in danger of forsaking Christ for Judaism. It begins with the thought of the final revelation of God through His Son, Who is presented in His office as High Priest. His faithfulness, appointment, and ministry as High Priest are explained with constant appeal to be faithful to Him.

Chapter Thirteen is given over to the conclusion, summarizing various points and giving one more strong appeal to leave Judaism and take a firm stand with Christ, the great Shepherd of the sheep. While urging Christians to leave Judaism, the opening verses of the chapter remind of virtues that were to continue. They had God's approval under the old covenant as well as under the new. The following are mentioned: (1) Brotherly love; (2) hospitality to strangers; (3) concern for the oppressed; (4) marriage as an institution to be held in honor; (5) trust in God as opposed to love of money.

The admonition to forsake Judaism and take a firm stand with Christ, begins with the appeal to remember those leaders who had spoken the word to them, as well as the ones watching over their souls. They were to imitate the faith of those who put their trust in Jesus Christ, Who is the same for all eternity. Consequently they are warned against being carried away with strange teachings about foods, etc., such as characterized much of Judaism. The plea is made to go out of the camp of Judaism to Christ who suffered outside the gate. Through Him make a sacrifice of praise to God. Submit to your leaders who watch over your souls.

The chapter closes with a request for prayer that the writer be restored to them, followed by the wonderful benediction which sums up the theme of the book about the great Shepherd of the sheep and the blood of the eternal covenant. The writer appeals for understanding as to the purpose of the brief epistle. He mentions Timothy and the hope of seeing them.

The closing word of greeting mentions their leaders (for the third time in the brief chapter) as well as all the saints. Those of Italy joined in the greetings.

A prayer closes the book: "Grace be with you all."